IRREGULAR MIGRATION AS A CHALLENGE FOR DEMOCRACY

IRREGULAR MIGRATION AS A CHALLENGE FOR DEMOCRACY

Edited by
Elżbieta Kużelewska
Amy Weatherburn
Dariusz Kloza

intersentia
Cambridge – Antwerp – Portland

Intersentia Ltd
Sheraton House | Castle Park
Cambridge | CB3 0AX | United Kingdom
Tel.: +44 1223 370 170 | Fax: +44 1223 370 169
Email: mail@intersentia.co.uk
www.intersentia.com | www.intersentia.co.uk

Distribution for the UK and Ireland:
NBN International
Airport Business Centre, 10 Thornbury Road
Plymouth, PL6 7PP
United Kingdom
Tel.: +44 1752 202 301 | Fax: +44 1752 202 331
Email: orders@nbninternational.com

Distribution for Europe and all other countries:
Intersentia Publishing nv
Groenstraat 31
2640 Mortsel
Belgium
Tel.: +32 3 680 15 50 | Fax: +32 3 658 71 21
Email: mail@intersentia.be

Distribution for the USA and Canada:
International Specialized Book Services
920 NE 58th Ave. Suite 300
Portland, OR 97213
USA
Tel.: +1 800 944 6190 (toll free) | Fax: +1 503 280 8832
Email: info@isbs.com

Artwork on the cover:
Jeffrey Smart (Italy; Australia, b.1921, d.2013)
Bus terminus (1973)
synthetic polymer paint and oil on canvas, 92 × 81 cm
Art Gallery of New South Wales
Bequest of Mrs John Minter 1998
Photo: Brenton McGeachie, AGNSW
© Estate of Jeffrey Smart
251.1998

ISBN 978-1-78068-622-6
D/2018/7849/35
NUR 828

GPRC
Guaranteed
Peer Reviewed
Content

British Library Cataloguing in Publication Data. A catalogue record for this book is available from the British Library.

FOREWORD

European Responses to Immigration – and its Critics: Democratic Dilemmas

Kristian Berg Harpviken*

Immigration has emerged as the defining issue of our times. Across the democratic states of Europe, there is deep resistance to immigration. From the vantage point of late 2017, it is hard to think of a topic more in need of analysis and understanding than the tensions between democracy and migration, so eloquently shed light on by the contributors to this volume, which brings together a wide spectrum of disciplinary and analytical perspectives. The editors deserve praise for their initiative – even courage – in taking on this topic, which is as pressing as it is delicate, raising dilemmas that can only be met through intellectual and ethical honesty. I am grateful to the authors and the editors alike, and I am honoured to be asked to contribute with the foreword.

The 2015 'migration crisis' has become a major reference point in European politics. The nature of the 'crisis' is contested. Some see the 'crisis' as the onset of a new era of mass migration, others emphasise the failure of international migration management. In either case, across Europe, we see the emergence of a strong anti-immigration movement. Relatedly, we see mounting polarisation within states and mounting scepticism to existent political elites, even to the way democracy works. We have become accustomed to take democratic progress for granted, but we may find ourselves on the verge of what late Charles Tilly would call 'de-democratization'[1] – a process where there is decreasing equality between state agents and citizens, where binding political consultation (state-citizens) is fading, and where protection of the population (particularly minorities) from arbitrary action by government agents is weakening. Are we entering an era of de-democratisation? The question is tied to the future of the European project

* Peace Research Institute Oslo (PRIO), Norway. E-mail: kristian@prio.org.

1 C. Tilly, *Democracy*, Cambridge University Press, Cambridge 2007, p. 13.

itself, where deepening dissatisfaction with the European Union both divides the citizenry of its Member States and creates deep rifts between Member States. The future of European integration and the future of democracy in Europe are intrinsically connected, with immigration as the central issue of contestation.

Anti-immigration sentiments in Europe have grown steadily at least since the 1970s. It has taken various expressions, from violent attacks (on immigrants, asylum centres or various care-takers) to regular parliamentary debates. Quite remarkably, anti-immigration has come to the fore in countries that differ fundamentally both in their policies and in the degrees and forms of immigration they have experienced. Poland, to take one example, is one of the most homogenous countries in Europe, yet anti-immigration has been a central mobilising issue and contributed to parliamentary majority for the Law and Justice Party, which pursues a very restrictive immigration policy, at odds with Brussels. Germany, which for decades has pursued perhaps the most generous immigration policy in Europe, and whose population is multi-cultural, sees similar sentiments, well beyond the support base of the *Alternative für Deutschland* (AfD), the party that landed 12.6 per cent of the vote in the 2017 national elections.

'Resistance against migration is the clearly most important cleavage line to appear in … European politics', argues Norwegian sociologist Lars Mjøset.[2] If so, it is quite remarkable how adaptable this movement is to various national contexts. It is equally remarkable, as Mjøset points out, that this is a movement that does not first and foremost take the shape of separate single-issue organisations – the ghost of national socialism has effectively prevented that – but, rather, the issue is picked up by political entrepreneurs tied to parties, often populist, largely on the right (although traditional labour milieus are not exempted). Anti-immigration sentiments, in most countries, have wide appeal and are also picked up by mainstream parties who seek to meet the threat from the political right by variations over the theme of being 'tough on immigration'.

It was the 2015 upsurge of immigrant arrivals to Europe – a large share being asylum seekers from Syria, followed by Eritrea and Afghanistan – that definitively brought the immigration debate to the top of the list of political priorities in most European countries. The 2017 Eurobarometer reveals that whereas terrorism is seen by most as the chief concern (44 per cent, up 12 per cent over the last year), immigration follows suit (with 38 per cent,

2 L. Mjøset, 'Old and New Social Movements in the Nordic Countries – History and Future in an International Perspective' in F. Engelstad, C. Holst and G.C. Aakvaag (eds.), *Democratic State and Democratic Society*, De Gruyter, Berlin 2018 (forthcoming).

down 7 per cent since 2016). These two issues dominate, with the topmost other issue being the economic situation, listed by 18 per cent. Climate change and the environment, are listed by, respectively, 8 per cent and 6 per cent, even though these issues are spearheaded by strong social movements, and are seen by many experts as threats of enormous magnitude in the longer term.[3]

The concerns of immigration sceptics were well known, but carried a different weight in 2015, with seemingly unstoppable mass arrivals, and a corresponding collapse in the institutions set up for migration management, particularly those at the European level. Many, but not all, of the concerns focus on Muslim immigrants. The sense of a threat to culture and values is prominent (and, parenthetically, may also take the form of a worry about the future of democracy, with new citizens coming from non-democratic states where there has been little reason to trust the institutions of power). Equally, some worry about the distribution of economic resources, as immigrants will need support (at least in the short term), in a climate where mechanisms of welfare and redistribution are already scaled back in many European countries. Security is another concern, exacerbated by an increase in the number of terror attacks in Europe and the 'foreign fighters' who have travelled to Syria to join violent extremist groups.

A dilemma – particularly for countries that already host large immigrant populations – is that the new policies adopted in order to prevent future large-scale immigration may be exacerbating problems within. Policies aimed at deterring immigration may make integration more difficult for those already here. Ultimately, policies aimed at constraining immigration may bring about exclusion, with the inherent risk that at least some immigrants turn to extremism, even violence, fulfilling the basic prophecy of immigrants as security threats. This is seen clearly when domestic integration programmes are revised, in part with a view to send a strong message to prospective immigrants that this is not a 'welcoming' country. Likewise, when strong messaging is used in media campaigns to deter prospective migrants, the message is picked up by those who are already accepted, who unavoidably feel less welcome. This relates to a broader concern over a possibly deepening cleavage between the majority population and groups of immigrants of non-Western origin.

In this book, however, the main interest is in the broader polarization we see in virtually all European states, with increasingly recalcitrant positions dividing the citizenry, and with immigration as the issue that crystallises the conflict. Norway, which has been ruled by a minority coalition of the Conservatives and the Progress Party since 2013 (a mandate renewed in the parliamentary

---

3 European Commission, 'Public Opinion in the European Union', *Standard Eurobarometer 87*, Brussels 2017, <http://ec.europa.eu/commfrontoffice/publicopinion/index.cfm/ResultDoc/download/DocumentKy/79565> accessed 19.03.2018.

elections in September 2017), is a case in point. The Progress Party, definitely at the moderate end among right-wing populist parties in Europe, pursues a strict immigration policy. The party has gained from it, so much so that other more mainstream parties are reluctant to challenge its views, with the net effect being a tangible shift on immigration policy overall. One element, amongst many, has been a grand push to return asylum-seekers who have not been granted a right to stay. An Amnesty International report from October 2017 pinpoints Norway as the country in Europe that returns the highest number of Afghans, in absolute numbers.[4] Asylum-seekers under 18, who would not receive appropriate care upon return, are being granted temporary protection, but are deported upon their eighteenth birthday. Since 2016 the Norwegian government has been working to open an orphanage in Kabul to enable the return of minors without care. The deputy minister for justice and public security at the time, Jøran Kallmyr, argued that:

> [m]any of those who come to Norway do so for economic reasons. If we have a consistent practice, where it is the basis for asylum that counts, there will be fewer who are sent on a dangerous trip to Europe. The families and kids will not achieve the goal of obtaining money.[5]

There have been strong negative reactions to these strict return measures from citizens in most parts of the political spectrum. Norway, where the relative consensus on most major issues has been so deep that this has often been pointed to as a problem, is an interesting case. Over the early parts of the twenty-first century, we see that consensus being challenged – with immigration as the issue where political emotions run the highest, and polarization goes the deepest.

Accommodating the anti-immigration movement through conventional politics is a challenge in its own right. Mjøset, with reference to Beck's conceptualisation of political mobilisation in 'risk society',[6] points out that whereas the political movements of the industrial area were offensive and focused on issues that could be addressed within the confines of the nation-state, the movements of the current times are fundamentally defensive and address issues that necessitate transnational solutions.[7] The labour movement, or the

---

4 Amnesty International, *Forced back to Danger: Asylum-seekers returned from Europe to Afghanistan*, London 2017, <https://www.amnesty.org/en/documents/asa11/6866/2017/en> accessed 19.03.2018.

5 T. Strand and S. Granviken, 'Norge vil sende afghanske gutter til barnehjem i Kabul: Afghanistan er positiv' [Norway would like to send Afghan boys to an orphanage in Kabul. Afghanistan is positive], *Aftenposten*, 01.02.2016, <https://www.aftenposten.no/norge/i/z7dw/Norge-vil-sende-afghanske-gutter-til-barnehjem-i-Kabul-Afghanistan-er-positiv> accessed 19.03.2018 (author's translation).

6 U. Beck, *Risk Society: Towards a New Modernity*, Sage, London 1992.

7 L. Mjøset, *supra* n. 2.

women's rights movement, to take two examples of the industrial era, both had proactive claims, which could be addressed through a variety of institutional innovations and political reforms at a national level. The movements of the present, of which anti-immigration is one example (other examples are anti-globalisation and environmental activism) are defensive – fighting to constrain a strong irreversible trend – and they engage with issues that fundamentally can only be managed through international cooperation. The uncomfortable paradox is evident for anti-immigration, which almost always goes hand in hand with a deep scepticism of supranational institutions, rooted in nationalism of some sort or another, and thereby undermines the very institutions that are so critical to managing the movement's main political concerns.

The polarisation within Europe's nation-states has its parallel in mounting tensions between those states, creating a deep rift within the Union itself. To the surprise of most observers, the Euro-crisis, serious as its after-effects are, was superseded by the 2015 migration crisis, which brought to light a deep political-cultural divide between the West and the East, between Old and New Europe. The Euro-crisis, no doubt, was a fundamental challenge, with countries of the Mediterranean (Greece and Cyprus in particular) pitted against Northern Europe. Germany spearheaded structural responses, widely unpopular further South, but stood out as the undisputed leader that saved the European project. The migration crisis, at first sight far less of a threat, proved to be the opposite. Germany received much of the blame for the immigration wave, given its generous welcome, and as an already reluctant leader of Europe, it lost legitimacy. While the South-North divide is also relevant for immigration, with the bulk of migrants arriving illegally by sea to Greece and Italy, the main fault line within the Union goes East-West.

The New Europe, argues German sociologist Christian Joppke, is sceptical of immigration in large part because decades under communism have shielded its populations from the liberal revolutions that had transformed the political debate in the capitalist West. Human rights writ large – with the acceptance of religious, ethnic, sexual, and other sorts of difference – has not taken hold.[8] Hence, writes Joppke, the illiberal Christian nationalism that Hungary's Prime Minister Viktor Orbán preaches is not an exception, but rather a representation of widely held sentiments. When Europe has failed to come up with effective joint responses to migration, the failure has been ultimately rooted in this divide, and for every effort that fails the divide grows wider. The EU's resettlement

---

8 C. Joppke, 'The Syrian Refugee Crisis and the Two Europes: Christian Europe & Liberal Multiculturalism', *The Critique*, 06.01.2016, <http://www.thecritique.com/articles/the-syrian-refugee-crisis-the-two-europes-5> accessed 14.11.2017.

scheme, for example, adopted against the loud protests of many of the EU's newest members, has proven virtually impossible to implement, and Brussels is at risk of exacerbating the problem as it moves towards imposing the scheme, penalising countries that resist. In this there is a painful irony, as the measures that have proven most effective in halting immigration to Europe – the border fences of Hungary, the naval policing of the Aegean Sea, the internment camps in Libya – are fundamentally at odds with the very values celebrated by the liberals of Old Europe.

But can the immigration challenge fundamentally threaten democracy in Europe? As should be clear from the discussion above, I am not here primarily concerned with the issue that new citizens may be lacking an understanding of – or respect for – the workings of the democratic state. Even though that is a real concern, it does not seem to me to be one that in its own right threatens democracy, simply because experience teaches us that the absolute bulk of immigrants learn to appreciate the majority's basic values (and for many, this was a major motivation for moving in the first place). No, I am more concerned with the deep rifts within Europe's nation-states, where anti-immigration is the galvanising issue for citizens who otherwise may differ widely in their political opinions, but nonetheless share one or several of the following broad orientations: economic protectionism; anti-elitism; nationalism; dismantling of (old or new) minorities' rights, guarding of traditional family values; and increasing use of force as a tool of governance (both in domestic and foreign affairs). The extent to which these orientations are at odds with basic democracy varies widely – some of them need not be so at all – but the totality, if coming together under one political umbrella, alongside anti-immigration, is a prescription for the onset of what Tilly termed 'de-democratization', a process where the binding political consultation between a government and its citizens lose out to other mechanisms of political decision-making and everyday rule.[9]

The challenge that the immigration issue poses to the future of European democracy is real. Immigration itself is a genuine challenge, but the fundamental challenge that immigration brings to the fore is a domestic one, it is about fundamentally different political visions that cut through the citizenry of Europe's nation-states. With that, it becomes critically important how these nation-states, through their democratic institutions, tackle immigration. Writing in the fall of 2017, so far, much of what we have seen is a dramatic shift towards stricter controls, deterrence, restrictions in transit and sending countries, measures also adopted by mainstream parties that not long ago embraced a much more liberal line. All of this, while ethically deeply problematic, is also understandable, not only because of the fear of mass immigration, but also

---

9 C. Tilly, *supra* n. 1, p. 164.

because of the fear of a popular reaction that threatens democracy itself. There is undoubtedly a need to develop policies that secure protection for those who need it the most; policies that does not imply a cessation of human mobility as we know it. But ultimately, while tackling immigration is necessary in order to secure continued democratisation of Europe's nation-states, it is not going to be sufficient, simply because the forces of de-democratisation span so much wider, and because once an anti-immigration sentiment is out of the bottle, it is hard to put it back in.

The resistance to supranational decision-making – here, in the form of the European Union – brings the dilemma to the fore. Such resistance is closely associated with the anti-immigration movement. Yet, the immigration itself transcends the borders between nation-states, and cries out for international responses, exactly at a time when European institutions falter, in large part, as a consequence of rifts both between and within its Member States. The fact that the Union struggles to stem political fragmentation, at a time – and on an issue – where a coordinated response is needed is deeply worrisome. In that situation, we need both the scholarly analysis and reflection presented in this volume, and we need informed political innovation within and between Europe's nation-states.

Oslo, October 2017

INTRODUCTION

Asking Big Questions: Migrants *Ante Portas* and What to Do with Them?

Elżbieta Kużelewska,* Amy Weatherburn** and Dariusz Kloza***

'Would you tell me, please, which way I ought to go from here?'
'That depends a good deal on where you want to get to,' said the Cat.
'I don't much care where–' said Alice.
'Then it doesn't matter which way you go,' said the Cat.
'–so long as I get somewhere,' Alice added as an explanation.
'Oh, you're sure to do that,' said the Cat, 'if you only walk long enough.'
Lewis Carroll,
Alice's Adventures in Wonderland (1865)[1]

I.

To what extent does the *status quo* of irregular migration to Europe pose a challenge for democracy?[2] The surge of people moving, predominantly from war-torn, repressed and impoverished countries in the Middle East and Africa

* Centre for Direct Democracy Studies (CDDS), Faculty of Law, University of Białystok, Poland. E-mail: ekuzelewska@gmail.com.

** Research Group on Fundamental Rights and Constitutionalism (FRC), Vrije Universiteit Brussel (VUB), Belgium. E-mail: amy.weatherburn@vub.be.

*** Research Group on Law, Science, Technology and Society (LSTS), VUB; Peace Research Institute Oslo (PRIO), Norway. E-mail: dariusz.kloza@vub.be.

1 L. Carroll, *Alice's Adventures in Wonderland and Through the Looking-Glass*, Random House, New York 2012 [Macmillan, London 1865], pp. 89–90.

2 The International Organization for Migration (IOM) offers definitions for a few key notions concerning migration that we find vital to mention at the outset of our analysis. Starting with the most basic concept, '*migration*' is a 'process of moving, either across an international border, or within a State. It is a population movement, encompassing any kind of movement of people, whatever its length, composition and causes; it includes migration of refugees, displaced persons, uprooted people, and economic migrants.' (Semantically speaking, migration is further split into '*immigration*', which – according to the Cambridge Dictionary

to the outer borders of Europe, which started in the early 2010s and which intensified in the summer of 2015 – and the implications for the Old Continent that this massive flow of people has caused – gave an impetus to the present book. It seeks to contribute to the contextualisation, better understanding of and drawing of lessons from the *status quo* of irregular migration to Europe and its relation to the values and principles on which Europe has been built.[3]

Migration in Europe (i.e. within, to and away from), as anywhere in the world, is by no means a novel phenomenon.[4] Immigration *to* the Old Continent once again gained its momentum and – consequently – public attention in the aftermath of the so-called Arab Spring. A sequence of protests against authoritarian political regimes in Africa and the Middle East that broke out on 17 December 2010 in Tunisia resulted in democratisation for some of them, but in others led to political unrest and even civil war. The latter caused an intensified emigration therefrom, largely towards Europe. The Italian island of Lampedusa – located less than 120 km from the Tunisian shore – and the vessels that have sunk around that island have become symbolic. Lampedusa perhaps marked the first sign that this influx of people constituted a serious problem and hence people started naming it a 'crisis'. Subsequent events only magnified the problem: perhaps the biggest mark has been left by the ongoing Syrian civil war.

In 2015 alone, irregular immigrants filed 1.25 million applications for asylum in the European Union (EU) with a combined total of 68,000 in Norway and Switzerland.[5] In parallel, an estimated 3,771 lives have been lost or went missing in the Mediterranean in the same year, which increased in the subsequent

of English – is 'the act of someone coming to live in a different country'. '*Emigration*' is its antonym, i.e. 'the process of leaving a country in order to live permanently in another country'. A comparable distinction is made between 'immigrants' and 'emigrants'.) Migration is *irregular* if this 'movement … takes place outside the regulatory norms of the sending, transit and receiving countries'. In turn, '*illegal* migration' – a part of irregular one – is often limited to cases of 'smuggling of migrants and trafficking in persons'. Concerning people *en route*, '*asylum seekers*' are those 'seeking to be admitted into a country as refugees and awaiting decision on their application for refugee status'. Asylum seekers are irregular migrants when they do not use regular means to claim the protection they seek. A '*refugee*', by contrast, is a person who already received a positive decision on his or her claim for asylum. (We acknowledge these definitions are not legally binding. Such a quality has been vested only e.g. for the definition of a refugee, which we cite *infra* n. 56.) Cf. IOM, *Glossary on Migration*, Geneva 2004, <http://www.iomvienna.at/sites/default/files/IML_1_EN.pdf>. All Internet links in this contribution have been verified on 25 November 2017.

3 By 'Europe' we understand a patchwork of economic and political integration processes nowadays taking place on the Old Continent, in particular the European Union (EU). We explain our understanding *infra* n. 42.

4 Z. Bauman, *Strangers at Our Door*, Polity Press, Cambridge 2016, p. 3.

5 Eurostat, 'Record number of over 1.2 million first time asylum seekers registered in 2015', press release, 44/2016, 04.03.2016.

year to 5,022[6] and, as of 25 November 2017, had already reached 2,992.[7] Europe has faced a situation in which human beings have been fleeing to European soil and a vast majority of them have been seeking – and we are confident this is the right term – some *help*. (Yet we are aware some of them might come with bad intentions.) As a result, Europe, to its series of recent big questions – for instance, the 'democratic deficit', the rejected 2004 Treaty establishing a Constitution for Europe, or the 2009 sovereign debt crisis – had to add another one: migrants stand *ante portas* and what to do with them?[8]

This recent, massive arrival of people to Europe caused a whole spectrum of reactions, from sympathy and enthusiasm to hostility, amongst all stakeholders and at all levels. Some commentators argued that because Europe has committed itself to the protection and promotion of high moral values and principles, and amongst them fundamental rights, it has to uphold them by welcoming and accommodating the irregular migrants. They see their arrival as a historical necessity, indispensable justice, economic opportunity and even as a new chapter in European history. Other commentators contrasted this viewpoint with an opinion that irregular migration is a multidimensional threat to the host polities. They have also called it an 'invasion' or a 'flood', linked to the rise of crime and terrorism; they have feared economic, social and cultural difficulties.

As a reaction, many people went to the streets. Some have marched with posters 'refugees welcome' in front of the many harbours and train stations where these people have been waiting to catch their connections whilst in transit on their journey.[9] There were many people who offered a helping hand to refugees, starting with first aid.[10] At the same time, there have been people protesting against the influx of migrants, carrying the slogan 'go home' and provoking racist and xenophobic reactions; the rates of hate crime have increased. Some

---

[6] European Parliament, *EU Migrant Crisis: Facts and Figures*, Strasbourg, 30.06.2017, <http://www.europarl.europa.eu/news/en/headlines/society/20170629STO78630/eu-migrant-crisis-facts-and-figures>.

[7] The United Nations' High Commissioner for Refugees (UNHCR) maintains up-to-date statistics at <http://data2.unhcr.org/en/situations>. So does, *inter alia*, the IOM at <http://migration.iom.int/europe> and the European Border and Coast Guard Agency (Frontex) at <http://frontex.europa.eu/trends-and-routes/migratory-routes-map>.

[8] D. Dinan, 'Crises in EU History' in D. Dinan, N. Nugent and W.E. Paterson, *The European Union in Crisis*, Macmillan, London 2017, pp. 16–32.

[9] E. Graham-Harrison, P. Kingsley, R. Waites and T. McVeigh, 'Cheering German crowds greet refugees after long trek from Budapest to Munich', *The Guardian*, 05.09.2015, <https://www.theguardian.com/world/2015/sep/05/refugee-crisis-warm-welcome-for-people-bussed-from-budapest>.

[10] Their actions often met with appreciation. For instance, the Vrije Universiteit Brussel (VUB), where two of the editors of this book work, in November 2017 awarded doctorates *honoris causa* to Emma Bonino for her 'determined efforts in relation to migration and refugees' and to the 'inhabitants of Lampedusa', represented by Pietro Bartolo, for their 'charity and helpfulness'. Cf. 'Honorary doctorate for Dr. Emma Bonino and the inhabitants of Lampedusa', *VUB Today*, 28.11.2017, <http://www.vubtoday.be/en/content/honorary-doctorate-dr-emma-bonino-and-inhabitants-lampedusa>.

other people have voiced their opposition in even stronger ways, for example, by attacking refugee shelters.[11]

Political leaders in Europe have split accordingly. The contrast between the actions of Angela Merkel of Germany (e.g. introducing an 'open border' policy for refugees in 2015)[12] and those of Viktor Orbán of Hungary (who built a barbed-wire fence throughout the Hungarian border with Serbia[13] and claimed, most recently, cultural 'incompatibility' of migrants and the European societies)[14] is illustrative of this discord. The EU and its Member States have responded with a combination of humanitarian- and security-oriented measures. For example, they reformed their legislative frameworks on external border control,[15] asylum and immigration as well as launched search and rescue (S&R) operations such as the Italian 'Mare Nostrum',[16] followed by the EU-coordinated border security operation 'Triton'[17] and the EU military operation 'Sophia'.[18] In order to ease the burden on Italy and Greece, the EU have temporarily introduced

11 P. Oltermann, 'Crowd cheer fire at hotel being converted into refugee shelter in Saxony', *The Guardian*, 21.02.2016, <https://www.theguardian.com/world/2016/feb/21/crowd-cheers-fire-hotel-refugee-shelter-saxony-germany>; V. Garza, 'Polish brothers plead not guilty for setting fire to asylum center', *Norway Today*, 10.10.2017, <http://norwaytoday.info/news/polish-brothers-pleas-not-guilty-setting-fire-asylum-center>.

12 E. Graham-Harrison, P. Kingsley, K. Rawlinson and W. Murray, 'First Refugees Arrive from Hungary after Austria and Germany Open Borders', *The Guardian*, 05.09.2015, <https://www.theguardian.com/world/2015/sep/05/refugees-travelling-from-hungary-can-enter-germany-and-austria>.

13 A. Sandford, 'Hungary Completes New Anti-Migrant Border Fence with Serbia', *Euronews*, 28.04.2017, <http://www.euronews.com/2017/04/28/hungary-completes-new-anti-migrant-border-fence-with-serbia>.

14 E. Zalan, 'Orban Vows to Defend Poland from EU's Inquisition', *EU Observer*, 24.07.2017, <https://euobserver.com/political/138586>.

15 Perhaps the most visible examples are: the reinforcement of the European Border and Coast Guard Agency (Frontex) and – what might have been noticed by many travellers – the amendment of the Schengen Border Code, effective from 7 April 2017, that reinforced checks of all people at the external borders, both at entry and at exit. Cf. Regulation (EU) 2016/1624 of the European Parliament and of the Council of 14 September 2016 on the European Border and Coast Guard ..., [2016] OJ L251/1; Regulation (EU) 2017/458 of the European Parliament and of the Council of 15 March 2017 amending Regulation (EU) 2016/399 as regards the reinforcement of checks against relevant databases at external borders, [2017] OJ L74/1. Cf. also S. Carrera S. Blockmans, D. Gros and E. Guild, 'The EU's Response to the Refugee Crisis. Taking Stock and Setting Policy Priorities', CEPS [Centre for European Policy Studies] Essay No. 20/16, Brussels 2015, <https://www.ceps.eu/publications/eu's-response-refugee-crisis-taking-stock-and-setting-policy-priorities>.

16 Ministero della Difesa [Repubblica Italiana], *Mare Nostrum*, [no date], <http://www.marina.difesa.it/cosa-facciamo/operazioni-concluse/Pagine/mare-nostrum.aspx>.

17 European Commission, *Frontex Joint Operation 'Triton' – Concerted efforts to manage migration in the Central Mediterranean*, memo 14/566, Brussels, 07.10.2014, <http://europa.eu/rapid/press-release_MEMO-14-566_en.htm>.

18 European External Action Service, 'Mission EUNAVFOR MED – Operation SOPHIA', factsheet, Brussels, 20.10.2017, <http://eeas.europa.eu/sites/eeas/files/october_2017_-_factsheet_on_eunavfor_med_mission_english.pdf>.

emergency 'relocation and resettlement' schemes between Member States (also known as 'migrant quotas'),[19] notwithstanding opposition from a few Member States, mainly due to the mandatory nature of these measures.[20] The EU even 'agreed' with Turkey that all irregular migrants arriving from Turkey at a Greek shore would be returned.[21] At the same time, courts of law from national ones, at all levels, to supranational ones, that is, the European Court of Human Rights (ECtHR) and the Court of Justice of the European Union (CJEU) – have been more and more often seized by cases concerning immigration and the implications these measures produce for the values and principles on which Europe has been built.

Finally, the media, both digital and more traditional outlets, also took two diverging stances. Those unfavourable to irregular migration, especially in the 'new' EU Member States, rarely said anything positive about migrants.[22] By contrast, those favourable attempted to counterbalance this negative coverage by, for example, depicting the many refugee ships and camps – such as in Calais, France – and paying special attention to death, illness and the living conditions therein.[23] The photograph of the dead body of a three-year-old Syrian boy on a Turkish shore, named Alan Kurdi, is illustrative here.[24] In parallel, artists – ranging from literature to cinematography – took a rather favourable stance towards irregular migration and migrants. For example, Ai Weiwei's recent art installation on the streets of New York City display sculptures of fences and invites a 'reflection on the profound social and political impulse to divide people from each other'.[25]

---

19 Council Decision (EU) 2015/1523 of 14 September 2015 establishing provisional measures in the area of international protection for the benefit of Italy and of Greece [2015] OJ L239/146; Council Decision (EU) 2015/1601 of 22 September 2015 establishing provisional measures in the area of international protection for the benefit of Italy and Greece [2015] OJ L248/80. Cf. also European Commission, *Twelfth Report on Relocation and Resettlement*, COM(2017) 260 final, Strasbourg, 16 May 2017.

20 European Commission, *Relocation: Commission launches infringement procedures against the Czech Republic, Hungary and Poland*, press release, IP/17/1607, Brussels, 14.06.2017; CJEU, Case C-643/15 *Slovak Republic and Hungary v. Council of the European Union*, Judgment of 06.09.2017.

21 European Council, *EU–Turkey Statement*, Press Release 144/16, Brussels, 18.03.2016, <http://www.consilium.europa.eu/en/press/press-releases/2016/03/18/eu-turkey-statement/pdf>.

22 J. Cieński, 'Why Poland Doesn't Want Refugees', *Politico*, 21.05.2017, <http://www.politico.eu/article/politics-nationalism-and-religion-explain-why-poland-doesnt-want-refugees>.

23 Human Rights Watch, *Greece: Dire Refugee Conditions on Islands, Transfer Asylum Seekers to Mainland*, 23.01.2017, <https://www.hrw.org/news/2017/01/23/greece-dire-refugee-conditions-islands>.

24 H. Smith, 'Shocking images of drowned Syrian boy show tragic plight of refugees', *The Guardian*, 02.09.2015, <https://www.theguardian.com/world/2015/sep/02/shocking-image-of-drowned-syrian-boy-shows-tragic-plight-of-refugees>.

25 A. Weiwei, *Good Fences Make Good Neighbors*, Public Art Fund, New York, NY, October 2017 – February 2018, <https://www.publicartfund.org/ai_weiwei_good_fences_make_good_neighbors/about>.

As with many aspects of public life, the reactions to irregular migration that we have sketched above are interrelated: media and politicians do influence the public opinion and *vice versa*. And we could continue recalling these stories from both ends of the spectrum, both positive and negative – as irregular migrants have not ceased to arrive in Europe; their journeys continue – but it is fair to conclude that migration remains a heated, multifaceted yet controversial topic. There exist two opposing viewpoints as to what to do in light of the fact that irregular migrants have already come to Europe, have been waiting *ante portas* or will arrive in the days to come – should Europe welcome them or send them back?

These two contrasting viewpoints stand behind the main idea for this book. We have chosen to look at the extent to which the past, the present and the future of irregular migration to Europe relates to the foundational values and principles on which Europe has been built, namely democracy, the rule of law (*Rechtsstaat*) and the respect for fundamental rights. We focus on those people who seek various forms of help in Europe, motivated by war or other injustices in the places where they come from. With this book we do not aim to offer any complete or ultimate answer – if this was ever possible – but rather we want to modestly partake in a debate on the appropriate way to deal with irregular migration.

II.

Let us set the scene before giving voice to the authors of the many chapters in this book. There are multiple ways of examining the past, the present and the future of irregular migration to Europe and the way it relates to the European foundational values and principles. We acknowledge these perspectives are neither exhaustive nor clear-cut, yet they have the advantage of clarifying the main drivers at stake.

1. Migration as an ethical question. The first amongst these perspectives, on our view, is to look from the moral philosophy (ethics) viewpoint, or – more concretely – theories of justice. We see the ethical reflection, in the context of irregular migration, as indispensable for minimum two reasons: first, we are concerned with human beings and thus the stakes are very high. Second, we have observed there has been too much noise in the debates on migration, yet there has not been enough wisdom therefrom; an ethical reflection is meant to remedy that. Ethics offers 'ideas about how to live'; it determines 'what we find acceptable or unacceptable, […] it determines our conception of what is due to us, and what is due from us, as we relate to others'.[26] It has an ambition to be a supreme set of normative dispositions that defines the

[26] S. Blackburn, *Ethics. A Very Short Introduction*, Oxford University Press, Oxford 2000, p. 1.

'standards of behaviour'.[27] Every day people make choices about their own lives and often about the lives of other people, for instance within a family or a group of friends or within a polity (e.g. governments). They frame their choices as a simple dichotomy between being 'good' or 'bad', between 'right' and 'wrong'; for many – a distinction between a sin or not. People probably do not necessarily realise their arguments and their decisions do have moral origins and ramifications, or – at least – that these arguments and decisions can be framed in ethical terms and analysed through the lens of formal 'tools' that ethics provides.

At the most rudimentary level, *normative* ethics offers a few approaches on how to decide what is the right thing to do. In Western philosophy, for example, if those favourable of migration claim that accepting refugees is all about human dignity, they believe in duty, for example to recognise this dignity and thus to help those in need; they are deontologists. They hold that all humans are worthy of respect, regardless of who they are or where they come from, and it is therefore wrong to treat them as mere instruments towards any given aim.[28] (This is the legacy of Immanuel Kant,[29] which often stands in opposition to e.g. Niccolò Machiavelli.)[30] Libertarians, in their belief in human freedom, would rather welcome anybody, as these people are entitled to do whatever they want with their life and their property, provided they respect other people's rights to do the same.[31] (This is the legacy of e.g. John Locke.)[32] If those favourable to the accommodation of irregular migrants claim this would maximise overall good – that is, a greater happiness for the greatest number of people – then they look at consequences of actions. They take, in other words, a consequentialist stance, or – more precisely – a utilitarian stance: they have 'calculated' the pros to outweigh the cons. Yet the utilitarian calculus can equally demonstrate that disadvantages outweigh advantages. (This is the legacy of e.g. Jeremy Bentham[33] and John Stuart Mill.)[34] Finally, those who follow virtue ethics (aretaic ethics), they would rather welcome and help a refugee since this would be a benevolent thing to do or because that would be what a virtuous person would do. (This is the legacy of Plato and Aristotle, revived by Elizabeth Ascombe in the twentieth century.)[35] We note that as virtues such as charity and altruism are rather straightforward, there are some – such as prudence (wisdom) – that can be variously interpreted in the context of migration.

---

27 *Ibid.*

28 M.J. Sandel, *Justice. What's the Right Thing to Do?*, Penguin, London 2009, p. 103.

29 Cf. e.g. I. Kant, *Grundlegung zur Metaphysik der Sitten* [Groundwork of the Metaphysic of Morals], 1785.

30 Cf. e.g. N. Machiavelli, *Il Principe* [The Prince], 1532.

31 M.J. Sandel, *supra* n. 28, pp. 59–60.

32 Cf. e.g. J. Locke, *Two Treatises of Government*, 1689.

33 Cf. e.g. J. Bentham, *An Introduction to the Principles of Morals and Legislation*, 1789.

34 Cf. e.g. J.S. Mill, *On Liberty*, 1859.

35 G.E.M. Anscombe, 'Modern Moral Philosophy', (1958) 33(124) *Philosophy* 1.

These schools of normative ethics take a different unit of measure (e.g. communitarian or individual well-being), they are often mutually exclusive and they rarely provide any ultimate answer. The reason why we just mentioned them is that they stand behind any legal statue, any political decision or any deed made in public and private lives, even though the importance of ethics might not initially be so visible.

At a more concrete level, *applied* ethics has already devoted considerable attention to the phenomenon of migration and to the migrant as a person, regardless of whether regular or not. From the richness of such discourse, we can immediately recall at least Emmanuel Levinas and his emphasis on the encounter with another human being, 'the Other'. Levinas claims not only that the meeting with the Other is the most important experience in human life, but also that 'I' has to take some responsibility and to care for 'the Other'.[36] A migrant is another human being and his or her arrival to a new polity would constitute such a profound experience, a meeting, and would demand the host to take some responsibility. It is fascinating that someone else is different; such an encounter often brings a totally different understanding of the world, thus enrichment.[37]

2. Migration as a legal question. The second perspective is that of law, including its ethical foundations as well as the legal practice. It is the law that has predominantly been used to regulate migration and the status, rights and duties of a migrant.[38]

Generally speaking, political systems in the majority of democratic polities have been built on some main values and principles, 'ideals that dominate [...] political morality', in particular democracy, the rule of law (*Rechtsstaat*), the respect for fundamental rights and economic freedom.[39] This is so because these ideals appeal to many as an appropriate way of public organisation and – as

---

36 E. Levinas, *Totalité et Infini. Essai sur l'extériorité* [Totality and Infinity: An Essay on Exteriority], Martinus Nijhoff, La Haye 1961. Cf. also R. Kapuściński, *Ten Inny* [This Other], Znak, Kraków 2006.

37 We recall here a media campaign run by Amnesty International in mid-2016, titled 'Look Beyond Borders', in which an experimental video film depicting a short encounter between a European and a recently-arrived refugee was shown to 'break down barriers'. The idea was based on a 'theory that four minutes of uninterrupted eye contact increases intimacy'. Cf. Amnesty International, 'Look refugees in the eye: Powerful video experiment breaks down barriers', press release, 24.05.2016, <https://www.amnesty.org/en/latest/news/2016/05/look-refugees-in-the-eye>.

38 There exist many mechanisms of regulation. For their classical overview, cf. e.g. C.C. Hood, *The Tools of Government*, Macmillan, London 1983, pp. 2–11.

39 J. Waldron, 'The Rule of Law and the Importance of Procedure' in J. Fleming (ed.), *Getting to the Rule of Law*, New York University Press, New York 2011, p. 3, <http://lsr.nellco.org/cgi/viewcontent.cgi?article=1235&context=nyu_plltwp>. Yet we acknowledge these 'ideals' have been, over the time, variously conceptualised. For the sake of clarity, it suffices here to explain that both the rule of law and *Rechtsstaat* doctrines serve multiple purposes in a

Dahl put it – amongst these ideals, democracy 'uniquely possesses a number of features that most people, whatever their basic political beliefs, would consider desirable'.[40] The laws of these polities, and in particular their highest legal norms – their *magnae cartae*, aim at the protection of these ideals (at minimum) and their promotion (at best). As Agnes Callamard, the UN Special Rapporteur on extrajudicial, summary or arbitrary executions – whilst reporting on migration – has observed:

> [t]he right not to be arbitrarily deprived of life is a foundational and universally recognized right, applicable at all times and in all circumstances, including during armed conflict or other public emergency. The right to life – a norm of *jus cogens* – is protected by international and regional treaties, customary international law and domestic legal systems.[41]

The legal provisions that are of our particular interest are those affecting the polity of Europe.[42] Generally speaking, human rights have become, at a certain

---

polity and one of them is to channel the exercise of 'public power through law'. They achieve their goals in different manners and hence function differently while sharing some common characteristics. The rule of law doctrine dominates on the British Isles, the *Rechtsstaat* – on the continental Europe. Cf. e.g. G. Lautenbach, *The Concept of the Rule of Law and the European Court of Human Rights*, Oxford University Press, Oxford 2013, p. 18.

40 R. A. Dahl, 'The value of democracy' *Encyclopædia Britannica*, 2017, <https://www.britannica.com/topic/democracy/The-value-of-democracy>.

41 United Nations, *Report of the Special Rapporteur of the Human Rights Council on extrajudicial, summary or arbitrary executions*, New York, 15.08.2017, A/72/335, §14.

42 The reader deserves a word of explanation. We understand Europe *sensu largo* – it is a patchwork of supranational arrangements of economic and political nature occurring on the European continent, of individual countries that partake in these arrangements as well as of their inhabitants, regardless if citizens or not. In geographical terms, this polity comprises the EU with the non-EU members of the European Economic Area (EEA), Switzerland as well as four microstates – Monaco, Andorra, San Marino and the Vatican City/Holy See – that partake with a varying degree in these policies. All of them but the Vatican City/Holy See are members of the Council of Europe (CoE). The Council of Europe, in turn, tasked with safeguarding and promoting democracy, the rule of law (*Rechtsstaat*), fundamental rights and social development, currently comprises 47 Member States, i.e. virtually all countries on the European soil, with a notable exception of Belarus. (Cf. the Statute of the Council of Europe, London, 05.05.1949; European Treaty Series (ETS) No. 1, as amended.) Eventually, the EU is a much more closely integrated economic and political union of 28 Member States. Its main *economic* component – the internal market – has been open to four other countries, i.e. Norway, Iceland and Liechtenstein (linked thereto *via* the EEA Agreement) – as well as Switzerland (linked *via* bilateral agreements). In parallel, a part of EU *political* output – e.g. common migration and asylum policy – affects, to a various degree, also these four counties and four microstates too and this is why our object of interest – geographically speaking – comprises 36 countries. In parallel, at the regional level, there exists also a few politico-economic unions, such as Benelux (Belgium, the Netherlands and Luxembourg) and a few loose, political alliances, such as the Visegrád Group (Poland, Hungary, the Czech Republic and Slovakia) or the Weimar Triangle (France, Germany and Poland). Let us borrow a commonly used phrase 'European integration project' to refer, for our purposes, to this patchwork of arrangements.

point, a narrative of the European integration project.[43] They can be analysed at three levels. Their first manifestation is the work of the Council of Europe. When we look at its legal system, the European Convention on Human Rights (ECHR, 1950)[44] affords the protection of fundamental rights of any person, i.e. regardless of their citizenship or lack thereof, who happens to find him- or herself under the jurisdiction (*sensu largo*) of any the Council's Member States. Therefore, irregular migrants benefit too. The Convention established the European Court of Human Rights (ECtHR), sitting in Strasbourg, and the bulk of the legal rules on migration originates from its judgments. Empirically speaking, in the context of migration, the Court has been seized thus far to adjudicate on cases concerning the prohibition of torture (Article 3 ECHR), right to liberty and security (Article 5), right to privacy (Article 8) and the right to effective remedy (Article 13).[45] In parallel, the European Social Charter (1961,[46] revised 1996)[47] is often seen as a complementing instrument to the ECHR, yet it lacks any strong enforcement mechanisms – the European Committee of Social Rights monitors the implementation of the Charter yet it has no binding powers whatsoever.[48] Concerning specifically irregular migration, the Council of Europe appointed in February 2016 its first Special Representative on Migration and Refugees and tasked him, *inter alia*, to monitor and 'gather information on how the fundamental rights of migrants and refugees are protected';[49] this is meant to aid policy-making.

The second manifestation of human rights as a narrative of the European integration project is the European Union (EU). Initially conceived as an economic endeavour to secure peace and prosperity,[50] what is now the EU has been gradually exercising more and more public authority in a growing number of fields and hence, at a certain point, the question of democratic legitimacy came to the fore. Following the decades of political and academic debates – and resulting constitutional changes – the foundational Treaties have progressively been reflecting the democratic nature (*sensu largo*) of the

---

43 S. Smismans, 'Fundamental rights as a political myth of the EU: can the myth survive?' in S. Douglas-Scott and N. Hatzis (eds.), *Research Handbook on EU Law and Human Rights*, Edward Elgar Publishing, London 2017, pp. 13–34; G. de Búrca, 'The Language of Rights and European Integration' in J. Shaw and G. More (eds.), *New Legal Dynamics of the European Union*, Oxford University Press, Oxford 1995, pp. 24–34.

44 Convention for the Protection of Human Rights and Fundamental Freedoms, Rome, 04.11.1950; ETS No. 5, as amended; most recently by Protocol No. 16, Strasbourg, 02.10.2013; ETS No. 214.

45 ECtHR, Press Unit, *Migrants in Detention*, factsheet, July 2017, <http://www.echr.coe.int/Documents/FS_Migrants_detention_ENG.pdf>.

46 ETS No. 35.

47 ETS No. 163.

48 Cf. <http://www.coe.int/t/democracy/migration/bodies/ecsr_en.asp>.

49 Cf. <https://www.coe.int/en/web/special-representative-secretary-general-migration-refugees/home>.

50 Cf. *supra* n. 42.

European integration project. In the most recent wording, amongst the values and principles on which the Union has been built, the 'respect for human dignity' stands *primus inter pares*. We read this from Article 2 of the Treaty on the European Union (TEU), as lately amended by the Treaty of Lisbon (2009):

> The Union is founded on the values of respect for human dignity, freedom, democracy, equality, the rule of law and respect for human rights, including the rights of persons belonging to minorities. These values are common to the Member States in a society in which pluralism, non-discrimination, tolerance, justice, solidarity and equality between women and men prevail'.[51]

We supplement this observation with a set of rules for the democratic functioning of the Union, such as the equality of citizens and the representative democracy (Articles 9–12 TEU),[52] and the entry into force of the legally binding Charter of Fundamental Rights of the European Union (CFR, 2009). The importance of the Charter is unparalleled: in order to ensure the practical, effective and efficient protection of human rights, the EU has bound itself by a 'bill of rights' that serves as a benchmark against which the secondary EU law and the law of the Member States implementing EU law is checked. Article 1 confirms the commitment to these values and principles as the Charter opens with the statement that '[h]uman dignity is inviolable. It must be respected and protected'.[53]

Third and finally, all European countries partake in the global system for the protection of fundamental rights. All are members of the United Nations (UN), the majority supported the adoption of the Universal Declaration of Human Rights (UDHR, 1948)[54] and all signed the legally binding International Covenant on Civil and Political Rights (ICCPR, 1976) as well as the many subsequent human rights treaties. The protection of fundamental rights is further enshrined in their national constitutions.

More concretely, when it comes to the regulation of irregular migration – this including the safeguarding of migrants' rights – we observe it occurs at four levels:

1. *International* – the UN, whose Convention Relating to the Status of Refugees, signed in Geneva in 1951 (i.e. 'the 1951 Refugee Convention'),[55] and a subsequent Protocol, signed in New York in 1967, constitute the key legal

---

51 [2016] OJ C202/389. Yet note Protocol No. 30 and declarations Nos. 53 and 61–62 by the UK, Czech Republic and Poland on the Charter of Fundamental Rights of the European Union, [2016] OJ C202/312 and 358.

52 A. von Bogdandy, 'The European lesson for international democracy: The significance of Articles 9 to 12 EU Treaty for international organizations' (2012) 23 *European Journal of International Law* 315.

53 *Supra* n. 51.

54 UN, General Assembly, Resolution 217 A, Paris, 10.12.1948.

55 United Nations Treaty Series (UNTS) Vol. 189 (1954), No. 2545.

framework in our field of interest, defining the status of a refugee, vesting in him or her some basic rights and requiring a state to take some action benefiting refugees.[56] The importance of both the Convention and its Protocol lies in the fact that these instruments constitute a worldwide reference framework for irregular migration, having been ratified by altogether 148 parties, and that the principle of non-refoulement they contain (i.e. a right of an asylum seeker not to be sent back to a country in which he or she would be in likely danger of persecution; Article 33) is nowadays widely considered a *jus cogens* norm (i.e. a pre-emptory norm with no derogation) in international law.[57] To manage irregular migration around the world, the UN created the office of the High Commissioner for Refugees (UNHCR) in 1950.

2. *Supranational, or regional* – in particular those arrangements in Europe, the Americas and Africa; each of these have undertaken legal steps to regulate irregular migration and migrants, within their competences and within their respective jurisdictions; while we overview the European legal framework *infra*, some notable examples from elsewhere could include the Organisation of African Unity's Refugee Convention (1969)[58] or the Cartagena Declaration on Refugees, concerning Latin America (1984).[59]
3. *National* – an individual country in which its national constitution, primary and secondary legalisation regulate migration and migrants. Concerning the right to asylum, for example, most countries provide this through domestic legislation, in particular by a statute incorporating the 1951 Refugee Convention. However, France, Italy, Germany and Poland stand out as four of very few European countries specifically to guarantee such a right in their national constitutions.[60]

---

56 Article 1(A)(2) defines *refugee* as a person, who 'owing to well-founded fear of persecution for reasons of race, religion, nationality, membership of a particular social group or political opinions, is outside the country of his nationality and is unable or, owing to such fear, is unwilling to avail himself of the protection of that country'. In other words, a refugee is a person not protected by his or her own state – however this link is understood – and thus the international community steps in to offer such a protection. Article 1(F) excludes from this group people 'to whom there are serious reasons for considering that: (a) he has committed a crime against peace, a war crime, or a crime against humanity, … (b) he has committed a serious non-political crime outside the country of refuge prior to his admission to that country as a refugee; (c) he has been guilty of acts contrary to the purposes and principles of the United Nations'.

57 J. Allain, 'The *Jus Cogens* Nature of Non-Refoulement' (2001) 13(4) *International Journal of Refugee Law* 533.

58 Convention governing the Specific Aspects of Refugee Problems in Africa, Addis Adaba, 10.09.1969; UNTS Vol. 1001 (1976), No. 14691.

59 Cartagena Declaration on Refugees, 22.11.1984, <http://www.refworld.org/docid/3ae6b36ec.html>.

60 H. Lambert, F. Messineo and P. Tiedemann, 'Comparative Perspectives of Constitutional Asylum in France, Italy, and Germany: Requiescat in Pace?' (2008) 27(3) *Refugee Survey Quarterly* 16. Cf. also Article 53-1 of the French Constitution (JORF [1958] 238/9151, as amended), Article 10 of the Italian Constitution (GU [1947] 298/1, as amended), Article 16a of the German Constitution (BGBl [1949] III/100-1, as amended) and Article 56 of Polish Constitution ([1997] OJ 78/483, as amended).

4. *Cross-institutional* – multiple stakeholders at multiple levels may become involved in the regulation of irregular migration and migrants; the most recent example is a code of conduct proposed by the Italian government for the many non-governmental organisations (NGOs) who, on their vessels, have attempted to save refugees on the Mediterranean.[61]

When we look at the EU and the regulation of migration, at a pragmatic level, the first key concept that comes to our minds is the so-called Schengen Area, which has abolished physical border controls among the vast majority of European countries and became one of the core pillars of the European integration project. The second is the Dublin system, introduced in the early 1990s, which is a set of rules overseeing the admission of asylum seekers; it states the principle that the country of the first entry of the asylum seeker is to examine his or her application and that the asylum seeker is prohibited from (re-)applying in other Member States.[62] These two are interlinked: the abolition of internal border controls requires the strengthening the control of external borders, which – in turn – necessitates a common policy on migration.

But this does not exhaust the whole picture. At a constitutional level, Article 18 CFR grants a right to asylum in accordance with the 1951 Refugee Convention and Article 19 prohibits the return of migrants should they face danger (i.e. *non-refoulement*). The Treaty on the Functioning of the European Union (TFEU)[63] calls on the EU to develop a 'common policy on asylum, immigration and external border control' (Article 67) as well as a common policy on 'asylum, subsidiary protection and temporary protection with a view to offering appropriate status to any third-country national requiring international protection and ensuring compliance with the principle of *non-refoulement*' (Article 78). Both the EU and its Member States have a say in the shape of these policies; in other words, irregular migration and asylum constitute a shared competence, as contrasted to, for example, the customs union, which constitutes an exclusive responsibility of the EU (Article 4 TFEU).[64]

---

61 C. Balmer, 'Italy Drafts Contested Code of Conduct for NGO Migrant Boats', *Reuters*, 13.07.2017, <https://af.reuters.com/article/topNews/idAFKBN19Y0MH-OZATP>. We refrain here from commenting on the contents of the said Code of Conduct.

62 Currently in its third iteration, cf. Regulation (EU) No 604/2013 of the European Parliament and of the Council of 26 June 2013 establishing the criteria and mechanisms for determining the Member State responsible for examining an application for international protection lodged in one of the Member States by a third-country national or a stateless person, [2013] OJ L180/31. However, Protocol 24 to the TEU and TFEU, generally speaking, rules out a possibility for a citizen of an EU Member State to seek asylum in another Member State; Belgium is a notable exception to that rule. Cf. S. Top, 'The European Arrest Warrant against Puigdemont: A Feeling of Déjà Vu?', *EJIL: Talk!*, 03.11.2017, <https://www.ejiltalk.org/the-european-arrest-warrant-against-puigdemont-a-feeling-of-deja-vu>.

63 *Supra* n. 51.

64 To conclude this part, the law on migration has been subject to prolific academic and professional commentary. Cf. e.g. European Union Agency for Fundamental Rights

Here we hasten to note that the focus of this book is not devoted to migration within a single country (i.e. internal migration). Neither is this book concerned with a key aspect of the European integration project – wherein intra-European migration has seen unprecedented freedom of movement of persons[65] – or regular migration, but rather this book is devoted to the arrival at the external borders of Europe of the 'outsiders', that is, third country nationals and, to some extent, stateless people, who are seeking either international protection as asylum seekers (i.e. humanitarian migration) or seeking a better way of life as economic refugees. In other words, this book is largely preoccupied with, as the IOM puts it, 'irregular migration' to Europe.

(FRA), *Handbook on European law relating to asylum, borders and immigration*, 2nd ed., Luxembourg 2015, <http://fra.europa.eu/en/publication/2013/handbook-european-law-relating-asylum-borders-and-immigration>; M. Kahanec and K.F. Zimmermann (eds.), *Labor Migration, EU Enlargement, and the Great Recession*, Springer, Berlin-Heidelberg 2016; S. Castles, H. de Haas and M.J. Miller (eds.), *The Age of Migration: International Population Movements in the Modern World*, Palgrave Macmillan, London 2013; M.N. Rosenblum and D.J. Tichenor (eds.), *The Oxford Handbook of the Politics of International Migration*, Oxford University Press, Oxford 2012; S. Peers, E. Guild, J, Tomkin, V. Moreno Lax and M. Garlick, *EU Immigration and Asylum Law (Text and Commentary): Second Revised Edition*, Martinus Nijhoff, Leiden 2012; R. Rubio-Marín, *Human Rights and Immigration*, Oxford University Press, Oxford 2014; F. Cherubini, *Asylum Law in the European Union: From the Geneva Convention to the Law of the EU*, Routledge, New York 2015; V. Mitsilegas, *The Criminalisation of Migration in Europe. Challenges for Human Rights and the Rule of Law*, Springer, Dordrecht 2015.

65 Again, the reader deserves a word of explanation. The EU, in its economic aspect, is built on a few bases and one of them is 'four freedoms' that ensure free movement of goods, capital, services and persons (labour) between the EU Member States. (Another base, a political one, is e.g. the already mentioned respect of human dignity, realised mainly by the protection of fundamental rights.) These four freedoms grew gradually, by a combination of some visionary thinking and trial-and-errors, since the European integration project commenced in 1950s. In the context of intra-European migration – in essence and with the risk of over-simplification – any citizen of the Union (a status conferred thereupon since 1993 by a mere fact of possessing a citizenship of one of the Member States) can freely travel, reside, study, work, retire and own immovable property in any Member State of the Union. (There are exceptions, of course.) These freedoms are extended to EEA States as well as to Switzerland, although, again, not without exceptions. These freedoms – or, to a large extent, the abolition of relevant restrictions – are further strengthened by the elimination of physical controls at national borders between the majority of countries on the European soil. The so-called Schengen Area (named for the place where the relevant agreement was signed in 1985) comprises, at the time of writing, 22 EU Member States, three EEA Member States and Switzerland. Some European 'micro-states' which have an open border with a neighbouring EU Member State, e.g. Monaco, are *de facto* included too. (But not Andorra.) By contrast, excluded are e.g. some parts of some Member States that are outside geographical Europe, e.g. Réunion (a French *région d'outre-mer*), or have a special status within Europe, e.g. Svalbard in Norway or Mount Athos in Greece. However, physical checks at some internal borders can be exceptionally, and for a short period of time, re-installed as a response to some threat or emergency. The recent migration 'crisis' to which the present book has been devoted, is one of such emergencies. Cf. further a classic: P. Craig and G. de Búrca, *EU Law: Text, Cases, and Materials*, 5th ed., Oxford University Press, Oxford 2011.

3. Migration as an uncertain question. The third perspective, on our view, looks at the future consequences of migration. In addition to the obvious advantages and disadvantages for migrants themselves, migration as a phenomenon – regardless of being regular or not – *might* bring multiple benefits to a hosting polity, but it *might* equally bring detriment thereto by, for instance, threatening their security and well-being. Correspondingly, migrants themselves *might* fall victim of hostility of a hosting polity, where – once legally admitted – they might feel less welcome, find it difficult to integrate and even fall victim of humiliation and hate crime. And while they await the result of their asylum application, they might suffer from the fear of rejection (and thus deportation) or – as doctors in Sweden put it – 'Uppgivenhetssyndrom' (resignation syndrome).[66]

Commentators usually explain the positive impact of migration in economic terms, in particular in the areas of the labour market, public purse and economic growth. Migrants fill important niches both in fast-growing and declining sectors of the economy by bringing new skills and abilities to their hosts and often contributing more to the state budget (e.g. in taxes) than they actually take therefrom (e.g. in benefits).[67] Migration, in parallel, profoundly – and, on some occasions, creatively – impacts the culture and heritage of the hosting polity, in areas ranging from less obvious ones, such as cuisine and food consumption, sport or fashion, to more visible ones, such as language and art. The landscape is often more diverse as a result as the migrants are present in all cultural sectors.

Some commentators contrast these positive, economic and cultural impacts of migration against the negative impacts, such as dangers to national security, political system, social structure and demography as well as economy and cultural heritage, among others. They see it as a 'Trojan horse' and argue it is difficult, if not impossible, to differentiate between those migrants who come as friends and those who come as foes. Thus, they claim, migrants increase the threat of petty crimes as well as of serious ones, including terrorism. More broadly, they see them as a threat to stability, safety and public security. They argue migrants threaten traditions, values and identity of hosting polities. These commentators most often claim that migrants 'steal jobs' as they tend to work for a lower wage than the hosts. They even point out that the different ethnical and cultural background of migrants makes it difficult, if not impossible, for them to integrate and – if this is desired – assimilate.[68] The experience of

66 R. Aviv, 'The Trauma of Facing Deportation', *The New Yorker*, 03.04.2017, <https://www.newyorker.com/magazine/2017/04/03/the-trauma-of-facing-deportation>.

67 Organization for Economic Cooperation and Development (OECD), *Migration Policy Debates: Is Migration Good for the Economy?*, Paris, May 2014, <https://www.oecd.org/migration/OECD%20Migration%20Policy%20Debates%20Numero%202.pdf>.

68 M. Haisler and Z. Layton-Henry, 'Migration and the Links between Social and Societal Security' in O. Wæver, B. Buzan, M. Kelstrup and P. Lemaitre (eds.), *Identity, Migration and the New Security Agenda in Europe*, Pinter, London 1993, pp. 148–166.

immigrants many times confirms such difficulties as their 'social acceptance' is often 'conditional upon [their] very best behaviour'.[69]

The stark contrast between the two positions outlined above can be also understood by differentiating between 'wanted' or 'unwanted' migration. Migrants are usually wanted when the hosting polity, due to labour shortages, either lacks high-skilled migrants or needs low-skilled migrants.[70] To that end, such a polity usually opens regular, legal channels for immigration. For instance, the 'green card lottery' in the United States is perhaps the most known example. In the EU, the so-called 'Blue Card' gives the right for highly qualified third-country nationals to reside and work in the territory of a EU Member State.[71] When it comes to 'unwanted' migration, the hosting polity would 'rather be without' it, yet it often *de facto* has to live with it. Such migrants are usually those whose return is impossible even if their claims for protection are rejected (i.e. 'unavoidable' migrants) and those who were granted asylum or who are admitted for family reunification (i.e. 'reluctantly accepted').[72]

This bring us to our third perspective on understanding migration, that is, one of profound uncertainty of the consequences of migration. Here we ask about the future, yet we do not possess enough knowledge to make any fully informed decision how to act. We not only do not know how a given issue of societal importance could develop (i.e. 'unknown knowns'), but – more importantly – we do not even know what other societal issues could possibly be affected or raised (i.e. 'unknown unknowns'). Regardless of the view that prevails (i.e. migration is good or bad) and, even if we take a consequentialist stance, regardless of whether the negative impacts that can be overcome and positive impacts maximised, the many effects that migration brings to the fore are impossible to be predicted in full, if ever. (This is true for many aspects of life.) This, in turn, scares people and often fuels opposition towards migration, both regular and irregular.

4. Migration as an omnipresent question. The fourth and final perspective, on our view, is that of history. Many commentators view the *status quo* of irregular migration to Europe as 'the defining issue of our times'.[73] A few others add that it has been an 'unprecedented' phenomenon, in a sense of the

69 M. Okwonga, 'The Ungrateful Country' in N. Shukla (ed.), *The Good Immigrant*, Unbound, London 2017, p. 231.

70 J. Carling, 'The European Paradox of Unwanted Migration' in J.P. Burgess and S. Gutwirth (eds.), *A Threat Against Europe? Security, Migration and Integration*, VUB Press, Brussels 2011, pp. 33–34.

71 Council Directive 2009/50/EC of 25 May 2009 on the conditions of entry and residence of third-country nationals for the purposes of highly qualified employment [2009] OJ L155/17. The 'Blue Card' system does not apply to Denmark, Ireland and the United Kingdom.

72 J. Carling, *supra* n. 70, pp. 34–35.

73 K.B. Harpviken, *Foreword*, in this volume, p. v.

scale, difficulty and the lack of any predecessor.[74] Conversely, other analysts claim the 'crisis rhetoric' has been only a media 'hype', fuelled by the quest to sensationalise the problem in order to grab public attention, and, in this way, constituting a useful political tool;[75] yet hard numbers do not necessarily support that view.[76] We agree that irregular migration nowadays is a 'defining' concern, yet we disagree it is anyhow 'unprecedented'. Migration has always been a part of Europe as it was a part of any other continent on this planet. From the beginning of history, the inhabitants of place X or Y either were moving to other places or other people were coming to place X or Y, in large or small numbers. Some of them have had very serious reasons, often ambiguous and concurring – to look for some form of help, to flee some injustice or to seek better living conditions – and strong motivation, only fuelled by despair since – as Bob Dylan has sung – 'when you ain't got nothing, you got nothing to lose'.[77] The UN adopted *The New York Declaration for Refugees and Migrants* in September 2016, admitting that:

> [s]ince earliest times, humanity has been on the move. Some people move in search of new economic opportunities and horizons. Others move to escape armed conflict, poverty, food insecurity, persecution, terrorism, or human rights violations and abuses. Still others do so in response to the adverse effects of climate change, natural disasters (some of which may be linked to climate change), or other environmental factors. Many move, indeed, for a combination of these reasons.[78]

Yet we acknowledge some other people have less pressing reasons, such as a wish for bettering their lives (predominantly in economic terms) or, simply, to satisfy their curiosity about the world. People have been, do and will be moving from one part of the world to another, for a shorter or longer period of time, or even permanently. Sometimes they would be expected and welcome, some other times – not or not so much. In other words, '[t]he story of humanity is essentially the story of human movement'[79] and, from this viewpoint, it will just continue to be so.

---

[74] D. Dinan, N. Nugent and W.E. Paterson, 'Conclusions: Crisis Without End?' in D. Dinan, N. Nugent and W.E. Paterson, *The European Union in Crisis*, Macmillan, London 2017, pp. 360–75.

[75] J. Ramji-Nogales, 'Migration Emergencies' (2017) 68(3) *Hastings Law Journal* 616.

[76] G.J. Abel and N. Sander, 'Quantifying Global International Migration Flows' (2014) 343 *Science* 1520; G.J. Abel, *Estimates of Global Bilateral Migration Flows by Gender Between 1960 and 2010*, working paper No. 2/2016, Vienna Institute of Demography, Vienna, pp. 1–32, <https://www.oeaw.ac.at/fileadmin/subsites/Institute/VID/PDF/Publications/Working_Papers/WP2016_02.pdf>.

[77] B. Dylan, *Like a Rolling Stone*, 1965.

[78] United Nations, General Assembly, *The New York Declaration for Refugees and Migrants*, New York, 19.09.2016, A/RES/71/1.

[79] P. Kingsley, *The New Odyssey: The Story of Europe's Refugee Crisis*, Guardian Faber Publishing, London 2016, p. 264.

Each country has had its own immigration and emigration trends and traditions. There are countries 'built' on migration, for instance the United States of America or Canada, and there are countries that have seen almost no immigrants, but only emigrants. (A list thereof would be quite long here.) To take the United Kingdom (UK) as an illustrative example, the British – following the end of the Second World War and the related shortage of labour – encouraged immigration from predominantly former colonies, gathered under the Commonwealth of Nations. It was clear that colonial links and networks (i.e. political, economic and cultural) constituted major determinants of the origins and composition of immigrants.[80] In addition, the UK recruited the so-called European Volunteer Workers, predominantly from Eastern European countries under Soviet influence. However, this initially favourable approach to immigration – manifested by, for example, the British Nationality Act 1948 affirming the right of Commonwealth citizens to settle in the UK[81] – changed a few decades later. For example, in 1972 the Leicester City Council placed an advertisement in an Ugandan newspaper to discourage the arrival of Ugandan Asians expelled by the regime of Idi Amin.[82] The British Nationality Act 1981 placed restrictions on the originally automatic right to citizenship.[83] The enlargement of the EU in 2004 invited a new wave of immigration from the East of Europe, as the UK was one of the few 'old' Member States that immediately granted free movement to these workers. The current political climate surrounding the so-called 'Brexit' process (i.e. the withdrawal of the UK from the EU) has placed migration at the fore of discussion, with little known about the future of other EU citizens living in the UK and significant resistance to the implementation of agreements to assist with the safe resettlement of asylum seekers.[84]

To take Poland as a further example, at several points in the nineteenth century – after the loss of independence from 1795 until 1918 – Poles have fled their country, for example seeking refuge from repressions after many failed uprisings against occupying powers. At the same time, many Poles were forcibly deported to Siberia. Then, they were escaping the atrocities of Second World War and – motivated, in addition, politically – in the aftermath thereof,

---

[80] M. Czaika and H. de Haas, *Determinants of Migration to the UK*, briefing, Migration Observatory, University of Oxford, 11.10.2017, <http://www.migrationobservatory.ox.ac.uk/wp-content/uploads/2016/04/Briefing-Determinants-of-Migration-17-1.pdf>.

[81] 11 & 12 Geo. 6 c. 56.

[82] BBC, *Ugandan Asians advert 'foolish', says Leicester councillor*, 08.08.2012, <http://www.bbc.com/news/uk-england-leicestershire-19165216>.

[83] 1981 c. 61.

[84] A. Gentleman, 'Legal Challenge to Cap on Dubs Child Refugee Scheme Fails', *The Guardian*, 02.11.2017, <https://www.theguardian.com/world/2017/nov/02/child-refugee-legal-challenge-dubs-government-scheme-fails>.

when the East of Europe was put into the sphere of the Soviet influence,[85] as well as after the introduction of martial law in 1981, as a consequence of the *Solidarność* movement. Notably, after the so-called 'March 1968' thousands of Polish Jews were forced to leave the country with a one-way passport. It was predominantly the United States, Canada, the UK and France that welcomed them.[86] After the restitution of democracy in 1989, migration to seek better living opportunities has also been present, which has intensified gradually since 2004 when Poland joined the EU, enabling Poles to freely live and work in other Member States of the EU/EEA and in Switzerland. In recent years, the trend has been changing: Poland has not only faced emigration to the West of Europe, but also it is slowly becoming a destination for many Eastern Europeans for a mixture of economic and political reasons: nowadays, Ukrainians constitute the biggest nationality migrating to Poland.[87]

Despite our emphasis on a single type of migration (i.e. irregular) in one particular geographical area (i.e. Europe) and in one particular direction (i.e. *to* Europe), we acknowledge that irregular migration is not solely a European phenomenon.[88] We recognise the *status quo* of irregular immigrants in other parts of the world is, at this moment in time, often much more in dire need of political and, arguably, academic attention.[89] Outside Europe, migration has recently made headlines with, for example, the United States President's executive orders to restrict immigration,[90] ongoing forced displacement in Colombia[91] and South Sudan,[92] the Rohingya refugee crisis in

---

85 For the account of the Polish intelligentsia fleeing the communist rule, cf. especially the memoirs of Henryk Grynberg, who claimed that in late 1940s '... anyone who could, slipped away ... the new *clique* did not care, quite the contrary: the more gone, the better' (translation ours). H. Grynberg, *Uchodźcy* [Refugees], Świat Książki, Warszawa 2004, p. 8.

86 D. Stola, *Kraj bez wyjścia? Migracje z Polski 1949–1989* [A Country with No Escape? Migrations from Poland 1949–1989], Instytut Pamięci Narodowej, Warszawa 2010; P. Milza (ed.) *L'émigration politique en Europe aux XIXe et XXe siècles*, École Française de Rome, Rome 1991.

87 I. Jóźwiak and M. Piechowska, *Crisis-driven Mobility between Ukraine and Poland. What Does the Available Data (Not) Tell Us*, working paper Nr 99(157), Centre of Migration Research, University of Warsaw, 2017, <http://www.migracje.uw.edu.pl/wp-content/uploads/2017/05/WP99157.pdf>.

88 F. Trauner, 'Asylum Policy: The EU's "Crises" and the Looming Policy Regime Failure' (2016) 38(3) *Journal of European Integration* 319.

89 Cf. e.g. the Uppsala Conflict Data Program at <http://ucdp.uu.se>.

90 D. Barrett, 'White House expands travel ban, restricting visitors from eight countries', *The Washington Post*, 24.09.2017, <https://www.washingtonpost.com/world/national-security/trump-administration-changes-travel-ban-countries/2017/09/24/1fef7cfe-a140-11e7-ade1-76d061d56efa_story.html>.

91 UNHCR, 'Forced displacement growing in Colombia despite peace agreement', briefing, 10.03.2017, <http://www.unhcr.org/news/briefing/2017/3/58c26e114/forced-displacement-growing-colombia-despite-peace-agreement.html>.

92 J. Burke, 'Bonded by spilt blood, South Sudanese refugees in Uganda reach million mark', *The Guardian*, 17.07.2017, <https://www.theguardian.com/global-development/2017/aug/17/south-sudan-refugee-families-uganda>.

Myanmar (Burma)[93] or Australia's highly controversial detention centres in, for example, Papua New Guinea and Nauru.[94]

III.

The present book is split into three main parts. Part I is entitled *The European Integration Project and Irregular Migration: Upholding Fundamental Values and Principles*. This volume begins by providing an overview of the regulatory framework for irregular migration currently in place at the supranational level. It highlights the key values and principles enshrined in European law and contrasts them with practice, that is, implementation and enforcement. Therefore, a recurring question that arises in this Part asks to what extent these values and principles and these practices are in conformity.

In Chapter 1, *Lonardo* uses the current legal framework to question who exactly is responsible for the management of migration: the EU or its Member States? As it is a shared competence, the discourse is split. The author analyses the Draft Articles on Responsibility of International Organizations (DARIO) and shifts away from the understanding that the EU should take responsibility. He purports that responsibility should eventually rest with the Member States. Indeed, the extent to which this is applied in practice can be further seen in the following two chapters.

Miglio pursues, in Chapter 2, an understanding of the governance and management of migration in accordance with the emerging principle of solidarity amongst the EU Member States, and the weight that is afforded to this concept when it comes to the Area of Freedom, Security and Justice (AFSJ). In principle, such solidarity has been forthcoming in a monetary sense. However, a shift towards non-monetary solidarity has not been without opposition from individual Member States, which have made legal challenges to contest the increased focus on the so-called 'fair sharing', which helps to define 'the content of the principle of solidarity in this particular policy area'.[95] Indeed, here a distinction is made between responsibility (cf. Chapter 1) and solidarity, which – as previously mentioned, and on this author's view – is increasingly being called upon as a tool for crisis management.

---

93 A. Ramzy, '270,000 Rohingya Have Fled Myanmar, U.N. Says', *The New York Times*, 08.09.2017, <https://www.nytimes.com/2017/09/08/world/asia/myanmar-rohingya-refugees-270000.html>.

94 Human Rights Watch, *Australia/PNG: Refugees face unchecked violence: Keeping People on Manus Island Leaves Hundreds at Risk*, 25.10.2017, <https://www.hrw.org/news/2017/10/25/australia/png-refugees-face-unchecked-violence>; cf. also 'The Nauru Files', *The Guardian*, <https://www.theguardian.com/australia-news/nauru-files>.

95 Chapter 2, in this volume, p. 38.

Another tool for crisis management is discussed in Chapter 3, where *Butler* provides an insight into the bilateral measures taken by EU Member States, on behalf of the EU but under the auspices of EU external relations, and in particular the Common Foreign and Security Policy (CFSP). The chapter considers the questionable legality of some of these agreements and demonstrates interconnections between these and the EU–Turkey Statement of 18 March 2016 that further elaborated upon the EU–Turkey Joint Action Plan of 15 October 2015, and its unprecedented presentation as a press release. This inevitably raises questions about the Statement's ability to be overseen judicially and the implications of such an action on the rule of law.

Chapter 4 provides an alternative perspective on migration to the EU, where this phenomenon is not considered as a crisis situation (as it is viewed in the common parlance). Instead, *Cudowska* argues that migration has been a steady and an unstoppable phenomenon for more than a decade and it has had a clear effect on economies and trade policies across the globe. Nowadays, migration is an unrelenting part of global society and drives social and economic changes.

In Chapter 5, *Drinóczi* and *Mohay* discuss the recent case of *Ilias and Ahmed v Hungary* (2017), in which the ECtHR upheld the protection of the fundamental rights of irregular migrants. The Court found the detention of the two asylum seekers to be arbitrary and that the Hungarian authorities had deprived them of the right to challenge the conditions they were put into. These authors see the Strasbourg Court's decision as a confirmation that 'the existing rights and standards are, in principle, appropriate for the handling of current emergency or crisis situations and no reinterpretation is necessary or warranted'.[96] The authors link the deeds of the Hungarian government with the negative political and social attitude towards irregular migration. To illustrate their point, the authors report on the populist moves of the Hungarian government in place and, as an example, they reproduce the entire text of the 'National Consultation on Immigration and Terrorism' that was run in 2015.

Gabrielsen Jumbert determines, in Chapter 6, the extent to which measures aimed at providing assistance and relief to migrants at sea *en route* to Europe create, in parallel, a so-called 'pull factor', that is, an encouragement for more migrants to come. The 'fear of saving lives' has been both dominant and powerful in popular perception and in policy debates since it seems to explain 'the otherwise inexplicable'.[97] This resulted in the emergence of controversial deterrent policies, including 'push back' operations, which was met, in response, with rescue operations run by some non-governmental organisations (NGOs). The author eventually asks for a 'broader picture' to be taken into account in the determination of what motivates (or not) migrants to come to Europe.

96 Chapter 5, in this volume, p. 110.
97 Chapter 6, in this volume, p. 121.

Part II is entitled *Migrants, their rights and the limits thereof.* Here the authors analyse whether the very basic concepts on which migration law and policy operate live up to the expectations vested therein nowadays. In particular, these authors ask after the limits of the concept of 'refugee' and the definition of certain crimes related to migration; they further consider how these relate to the values and principles on which Europe has been built.

In Chapter 7, *Piekutowska* and *Kużelewska* focus upon the notion of economic refugees and the need to differentiate between those who require humanitarian protection (e.g. as a result of dire economic necessity) and those who qualify as economic migrants (i.e. those seeking improvement of their life economically, but whose choice to migrate has been made rather voluntarily, without the coercion present in humanitarian migration). This Chapter departs from a statistical analysis of international migration and determines the causes and barriers faced by economic refugees. Whilst the authors acknowledge that the impact of economic refugees on the *status quo* of migration to Europe is rather limited, this phenomenon requires more attention in the context of the EU external relations, especially concerning the regions that are most severely affected by poverty. The authors leave the reader pondering on the limits of the current legal framework, providing for international protection *solely* to those who are the most vulnerable. Therefore, they stress that economic refugees are not considered refugees according to the Geneva Convention as the decision to leave the country is not based on political persecution, but rather on economic factors. It thus seems that the 1951 Refugees Convention does not entirely correspond to the current migratory needs.

Chapter 8, the first to deal with the criminalisation of migration, looks at the EU response to the smuggling of migrants. *Brière* commences by comparing the EU definition of this crime with its counterpart in international law. She discusses how legislators decide to define the offence of migrant smuggling and how their decisions may encroach upon democratic principles. The author underlined conflicting perceptions and arguments within both the EU and its Member States.

In Chapter 9, *Top* discusses the legal evolution of the so-called political offence exemption in extradition law. The author discusses the legal developments made in relation to terrorism and the impact that these have had not only on the attitude towards migrants arriving in Europe, but also on the legitimacy of the European integration project, where values such as 'respect for human dignity, freedom, … equality, … human rights, including the rights of persons belonging to minorities'[98] are put into question.

98 Chapter 9, in this volume, p. 178.

Part III is entitled *The* status quo *of migration in Europe: selected national perspectives* and moves the focus of this book from the European to a national level. These chapters do not only act as 'national reports' but they also demonstrate how various stakeholders, working at a national level, deal with irregular migration. The latter is of crucial importance as migration policy is a shared competence between the EU and its Member States; this part provides an insight into some of the unilateral measures implemented by Member States to regulate and manage migration.

Chapter 10 provides an overview, portrayed by *Panzeri*, of the Italian response to the migrant 'crisis'. The author focuses on Italian legislative developments regarding migrants' reception and integration. He criticises the lack of solidarity among the EU Member States, especially from the Visegrád Group,[99] which is leading in populism, instead of a rational migrant policy. The author also notes obvious shortcomings regarding Italian and European management of the 'migrant crisis'. He eventually criticises the insufficient measures of social inclusion addressed to irregular migrants in Italy.

Chapter 11 addresses the criminalisation of migration at a national level. *Perkowska* elaborates upon the 'crimmigration' – the interception of criminal and immigration law – that is a central feature of current migration law in Poland and its reforms in the past decade. This has led to some disproportionality in the response towards the *status quo* of migration, premised upon the perceived threat to public order and security. However, the Chapter clearly demonstrates that such reforms are a necessary step towards the harmonisation and approximation of national law with EU law. Yet the Chapter thought-provokingly engages with controversial domestic legal reform that is merely proscribing democratic standards and encourages 'crimmigration'. In result, the effective protection of fundamental rights has been put into question.

In Chapter 12, *Roots* discusses a new stakeholder in the governance and management of migration: NGOs. She suggests their involvement owes much to the inefficiency of the way in which irregular migration has been handled thus far. In her chapter, she considers the involvement of these organisations at a national level in the development of the Estonian migration policy. The author outlines the key attributes of NGOs that are necessary to ensure that civil society participation is effective. She subsequently evaluates the actual impact these organisations have had in the Estonian context against the backdrop of the current migration situation in Europe. She also notes that the involvement of NGOs began in 2013, which demonstrates an ongoing engagement with legal and policy development that pre-dates the current situation.

---

99 Cf. *supra* n. 42.

Finally, in Chapter 13, *Sierocka* discusses language as a significant factor contributing towards the integration of migrants into their host polities. She stresses that linguistic integration is a key response when combatting the hostile and populist discourse against irregular migrants. In her Chapter, she describes the existing European and national responses to linguistic integration and concludes that it is, more than ever, vital that Europeans engage in a 'dialogue' with irregular migrants in order to positively affect social cohesion and integration of immigrants into host societies.

IV.

Taking into account the topics discussed in the contributions to this volume, we cannot help but offer in the following a few points of reflection on irregular migration to Europe. Building on the past and the present of migration, here we focus – perhaps more importantly – on its future.

1. Migration is quite like the weather. Migration is nothing new: it has been here and there in the past, it is a phenomenon of the present times and it will never cease to occur, regardless whether we like it or not. (And, as some predict, because 'as intercountry inequality widens and climate change threatens livelihoods', the numbers of migrating people will only increase.)[100] Neither is migration limited to Europe; quite the contrary: all parts of the world have faced it. Consequently, we see the weather (sic!) as an apt allegory for migration. Migration, similarly to the weather, has always been here.

To further illustrate the omnipresence of migration, and in line with the tradition that *European Integration and Democracy* book series has established, we have reproduced on the front cover of this volume – with the kind permission of the Art Gallery of New South Wales in Sydney, Australia – one of the masterpieces of Jeffrey Smart (1921–2013), titled *Bus Terminus* (1973).[101] In this modernist picture, these buses – of various shapes and colours – have either just completed their journeys or they wait to embark on some other. We do not know where these buses have come from and where they soon might go. We know nothing about their passengers and their luggage – if there are few or many of them, what motivates them to go, whether their journey is comfortable enough, if someone awaits them, etc. Yet one thing is sure: these buses have been carrying people and will not cease to do so. The same can be said about migration.

---

100 I. Goldin, G. Cameron and M. Balarajan, *Exceptional People: How Migration Shaped Our World and Will Define Our Future*, Princeton University Press, Princeton 2012, p. 6.

101 J. Smart, *Bus terminus*, 1973; Art Gallery of New South Wales, Sydney, Australia; No. 251.1998, 92.0 x 81.0 cm; copyright by Estate of Jeffrey Smart, <https://www.artgallery.nsw.gov.au/collection/works/251.1998>.

2. Migration – as an unavoidable fact of life and like many aspects of public life – requires both responsible and visionary governance and management.[102] Many meanings can be asserted to these qualifying terms, yet in the context of migration, we would like to point out a few characteristics thereof.

2a. The first step is perhaps to realise the unavoidability of migration and, as a consequence, to start responding thereto. As we have suggested, migration is quite like the weather, yet while people cannot do much about the weather, they could – and should – do something about migration.[103] Thus we agree with Patrick Kingsley that '[t]he sooner we recognise the inevitability of this movement, the sooner we can try to manage it'.[104] François Crépeau, the UN Special Rapporteur on the human rights of migrants, added '[a]s mobility is increasing with globalisation, instead of resisting it, we should organise it'.[105] The simplest way is to organise channels for legal migration, as, for example, with the Hungarians after the Budapest Revolution in 1956[106] or with the Indochinese in late 1970s.[107] Thus, Jean-Claude Juncker announced in his 2017 State of the Union Address that '[w]e will also work on opening up legal pathways. Irregular migration will only stop if there is a real alternative to perilous journeys.'[108]

2b. Yet having the mere governance and management of migration in place is not sufficient. This governance and management has to adhere to certain qualities – in our view: responsibility and vision. Responsible governance and management adheres, at minimum, to democratic standards, the rule of law (*Rechtsstaat*) and respect for human rights. Migrants are human beings and

---

102 We distinguish between 'governance' and 'management'. Simplifying, the former signifies leadership, policy-making, regulation, etc. The latter comes second and implements such 'governance' into practice.

103 We have been inspired here by Gary T. Marx. In early 2010s, he compared privacy to the weather and argued that – contrary to the weather – 'there is much that should, and can, be done' about the governance and management of privacy. G.T. Marx, 'Privacy Is Not Quite Like the Weather' in D. Wright and P. De Hert (eds.), *Privacy Impact Assessment*, Springer, Dordrecht 2012, p. v.

104 P. Kingsley, *supra* n. 79, p. 264.

105 G. Jackson, 'UNs François Crépeau on the Refugee Crisis: 'Instead of Resisting Migration, Let's Organise It'', *The Guardian*, 22.04.2015, <https://www.theguardian.com/world/2015/apr/22/uns-francois-crepeau-on-the-refugee-crisis-instead-of-resisting-migration-lets-organise-it>.

106 M. Zieck, 'The 1956 Hungarian Refugee Emergency, an Early and Instructive Case of Resettlement' (2013) 5(2) *Amsterdam Law Forum*, <http://amsterdamlawforum.org/article/viewFile/314/487>; K. Kovačević, 'The Refugee Problem in Yugoslavia', in: J.M. Rainer, K. Somlai (eds.), *The 1956 Hungarian Revolution and the Soviet Bloc Countries: Reactions and Repercussions*, The Institute for the History of the 1956 Hungarian Revolution, Budapest 2007, pp. 111–128, <http://www.rev.hu/rev/htdocs/hu/kiadvanyok/Hungarian_revolution_2007/The_1956HungarianRev.pdf>.

107 B. Stein, 'The Geneva Conferences and the Indochinese Refugee Crisis' (1979) 13(4) *The International Migration Review* 716.

108 J.C. Junker, *State of the Union Address*, Strasbourg, 13.09.2017.

hence holders of inalienable rights, and Europe, like many other democratic polities, has promised to respect them.

All European countries and the EU itself, each have their *magnae cartae* and each promised to live up to their commitments therein; as we outlined at the beginning of this contribution. They promised to respect human rights of 'everyone within [their] jurisdiction'.[109] The European Court of Human Rights in Strasbourg has emerged as the ultimate guardian of these commitments – as *Drinóczi* and *Mohay* observe – as the many polities in Europe have failed to do so. We thus argue even further: compliance with international human rights law is indispensable, but more is needed. The stakes here are rather high: migrants are human beings (a repetition, we know) and, if they are refugees, their life is often in peril. Therefore this compliance with the highest legal norms, we argue, must be complemented by an ethical reflection.

There are 'big' ethical dilemmas that both individuals and those who govern them must ask themselves. For the latter, the main question would ask what constitutes a good government. How should a just government act? Should such a government take moral responsibility for the well-being of refugees? Would the acceptance of irregular migrants be one of Aristotelean virtues? Is a good government bound by a duty to help? Taking a utilitarian stance, should those who govern strive only for the greater good for their own people or, rather, should they strive for the entire humankind? (In contrast, those who want to reject refugees often adopt similar arguments and claim that welcoming refugees would result in a reduction of their own 'good'.)[110] The answer to each of these questions depends on the ethical stance chosen by the individual and those who govern and manage the polity; we outlined this earlier in our discussion on ethics and migration.

To solve such a dilemma, Europe could ask itself what we call a kind of 'reversed democracy question'. ('Reversed' because now it is Europe who is being asked for help. In the future, the situation might reverse: Europe might ask for help.) This is an inquiry that Bentham and Mill perhaps would embark on too. If, for instance, a humanitarian crisis hit Europe and forced thousands or millions of Europeans to flee the Old Continent in a quest for survival, what would Europe want the other democratic countries around the world to do? Would it want them to build fences with barbed wire and keep Europeans in refugee camps for months, if not years? Or would Europe want these countries – built equally on the respect for human dignity and governed by democracy, rule of law (*Rechtsstaat*) and the respect for fundamental rights – to stick to these values and principles?

---

109 Convention for the Protection of Human Rights and Fundamental Freedoms, *supra* n. 44, Art. 1.

110 We thank Iris Huis in 't Veld for bringing this matter to our attention.

Another way could be to ask what does Europe owe to refugees. *Harpviken* speculated that Angela Merkel would be awarded the Nobel Peace Prize for 2015 as she had demonstrated a 'true leadership and risen above politics, taking a humane approach in a difficult situation'[111] with her opening of German borders for irregular migrants in 2015. Merkel perhaps asked herself a few questions Kant would have asked himself: is it a moral duty to treat everybody with respect? Should we show some sincere solidarity with fellow human beings? Should we treat all people as an end in themselves and not merely as a means to some end? Or should we allow robbing them of their dignity?

Furthermore, ethical reflection requires also thinking about more practical aspects. First and foremost, ethics goes beyond the law and ethical reflection asks an elementary question after the contents of the law. It was observed already in ancient Rome that *non omne quod licet honestum est.*[112] For example, should the law differentiate between vulnerable and non-vulnerable migrants? What constitutes a good cause for fleeing a collapsed homeland to be accepted in a host polity? Is fleeing a war a better reason than fleeing dictatorships, religious extremism or poverty? Is a child or a pregnant woman a more vulnerable migrant than any other migrant?

In this ethical reflection, a few chapters in this volume analysed criminal justice aspects and the allocation of responsibility (*Brière*, *Top* and *Lonardo*). We would point out one more issue. Those who unjustifiably act against migrants shall face liability for their deeds and criminal law must be apt to address these crimes. In this context, we can immediately think of human smuggling and trafficking, but the picture is actually much broader. For example, Kalpouzos and Mann pointed out to the 'banality of crimes against migrants', as '[a]round the world, migrants are locked up in camps, abused and often driven to the brink of starvation. Many die as a result.'[113] Therefore it is not surprising that the International Criminal Court and its Prosecutor have been asked to examine the alleged 'migrant-related crimes in Libya'[114] or to 'launch an investigation

111 Peace Research Institute Oslo, 'Nobel Peace Prize 2015: PRIO Director's Speculations', October 2015, <https://www.prio.org/About/PeacePrize/PRIO-Directors-Speculations-2015>. Eventually, the Prize was awarded to the Tunisian National Dialogue Quartet. Cf. 'The Nobel Peace Prize 2015'. *Nobelprize.org*, press release, <http://www.nobelprize.org/nobel_prizes/peace/laureates/2015/press.html>.

112 Latin for 'not all that is permitted is honest'.

113 I. Kalpouzos and I. Mann, 'The Banality of Crimes against Migrants', *Der Spiegel*, 28.10.2017, <http://www.spiegel.de/international/world/editorial-on-crimes-against-migrants-a-1175239.html>.

114 International Criminal Court, 'Statement of the ICC Prosecutor to the United Nations Security Council on the situation in Libya', New York, 09.05.2017, §29, <https://www.icc-cpi.int/Pages/item.aspx?name=170509-otp-stat-lib>.

regarding crimes against humanity which may have been committed against asylum seekers and refugees in Nauru and Manus Island'.[115]

In parallel, the needs of asylum seekers and refugees are not limited to their most basic needs, especially to the respect for their dignity and fundamental rights. There have some rudimentary needs too. They need to live as normally as possible and thus – as *Cudowska* pointed out – they need access to the labour market. They too need integration with the hosting polity (as *Panzeri* argued) and the acquisition of language skills (as *Sierocka* asserted) – as well as access to education – constitute perhaps the first steps thereto.[116] By contrast, the hosting polity also has its own needs that are of ethical importance, for example, how to ensure safety and security for everyone?

2c. Responsible governance and management of migration, which is a global phenomenon, requires coordinated answers. It was Beck who famously observed that 'global risks require global responses' and no country could cope alone which such challenges.[117] Migration is such a 'global risk' and *Harpviken* strikes the same chord by arguing that migration 'necessitate[s] transnational solutions'.[118] In the context of Europe, what is clear is that there needs to be consistency in the response towards irregular migrants. Indeed, whilst the Dublin system is considered as the 'baseline' approach to asylum in the EU, it cannot but be noted that both its design and implementation are questionable.[119] Its application is doomed either way: either acceptance of EU rules will lead to the overburdening of Southern EU Member States or ignorance of EU rules will lead to the overburdening of Northern EU Member States.[120] Furthermore, the governance and management of migration requires cooperation and solidarity. We do not only mean that the EU Member States should cooperate and mutually support each other in governing migration, financially and politically (as required per the Treaties and as *Miglio* discussed), but also, in its daily management multiple stakeholders, from public authorities to NGOs (as *Roots* suggests), should be involved and should cooperate and mutually support each other.

---

115 'The Situation in Nauru and Manus Island: Liability for crimes against humanity in the detention of refugees and asylum seekers', communiqué to the Office of the Prosecutor of the ICC, 13.02.2017, <http://docs.wixstatic.com/ugd/b743d9_e4413cb72e1646d8bd3e8a8c9a466950.pdf>.

116 For example, the VUB since 2016 maintains the 'Welcome Student-Refugee Program'. For those who had to 'abruptly stop their studies and flee', the University wants to give them a 'fair chance to continue their studies'. Cf. <http://www.vub.ac.be/en/welcome-student-refugees-programme>.

117 U. Beck, 'The Cosmopolitan Condition: Why Methodological Nationalism Fails' (2007) 24(7) *Theory, Culture & Society* 288.

118 K.B. Harpviken, *Foreword*, in this volume, p. viii.

119 European Parliament, *Reform of the Dublin System*, briefing No. PE 586.639, 10.03.2017.

120 F. Trauner, *supra* n. 88.

However, we acknowledge there is also a negative side of migration. We have already mentioned a widespread argument that migration might not only bring profound changes to the society but also, in some instances, the migratory process could lead to a security threat. This matter has been frequently discussed in this volume. However, both the governance and the management of such a situation call for putting a 'thin red line' between benefits and threats posed by migration. This could take a form of the classically understood legal concepts of 'proportionality' – that is, legitimately and not excessively justifying any interference with a fundamental right[121] – or 'practical concordance' (*praktische Konkordanz*) – that is, preserving as much as possible of each competing interest at stake.[122] Yet, whenever the existence of a threat posed by irregular migrants cannot be satisfactorily established, the law already knows the solution: *in dubio pro reo*.

2d. We further argue that visionary governance and management of migration is needed. The measures taken now to address migration will impact on future generations. The entire body of migration law and policy was conceived in the aftermath of military conflicts in Europe in the twentieth century, with a particular cause for migration in mind: fleeing a war. Thus, it is often called an 'antiquated refugee regime'.[123] Yet the governance and management of migration, in the same way as many aspects of public life, face changes in the society and thus must be responsive thereto. We have hinted at this already and we can take it for granted that the future will bring more examples of so-called 'survival migration'.[124] This requires thinking about the future in a long term and refraining from *ad hoc*, quick and thus incompetent responses. *Harpviken* calls for 'informed political innovation'. A few authors in this book have discussed some brave proposals: from a simple need for long-term solutions, to an addressing of the root causes of irregular migration (*Butler*); and from the establishment of a centralised procedure for examining asylum claims in the EU (*Miglio*); to a re-definition of basic concepts such as 'refugee' (*Piekutowska* and *Kużelewska*); and migration-related crimes (*Brière, Top*). Furthermore, New Zealand's incoming Labour-led coalition government has already hinted at the introduction of an experimental humanitarian visa category for those

121 Cf. D. Lindsay, 'The Role of Proportionality in Assessing Transatlantic Flows of Personal Data', in D.J.B. Svantesson and D. Kloza (eds.), *Trans-Atlantic Data Privacy Relations as a Challenge for Democracy*, Intersentia, Cambridge 2017, pp. 49–84.

122 O. De Schutter and F. Tulkens, 'The European Court of Human Rights as a Pragmatic Institution' in E. Brems (ed.), *Conflicts Between Fundamental Rights*, Intersentia, Antwerp 2008, pp. 169–216.

123 J. Ramji-Nogales, *supra* n. 75.

124 A. Betts, *Survival Migration: Failed Governance and the Crisis of Displacement*, Cornell University Press, Ithaca 2013.

who are adversely affected by climate change.[125] We thus argue for the need for migration law to adapt to the reality of changing society, regardless whether at a national, supranational or international level. It is perhaps for these reasons that the UN is currently considering two new 'global compacts' on migration, one on refugees and the other on safe, orderly and regular migration, both of which are to be adopted in 2018.[126] Yet we acknowledge that the difficulty of adhering to these qualities of governance and management of migration – i.e. being responsible and visionary – is magnified by the importance of the human lives at stake, the profound uncertainty of the consequences of migration and its omnipresence.

3. *However, thus far, the way in which Europe has managed the influx of irregular migrants has created multifaceted crises.* We agree with Kingsley that this migration situation is 'predominantly a problem with Europe, not with the people trying to breach its borders'.[127] Many of the authors in this book have highlighted the incompetence and inadequacy of European and national responses to the migration crisis – especially their fragmented, improvised and chaotic character – and perhaps most acutely *Panzeri* with his snapshot of migration governance in Italy. In conclusion, both the EU and some of its Member States have, at times, encountered troubles with conforming to democratic standards, the rule of law (*Rechtsstaat*) and the protection of fundamental rights.

In an attempt to adequately name this problem, many commentators have called it a migration 'crisis' and highlighted the sense of urgency. Yet this crisis is multidimensional, having at least four aspects.[128] Indeed, if we look narrowly, it is a 'refugee crisis', having a predominantly political and legal nature, and caused by, for example, the narrow understanding of international refugee law (e.g. including in its scope the escape from persecution, but excluding the e.g. 'survival' migration or economic refugees), the lack of coherence in the EU migration and asylum policy (e.g. shared responsibility between the EU and its Member States), or the lack of 'extraterritoriality' of refugee law (which requires those who need protection to have already accessed the territory of a country whose help they seek, rather than to be offered safe and regular channels for

---

125 Ch. Anderson, 'New Zealand considers creating climate change refugee visas', *The Guardian*, 31.10.2017, <https://www.theguardian.com/world/2017/oct/31/new-zealand-considers-creating-climate-change-refugee-visas>.

126 United Nations, *Report of the Special Rapporteur of the Human Rights Council on extrajudicial, summary or arbitrary executions*, New York, 15.09.2017, A/72/335, §§4 and 84.

127 P. Kingsley, *supra* n. 79, p. 294.

128 We thank Marta Pachocka for bringing this matter to our attention. Cf. further M. Pachocka, 'Looking beyond the current migration and refugee crises in Europe: a common policy of the EU and the outlook for the future – in search of solutions' in *Migrations: Jean Monnet Seminar 2016*, Publications Office of the European Union, Luxembourg 2016, pp. 73–84.

reaching such a country).[129] Second, it is an '(im)migration crisis', having rather demographic nature, caused by the massive number of irregular migrants *ante portas* and bringing 'consequences ... for the transit and migrant-receiving countries'.[130] Third, it is a 'humanitarian crisis', due to the perilous journeys that the irregular migrants undertake, often resulting in death, as well as due to the reasons therefor, such as fleeing war-torn and impoverished countries. Fourth, in a broader sense, it is a 'solidarity crisis' between the European countries, wherein the political wrangling and lack of reciprocity has led to a 'divided Europe' and no real and effective system of 'fair-sharing of responsibility' (cf. *Lonardo*, *Miglio* and *Butler*).

However, the perception of irregular migration as a threat must be contextualized. Not all European countries have been equally affected by irregular migrants; there are countries of first-reception (e.g. Greece and Italy), from which irregular migrants transit – *via*, for example, Hungary – to target countries (e.g. Germany or Sweden); some countries seem not to be affected at all (e.g. some Baltic States). In other countries there have been wide-reaching legal reforms that are being attributed to a threat that is not so evident, as *Perkowska* demonstrated in the Polish context.

The EU has sought to overcome many obstacles it has faced by deepening its integration towards 'an ever closer Union',[131] often on a paradigm 'crisis as an opportunity'. *Miglio* takes the most recent example of the sovereign debt crisis. A response thereto saw many initiatives adopted at multiple levels that have sought to strengthen and facilitate the stability of the monetary union. For instance, the euro crisis resulted in the creation of new, and a strengthening of existing, supranational institutions such as the European Stability Mechanism, the enhancement of fiscal surveillance powers of the Commission, and the construction of the banking union.[132] Nevertheless, approaches to tackling a common migration and asylum policy are inevitably more complex and sensitive processes than those that created the monetary union. What can be seen from the recent migration 'crisis' is that Europe nowadays resists, to a large extent, supra-national decision-making and that it is rather more polarised than any more integrated as 'for every effort that fails, the divide grows wider'.[133]

Notwithstanding, migration is a dynamic process and its responsible and visionary management and governance is shaped by experience. The current migration situation offers a valuable lesson to be learnt quickly.

---

129 J. Ramji-Nogales, *supra* n. 75.

130 M. Pachocka, *supra* n. 128, p. 74.

131 D. Dinan, *Ever Closer Union: An Introduction to European Integration*, 4th ed., Lynne Rienner Publishers, Boulder 2010.

132 T.A. Börzel and T. Risse, 'From the Euro to the Schengen Crises: European Integration Theories, Politicization, and Identity Politics' (2018) 25(1) *Journal of European Public Policy* 1.

133 K.B. Harpviken, *Foreword*, in this volume, p. ix.

4. A responsible and visionary governance and management of migration requires, at minimum, 'best available information' and a debate carried out in moderation. Both public debate and policy-making run on information, be it information sought for a discourse and to make decisions, and information disseminated in order to influence such a discourse and decision-making.[134] For such information to support responsible and visionary governance and management of migration, it has to satisfy a few quality criteria.

It will sound like a truism, but debates and decision-making that are *not* based on facts, that is, information that is 'known or proved to be true',[135] and that are *not* based, as far as possible, on 'best available information' would create only confusion and bring bad results. We are fully aware that a 100 per cent certainty is unachievable, yet it is an ideal to which debates and decision-making should aspire. We have attempted to demonstrate these tensions at the beginning of our contribution and the many authors in this book have analysed them in a greater detail. Perhaps the prime example from the present book would be the concept of 'rescue as a pull-effect' that, in the words of *Gabrielsen Jumbert*, 'allows a seemingly logical explanation to the otherwise inexplicable' and hence remained 'powerful', guiding 'official responses to the crisis'.

The 'best available information' implies – as far as possible – the need for a complete picture. Therefore we argue for a more holistic approach to the governance and management of migration, in order to encompass many different, inevitable perspectives and understandings that are sometimes lacking in rather narrowly focused or one-sided approaches. This is clearly visible when *Piekutowska* and *Kużelewska* consider the concept of 'economic refugees', when *Brière* analyses the difficulties with defining the crime of 'migrant smuggling', or *Top* discusses the 'political offence' exemption in extradition law.

Yet plain facts do not always speak to popular imagination. It is difficult to understand what migrants are going through without meeting them, or without seeing the places they are fleeing from or without paying a visit to the places where they have been forced to live, such as refugee camps or detention centres. We argue for going beyond media coverage. Especially for those concerned with policy-making, we suggest a retrospective visit, for example, to Sarajevo in contemporary Bosnia and Herzegovina to better understand what its inhabitants went through barely a quarter of century ago, just on the doorstep of the European integration project, and why some of them wanted to flee.[136] For those less inclined to travel, we suggest reading some of the voluminous accounts of post-2010 refugees' journeys.[137]

---

134 C.C. Hood, *supra* n. 38, pp. 21–39.

135 *Oxford Dictionary of English*, 3rd ed., Oxford University Press, Oxford 2010.

136 M. Glenny, *The Balkans: Nationalism, War, and the Great Powers, 1804–1999*, Penguin, New York 1999.

137 Cf. e.g. P. Kingsley, *supra* n. 79; A. Björk and M. Beijmo, *Båt 370. Döden på Medelhavet*, Norstedts, Stockholm 2017.

Eventually, as *Harpviken* puts it, migration requires 'intellectual and ethical honesty'[138] and this equally applies to the debates thereon. We propose this in contrast to the contemporary quality of this discourse, rather full of misleading statements and too much (negative) emotion.[139] The media, to a large extent, control the circulation of information and one of the greatest sins of some – but not all – of the media outlets is the inaccurate portrayal of migrants and, correspondingly, of the risk of a threat to public security and safety. By increasing their subjectivism and the pursuit of income, these media are congruently losing their function in a democratic polity, which, in turn, creates only an 'illusion of the fourth estate'. For example, in some European countries, due to the media influence – and in particular in rural areas where only the public media could reach – the term 'migrant', while semantically a neutral term, nowadays provokes only negative connotations and the popular attitude towards irregular migrants has quickly shifted from acceptance towards strong opposition (cf. *Drinóczi* and *Mohay*).[140] This observation is valid not only for 'traditional' media, such as the printed press or television, but also for 'new' ones, including social media sites. Yet it is edifying that some steps have been undertaken to restore public trust in the media, for example the 2016 Code of Conduct on illegal online hate speech, endorsed by the European Commission and four major technology companies from the Silicon Valley.[141] (Yet we refrain here from assessing its effectiveness.) We therefore suggest that some media outlets should ask their reporters and commentators to revisit a textbook to journalism ethics and standards.

5. A direction to go. All in all, there are irregular migrants standing *ante portas* of Europe. And this Europe finds itself on the crossroads and asks, like Alice – to paraphrase Carroll from the epigraph, 'which way I ought to go from here?'. Indeed, it 'depends a good deal on where [it] want[s] to get to'. If Europe does not 'much care', or does not want to care, for the values and principles it chose to be built on, for responsible and visionary governance and management of public affairs, including (irregular) migration, for its legitimacy and reputation, then, as the Cheshire Cat hints, 'it doesn't matter which way [it] go[es]', even though it might ultimately get 'somewhere'. A crisis provoking another crisis is just 'some' solution, but it would not be a preferable one. (This observation is also valid for many other polities around the world that have been concerned

---

138 K.B. Harpviken, *Foreword*, in this volume, p. v.

139 BBC, *Reality Check: Migration to the UK*, 25.05.2017, <http://www.bbc.com/news/election-2017-40015269>.

140 We thank István Hegedűs for bringing this matter to our attention. Cf. e.g. A. Földes, 'The villagers were so horrified of the refugees that they even banished their mayor', *index.hu*, 05.10.2017, <https://index.hu/mindekozben/poszt/2017/10/05/ocsenyi_videonk_angolul_is_the_villagers_were_so_horrified_of_the_refugees_that_they_even_banished_their_mayor>.

141 European Commission, *European Commission and IT Companies announce Code of Conduct on illegal online hate speech*, press release, Brussels, 31.05.2016, IP/16/1937.

with the governance and management of migration.) Therefore, the main aim of our book was to join the voluminous professional and academic literature on migration and to offer a few modest suggestions regarding the direction in which Europe should go whenever irregular migrants stand *ante portas*.

V.

This book constitutes the fifth volume in *European Integration and Democracy* Series. The Series was launched in 2011 and is edited at the Centre for Direct Democracy Studies (CDDS) at the University of Białystok, Poland. Since 2014, the Series has been published by Intersentia, a reputable publishing house based in Belgium and the UK. Each volume in the Series tackles a pressing issue that is of utmost importance for the European integration project and, at the same time, that poses a challenge to the values and principles on which this project has been built. Because our books are titled *in fine* '... as a challenge to democracy', we hasten to explain that, for this Series, we see the term 'challenge' rather neutrally. We approach each subject-matter as a 'task or situation that tests someone's abilities'[142] and not necessarily as something negative, especially as a threat to broadly understood democracy. Thus far, our books have discussed – through that lens – topics such as the elections to the European Parliament or trans-Atlantic data privacy relations.[143]

As all volumes thus far in our Series, this book originated from a call for papers, which we issued in May 2016. The response we received was indicative of the topicality of our chosen subject-matter and the variety of interest from academic scholarship. All submissions underwent a double-blind peer-review process in accordance with the Guaranteed Peer-Review Content (GPRC) scheme, a standard used by Intersentia.[144] In result of this careful selection process, we have accepted 10 submissions. We have subsequently enriched the contents of the volume with three invited contributions from prominent scholars and commentators.

This book does not aspire to be a monograph on irregular migration to Europe; it is, rather, an anthology compiling diverse yet rich academic comments

---

142 *Oxford Dictionary of English*, *supra* n. 135.

143 The previous volumes are: E. Kużelewska and D. Kloza (eds.), *The Challenges of Modern Democracy and European Integration*, Aspra-JR, Warsaw 2012; E. Kużelewska and D. Kloza (eds.), *Elections to the European Parliament as a Challenge for Democracy*, Aspra-JR, Warsaw 2013; E. Kużelewska, D. Kloza, I. Kraśnicka and F. Strzyczkowski (eds.), *European Judicial Systems as a Challenge for Democracy*, Intersentia, Cambridge 2015; D.J.B. Svantesson and D. Kloza (eds.), *Trans-Atlantic Data Privacy Relations as a Challenge for Democracy*, Intersentia, Cambridge 2017.

144 Cf. <http://www.gprc.be/en/content/what-gprc>.

on a wide range of pressing issues within a broad topic. (We acknowledge there are issues we would have liked to see discussed in this volume, yet – due to the chosen format, i.e. chapters deriving predominantly from a call for papers – we have not received, even for consideration, any contribution devoted thereto.)[145] We have been exceptionally careful in allowing the authors to express their ideas as they want to do so, with only minimal editorial intervention. We wish for this book to be both a commentary and reference work, and to reach not only our fellow academics in Europe and beyond, but also policy makers, civil society organisations and journalists concerned with (irregular) migration.

VI.

Many have helped in the gestation of this book and in ensuring its quality. In particular, we thank the authors as well as congratulate them for their strong academic scholarship, which has been further bolstered by the apt and thought-provoking Foreword. For that, our gratitude and thanks go to Kristian Berg Harpviken, Research Professor, and former Director, of the Peace Research Institute Oslo (PRIO). We thank the anonymous peer-reviewers who have all contributed to ensuring the scientific quality and integrity of this volume. We are grateful to the panellists and participants of the policy forum *Migration crisis as a challenge for democracy*, held on 14 November 2017 at the University of Warsaw and co-organised by the CDDS; their interventions gave us further impetus and ideas to refine the present Introduction. We have received with gratitude further help from – in alpha order – Rocco Bellanova, Karolina Boiret, István Böröcz, Raphaël Cahen, Iris Huis in 't Veld, Lucas Melgaço, Marta Pachocka, Sibel Top, Florian Trauner and Marta Witkowska. Once again, we thank Intersentia and our publisher Tom Scheirs. (It is our third book together!) Finally, we gratefully acknowledge the intellectual and financial support received for this book from the Research Group on Fundamental Rights and Constitutionalism (FRC) at the Faculty of Law and Criminology of the Vrije Universiteit Brussel (VUB).

Białystok/Brussels, November 2017

[145] The issues include, *inter alia*, the role of new technologies in migratory processes and the position of various religious groups on irregular migration.

CONTENTS

LIST OF ABBREVIATIONS

AA	Association Agreement
ABW	Agencja Bezpieczeństwa Wewnętrznego [Internal Security Agency] [Poland]
AFSJ	Area of Freedom, Security and Justice
AGIPA	Act on Granting International Protection to Aliens [Estonia]
AMIF	Asylum, Migration and Integration Fund [EU]
BIT	Bilateral Investment Treaty
CBP	Common Basic Principle
CEAS	Common European Asylum System
CEFR	Common European Framework of Reference for Languages
CFSP	Common Foreign and Security Policy
CIE	Identification and Expulsion Centre [Italy]
CISA	Convention implementing the Schengen Agreement
CJEU	Court of Justice of the European Union
CMR	Central Mediterranean Route
COMPAS	Centre on Migration, Policy and Society
CPA	Criminal Procedure Act [Hungary]
CPTA	Centre for Temporary Residence and Assistance [Italy]
CPT	European Committee for the Prevention of Torture and Inhuman or Degrading Treatment or Punishment
CSDP	Common Security and Defence Policy
DARIO	Draft Articles on Responsibility of International Organizations
DG	Directorate-General [European Commission]
EASO	European Asylum Support Office
EAW	European Arrest Warrant
EC	European Commission; European Community
ECB	European Central Bank
ECHR	European Convention on Human Rights
ECI	European Citizens' Initiative
ECRE	European Council on Refugees and Exiles
ECSC	European Coal and Steel Community
ECtHR	European Court of Human Rights
EDA	European Defence Agency
EEA	European Economic Area
EEAS	European External Action Service

EEC	European Economic Community
EFSF	European Financial Stability Facility
EFSM	European Financial Stabilisation Mechanism
EHRC	Estonian Human Rights Centre
EIO	European Investigation Order
EMU	Economic and Monetary Union
ENP	European Neighbourhood Policy
ERC	Estonian Refugee Council
ERF	European Refugee Fund
ESM	European Stability Mechanism
ESMA	European Securities and Markets Authorities
EU	European Union
EUBAM	EU Border Assistance Mission in Libya
EUMC	EU Military Committee
FRA	European Union Agency for Fundamental Rights
Frontex	Frontières extérieures, European Border and Coast Guard Agency
GATT	General Agreement on Tariffs and Trade
ICJ	International Court of Justice
ICT	Information and Communications Technologies
IGC	Intergovernmental Conference
ILC	International Law Commission
ILO	International Labour Organization
IMO	International Maritime Organization
IOM	International Organization for Migration
JHA	Justice and Home Affairs
JMC	Johannes Mihkelson Centre
KFOR	Kosovo Force
LIAM	Linguistic Integration of Adult Migrants
LIBE	Committee on Civil Liberties, Justice and Home Affairs [European Parliament]
MEP	Member of the European Parliament
MIPEX	Migrant Integration Policy Index
MSF	Médecins Sans Frontières
NATO	North Atlantic Treaty Organization
NGO	Non-governmental Organisation
OECD	Organisation for Economic Co-operation and Development
PPU	Procédure Préjudicielle d'Urgence [Urgent Preliminary Ruling Procedure]
PSC	Political and Security Committee of the EU
RRO	Roundtable of Refugee Organisations
SAR	Search and Rescue

SOLAS	International Convention for the Safety of Life at Sea 1974
SPRAR	Protection System for Asylum Seekers and Refugees
TEC	Treaty Establishing the European Community
TEU	Treaty on European Union
TFEU	Treaty on the Functioning of the European Union
UK	United Kingdom of Great Britain and Northern Ireland
UN	United Nations
UNCLOS	United Nations Convention on the Law of the Sea
UNHCR	United Nations High Commissioner for Refugees
UNSC	UN Security Council
UNTS	United Nations Treaty Series

PART I

THE EUROPEAN INTEGRATION PROJECT AND IRREGULAR MIGRATION: UPHOLDING FUNDAMENTAL VALUES AND PRINCIPLES

1. THE 'MIGRANT CRISIS': MEMBER STATES' OR EU'S RESPONSIBILITY?

Luigi LONARDO*

1. INTRODUCTION

The so-called 'migration crisis', which unfolded in the summer 2015, has seemed to pose, excluding the exaggerations of political discourses, a threat to the European Union's (EU) politics, security and ultimately values. Migratory fluxes are physiological and familiar to EU Member States.[1] However, the extreme conditions resulting from the arrival and presence of a significant additional number of people in need of protection[2] has acted as a trigger which 'exert[s] pressure on host countries, including their reception capacities, national asylum processes, economies and security'.[3] Policy-makers have devoted increased attention to the study of migration, and have attempted to deal with trafficking, migrant smuggling and related exploitation at the national, regional and international levels.[4] Despite these efforts, the International Organization for Migration has called Europe the most dangerous destination for irregular migrants in the world, and the Mediterranean the world's most dangerous border crossing.[5] While European politicians and citizens alike have hurried to

* King's College London, United Kingdom. E-mail: luigi.lonardo@kcl.ac.uk.

1 See D. ABOULAFIA, *The Great Sea. A Human History of the Mediterranean*, Oxford University Press, Oxford 2011. Significantly, the author uses the word 'refugee', which is now mainstream, to indicate any group of migrants through the history of the Mediterranean.

2 See P. CONNOR, 'Number of Refugees to Europe Surges Record 1.3 Million in 2015', *Pew Research Center*, 02.08.2016, <http://www.pewglobal.org/2016/08/02/number-of-refugees-to-europe-surges-to-record-1-3-million-in-2015/> accessed 29.12.2016.

3 GRADUATE INSTITUTE OF INTERNATIONAL AND DEVELOPMENT STUDIES, 'Onward Movement of Asylum-Seekers and Refugees: Discussion paper prepared for the Expert Roundtable on Onward Movement' (1–2 October 2015) p. 1, <http://www.unhcr.org/562f81c39.pdf> accessed 29.12.2016.

4 A. GALLAGHER, 'Human Rights and the New UN Protocols on Trafficking and Migrant Smuggling: A Preliminary Analysis' (2001) 23 *Human Rights Quarterly* 975, 1004.

5 INTERNATIONAL ORGANIZATION FOR MIGRATION, *Fatal Journeys. Tracking Lives Lost During Migration*, International Organization for Migration, Geneva 2014.

organise the response they best deemed fit to welcome (or not) the refugees, a key question has arisen for lawyers, philosophers and policy-makers in the EU: who should be held responsible for the people who seek protection?

This question has far-reaching moral, political and legal implications. This chapter focuses on the latter, with a twofold purpose. First, it discusses the question of legal responsibility of international organisations, under the Draft Articles on Responsibility of International Organizations (DARIO).[6] Second, it seeks to contribute to a conceptualisation of the impact of the migration crisis on the role of the EU in the international sphere. In particular, the chapter discusses some of the challenges arising from the EU and Member States' involvement in three activities: search and rescue operations; border controls; and onward journeys of migrants within the EU. It considers the relevant public international law and EU law obligations applicable to these operations in the Mediterranean Sea. Under the current DARIO, there are, in principle, two possibilities: a wrongdoing is either attributable to an international organisation, or it is not – hence, in the case of the EU, it is attributed to its Member States.

The main idea proposed and defended in the chapter is that the EU should not be held legally responsible, under international law, for the deficiencies and wrongful acts of its Member States in matters, such as immigration, that fall under the 'shared competences',[7] and where Member States thus retain a large amount of discretion and mostly employ their own resources. The chapter presents the case that the responsibility for a breach of international law, instead, lies with the Member State committing the wrongdoing. The fundamental test for deciding who is responsible – a state or an international organisation – is that of 'direct attribution' of a conduct to an actor. This concept figures in a robust jurisprudence of the European Court of Human Rights (ECtHR), which applied it to missions conducted under UN mandate.[8] The ECtHR considered, in *Behrami*, its jurisdiction *ratione personae* in relation to the conduct of forces placed in Kosovo at the disposal of the UN (UN Interim Administration Mission in Kosovo) or authorised

---

6 International Law Commission, 'Draft Articles on Responsibility of International Organizations, 2011', *Yearbook of the International Law Commission*, 2011, vol. II, Part Two.

7 Article 4 of the Treaty on the Functioning of the European Union (TFEU) provides that the Area of Freedom, Security and Justice will be a shared competence between the EU and its Member States. And Article 67(2), in Title V on the 'Area of Freedom, Security and Justice' explains that the Union 'shall ensure the absence of internal border controls for persons and shall frame a common policy on asylum, immigration and external border control, based on solidarity between Member States, which is fair towards third-country nationals. For the purpose of this Title, stateless persons shall be treated as third-country nationals.'

8 See ECtHR, *Behrami and Behrami v. France; Saramati v. France, Germany and Norway*, Applications Nos. 71412/01 and 78166/01, 02.05.2007.

by the UN (Kosovo Force (KFOR)). The ECtHR referred to the criterion of 'effective control', which had been provisionally adopted by the International Law Commission in its Draft Articles on State Responsibility.[9] The ECtHR considered that the decisive factor was whether 'the United Nations Security Council retained ultimate authority and control so that operational command only was delegated'.[10] While acknowledging 'the effectiveness or unity of NATO command in *operational* matters' concerning KFOR,[11] the Court noted that the presence of KFOR in Kosovo was based on a resolution adopted by the Security Council and concluded that 'KFOR was exercising lawfully delegated Chapter VII powers of the UNSC so that the impugned action was, in principle, "attributable" to the UN within the meaning of the word outlined [in article 4 DARIO]'.[12] Despite the institutional differences between the EU and the UN, the test of 'direct attribution' is applicable to the EU,[13] in so far as the EU meets the criteria to be considered an international organisation under DARIO.[14] While this line of inquiry brought the ECtHR to the conclusion that the UN was exercising effective control, it yields a different result when it is applied to the EU.

The argument proposed in this chapter is that Member States are responsible for conducting the operations with regards to migration and therefore are not under the 'effective control' of the EU.[15] Thus, they should be held accountable for their breaches. The conceptualisation is not only useful for academic purposes but it also aims to contribute to the policy tackling the important symptoms of the catastrophe, in terms of protection on migrants. The author believes that the causes of the problems are deep and consist of troubled relationships and longstanding behaviours rooted in the long-run of historical

---

9 On these, see the discussion below.

10 *Behrami*, *supra* n. 8, para. 113.

11 *Ibid.*, para 139.

12 *Ibid.*, para 141. See also the formulation in ECtHR, *Nada v. Switzerland*, Grand Chamber, Application No. 10593/08, 12.09.2012, distinguishing *Behrami* on the facts and finding that the conduct of France was not directly attributable: in *Nada*, the Court stated that it 'found in Behrami and Saramati that the impugned acts and omissions of the Kosovo Force, whose powers had been validly delegated to it by the Security Council under Chapter VII of the Charter, and those of the United Nations Interim Administration Mission in Kosovo, a subsidiary organ of the United Nations set up under the same Chapter, were directly attributable to the United Nations' (at para. 120).

13 Quoting P. Koutrakos: 'The European Union is endowed with express legal personality. Therefore, by applying the famous dictum of the International Court of Justice about international organizations, it "is a subject of international law and capable of possessing international rights and duties"', in P. Koutrakos, *The Common Security and Defence Policy*, Oxford University Press, Oxford 2015, p. 126. The case cited is ICJ, *Reparation for Injuries Suffered in the Service of the United Nations* (1949) ICJ Reports 174 p. 179.

14 And as discussed in more detail in section 4 below.

15 A similar argument was proposed by P. Koutrakos, *supra* n. 13, p. 126, with regard to EU military operations.

processes: political upheavals, demographic changes and international power dynamics.[16] While the causes are hard to identify and barely possible to address directly, it is nonetheless felt that the symptoms must be addressed in order to alleviate the sufferings of those who are involved.

The discussion in this chapter is structured in four parts. First, it will locate the source of Member States' obligations (section 2). This is the current international legal framework binding EU Member States as far as search and rescue operations are concerned. Second, it addresses the key practice of EU Member States under EU law, and it highlights and discusses the main legal challenges (section 3). Third, the chapter makes the case for individual responsibility of EU Member States' under international law – rather than for the EU as a whole (section 4). The chapter concludes by elaborating on the significance of the lack of recognition of the EU's responsibility for the role of the Union in the international sphere (section 5).

2. INTERNATIONAL LAW OBLIGATIONS

Public international law protects the rights of certain groups of individuals deemed worthy of specific care. The obligations stem from several bodies of law which bind the EU and its Member States (Article 2 and Article 3(5) of the Treaty on European Union (TEU)),[17] namely international human rights law, international refugee law, the law of the sea, and international criminal law.[18] The groups who enjoy the rights in question include, on the one hand, refugees,

16 See Human Rights Watch, *Europe's Migration Crisis*, <https://www.hrw.org/tag/europes-migration-crisis> accessed 29.12.2016: 'Over 55 per cent of those taking the dangerous journey originate from countries beset by war or generalized violence, or having repressive governments, such as Syria, Afghanistan, Nigeria, Eritrea, and Iraq.'

17 Article 2 TEU: 'The Union is founded on the values of respect for human dignity, freedom, democracy, equality, the rule of law and respect for human rights, including the rights of persons belonging to minorities …' Article 3(5) TEU: 'In its relations with the wider world, the Union shall uphold and promote its values and interests and contribute to the protection of its citizens. It shall contribute to peace, security, the sustainable development of the Earth, solidarity and mutual respect among peoples, free and fair trade, eradication of poverty and the protection of human rights, in particular the rights of the child, as well as to the strict observance and the development of international law, including respect for the principles of the United Nations Charter.'

18 Costello has a slightly different categorisation in her book on *The Human Rights of Migrants and Refugees in European Law*: 'There are thus two, if not three, dynamic bodies of law under scrutiny here: The case law of the ECtHR on migrant rights, which contains notable unstable features, which are highlighted and, where appropriate, critiqued throughout. Then, there is EU law on migration and asylum, which has been subject to legislative revision and progressive judicial interpretations. Thirdly, we have international refugee law, in particular the [Convention Relating to the Status of Refugees], which lacks a central enforcement authority, but is characterized by dynamic interpretation and cross-fertilization across jurisdictions, viewed by many as an exemplar of transnational judicial dialogue.' C. Costello, *The Human Rights of Migrants and Refugees in European Law*, Oxford University Press, Oxford 2015, p. 6.

who are themselves a 'special class' of migrants who deserve specific protection by their host state.[19] On the other hand, international law protects any person who is at sea. Measures in this regard include, for example, the obligation to provide assistance to people in distress,[20] policies on visas,[21] carrier sanctions and interception of migrants at sea.[22] The Member States' legal duties originate from the interplay between these obligations.

The codification of much of the legal framework for the protection of refugees predominantly took place in the wake of the Second World War. However, despite being quite dated, the normative instruments have been interpreted by the ECtHR as extending so as to afford the protection deemed appropriate to the migrants. This chapter will offer a few considerations on the content and scope of this framework.

2.1. REFUGEE LAW

The definition of refugee is contained in Article 1 of the 1951 Convention Relating to the Status of Refugees (Refugee Convention).[23] A refugee is a person who 'owing to well-founded fear of being persecuted for reasons of race, religion, nationality, membership of a particular social group or political opinion, is outside the country of his nationality and is unable or, owing to such fear, is unwilling to avail himself of the protection of that country'. The instruments for the protection of refugees provide for the duty of care recognised by the Refugee Convention, and which is thought to reflect customary international law. The duty of care is grounded in Article 14 of the Universal Declaration of Human Rights (1948), which recognises the right of persons to seek asylum from persecution in other countries.[24] However, the duty of care does not

---

19 I. Zamfir, 'Refugee Status under International Law', European Parliamentary Research Service (October 2015), <http://www.europarl.europa.eu/RegData/etudes/ATAG/2015/569051/EPRS_ATA(2015)569051_EN.pdf> accessed 29.12.2016.

20 Apart from it being a long-standing maritime custom, this is also further elaborated upon later in this chapter.

21 A. Zolberg, 'Guarding the Gates in a World on the Move' (2002) *Social Science Research Council, After September 11.*

22 B. Ryan, 'Extraterritorial Immigration Control: What Role for Legal Guarantees?' in B Ryan and V Mitsilegas (eds.), *Extraterritorial Immigration Control*, Martinus Nijhoff Publishers, Leiden 2010.

23 UN General Assembly, *Convention Relating to the Status of Refugees*, 28.07.1951, 189 UNTS 137, <http://www.refworld.org/docid/3be01b964.html> accessed 28.12.2016. The Article has to be read in conjunction with the 1967 Protocol Relating to the Status of Refugees, which does away with the original time limitation that restricted the scope of application of the Refugee Convention to people who became refugees by reason of events occurring before 01.01.1951.

24 UN General Assembly, *Universal Declaration of Human Rights*, 10.12.1948, 217 A (III), <http://www.refworld.org/docid/3ae6b3712c.html> accessed 28.10.2016.

extend so far as to be translated into an entitlement to asylum for the individuals concerned, nor does it impose an obligation on states to grant asylum. For example, the Refugee Convention does not guarantee asylum seekers the right to be granted refugee status, even if they fulfil the conditions to be considered refugees. The existence of refugee status is ultimately for states to determine: obviously, this determination does not affect the obligations deriving from the Refugee Convention and customary international law.[25]

States are under the positive obligation to refrain from actions that would endanger refugees, and especially from returning them to a country where they would be at risk of persecution.[26] The latter is the so-called *refoulement*, and the prohibition of this act is a fundamental principle of international law. In particular, even though immigrants may be forced to enter the country of refuge unlawfully, this situation does not *per se* forfeit protection: illegal entrants can still qualify as refugees if they fulfil the relevant criteria, and should not be punished for their illegal entry if they come directly from the territory where their life and freedom was threatened, provided they present themselves without delay to the authorities and show good cause for their illegal entry or presence (Article 31). There is no definition, in the Refugee Convention, of what constitutes the illegal entry or presence of a refugee. Within the limits imposed by the Refugee Convention, and pursuant to its object and purpose, therefore, the determination over the legality of the refugee's presence on the territory of a Member State is a matter of national and EU law.

States also have a duty to accord certain rights to those seeking refuge on their territories, independent of the legality of these people's situation. Such rights include: freedom of religion (Article 4); property rights (Article 13); the right to primary education (Article 22); the right to access to the courts (Article 16(1)); a limited right to move freely, subject to justifiable restrictions (Article 31(2)) etc. Other rights are granted when refugees are 'lawfully present' in the host state (for example while their asylum claim is processed), including the right to self-employment (Article 18) and the right to move freely, subject to regulations applicable to aliens in general (Article 26). Other rights shall be granted when refugees are 'lawfully staying' in a state party (usually after recognition of their refugee status by the State concerned), including the right to paid employment (Article 17) under conditions no less favourable than for other aliens.

An overview of EU refugee law and its Common European Asylum System (CEAS) is beyond the scope of this chapter, but it is nonetheless worth noting

---

25 See e.g. J.C. Hathaway and M. Foster, *The Law of Refugee Status*, 2nd ed., Cambridge University Press, Cambridge 2014, p. 23 ff.

26 Article 3 of the 1984 Convention against Torture affords the same protection where there are substantial grounds for believing that a person to be returned would be in danger of being tortured.

that the interplay between the Refugee Convention and the fundamental EU Treaties is evident. The Refugee Convention's framework is dominant in Article 78 TFEU, which provides that:

> The Union shall develop a common policy on asylum, subsidiary protection and temporary protection with a view to offering appropriate status to any third-country national requiring international protection and ensuring compliance with the principle of *non-refoulement*. This policy must be in accordance with the Geneva Convention of 28 July 1951 and the Protocol of 31 January 1967 relating to the status of refugees, and other relevant treaties.

Furthermore, Article 18 of the EU Charter of Fundamental Rights is worded as follows: 'The right to asylum shall be guaranteed with due respect for the rules of the Geneva Convention of 28 July 1951 and the Protocol of 31 January 1967 relating to the status of refugees and in accordance with the Treaty on European Union and the Treaty on the Functioning of the European Union.'

Under EU law, the European Border and Coast Guard Agency and the national authorities of Member States which are responsible for border management, including coast guards to the extent that they carry out border control tasks, constitute the European Border and Coast Guard, responsible for search and rescue operations.[27] These entities have shared responsibility over integrated border management – but the management of the section of borders of each Member State remains the primary responsibility of that State.[28] In particular, with regard to these operations, Member States have an obligation to cooperate so that persons rescued at sea are disembarked in a place of safety as soon as possible.[29] To this aim, Member States cooperate[30] in search and rescue operations with the EU border agency Frontex,[31] which are coordinated thereby. Article 4(1) of Regulation 656/2015 on joint operations between Member States and Frontex, states that no-one can be 'disembarked in, forced to enter, conducted to or otherwise handed over to' an unsafe country as further defined in the Regulation; and the subsequent Article 4(2) mandates that, when considering disembarkation to a third country, Member States must

---

27 Regulation (EU) 2016/1624 of the European Parliament and of the Council of 14 September 2016 on the European Border and Coast Guard [...] [2016] OJ L251/1 Article 4(b).

28 Article 5(1) of Regulation 2016/1624, *ibid.*

29 Regulation (EU) No 656/2014 of the European Parliament and of the Council of 15 May 2014 establishing rules for the surveillance of the external sea borders in the context of operational cooperation coordinated by the European Agency for the Management of Operational Cooperation at the External Borders of the Member States of the European Union [2014] OJ L189/93.

30 Notably through existing information exchange tools, such as the European Border Surveillance System established by Regulation (EU) No 1052/2013 [2013] OJ L95/11.

31 On which see further section 3 below.

take into account the general situation in that third country.[32] It is also worth recalling at this point that Costello identifies a fundamental flaw in the CEAS. In her opinion, the system 'imposes legally binding standards on procedures, status and living conditions while refugee status is being determined. The CEAS requires individuals to be on the territory, not of the EU, but of the state in question, in order to claim asylum. However, EU law makes it virtually impossible to get to that country safely and legally.'[33]

2.2. LAW OF THE SEA

It is a longstanding custom in international law, now enshrined in Treaty law, that the master of a ship has an obligation to render assistance to those in distress at sea, regardless of their nationality, status or the circumstances in which they are found. Compliance with this obligation is essential to preserve the integrity of maritime search and rescue services. The obligation stems from two essential texts.[34]

Article 98(1) of the 1982 UN Convention on the Law of the Sea (UNCLOS)[35] provides that:

> Every State shall require the master of a ship flying its flag, in so far as he can do so without serious danger to the ship, the crew or the passengers: (a) to render assistance to any person found at sea in danger of being lost; (b) to proceed with all possible speed to the rescue of persons in distress, if informed of their need of assistance, in so far as such action may reasonably be expected of him.

Regulation 10 of the 1974 International Convention for the Safety of Life at Sea (SOLAS Convention)[36] provides that:

> The master of a ship at sea, on receiving a signal from any source that a ship or aircraft or survival craft thereof is in distress, is bound to proceed with all speed to the assistance of the persons in distress informing them if possible that he is doing so.

32 For an analysis of the Regulation, see S. Peers, 'New EU Rules on Maritime Surveillance: Will They Stop the Deaths and Push-Backs in the Mediterranean?' (27.06.2014, EU Law Analysis), <http://eulawanalysis.blogspot.fr/2014/06/new-eu-rules-on-maritime-surveillance.html> accessed 05.01.2018.

33 C. Costello, 'It Need Not Be Like This' (2016) *FM Review* 14, <http://www.fmreview.org/sites/fmr/files/FMRdownloads/en/destination-europe/costello.pdf> accessed 29.12.2016.

34 For a detailed discussion see R. Barnes, 'The International Law of the Sea and Migration Control' in B. Ryan and V. Mitsilegas (eds.), *Extraterritorial Immigration Control*, Martinus Nijhoff Publishers, Leiden 2010.

35 UN General Assembly, *Convention on the Law of the Sea*, 10.12.1982, <http://www.refworld.org/docid/3dd8fd1b4.html> accessed 29.12.2016.

36 International Maritime Organization (IMO), *International Convention for the Safety of Life At Sea*, 1 November 1974, 1184 UNTS 3, <http://www.refworld.org/docid/46920bf32.html> accessed 29.12.2016.

It is now necessary to consider the interplay between the duties spelt out by refugee law and the law of the sea. In its landmark decision *Hirsi*,[37] the ECtHR has ruled that countries subject to its jurisdiction have to respect human rights obligations even in the high seas. In this case, the applicants, part of a group of about 200 individuals who left Libya in 2009 aboard three vessels with the aim of reaching the Italian coast, were intercepted by ships from the Italian Revenue Police and the Coastguard. The migrants who were on the intercepted vessels were transferred onto Italian military ships and returned to Tripoli. The applicants stated that during that voyage the Italian authorities did not inform them of their destination and took no steps to identify them. In Tripoli, the Italian authorities handed over the migrants to the Libyan authorities, and this despite the objections of the migrants themselves.

This was the first case in which the Court had to examine the removal of aliens taking place outside national territory. The Court found that returning the migrants to Libya without examining their case exposed them to a risk of ill-treatment and amounted to a collective expulsion. The Court for the first time examined whether Article 4 of Protocol No. 4 to the European Convention on Human Rights (ECHR) ('Collective expulsion of aliens is prohibited') applied outside national boundaries. The Court reasoned that neither Article 4 of Protocol No. 4 nor the *travaux préparatoires* of the ECHR precluded extraterritorial application of that Article. Crucially, the Court found that limiting its application to collective expulsions from the national territory of Member States would entail that a high number of migrants would be excluded from the protection of that provision, given the dynamics and forms of contemporary migratory fluxes. Limiting its scope would deprive migrants of an examination of their personal circumstances before being expelled. This case of extra-territorial jurisdiction set an important precedent for the protection of migrants who try to reach the EU. As one commentator summed up:

> There are three crucial reasons why *Hirsi* is a fundamental decision. The first is that it clarified that the Court's *Soering* jurisprudence on *non-refoulement* under Article 3 ECHR also applies in the high seas. This is bound to have important consequences not only for the debates over the interpretation of the term 'jurisdiction' in Article 1 ECHR, but also, arguably, for the analogous long-standing debate over the applicability of *non-refoulement* obligations arising from the Geneva Convention on Refugees in the high seas. Secondly, it is only the second time (after *Čonka v. Belgium*, no. 51564/99, 2002) that the Court finds a State to have breached Article 4 of Protocol 4 ECHR, which prohibits the 'collective expulsion of aliens'. In order to reach such a conclusion, the Court had to interpret the term 'expulsion' somewhat counter-textually. Thirdly, *Hirsi* stands as a landmark judicial reaffirmation of the long-standing

[37] ECtHR, *Hirsi Jamaa and Others v. Italy*, Application No. 27765/09.

jurisprudence of the Court on the protection of migrants from the risk of torture and inhuman treatment, and must be read in the context of European migration policy.[38]

The duty of care and to render assistance was restated by the ECtHR in its decision *M.S.S. v. Belgium and Greece*,[39] who spoke of asylum seekers as a 'particularly underprivileged and vulnerable population group in need of special protection'. The Court 'note[d] the existence of a broad consensus at the international and European level concerning this need for special protection, as evidenced by the Geneva Convention, the remit and the activities of the UNHCR and the standards set out in the Reception Directive'.[40] It is worth mentioning that this status is also recognised in the Protocol to Prevent, Suppress and Punish Trafficking in Persons Especially Women and Children, supplementing the United Nations Convention against Transnational Organized Crime (2000), where coercion, in this case against victims of trafficking, does not need to involve physical force, or even mental domination, but simply an 'abuse of a position of vulnerability'. Furthermore, it is noteworthy that the duty – and the breach thereof – pertains to individual Member States.

3. MEMBER STATES' PRACTICE – SEARCH AND RESCUE, BORDER CONTROLS AND ONWARD JOURNEYS

The way search and rescue operations are regulated by EU law, and are conducted by Member States, give rise to the facts whose wrongfulness, it is argued, may trigger EU Member States' responsibility. While Goodwin-Gill was undoubtedly correct in pointing out how there is an obligation gap in international law itself,[41] the imperfection of international law is only a small part of the picture.

There are indeed areas of friction between the obligations under international law mentioned above and the conduct of Member States. One such area is, for example, the obligation deficit with regard to disembarkation: while single states are responsible for a Search and Rescue Region to ensure cooperation

---

38 F. Messineo, 'Yet another mala figura: Italy breached non-refoulement obligations by intercepting migrants' boats at sea, says ECtHR' (*EJIL: Talk!*, 24.02.2012), <http://www.ejiltalk.org/yet-another-mala-figura-italy-breached-non-refoulement-obligations-by-intercepting-migrants-boats-at-sea-says-ecthr/> accessed 29.12.2016.

39 ECtHR, *M.S.S. v. Belgium and Greece*, Application No. 30696/09, para. 251.

40 *Ibid.*, para. 251.

41 'There is a gap, then, or the perception of a gap, in the regulatory framework [of international law].' G. Goodwin-Gill, 'Notes for a Keynote Address: Regulating 'Irregular' Migration: International Obligations and International Responsibilities', National and Kapodistrian University of Athens Faculty of Law (20.03.2015), <http://www.kaldorcentre.unsw.edu.au/sites/default/files/GSGG-IrregularMigration-Athens.pdf> accessed 29.12.2016.

and coordination, disembarkation to a safe place was not regulated[42] until the adoption of the Border and Coast Guard Regulation in late 2016.[43] Another area concerns the problems deriving from some activities of the EU border agency Frontex. Established in 2004,[44] the EU Border and Coast Guard Agency has as a mission to 'promote, coordinate and develop European border management in line with the EU Charter of Fundamental Rights and the concept of Integrated Border Management'.[45] Frontex takes part in 'joint operations' between the EU and the Member States. For example, the joint operation Triton brings together border guard authorities and assets from 25 Member States and it is hosted by Italy. Frontex covers the subsistence costs of the officers, while it relies on the vessels and aircraft as well as border guards provided by various EU Member States. During the peak of summer of 2015, Triton deployed three airplanes, six Offshore Patrol Vessels, 12 patrol boats, two helicopters, nine debriefing and six screening teams.[46]

Issues arise from the extraterritorial involvement of Frontex. Even though it is contested whether there even exists a legal basis for the involvement of Frontex in operations beyond EU territory,[47] Frontex coordinates operations outside the territory of the EU, which include patrols on the high seas as well as the territorial waters of third states. Such operations also involve so-called 'working arrangements' concluded between Frontex and the respective authorities of third countries. As Fink convincingly shows in her work, in their current form, the working arrangements show considerable deficiencies.[48] The inadequacy is evident from the standpoint of the rule of law, democracy and human rights protection. Since working arrangements are not considered to be international treaties, they are not subject to judicial review, Parliament is not involved in their conclusion, they are not disclosed to the public, and the human rights record of cooperating authorities is not duly taken into account.

42 *Ibid.*

43 Article 34(2) of that Regulation mandates that 'in performing of its tasks, the European Border and Coast Guard shall ensure that no person is disembarked in, forced to enter, conducted to, or otherwise handed over or returned to, the authorities of a country in contravention of the principle of non-refoulement, or from which there is a risk of expulsion or return to another country in contravention of that principle'.

44 Council Regulation (EC) No 2007/2004 of 26 October 2004 Establishing a European Agency for the Management of Operational Cooperation at the External Borders of the Member States of the European Union [2004] OJ L349/1.

45 Frontex, 'Mission and Tasks', <http://frontex.europa.eu/about-frontex/mission-and-tasks/> accessed 29.12.2016.

46 Frontex, 'Frontex Expands its Joint Operation Triton', <http://frontex.europa.eu/news/frontex-expands-its-joint-operation-triton-udpbHP> accessed 29.12.2016.

47 A. Baldaccini, 'Extraterritorial Border Controls in the EU: The Role of FRONTEX in Operations at Sea' in B. Ryan and V. Mitsilegas (eds.), *Extraterritorial Immigration Control: Legal Challenges*, Martinus Nijhoff Publishers, Leiden 2010.

48 M. Fink, 'Frontex Working Arrangements: Legitimacy and Human Rights Concerns Regarding "Technical Relationships"' (2012) 28 *Merkourios Utrecht Journal of International and European Law* 20.

Following Fink's conclusion, the attempts to dispel concerns in this regard are not convincing. Some try to justify the current deficiencies of the working arrangements by recourse to their 'technical' as opposed to 'political' nature.[49] Likewise, the Regulation establishing Frontex appear to assume that merely 'technical relationships' cannot affect individuals.[50] However, and quite to the contrary, conformity with human rights, which include for example the right to an effective remedy,[51] is mandatory for the institutions and bodies of the EU[52] – like Frontex.

Border control, which as mentioned is the responsibility of Member States' authorities as coordinated by the European Border and Coast Guard Agency, must obviously comply with fundamental rights and the Regulation on Border and Coast Guard establishes mechanisms to report compliance of operations with the Union's *acquis* on human rights.[53]

---

49 With regard to cooperation with neighbouring countries, Frontex Executive Director General Ilkka Laitinen pointed out that because such arrangements are not concluded with the respective governments but with the border control authorities, Frontex does 'not establish a partnership with a country or a government but [with] the border control authority of that third country'.

50 Article 14(1) and 14(2) of the Frontex Regulation, as interpreted by Fink: 'Article 14(2) of the Regulation states that Frontex' own cooperation with third countries "shall be purely related to the management of operational cooperation". It appears that this is meant to "codify" that Frontex' "external relations" shall only be of a technical nature. An explicit mention that the cooperation with third countries shall be in full compliance with human rights was omitted is as such not surprising, as Frontex is bound to respect human rights regardless. However, interestingly, Article 14(1) of the Regulation, which is related to the agencies' facilitation of cooperation between Member States and third countries, adopts a different approach. It establishes that it will have to take place "in the framework of the European Union external relations policy, *including with regard to human rights* [emphasis added]". Furthermore, it sets out, "the Agency and the Member States shall comply with the norms and standards at least equivalent to those set by the EU legislation also when cooperation with third countries takes place on the territory of those countries". This difference in Article 14(1) and (2) of the Regulation is indeed remarkable. The omission of a reference to compliance with human rights in Article 14(2) of the Regulation appears to be based on the assumption that technical cooperation cannot affect individuals. It is, however, difficult to see how the mere facilitation of operational cooperation requires explicit mention of human rights, whereas it seems to be understood that operational cooperation itself does not. In the following sections these two assumptions will be tested as to their validity'. M. Fink, *supra* n. 48, 31.

51 Article 47 of the EU Charter of Fundamental Rights.

52 Article 51 of the EU Charter of Fundamental Rights.

53 E.g. Article 16(3): operation plans for joint actions shall include a reporting and evaluation scheme containing benchmarks for the evaluation report, including with regard to the protection of fundamental rights; and procedures setting out a mechanism to receive and transmit to the Agency a complaint against all persons participating in a joint operation or rapid border intervention, including border guards or other relevant staff of the host Member State and members of the European Border and Coast Guard teams alleging breaches of fundamental rights in the context of their participation in a joint operation or rapid border intervention.

Another problematic area is the management of the so-called 'onward journeys' of refugees after they arrive in the EU. Not all refugees remain in the country of arrival. Some, instead, continue their journeys to other Member States further afield, but always within the EU. It is necessary for the legal framework to take this phenomenon into account, and therefore provide the necessary safeguards with regards to asylum claim processing arrangements and adjudication processes to people seeking protection who may have moved, or will move, onwards.

4. RESPONSIBILITY OF THE EU OR OF THE MEMBER STATES?

The question on the responsibility under international law of the EU or of the Member States should be resolved with the answer that, in the current framework, it is, and it ought to be, responsibility of the Member States.

The case for the responsibility of the EU – collectively – could be made by having recourse to the 2011 Draft Articles on the Responsibility of International Organisations, adopted by the UN General Assembly (A/66/10) (DARIO).[54] While the DARIO have not received as much attention and recognition as the Draft Articles on State Responsibility on whose pattern they are modelled,[55] they have nonetheless been referred to by European Courts.[56] Despite this, however, these Articles are not legally binding, and indeed the necessity of the very existence of the DARIO has been questioned.[57] In particular, DARIO leaves open the question on the relationship between the international organisation and its Member States.

The argument presented here is that DARIO, even if applicable to the EU,[58] does not engage its responsibility. It is still the Member States that should be held accountable, even when applying DARIO rules. The key concept that leads

54 International Law Commission, 'Draft Articles on Responsibility of International Organisations, 2011', *supra* n. 6, vol. II, Part Two, ch.IV.E.1.

55 International Law Commission, 'Draft Articles on Responsibility of States for Internationally Wrongful Acts', November 2001, Supplement No. 10 (A/56/10), ch.IV.E.1.

56 ECtHR, *Behrami*, *supra* n. 8; ECtHR, *Al-Jedda v. United Kingdom*, No. 27021/08; House of Lords, United Kingdom of Great Britain and Northern Ireland, *R (on the application of Al-Jedda) v. Secretary of State for Defence* [2007] UKHL 58; Supreme Court of the Netherlands 06.09.2013, *The State of the Netherlands v. Hasan Nuhanović*, No. 12/03324.

57 N. Blokker and R. Wessel, 'Introduction: First Views at the Articles on the Responsibility of International Organizations' (2012) 9 *International Organizations Law Review* 2.

58 It is now widely accepted that the EU as such may be responsible for an internationally wrongful act. See E. Paasivirta and P.J. Kuijper, 'Does one size fit all? The European Community and the Responsibility of International Organisations' (2007) 36 *Netherlands Yearbook of International Law 2005* 169.

to this conclusion is that of attribution, which in the case of the EU flows from the rules on competence:[59] in migration matters, the Member States mostly use their own resources and enjoy discretion in how they conduct the operations. It is true that the EU framework encompasses also a Regulation[60] – and there are talks to adopt a Qualification and Procedure Regulation as well – but as far as search and rescue operations are concerned, Member States are in command. Article 5(1) of the European Border and Coast Guard Regulation – adopted in 2016 – explicitly states that 'Member States shall retain primary responsibility for the management of their sections of the external border', and the European agency only has coordination and training tasks.

For the responsibility of the international organisation to be engaged, three criterion must be met: (i) an international organisation has to (ii) breach an international obligation, and (iii) the breach must be attributable to the organisation. As far as (i) is concerned, the EU is an international organisation for the purposes of DARIO. Article 2(a) DARIO provides: '"[I]nternational organisation" means an organisation established by treaty or other instrument governed by international law and possessing its own international legal personality. International organizations may include as members, in addition to States, other entities.' As required by Article 2(a) DARIO, the EU has legal personality (Article 47 TEU), and according to the commentary of the law commission on DARIO (A/66/10 suppl. 10) and an old authority, the International Court of Justice (ICJ) 1949 Advisory Opinion on the Reparation for Injuries Suffered in the Service of the UN,[61] the legal personality has to be objectively ascertained and be separate from that of its members.[62] In that case, the ICJ also stated about the UN that 'it must be acknowledged that its Members, by entrusting certain functions to it, with the attendant duties and responsibilities, have clothed it with the competence required to enable those functions to be effectively discharged'.[63] We will see that this is not entirely the

59 Focusing, correctly, on competences, see E. Paasivirta, 'The Responsibility of Member States of International Organisations. A Special Case for the European Union?' in A.S. Barros, C. Ryngaert and J. Wouters, *International Organisations and Member State Responsibility*, Brill Nijhoff, Leiden 2016, pp. 165ff.

60 Regulation (EU) No 604/2013 of the European Parliament and of the Council of 26 June 2013 establishing the criteria and mechanisms for determining the Member State responsible for examining an application for international protection lodged in one of the Member States by a third-country national or a stateless person [2013] OJ L180/31.

61 *Reparation for Injuries*, *supra* n. 13.

62 See, for a discussion, J. Crawford, *Brownlie's Principles of Public International Law*, Oxford University Press, Oxford 2012, p. 169 who identifies three criteria: (1) a permanent association of states, or other organisations, with lawful objects, equipped with organs; (2) distinction, in terms of legal powers and purposes, between the organisation and its member states; and (3) the existence of legal powers exercisable on the international plane and not solely within the national systems of one or more states.

63 *Reparation for Injuries*, *supra* n. 13, 179.

case for the EU in migration matters, which are a shared competence with Member States.[64] However, there is no doubt that the EU is a subject of international law and has a capacity to maintain its rights by bringing international claims, and it can be sued (Article 340 TFEU). It follows that it can also be liable for harm inflicted by it on third parties.

As far as (ii) and (iii) are concerned, they are considered together in Article 4 DARIO, which states, with a similar formulation to Article 2 of the Draft Articles on State Responsibility, that: 'There is an internationally wrongful act of an international organisation when conduct consisting of an action or omission: (a) is attributable to that organisation under international law; and (b) constitutes a breach of an international obligation of that organisation.'

Internationally wrongful acts are defined with reference to international law (Article 5 DARIO), whatever their source is (Article 10 DARIO). In light of the EU's special character,[65] a plea emerged to clarify its position on the international regime of responsibility. A proposal was issued to recognise a *lex specialis* principle[66] for the EU: any conduct on the part of the Member States (regarded as *de facto* organs of an international organisation), namely when the conduct of States consists of implementing or enforcing EU decisions, would be attributed to the EU and considered to be an act of the EU under international law. This would have established a criterion for attributing exclusive responsibility to the EU. However, no definitive conclusion was reached and the question is left open.[67]

In the operations discussed in this chapter, however, Member States are mainly taking part in joint operations, where they 'coordinate' and 'cooperate' with EU agencies. For example, the ships used for the search and rescue operations have the nationality of the Member States: UNCLOS affirms the general principle enunciated by the Permanent Court in the *Lotus Case*: 'Vessels on the high seas are subject to no authority except that of the State whose flag they fly. In virtue of the principle of the freedom of the seas, that is to say, the

---

64 In its submission to the ILC regarding DARIO, the EC Commission took the same view with regards to shared competences. It explicitly wrote, concerning external commitments, that: 'The EC is a party to many international agreements with third parties within its areas of competence. Quite often the EC concludes such agreements together with its member States, each in accordance with its own competencies. In that case the specificity of the EC lies in the fact that the EC and the member States each assume international responsibility with respect to their own competencies', p. 21, <http://legal.un.org/ilc/documentation/english/a_cn4_545.pdf> accessed 29.12.2016.

65 E. Paasivirta, *supra* n. 59.

66 J. D'Aspremont, 'The Articles on the Responsibility of International Organisations' (2013) *International Organisation Law Review* 15.

67 See, for an example of problems arising with the EU, ILC report on DARIO Yearbook of the International Law Commission, 2011, vol. II, Part Two 32, 40–42; see further N. Blokker and R. Wessel, *supra* n. 57, 5.

absence of any territorial sovereignty upon the high seas, no State may exercise any kind of jurisdiction over foreign vessels upon them.'[68] Thus UNCLOS Article 92(1) provides that '[s]hips shall sail under the flag of one State only and, save in exceptional cases expressly provided for in international treaties or in these articles, shall be subject to its exclusive jurisdiction on the high seas'.

Some authors have, more or less explicitly, advanced the proposition that the EU should be the responsible party. The key contention is that the fragmentation of responsibility results in a lack of protection. Thus Human Rights Watch has stated that the 'European Union countries failed to take collective action to share responsibility equitably for asylum seekers or to create safe and legal channels to Europe'.[69] Goodwin-Gill starts from the proposition that

> [t]he strategy of implementing a common policy through twenty-eight national systems, I suggested, was always bound to fail, no matter how comprehensive the top-down, legislative agreement on qualification, standards and criteria. The Dublin scheme, too, for all that it guarantees a decision for the asylum seeker somewhere, contributes nothing to what is and always was clearly needed in Europe, namely, effective, equitable sharing of protection responsibilities among a community committed to common, fundamental principles.[70]

His conclusion is utopic and, albeit commendable in principle, it is not shared by the author of this chapter.

> I suggested that, given the nature of the Union, its basis in common values and shared international obligations, what was needed was a truly European response, in which 'Europe's refugees' would enjoy European asylum, European protection and the rights and benefits accorded by European law. This would require, in turn, an EU institution, a *European Migration and Protection Agency* competent to fulfil collectively and to implement the individual obligations of Member States and the policy and protection goals of the EU. Moreover, it is essential to add 'migration', along with refugees and asylum seekers, precisely because the arrival of those in an irregular situation, whether directly or following interception or rescue at sea, presents Member States with legal and practical challenges that demand a community-based response.[71]

Costello, whose central contention is that moving immigration and asylum policy into EU law has greater potential than abiding by the statist paradigm,

---

68 (1927) PCIJ Ser. A No. 10, 25.

69 Human Rights Watch, *supra* n. 16.

70 G. Goodwin-Gill, 'Refugees and Migrants at Sea: Duties of Care and Protection in the Mediterranean and the Need for International Action', Jean Monnet Centre of Excellence on Migrants' Rights in the Mediterranean (Naples, 11.05.2015), <http://www.jmcemigrants.eu/jmce/wp-content/uploads/2015/06/GSGG-Naples-Final-May2015.pdf> accessed 29.12.2016.

71 *Ibid.* (emphasis in the original).

takes a similar view. The potential, in her view, derives from the EU's distinctive constitutional and institutional framework. 'At the constitutional level, the aim of the creation of an Area of Freedom, Security and Justice has transformative potential. The institutional dimension includes shared competences, minimum standards legislation, and the institutionalization of mutual recognition across the EU.'[72] The Europeanisation of immigration law is, according to Costello, a process of self-definition of the EU.

However, there are three key notions that must be taken into account. First, immigration falls under the Area of Freedom, Security and Justice, which is a shared competence between the EU and its Member States (Article 4(2) TFEU). Second, national security is the sole responsibility of the Member States. Third, considerations of democratic accountability tilt the balance of the normative argument towards Member States' responsibility.

Shared competences imply, if anything, shared responsibility (not the exclusive responsibility of the EU). But in the case of the international law obligations considered here, they tend to be the responsibility of Member States, rather than the EU. With regards to public international law, the rule of the Vienna Convention of the Law of Treaties is that a treaty binds only the parties to it (Article 26).[73] It is the Member States, and not the EU, who are parties to the conventions discussed above and whence the discussed legal obligations flow. The EU, which is not a party to those treaties, is only bound in so far as the provisions or the definitions of those conventions are referred to in the fundamental Treaties. However, at close scrutiny, the obligations in the area of migrations are, even under EU law, principally for the Member States: it is their responsibility to carry out the operations. Customary international law, instead, is considered by the Court of Justice of the EU to be binding on both the Union and its Member States.[74] However, there is still uncertainty on whether customary international law is also directly effective in the EU legal order.[75]

Article 4 TEU establishes without doubt that 'national security remains the sole responsibility of each Member State'. The issue of 'securisation' of borders – that is, to what extent border control is, or ought to be, a matter of security – is a debated one, but there is an increasing tendency to see it as a

[72] C. Costello, *supra* n. 18.

[73] Vienna Convention on the Law of Treaties, Article 26: 'Every treaty in force is binding upon the parties to it and must be performed by them in good faith.'

[74] See e.g. ECJ, Case C-286/90, *Anklagemyndigheden v. Poulsen and Diva Navigation* [1992] ECR I-6019.

[75] ECJ, Case C-162/96, *Racke* [1998] ECR I-3655, paras. 45–47. The ECJ referred to the direct effect of the agreement rather than of customary international law. But see also P. Eeckhout, *EU External Relations Law*, Oxford University Press, Oxford 2011, p. 386.

matter of national security.[76] The same concern is reflected in the fourth recital of the Regulation establishing Frontex, 'The responsibility for the control and surveillance of external borders lies with the Member States', and Article 1(2) thereof, 'While considering that the responsibility for the control and surveillance of external borders lies with the Member States, the Agency shall facilitate and render more effective the application of existing and future Community measures relating to the management of external borders'.

Finally, the normative argument gains strength if one considers that the Member States' accountability would imply more democratic control. As shown earlier, Frontex operational arrangements currently fall foul of the democratic control and the rule of law on which the EU should be based. Member States' resources, instead, are deployed through mechanisms that observe the democratic process – unlike in the EU case, which has delegated the arrangements to an Agency.

5. CONCLUSION

One of the main challenges of the 'migration crisis' lies in the attribution of responsibility. In principle, two options are conceivable under DARIO: responsibility for any breaches of international law can either be attributed to the EU or to Member States.

This chapter has proposed that the correct legal solution under international law is the engagement of the responsibility of the Member States who carry out the operations, with joint responsibility as a subsidiary principle, as Paasivirta suggests.[77] It has shown why the Draft Articles on State Responsibility are not conducive to attribution of acts to the EU in the migration matters considered (border control, search and rescue operations, and onward journeys of migrants). It has presented arguments based on the text of the Treaties and on the Frontex Regulation, and on democratic accountability.

While it may be commendable that Member States devolve more competence to the EU in the future, the current state of the law, and the practical reality of the operations, both point towards Member States' responsibility. Migration and refugee law are the most likely areas in which Member States would gain dramatically from putting their strength together in view of further cooperation.

---

76 J. Monar, 'Problems of Balance in JHA and the Impact of 11 September' in M. Anderson and J. Apap (eds.), *Police and Justice Cooperation and the New European Borders*, Kluwer Law International, The Hague 2002. A. Palm, 'Did 2016 Mark a New Start for EU External Migration Policy, or Was It Business as Usual?' (2016) *Istituto di Affari Internazionali Working Paper* 4, <http://www.iai.it/sites/default/files/iaiwp1633.pdf> accessed 29.12.2016.

77 E. Paasivirta, *supra* n. 59, 176.

Ghastly examples of deaths of refugees, which are tragically familiar to the contemporary reader, have been brought to the attention of the public by media, and the failure of single Member States, or at least their inability to cope with the sheer number of migrants, is apparent. This chapter ends with the lofty aspiration that the EU, once it is fully empowered in the field of migration, will help its Member States and, obviously, take on its own part of responsibility: morally as well as legally.

2. SOLIDARITY IN EU ASYLUM AND MIGRATION LAW: A CRISIS MANAGEMENT TOOL OR A STRUCTURAL PRINCIPLE?

Alberto MIGLIO*

1. INTRODUCTION

In recent years, the European Union (EU) has arguably been experiencing the deepest crisis in its history. The most acute phase of the economic and sovereign debt crisis had just been overcome, when a new crisis, driven by the increased flow of migrants and asylum seekers from the Southern and Eastern Mediterranean coasts, exposed the weaknesses of the European asylum system and led to an unprecedented level of confrontation between the Member States.

The two crises are not only interconnected,[1] but also share some common features and raise similar concerns.

The crisis of sovereign debt and the ensuing threat to the common currency have revealed the deep flaws existing in the architecture of the Economic and Monetary Union (EMU) and led to mounting dissatisfaction with EU policies among European citizens. In some Member States, the EU is viewed as responsible for detested austerity, shrinking budgets and ultimately the demise of the welfare state, whilst in others financial solidarity is fiercely contested as an unacceptable challenge to the principle of democracy.

Looking at the migration crisis and its perception in public opinion offers an equally depressing picture. The crisis has exposed a failure in the governance of migration[2] and generated a widespread sense of insecurity, prompting calls

* Department of Law, University of Turin, Italy. E-mail: alberto.miglio@unito.it. This chapter has been written in the context of the REScEU Project (Reconciling Economic and Social Europe, <www.resceu.eu>), funded by the European Research Council (grant no. 340534).

1 See A.J. MENÉNDEZ, 'The Existential Crisis of the European Union' (2013) 14 *German Law Journal* 453.

2 See D. THYM, 'The "Refugee Crisis" as a Challenge of Legal Design and Institutional Legitimacy' (2016) 53 *CMLR* 1545.

for border closure and repatriation of powers. The EU's intervention has been perceived as ineffective in the control of the external borders and in aiding the Member States in the allocation and reception of asylum seekers.

Both the sovereign debt crisis and the migration crisis can be explained as the product of a 'perfect storm',[3] a combination of external events, incorrect behaviours and ill-designed legal rules. The reason why they are so concerning, however, is that they also question some of the foundational values that are supposed to be shared within the Union,[4] solidarity in the first place.[5]

Against this background, the present chapter aims to assess the role of the principle of solidarity in the context of EU migration and asylum policies.

At the outset, by briefly sketching the evolution of references to solidarity in the EU Treaties, it shows that solidarity has emerged as a legal principle capable of imposing obligations (section 2). Building on this premise, the chapter subsequently attempts to better grasp the elusive nature of this principle by classifying its manifestations (section 3). It argues that the principle of solidarity can be better understood by distinguishing the different dimensions in which it operates: in inter-state relations, within each Member State and across Member States. The rest of the chapter focuses exclusively on the inter-state dimension, comparing the role of solidarity in the two main policy areas where its invocation has been so far controversial: the EMU and the EU policies on asylum and migration. While the purpose of this chapter is not to discuss in detail the relevance of solidarity in the EMU, it is submitted that the comparison can shed some light on the functions that the principle fulfils in the context of EU asylum and migration policies. Indeed, in the EMU, solidarity represents a counterweight to the dominant logic of individual responsibility of each Member State for its economic policy and for its budget, undoubtedly significant but confined to situations of emergency (section 4). By contrast, in the Area of Freedom, Security and Justice (AFSJ) and especially in the context of migration, asylum and border control, solidarity is not opposed to individual responsibility but is designated as one of the guiding principles of EU action (section 5). Yet, a critical analysis of the rules contained in the Dublin III Regulation on the allocation of responsibility for the processing of asylum application reveals that the promise of solidarity has not been fulfilled. Corrective mechanisms

3 T. Spijkerboer, 'Minimalist Reflections on Europe, Refugees and Law' (2016) 1 *European Papers* 533, 536; F. Munari, 'The Perfect Storm on EU Asylum Law: The Need to Rethink the Dublin Regime' (2016) *Diritti umani e diritto internazionale* 517, 525.

4 J.-P. Jacqué, 'Crise des valeurs dans l'Union européenne' (2016) *RTDE* 213, 215.

5 The crises certainly call into question solidarity among Member States, but arguably also solidarity among individuals and groups within and across national polities. The interactions between these levels are effectively captured, in relation to the financial and sovereign debt crisis, by M. Ferrera, 'Solidarity in Europe after the Crisis' (2014) 21 *Constellations* 222. On the different dimensions of solidarity in EU law, see section 3 below.

implemented so far also fall short of this objective, since they are premised on a short-term, emergency-driven logic (section 6). The chapter concludes that the construction of a European asylum system truly based on the principle of solidarity would require more ambitious plans and highlights the legal and political obstacles that they would have to overcome (section 7).

2. SOLIDARITY IN THE TREATIES: THE GRADUAL EMERGENCE OF A LEGAL PRINCIPLE

Solidarity has underpinned the project of European integration since its very inception. Famously, the Schuman Declaration foresaw the progressive making of Europe 'through concrete achievements which first create a *de facto* solidarity'. The Schuman Declaration, inspired and partly drafted by Jean Monnet, relied on his vision of integration as a gradual process similar to a chain reaction: integration in one sector of common policy would generate spillover effects and create the need for integration in related policy areas. This, in turn, would generate more spillover and eventually further integration. In his *Memoirs*, Monnet referred to this dynamic as a chain of solidarities, whereby solidarity in the limited sectors envisaged in the founding Treaties would call for solidarity in related sectors, gradually leading to deep integration.[6]

If solidarity, albeit only *de facto*, has proven to be quite successful as a driving force of European integration, translating it onto the plane of legal principles has required a long and difficult process.

References to solidarity in the founding Treaties were almost non-existent. On the one hand, it was evoked in the preamble of the European Coal and Steel Community (ECSC) Treaty, which essentially paraphrased the wording of the Schuman Declaration. On the other hand, the European Economic Community (EEC) Treaty only mentioned solidarity with regard to the relationship between the Member States and overseas countries, hardly an expression of the bond of solidarity to be created among the members of the Community. However, a solidarity-related mechanism was already present in Article 108 EEC, a provision pertaining to Title II of the Treaty on economic policy whereby the Council could, in certain circumstances, grant 'mutual assistance' to Member States facing difficulties in their balance of payments.

Subsequent Treaty revisions slowly but steadily strengthened the relevance of solidarity in primary law. On the one hand, some general references to solidarity progressively consolidated the impression that solidarity could transcend mere rhetoric and amount to a true principle of EU law. The Treaty on European Union (TEU) concluded in Maastricht set out a commitment

---

6 J. Monnet, *Mémoires*, Fayard, Paris 1976, pp. 598–99.

to organise relations between the Member States and between their peoples 'in a manner demonstrating … solidarity'[7] and called for the Member States to 'support the Union's external and security policy actively and unreservedly in a spirit of loyalty and loyal solidarity'.[8] Since the Amsterdam Treaty, solidarity has also been mentioned among the objectives of the Union (Article 2 TEU).

On the other hand, general references were supplemented by specific provisions relating to certain sectors. The Maastricht Treaty, building upon a pre-existing but more generic provision, introduced a mechanism whereby the Council, acting unanimously on a proposal from the Commission, could adopt 'measures appropriate to the economic situation' especially in the event of shortages in the supply of certain products (Article 103a(1) EC). In addition, the second paragraph of Article 103a EC allowed the Council, again by a unanimous vote, to grant Community financial assistance to a Member State 'in difficulties or … seriously threatened with severe difficulties caused by exceptional occurrences beyond its control'.[9] The Amsterdam Treaty, for the first time, also introduced a solidarity mechanism in the area of migration and asylum, authorising the Council to adopt temporary measures in support of Member States stricken with a sudden inflow of third-country nationals.[10]

Finally, while the Nice Treaty introduced no significant modifications, the Lisbon Treaty multiplied references to solidarity. First, it greatly strengthened the systematic dimension of the principle. Solidarity is now not only a value of the Union (Article 2 TEU), but is also listed among its objectives. According to Article 3(3) TEU, the Union shall promote 'solidarity between generations' and 'solidarity among Member States'. Moreover, 'solidarity and mutual respect among peoples' are mentioned, alongside a variety of other goals, as objectives that the Union should pursue in its external relations.[11]

In addition to general provisions variously qualifying solidarity as a value or an objective of the Union, the Treaty of Lisbon has also inserted several new rules referring to solidarity in specific policy areas: the Common Foreign and Security Policy (CFSP), the AFSJ and energy policy.

In the context of CFSP, Article 24(2) TEU calls for the development of mutual political solidarity as one of the bases for the definition, the conduct and the implementation of a common policy. The following paragraph adds that the Member States shall support the Union 'in a spirit of loyalty and

7 Article A TEU, later renumbered Article 1 TEU.

8 Article J.1 TEU, which later became Article 11 TEU.

9 Where difficulties were caused by natural disasters, the Council could act by qualified majority. The latter distinction was later abolished by the Treaty of Nice, which replaced unanimity with qualified majority voting altogether.

10 Article 64(2) EC.

11 This statement is echoed by a reference to solidarity as one of the guiding principles of external action in Article 21(1) TEU.

mutual solidarity' and cooperate to 'enhance and develop their mutual political solidarity'. Similarly, a 'spirit of mutual solidarity' should guide both the conduct of a Member State exercising constructive abstention, which shall not impede Union action, and that of the other Member States, which are bound to respect its position (Article 31(1) TEU). A display of solidarity between Member States is also at the core of the mutual defence mechanism laid down in Article 42(7) TEU: despite not containing the word 'solidarity', the obligation of assistance in case of armed aggression on the territory of a Member State is in fact a clearer expression of solidarity than most provisions mentioning it explicitly.[12]

As regards energy policy, the Treaty of Lisbon has introduced a new provision indicating that the Union policy in the energy sector shall be based on a spirit of solidarity (Article 194(1) of the Treaty on the Functioning of the European Union (TFEU)).

Arguably the most significant development, however, is the reference to solidarity as a guiding principle in the EU policies on migration, asylum and border control, one of the three components of the AFSJ together with cooperation in civil and in criminal matters (Article 67(2) TFEU). The claim that such policies shall be based on solidarity is reiterated by Article 80 TFEU, which contains further specifications as to the implementation of this principle. Both provisions will be examined in detail in section 5.

Besides references limited to particular policy areas, it is also worth mentioning that the Lisbon Treaty introduced a special assistance mechanism commonly known as 'solidarity clause' (Article 222 TFEU) with a view to helping Member States cope with specific and exceptional threats. It provides for an obligation on the Union and its Member States to 'act jointly in a spirit of solidarity if a Member State is the object of a terrorist attack or the victim of a natural or man-made disaster'.[13]

Finally, the Treaty provisions allowing for the adoption of measures 'appropriate to the economic situation' or tackling the consequences of exceptional occurrences beyond a Member State's control were reformulated and their scope expanded (Article 122 TFEU).

The Treaty of Lisbon has therefore marked an important step in the progressive emergence of an authentic principle of solidarity, capable of imposing obligations on the Member States and the Union. On the one hand, this reflects the strengthened commitment to constitutional principles, which, despite the

---

12 Cf. P. Hilpold, 'Filling a Buzzword with Life: The Implementation of the Solidarity Clause in Article 222 TFEU' (2015) 42 *LIEI* 209, 211, 215.

13 See M. Gestri, 'EU Disaster Response Law: Principles and Instruments' in A. de Guttry, M. Gestri and G. Venturini (eds.), *International Disaster Response Law*, T.M.C. Asser Press, The Hague 2012, p. 109; S. Blockmans, 'L'Union fait la Force: Making the Most of the Solidarity Clause (Article 222 TFEU)' in I. Govaere and S. Poli (eds.), *EU Management of Global Emergencies*, Martinus Nijhoff Publishers, Leiden 2014, p. 11; P. Hilpold, *supra* n. 12.

abandonment of the most visible symbolic elements, has largely survived the demise of the Constitutional Treaty.[14] On the other hand, such recognition is in line with the case law of the Court of Justice of the EU, which has long explicitly qualified solidarity as a 'principle'.[15]

Recently, the Court confirmed this statement in a judgment concerning the validity of Council Decision 2015/1601 on the relocation of asylum seekers,[16] where it held that, based on the principle of solidarity, the Council was 'bound ... to take measures which could be swiftly put in place and actually have an effect' in alleviating the pressure of migration flows on Italy and Greece.[17]

It is debatable whether defining solidarity as a 'constitutional principle',[18] as a 'founding and existential value'[19] or as 'the quintessence of what is both the *raison d'être* and the objective of the European project'[20] really has any added value from a legal perspective. It is also uncertain whether it qualifies as a *general* principle.[21] There can be no doubt, however, that it amounts to a *principle* of EU law[22] from which legal obligations arise and that Treaty provisions imposing a display of solidarity cannot be dismissed as mere rhetoric statements devoid of legal significance.[23]

---

14 See M. Dougan, 'The Treaty of Lisbon 2007: Winning Minds, not Hearts' (2008) 45 *CMLR* 617, 698.

15 ECJ, Case 77/77, *Benzine en Petroleum Handelsmaatschappij BV and others v. Commission*, ECLI:EU:C:1978:141, para. 15.

16 Council Decision 2015/1601 of 22 September 2015 establishing provisional measures in the area of international protection for the benefit of Italy and Greece [2015] OJ L248/80.

17 ECJ, Joined Cases C-643/15 and C-647/15, *Slovak Republic and Hungary v. Council*, ECLI:EU:C:2017:631, para. 249.

18 A. Von Bodgandy, 'Founding Principles' in A. Von Bodgandy and J. Bast (eds.), *Principles of EU Constitutional Law*, Hart, Oxford 2010, p. 53; R. Bieber, 'Gegenseitige Verantwortung – Grundlage des Verfassungsprinzips der Solidarität in der Europäischen Union' in C. Calliess (ed.), *Europäische Solidarität und nationale Identität – Überlegungen im Kontext der Krise im Euroraum*, Mohr Siebeck, Tübingen 2013, p. 67.

19 Opinion of AG Bot, Joined Cases C-643/15 and C-647/15, *Slovak Republic and Hungary v. Council of the European Union*, ECLI:EU:C:2017:618, para. 17.

20 *Ibid.*, para. 18.

21 On the difficulties surrounding the exact identification of general principles see C. Flaesch-Mougin, 'Typologie des principes de l'Union européenne' in *Le droit de l'Union européenne en principes – Liber amicorum en l'honneur de Jean Raux*, Apogée, Rennes 2006, p. 99; T. Tridimas, *General Principles of EU Law*, Oxford University Press, Oxford, 2006, pp. 2–3.

22 Cfr. C. Barnard, 'Solidarity and New Governance in Social Policy' in G. de Burca and J. Scott (eds.), *Law and New Governance in the EU and the US*, Hart, Portland 2006, p. 153, 156; A. McDonnell, 'Solidarity, Flexibility, and the Euro-Crisis: Where Do Principles Fit In?' in L.S. Rossi and F. Casolari (eds.), *The EU after Lisbon. Amending or Coping with the Existing Treaties?*, Springer, Heidelberg 2014, pp. 57, 61; J. Bast, 'Deepening Supranational Integration: Interstate Solidarity in EU Migration Law' (2016) 22 *European Public Law* 289; E. Küçük, 'Solidarity in EU Law: An Elusive Political Statement or a Legal Principle with Substance?' (2016) *Maastricht Journal of European and Comparative Law* 965, 966.

23 Therefore, it is no longer arguable that the principle of solidarity is merely 'political and non-binding' (M. Klamert, *The Principle of Loyalty in EU Law*, Oxford University Press, Oxford 2014, p. 35).

3. 'SOLIDARITY': WHAT'S IN A NAME?

This conclusion, however, is of little help when it comes to identifying the content of the solidarity obligations that EU law may impose. Indeed, while solidarity is mentioned 21 times in the text of the Treaties, the inflation of references in the most diverse contexts, rather than clarifying its meaning, reveals a fragmented and confusing picture.

Such perception of incoherence largely depends on the polysemy of the notion of solidarity, which may refer to rather different things.[24]

The first level of ambiguity relates to the various characterisations of solidarity in the EU legal order. In the Treaties, solidarity is explicitly mentioned not just as a principle, but also as a value and as an objective. This multiple characterisation suggests that solidarity may serve different functions. While it is established that at least in certain sectors it may operate as an interpretative instrument and as a yardstick in judicial review,[25] solidarity does not appear to have an equally strong normative dimension in all policy areas.

The second challenge in assessing the significance and implications of solidarity stems from the variety of factual contexts in which it may be invoked. Since solidarity is necessarily a relational concept – that is, one that implies a relationship between at least two subjects – a useful way of classifying its manifestations is to look at the different relations that it applies to. Following this criterion, three distinct dimensions of solidarity emerge in EU law.[26]

In some instances, solidarity is conceived of as a principle governing the joint production of collective goods regardless of borders. For instance, where the Treaty mentions solidarity between generations (Article 3(3), TEU), solidarity is identified as a value that should be safeguarded and promoted in the civil society at large, across national borders but equally within each Member State.

By contrast, the objective of promoting 'solidarity among peoples' (Article 3(5), TEU) refers to the cross-border solidarity that EU law establishes between citizens of different Member States. This kind of transnational solidarity[27] lies at the heart of European citizenship and is most clearly expressed

---

24 See S. De La Rosa, 'La transversalité de la solidarité dans les politiques matérielles de l'Union' in C. Boutayeb (ed.), *La solidarité dans l'Union européenne. Éléments constitutionnels et matériels*, Dalloz, Paris 2011, p. 165, noting that solidarity is a concept that defies definition.

25 C. Barnard, *supra* n. 22, p. 156. See also A. McDonnell, *supra* n. 22, pp. 57, 60–63.

26 For similar classifications see I. Domurath, 'The Three Dimensions of Solidarity in the EU Legal Order: Limits of the Judicial and Legal Approach' (2013) 35 *European Integration* 459, 460; A. Sangiovanni, 'Solidarity in the European Union' (2013) 33 *OJLS* 213, 221.

27 A. Sangiovanni, *ibid.*, 232–41; F. de Witte, *Justice in the EU – The Emergence of Transnational Solidarity*, Oxford University Press, Oxford 2015.

by the prohibition of discrimination on grounds of nationality.[28] In this sense, solidarity may refer, in particular, to the access to healthcare and social benefits in the Member State of residence by nationals of other Member States, epitomising the challenge to the boundaries of national welfare states posed by European integration.[29]

Finally, the third dimension of solidarity operates on the inter-state level, imposing upon the Member States a certain course of action in their reciprocal relations or in their relations with the Union. Most Treaty provisions expressly mentioning solidarity seem in fact to refer to this inter-state dimension of solidarity. Consider, for instance, the various provisions requiring action 'in a spirit of solidarity' or the statement that CFSP shall be 'based on the development of mutual political solidarity among Member States' (Article 24(2), TEU). Here solidarity, requiring 'joint action', clearly operates at the level of relations between Member States and, possibly, between the Member States and the Union.

Even if one only considers its role in governing the relations among Member States – the inter-state dimension – solidarity still appears as a composite concept. In this regard, scholars have distinguished between a procedural and a substantive dimension of solidarity.[30] The procedural dimension can in fact be viewed more appropriately as an implication of the principle of loyalty.[31] It does not address the allocation of collective goods but dictates to the Member States – and sometimes to the Union – obligations of conduct premised on their commitment to achieve the objectives set out in the Treaties.

The 'spirit of mutual solidarity' evoked by Article 31(1) TFEU on constructive abstention provides a good example of this understanding of solidarity. Despite the express reference to solidarity, the provision seems actually to be concerned with loyalty. Indeed, it only sets out reciprocal obligations of non-interference that strongly resemble similar mutual duties arising in the implementation of

---

28 See the essays collected in Y. Borgmann-Perbil and M. Ross (eds.), *Promoting Solidarity in the European Union*, Oxford University Press, Oxford 2010.

29 See M. Ferrera, *The Boundaries of Welfare: European Integration and the New Spatial Politics of Social Protection*, Oxford University Press, Oxford 2005.

30 See C. Tomuschat, 'Das europäische Solidaritätsprinzip und die Kruse des Euro – Von der Rechtsgemeinschaft zur Solidaritätsgemeinschaft?' in I. Pernice and R. Schwarz (eds.), *Europa in der Welt – Von der Finanzkrise zur Reform der Union*, Nomos, Baden-Baden 2013, pp. 153, 165; R. Bieber and F. Maiani, 'Sans solidarité point d'Union européenne – Regards croisés sur les crises de l'Union économique et monétaire et du Système européen commun d'asile' (2012) 48 *RTDE* 295, 296.

31 On the relationship between loyalty and solidarity see further M. Blanquet, *L'article 5 du traité C.E.E.: recherche sur les obligations de fidelité des États membres de la Communauté*, L.G.D.J., Paris 1994; A. Berramdane, 'Solidarité, loyauté dans le droit de l'Union européenne' in C. Boutayeb (ed.), *La solidarité dans l'Union européenne. Éléments constitutionnels et matériels*, Dalloz, Paris 2011, p. 53; F. Casolari, 'EU Loyalty after Lisbon: An Expectation Gap to Be Filled?' in L.S. Rossi and F. Casolari (eds.), *The EU after Lisbon: Amending or Coping with the Existing Treaties*, Springer, Heidelberg 2014, pp. 93–133.

enhanced cooperation:[32] the participating Member States cannot be hindered from proceeding further but also the position of the non-participating Member States must be respected and their rights and competences safeguarded. The first obligation is nothing but a reminder of the general duty that Member States have under Article 4(3) TEU not to jeopardise the attainment of Union objectives. The second, by contrast, is specific to some cases of differentiated integration where one or more Member States may be excluded from the scope of application of an EU measure: in such hypotheses, loyalty obligations are mutual since they protect not only the achievement of EU objectives, but also the expectation of non-participating Member States that their rights and competences will be preserved from encroachment.

The case law of the Court of Justice of the EU often reveals the same understanding of solidarity as a proxy for sincere cooperation. In most instances where the Court expressly mentioned solidarity, it actually imposed obligations that should rather be viewed as flowing from the duty of loyalty.[33] For instance, in one case the Court expressly linked solidarity, identified as 'the basis' of the Member States' obligation to fully comply with Community law, to Article 5 of the EEC Treaty expressing the principle of loyalty.[34] In another case, it deemed that the incomplete or selective application of a Community regulation was contrary to the 'duty of solidarity accepted by Member States by the fact of their adherence to the Community'.[35] The overlap between loyalty and solidarity may explain why the Court later stopped referring to solidarity altogether: given the tremendous development of duties of cooperation under the principle of loyalty,[36] solidarity was eventually overshadowed by the latter principle.

Nevertheless, the relevance of solidarity in the relations among Member States is not confined to a special dimension or implication of the duty of loyalty. In some cases, the Treaties also require a certain course of action to be taken in support of a Member State that is confronted with a particularly dire situation. In other instances, they indicate that a common policy shall be 'based on solidarity'. In such cases, solidarity does indeed operate as a principle distinct from loyalty and as an autonomous source of obligations. Instead of merely obliging the Member States to cooperate in ensuring the effectiveness of Union action, solidarity is intended as a condition enabling specific actions – such as support to a Member State – or as a criterion orientating the choice between different policy options.

---

32 See Article 327 TFEU.

33 R. Bieber and F. Maiani, *supra* n. 30, 296.

34 ECJ, Joined Cases 6 and 11/69, *Commission v. France* [1969], ECLI:EU:C:1969:68, para. 16.

35 ECJ, Case 128/78, *Commission v. United Kingdom* [1979], ECLI:EU:C:1979:32, para. 12.

36 See J. Temple Lang, 'The Development by the Court of Justice of the Duties of Cooperation of National Authorities and Communities Institutions under Article 10 EC' (2007) 31 *Fordham International Law Journal* 1483; M. Klamert, *supra* n. 23.

This substantive or material dimension of solidarity – as opposed to the procedural dimension discussed above – appears to have a limited scope, since solidarity-based mechanisms are only envisaged in specific sectors, creating what have been described as 'islands of solidarity'.[37] Specific solidarity-related obligations are in fact present only in four policy areas: the CFSP, energy policy, the EMU and the AFSJ, with particular reference to migration, asylum and border control. In the following sections, the role of solidarity in two of these policy fields – the EMU on the one hand, the AFSJ, especially the Common European Asylum System (CEAS), on the other – will be examined.

4. RESPONSIBILITY AND SOLIDARITY IN THE ECONOMIC AND MONETARY UNION

Within the EMU, inter-state solidarity was not adopted as a major organising principle. Rather, the opposite is true: the overall architecture of the EMU shaped by the Maastricht Treaty is premised on the autonomy and individual responsibility of each Member State for its budget.[38]

The reliance on autonomy and responsibility instead of solidarity is, on the one hand, a consequence of the philosophy underpinning the establishment of the EMU with its emphasis on price and financial stability.[39] On the other hand, it is a substitute for a comprehensive harmonisation of economic policies and the creation of a strong federal budget, which the Member States were not ready to consent to.[40] In the absence of a truly common economic policy and of a strong EU budget, a commitment of the Member States to budgetary discipline appeared necessary to guarantee stability.

In order to entrench this commitment and ensure that the Member States would conduct their economic and budgetary policy in line with the objective of stability, the Treaty introduced three different tools.

The first is the coordination of the economic policies of the Member States, which according to Article 121 TFEU is carried out through soft-law instruments and whose implementation is monitored through a multilateral surveillance procedure.

---

37 P. Hilpold, 'Understanding Solidarity within EU Law: An Analysis of the 'Islands of Solidarity' with Particular Regard to Monetary Union' (2015) 34 *YEL* 257, 265.

38 J.-V. Louis, 'Solidarité budgétaire et financière dans l'Union européenne' in C. Boutayeb (ed.), *La solidarité dans l'Union européenne. Éléments constitutionnels et matériels*, Dalloz, Paris 2011, p. 110.

39 See M. Herdegen, 'Price Stability and Budgetary Restraints in the Economic and Monetary Union: The Law as Guardian of Economic Wisdom' (1998) 35 *CMLR* 9.

40 J.-V. Louis, *supra* n. 38, 111.

The second is the Member States' obligation to avoid excessive deficits set out in Article 126(1) TFEU and the Stability and Growth Pact. Article 126 TFEU provides for a mechanism of monitoring and coordination to ensure compliance with this obligation, which could ultimately lead to sanctions against the Member State concerned according to Article 126(11) TFEU.[41]

The third and most significant safeguard consists of the prohibitions laid down in Articles 123, 124 and 125 TFEU. The first of these provisions is addressed to the European Central Bank (ECB) and the national central banks and prohibits the monetary financing of public authorities, whereas Article 124 TFEU precludes the latter from receiving privileged access to financial institutions. Finally, Article 125 codifies the no-bailout rule, stipulating that the Union and the Member States 'shall not be liable for or assume the commitments' of governments or other authorities of any Member State.

All such prohibitions pursue a common objective. By making each Member State solely and individually responsible for its own debt, they are meant to force the pursuit of a sound budgetary policy.[42] On the premise that they cannot rely on help from the Union, from the other Member States or from central banks, the Member States should have no incentive to disregard their budgetary commitments. As such, all the prohibitions embody clear anti-solidarity elements.[43]

In fact, some solidarity-based tools do exist in the context of the EMU, but their structure and the preconditions for their operation do not call into question the reliance of the overall EMU architecture on autonomy and responsibility.

The first is the mutual assistance mechanism in favour of Member States in difficulties relating to their balance of payments (Article 143 TFEU). Crucially, however, this tool can only operate to the benefit of Member States with a derogation,[44] revealing that the Treaty apparently allows for a higher degree of solidarity towards non-euro area Member States than among the Member States that share the common currency.

In addition, Article 122 TFEU provides for two further solidarity mechanisms. Article 122(1) TFEU derives from Article 103 EEC, a provision that allowed for the adoption of measures to mitigate difficulties arising in connection with the supply of products. The mechanism now has a much wider scope: since Article 122(1) TFEU refers to difficulties in the supply of products only as an

---

41 Both the coordination of economic policies and the Stability and Growth Pact have been strengthened as a response to the crisis with the adoption of the measures comprised in the so-called 'Six-Pack' in 2011.

42 P. Athanassiou, 'Of Past Measures and Future Plans for Europe's Exit from the Sovereign Debt Crisis: What is Legally Possible (and What is Not)' (2011) *ELR* 558, 560.

43 P. Hilpold, *supra* n. 37, 276.

44 By virtue of Article 1 of Protocol No. 16, it also applies to Denmark, to whom all provisions referring to a derogation are applicable, albeit Denmark benefits from an 'exemption'.

example, its scope of application also covers different 'economic situations'. In this vein, it recently provided the legal basis for granting financial assistance to the Member States most affected by the inflow of migrants and asylum seekers.[45] The broadening of its scope of application will arguably also affect judicial interpretation: while in the past the case law followed a restrictive approach, excluding reliance on this mechanism in areas falling within the scope of common policies,[46] this reading may no longer be justified. It seems therefore that Article 122(1) TFEU has some potential for giving substance to the principle of solidarity, even outside the context of economic policy. Nevertheless, it is clear from its wording that this tool is only intended to operate under exceptional circumstances in order to address specific situations of emergency.

Similarly premised on the existence of exceptional circumstances is the mechanism envisaged by the second paragraph of Article 122 TFEU, which has a partially different and more limited scope, since it is applicable only where difficulties affecting a Member State are 'caused by natural disasters or exceptional occurrences beyond its control'. Article 122(2) TFEU provided the legal basis for the establishment of the European Financial Stabilisation Mechanism (EFSM), the first institutional mechanism devised to grant financial assistance to Greece in 2010.[47] However, doubts regarding the legality of recourse to such tool in the context of the sovereign debt crisis, but above all the limited capacity of the EU budget, motivated recourse to instruments external to the EU legal order in order to channel further financial assistance directly from the Member States.[48]

Eventually, the need to introduce mechanisms of financial assistance to support the Member States most affected in order to prevent the crisis from spreading and ultimately to avoid the collapse of the common currency, posed the question of compatibility of such measures with the no-bailout clause.[49]

---

45 Council Regulation (EU) 2016/369 of 15 March 2016 on the provision of emergency support within the Union [2016] OJ L70/1. See A. Miglio, 'The Regulation on the Provision of Emergency Support within the Union: Humanitarian Assistance and Financial Solidarity in the Refugee Crisis' (2016) 1 *European Papers* 1171.

46 ECJ, Case 5/73, *Balkan-Import-Export GmbH v. Hauptzollamt Berlin-Packhof*, ECLI:EU:C:1973:109, para. 13; ECJ, Case 9/73, *Carl Schlüter v. Hauptzollamt Lörrach*, ECLI:EU:C:1973:110, para. 13; ECJ, Case 31/74, *Filippo Galli*, ECLI:EU:C:1975:8, para. 24.

47 Council Regulation (EU) 407/2010 of 11 May 2010 establishing a European financial stabilisation mechanism [2010] OJ L118/1.

48 The EFSF was set up in May 2009 as a special purpose vehicle in the form of a private company under Luxembourg law; the ESM was instituted by an international agreement concluded among the euro area Member States.

49 For an overview of the different interpretations put forward in the legal literature, see P.-A. van Malleghem, '*Pringle*: A Paradigm Shift in the European Union's Monetary Constitution' (2013) 14 *German Law Journal* 141, 160–62.

When it had to review the legality of the establishment of the European Stability Mechanism (ESM) in the *Pringle* case,[50] the Court of Justice of the EU, by exploiting the semantic ambiguities in Article 125 TFEU, interpreted the prohibition with a certain degree of flexibility. It held that financial assistance from the Member States is not forbidden, as any Member State remains responsible for its commitments to its creditors provided that support is subject to conditions prompting the requesting Member State to pursue a sound budgetary policy.[51] Additionally, it noted that under the ESM Treaty financial assistance cannot be granted as soon as a Member State encounters budgetary difficulties, but is only available as *extrema ratio*, when it is indispensable to safeguard the stability of the euro area as a whole.[52] Interestingly, whereas the Court did not mention the principle of solidarity in its reasoning, Advocate General Kokott did. In the Advocate General's view, the principle of solidarity could be relied upon, as an interpretative tool, in order to exclude an extensive interpretation of the prohibition.[53]

The Court also adopted a moderately permissive reading of the prohibition of monetary financing in the *Gauweiler* case, holding that whilst Article 123(1) TFEU prevents all financial assistance from the ECB to a Member State, it does not preclude the purchase by the European System of Central Banks of sovereign bonds of a Member State on the secondary market.[54] Such operations, however, are only permissible as long as they do not have an effect equivalent to a direct purchase from the authorities of the Member State concerned.[55] Given that Article 123(1) TFEU, like Article 125, is intended to support the Member States' commitment to budgetary discipline,[56] purchases of government bonds on secondary markets must be assisted by adequate safeguards ensuring that they do not amount to a circumvention of the prohibition of monetary financing.[57]

In *Pringle* and in *Gauweiler*, the Court thus mitigated the frictions between the logic of individual responsibility and the commitment to solidarity through a flexible interpretation of the anti-solidarity provisions.[58] Nevertheless, by emphasising the objective of budgetary discipline, it upheld individual

50 ECJ, Case C-370/12, *Pringle*, ECLI:EU:C:2012:756. Among the numerous comments, see B. De Witte and T. Beukers, 'The Court of Justice approves the creation of the European Stability Mechanism outside the EU legal order: *Pringle*' (2012) 50 *CMLR* 805; D. Thym and M. Wendel, 'Préserver le respect du droit dans la crise: la Cour de justice, le MES et le mythe du déclin de la communauté de droit' (2012) *CDE* 733.

51 *Pringle*, *ibid.*, para. 137.

52 *Ibid.*, para. 142.

53 View of AG Kokott, Case C-370/12, *Pringle*, ECLI:EU:C:2012:675, paras. 142–43.

54 ECJ, Case C-62/14, *Gauweiler*, ECLI:EU:C:2015:400, para. 95.

55 *Ibid.*, para. 97.

56 *Ibid.*, para. 100.

57 *Ibid.*, para. 102.

58 Cf. R. Bieber and F. Maiani, *supra* n. 30, 299.

responsibility as a guiding principle and made solidarity appear as an exception to the ordinary course of business.[59] Albeit responsibility and solidarity are not in a rule-exception relationship in a literal sense, financial assistance, as the foremost expression of economic solidarity between Member States, is only admissible in exceptional circumstances and in a form – loans subject to strict conditionality – that does not hinder the pursuit of budgetary stability.[60]

5. SOLIDARITY AS A GUIDING PRINCIPLE OF EU MIGRATION AND ASYLUM POLICIES

Whilst the architecture of the EMU is premised on autonomy and responsibility, with solidarity operating only as an exceptional corrective mechanism, responsibility and solidarity are not conceived of as opposing concepts within the framework of the AFSJ.

In laying down the fundamental principles for the establishment of the AFSJ, Article 67(2) TFEU provides that the Union '[s]hall ensure the absence of internal border controls for persons and shall frame a common policy on asylum, immigration and external border control, based on solidarity between Member States, which is fair towards third-country nationals'. The reference to solidarity in Article 67(2) TFEU is supplemented by Article 80 TFEU, which stipulates that the Union policies in this sector and their implementation 'shall be governed by the principle of solidarity and fair sharing or responsibilities, including its financial implications'. The second sentence adds that, 'whenever necessary', EU secondary law shall 'contain appropriate measures to give effect to this principle'.

Both Article 67(2) and Article 80 TFEU define inter-state solidarity as a legal principle underlying the EU policies on border checks, asylum and immigration. Their wording ('*shall* frame a … policy … *based* on solidarity', '*shall* be governed')[61] indicates that the principle is intended to be legally binding,[62] a conclusion that the Court of Justice of the EU has explicitly endorsed.[63] In addition, Article 80 is more specific than Article 67(2) TFEU, in that it not

---

59 V. Borger, 'The ESM and the European Court's Predicament in *Pringle*' (2012) 14 *German Law Journal* 113, 120.

60 For a critique of the Court's approach see H. Schepel, 'The Bank, the Bond, and the Bail-out: On the Legal Construction of Market Discipline in the Eurozone' (2017) 44 *Journal of Law and Society* 79.

61 Emphasis added.

62 See M. Gestri, 'La politica europea dell'immigrazione: solidarietà tra Stati membri e misure nazionali di regolarizzazione' in A. Ligustro and G. Sacerdoti (eds.), *Problemi e tendenze del diritto internazionale dell'economia.* Liber amicorum *in onore di Paolo Picone*, Editoriale Scientifica, Naples 2011, pp. 895, 903; J. Bast, *supra* n. 22, 292.

63 *Slovak Republic and Hungary v. Council*, *supra* n. 17, para. 249.

only sets out a guiding principle but also imposes on EU institutions concrete obligations to act[64] 'whenever necessary'.

It is therefore a rather straightforward conclusion that in this area the principle of solidarity may operate as a yardstick against which the validity of EU measures can be tested in annulment actions or in the context of a reference for preliminary ruling.[65] In the same vein, it may form the basis for an action for failure to act.[66] It has to be noted, however, that the Treaty grants the EU legislature broad discretion in shaping a common policy on migration, asylum and border control.[67] This view is further confirmed by the reference to 'appropriate measures', which suggests that it is for the competent EU institutions to decide which measures are suitable to give effect to the principle of solidarity. In light of this framework, it is hardly surprising that the Court of Justice of the EU has applied a lenient standard of review, stating that it would only strike down measures which are 'manifestly inappropriate' to attain the objective pursued.[68] As a consequence, EU measures are unlikely to be invalidated for failure to comply with the principle of solidarity, a conclusion further supported by the Court's traditional reluctance to resort to solidarity even as an interpretative tool in the context of the CEAS, despite explicit suggestions that it should do so from national courts[69] or from Advocates General.[70]

In addition to solidarity, Article 80 TFEU also mentions responsibility sharing. Such reference is not surprising in this context, given that responsibility sharing – or burden sharing[71] – is one of the principles of international refugee law and is mentioned in the preamble of the 1951 Geneva Convention relating to the status of refugees.[72]

It is interesting, however, to compare the relationship between responsibility and solidarity in this context and within the EMU. Whereas in the latter context solidarity operates as a countervailing principle to the dominant logic of individual responsibility of each Member State, Article 80 TFEU does not oppose responsibility and solidarity. On the contrary, since it indicates how

---

64 M. Kotzur, 'Article 80 TFEU' in R. Geiger, D.-E. Kahn and M. Kotzur (eds.), *European Union Treaties. A Commentary*, C.H. Beck-Hart, München-Oxford 2015, p. 437.

65 M. Gestri, *supra* n. 62, 903; J. Bast, *supra* n. 22, 293; *contra*, D. Thym, *supra* n. 2, 1550.

66 J. Bast, *supra* n. 22, 297.

67 See, to this effect, *Slovak Republic and Hungary v. Council*, *supra* n. 17, paras. 207–08.

68 *Ibid.*, para. 207.

69 See ECJ, C-528/11, *Halaf*, ECLI:EU:C:2013:342, para. 25.

70 Opinion of AG Mengozzi, Case C-638/16 PPU, *X and X v. Belgium*, para. 174.

71 See M. Gottwald, 'Burden Sharing and Refugee Protection' in E. Fiddian-Qasmiyeh, G. Loescher, K. Long and N. Sigona (eds.), *The Oxford Handbook of Refugee and Forced Migration Studies*, Oxford University Press, Oxford 2014, p. 525.

72 See A. Hans and A. Surhke, 'Responsibility Sharing' in J.C. Hathaway (ed.), *Reconceiving International Refugee Law*, Martinus Nijhoff Publishers, The Hague 1997, pp. 83–109; J. Milner, 'Burden Sharing' in M. Gibney and R. Hansen (eds.), *Immigration and Asylum: From 1900 to the Present*, ABC-CLIO, Santa Barbara 2005, p. 56.

responsibilities shall be allocated, the concept of fair sharing should be viewed as an element of solidarity[73] or, to be more precise, as a criterion that helps define the content of the principle of solidarity in this particular policy area.

Finally, as to the scope and content of solidarity obligations, other indications can be inferred from the wording of Article 80 TFEU. The first sentence provides, in particular, that 'financial implications' must be addressed, but by no means confines the implementation of solidarity and fair sharing to financial contributions, as the word 'including' indicates. This is another significant difference between the concept of solidarity that emerges in the EMU and the principle of solidarity set out in Article 80 TFEU. Within a framework based on the principle of individual responsibility of each Member State, solidarity may be understood as an exceptional remedy to a situation of emergency, where intervention is required to redress the consequences of events beyond ordinary business. By contrast, the reference to solidarity as an underlying policy principle contained in Article 80 TFEU points to a different and far more comprehensive understanding of solidarity, governing the relations between Member States beyond the emergency, in the ordinary process of decision-making and implementation of common policies.[74] In order to give effect to this principle, emergency-driven measures may prove insufficient.

6. THE COMMON EUROPEAN ASYLUM SYSTEM AND THE UNFULFILLED PROMISE OF SOLIDARITY

In reviewing the implementation of the principle of solidarity, the remaining section of this chapter will take a closer look at the allocation of responsibility for the reception of asylum seekers and for the processing of their applications, since it is on this issue that the debate on solidarity in the AFSJ has mostly concentrated so far. It should not be forgotten, however, that the principle of solidarity, as it also underpins the policies on migration and border checks, may be of relevance in other contexts as well.[75]

In order to assess how the principle of solidarity and fair sharing of responsibilities has been implemented in the CEAS, it is useful to rely on Noll's classification of different types of sharing.[76] According to this conceptual

73 See H. Gray, 'Surveying the Foundations: Article 80 TFEU and the Common European Asylum System' (2013) 34 *Liverpool Law Review* 175, 177, 182.

74 Cf. I. Goldner Lang, 'Is there Solidarity on Asylum and Migration in the EU?' (2013) 9 *CYELP* 1, 8–9.

75 See, for instance, M. Gestri, *supra* n. 62, 911–25, discussing the constraints that the principle of solidarity might impose on the regularisation of illegal migrants.

76 G. Noll, *Negotiating Asylum. The EU Acquis, Extraterritorial Protection and the Common Market of Deflection*, Martinus Nijhoff Publishers, The Hague 2000, p. 270.

framework, responsibility sharing can be achieved through three different instruments: the harmonisation of refugee and asylum legislation ('sharing norms'); the provision of financial assistance as a measure to redistribute between Member States the cost of reception ('sharing money'); and the distribution of protection seekers (rather awkwardly defined as 'sharing people').

As far as 'sharing norms' is concerned, harmonisation of the asylum laws of the Member States has so far been rather intense, but far from exhaustive. The Union has adopted, *inter alia*, directives on qualifications,[77] on common procedures for granting and withdrawing international protection[78] and on reception conditions.[79] Although these measures, as part of the second stage of harmonisation launched after the entry into force of the Lisbon Treaty, are more precise and comprehensive than the acts they have replaced,[80] EU law still does not provide for exhaustive harmonisation and does not entirely replace national law.[81]

Additionally, common rules are not uniformly applied throughout the Union. Huge disparities exist between Member States in relation to crucial aspects of

---

77 Directive 2011/95/EU of the European Parliament and of the Council of 13 December 2011 on standards for the qualification of third-country nationals or stateless persons as beneficiaries of international protection, for a uniform status for refugees or for persons eligible for subsidiary protection, and for the content of the protection granted [2011] OJ L 337/9.

78 Directive 2013/32/EU of the European Parliament and of the Council of 26 June 2013 on common procedures for granting and withdrawing international protection [2013] OJ L180/60.

79 Directive 2013/33/EU of the European Parliament and of the Council of 26 June 2013 laying down standards for the reception of applicants for international protection [2013] OJ L180/96.

80 Respectively, Council Directive 2004/83/EC of 29 April 2004 on minimum standards for the qualification and status of third country nationals or stateless persons as refugees or as persons who otherwise need international protection and the content of the protection granted [2004] OJ L304/12; Council Directive 2005/85/EC of 1 December 2005 on minimum standards on procedures in Member States for granting and withdrawing refugee status [2005] OJ L326/13; Council Directive 2003/9/EC of 27 January 2003 laying down minimum standards for the reception of asylum seekers [2003] OJ L31/18.

81 In 2016, the Commission tabled proposals for a comprehensive overhaul of EU asylum law, including the replacement of the Qualification Directive and the Asylum Procedures Directive by regulations. However, none of these measures have been adopted at the time of writing. See Proposal for a Regulation of the European Parliament and of the Council on standards for the qualification of third-country nationals or stateless persons as beneficiaries of international protection, for a uniform status for refugees or for persons eligible for subsidiary protection and for the content of the protection granted and amending Council Directive 2003/109/EC of 25 November 2003 concerning the status of third-country nationals who are long-term residents, COM(2016) 466 final; Proposal for a Regulation of the European Parliament and of the Council establishing a common procedure for international protection in the Union and repealing Directive 2013/32/EU, COM(2016) 467 final. The Commission also proposed a reform of the Reception Conditions Directive (see Proposal for a Directive of the European Parliament and of the Council laying down standards for the reception of applicants for international protection (recast), COM(2016) 465 final).

asylum law.[82] This is true not only for reception conditions and opportunities of integration for persons in need of international protection, but also for the speed and effectiveness of procedures for the recognition of asylum status, which vary wildly across the EU.[83] Even more stunningly divergent from Member State to Member State are recognition rates according to the country of origin of the applicant.[84]

In any event, common rules, even if they were uniformly applied, would not suffice to build a common asylum system based on solidarity and a fair sharing of responsibilities. Indeed, the fact that Member States apply the same law does not alone guarantee that responsibilities are fairly distributed. Common rules may very well allocate burdens unequally between Member States, exactly as they may be more of less fair to third-country nationals. Compliance with the principles set out in Article 67(2) and in Article 80 TFEU bears no relation to the mere existence of harmonised rules, but depends on their actual content.

As widely recognised, the Dublin III Regulation[85] provides precisely an example of an unbalanced approach not in line with the principle of solidarity.[86] Under the Regulation, the main criterion for the allocation among the Member States of responsibility for processing asylum applications and providing for the reception of asylum seekers is based on the place of crossing of the EU frontier. When a third-country national has irregularly crossed the external border of a Member State, that state will be responsible for examining that person's application.[87] Although this criterion is designed to be only subsidiary according to the hierarchy laid down in the Regulation, it has in fact become the most important one, since the overwhelming majority of migrants enter the EU territory irregularly.

Consequently, the task of processing asylum applications and providing for the reception of asylum seekers is unequally distributed among the Member States. Those at the Southern border of the Union are disproportionately affected

---

82 For an overview, see E. Jurado et al., 'Evaluation of the Implementation of the Dublin III Regulation', report prepared for the European Commission, March 2016.

83 See E. Guild et al., 'Enhancing the Common European Asylum System and Alternatives to Dublin', Study for the LIBE Committee of the European Parliament, 2015, p. 55, also for further references.

84 For the most recent data, see Eurostat, *Asylum Quarterly Report*, 12 December 2017, <http://ec.europa.eu/eurostat/statistics-explained/index.php/Asylum_quarterly_report> accessed 15.12.2017.

85 Regulation (EU) No 604/2013 of the European Parliament and of the Council of 26 June 2013 establishing the criteria and mechanisms for determining the Member State responsible for examining an application for international protection lodged in one of the Member States by a third-country national or a stateless person [2013] OJ L180/31.

86 See, among others, E. Küçük, 'The Principle of Solidarity and Fairness in Responsibility Sharing: More than Window Dressing?' (2016) 22 *ELJ* 448, 452–51; A.J. Menéndez, 'The Refugee Crisis: Between Human Tragedy and Symptom of the Structural Crisis of European Integration' (2016) 22 *ELJ* 388, 395; F. Munari, *supra* n. 3, 543.

87 Article 13(1) of Regulation 604/2013.

by the inflow of migrants and asylum seekers because of their geographical position and the current migration patterns. Instead of alleviating the unavoidable unbalance produced by objective, geographical factors, the choice of the entry criterion for allocating responsibility actually aggravates its consequences. One of the fundamental features of the system of allocation of responsibilities designed by the Dublin Regulation is that only one Member State can be responsible for deciding on the status of each asylum seeker (Article 3(1) of the Regulation). This is a necessary rule in a system where the application of asylum law is not fully centralised in the hands of a federal agency but relies on national authorities, as allowing more than one Member State to decide on the fate of a single applicant would be a waste of resources and entail the risk of conflicting decisions. However, the subjection of asylum seekers to one single national law generates a paradox, as the creation of a European area without internal borders is ironically made dependent on the 'nationalisation' of refugees.[88]

In order to prevent the circumvention of the rules allocating responsibility among the Member States, the Regulation lays down procedures for 'taking charge' and 'taking back'. In essence, they permit a Member State where an application for international protection has been lodged, if it considers that a different Member State is responsible under the Regulation or if an application has already been lodged in another Member State, to request that Member State to take charge of the applicant. In such cases, according to Article 18(1) of the Regulation, Member States are obliged to exercise the competence attributed by the rules on allocation of responsibility.

In practice, this system has turned out to be problematic from several points of view. First, as both the European Court of Human Rights[89] and the Court of Justice of the EU[90] have recognised, serious human rights concerns emerge when a Member State does not dispose of an effective asylum system or adequate reception capacity. As a result, the procedure for sending applicants back to the Member State of first entry cannot be applied if, due to systemic deficiencies in the asylum procedure and in the reception conditions of asylum seekers in the designated state, it would lead to a serious risk of breach of the applicants' fundamental rights.[91] This has led to a suspension of transfers to Greece on the basis of the Regulation since 2011.

Secondly, while the whole system is premised on cooperation and effective application of the common rules on the part of the Member States, this premise

---

88 A.J. Menéndez, *supra* n. 86, 393.

89 ECtHR 21.1.2011, *M.S.S. v. Belgium and Greece*, Application No. 30696/09; ECtHR 21.10.2014, *Sharifi and others v. Italy and Greece*, Application No. 16643/09; ECtHR 4.11.2015, *Tarakhel v. Switzerland*, Application No. 29217/12.

90 ECJ, Case C-411/10 and C-493/10, *N.S.*, ECLI:EU:C:2011:865, ECJ, Case C-578/16 PPU, *C.K. and others v. Republika Slovenija*, ECLI:EU:C:2017:127.

91 *N.S.*, *ibid.*, para. 106.

is undermined by the lack of solidarity and fairness in the distribution of burdens. On the one hand, divergent national protection standards generate an incentive for individuals seeking international protection to move away from the border states and attempt to reach other countries where they feel their applications have better chances of success or where they have better integration opportunities.[92] On the other hand, a system placing the task of managing the inflow of migrants and providing for the reception and integration of refugees exclusively on the country of first entry also creates an incentive for border states to disregard their EU law obligations to register asylum seekers and migrants and to prevent their secondary movement.[93] This is exactly what Greece and Italy did repeatedly, especially during the critical months of 2015, permitting migrants to travel North towards their intended destinations.[94]

In order to alleviate the unequal burdens due to the design of the CEAS and to some Member States being more exposed than others to migration flows, corrective mechanisms may be envisaged. They may entail either a redistribution of asylum seekers or refugees (sharing people) or the transfer of financial resources (sharing money).

None of those options is, in fact, new under EU law. The first mechanism of responsibility sharing, albeit non-binding, dates back to 1995, when the Council adopted a resolution calling for burden sharing in relation to the reception of people displaced by the conflict in former Yugoslavia.[95] In light of this experience, the Treaty of Amsterdam introduced a specific legal basis for the adoption of temporary measures to the benefit of affected Member States (current Article 78(3) TFEU). It provided the basis for the adoption, *inter alia*, of a directive on temporary protection,[96] which, however, has not yet been applied.

---

92 See M. Den Heijer, J. Rijpma and T. Spijkeboer, 'Coercion, Prohibition, and Great Expectations: The Continuing Failure of the Common European Asylum System' (2016) 53 *CMLR* 607, 610–11.

93 M. Den Heijer, J. Rijpma and T. Spijkeboer, *ibid.*, 612; E. Küçük, *supra* n. 86, 452–53; D. Thym, *supra* n. 2, 1548.

94 See, with reference to events in 2015, European Council Conclusions of 19 February 2016. On previous examples of recourse to this practice on the part of Italy and the ensuing Franco-Italian row over the border at Ventimiglia, see S. Montaldo, 'Le dichiarazioni (ritrattate) del governo ungherese sulla sospensione unilaterale del regolamento Dublino III e la nuova *querelle* franco-italiana: il problema delle frontiere europee' in *Sidiblog*, 09.07.2015.

95 Council Resolution of 25 September 1995 on burden-sharing with regard to the admission and residence of displaced persons on a temporary basis [1995] OJ C262/1.

96 Council Directive 2001/55/EC of 20 July 2001 on minimum standards for giving temporary protection in the event of mass influx of displaced persons and on measures promoting a balance of efforts between Member States in receiving such persons and bearing the consequences thereof [2011] OJ L212/12. See European Commission, Study on the Temporary Protection Directive, Final Report, January 2016, <http://ec.europa.eu/home-affairs/sites/homeaffairs/files/e-library/documents/policies/asylum/temporary-protection/docs/final_report_evaluation_tpd_en.pdf> accessed 15.12.2017.

In fact, efforts to cope with the unbalanced design of the CEAS have mostly focused on the provision of financial assistance to Member States in the managing of migration flows and in the control of external borders. In particular, an important instrument of financial solidarity was created with the establishment of the European Refugee Fund (ERF),[97] replaced in 2014 by the Asylum, Migration and Integration Fund (AMIF).[98] More recently, as part of the EU response to the increased inflow of migrants and asylum seekers in 2015, new instruments have been adopted, based on the assumption that an effective strategy for tackling the crisis requires significant funding.[99] One of those instruments, perhaps the most prominent given its broad scope of application which includes but is not limited to humanitarian assistance to refugees, is Regulation 2016/369 on the provision of emergency support within the Union.[100]

Whilst recourse to mechanisms of financial assistance has traditionally been the preferred option to compensate for the unequal allocation of responsibilities, relocation mechanisms have met with scepticism and even outright hostility from certain Member States.

The first binding schemes for the relocation of refugees were only adopted in the second half of 2015, when the crisis of the CEAS was at its peak and corrective measures were urgently needed. On 14 and 22 September 2015, the Council adopted two decisions intended to alleviate the pressure on the Member States most affected by the inflow of asylum seekers.[101] These are provisional emergency measures based on Article 78(3) TFEU, providing for the relocation of a total of 160,000 people in need of international protection from Greece and Italy to other Member States according to a system of quotas.

---

97 Council Decision 2004/904/EC of 2 December 2004 establishing the European Refugee Fund for the period 2005 to 2010 [2004] OJ L381/52; Decision 573/2007/EC of the European Parliament and the Council of 23 May 2007 establishing the European Refugee Fund for the period 2008 to 2013 as part of the General programme Solidarity and Management of Migration Flows and repealing Council Decision 2004/904/EC [2007] OJ L144/1.

98 Regulation (EU) 516/2014 of the European Parliament and of the Council of 16 April 2014 establishing the Asylum, Migration and Integration Fund [2014] OJ L150/168.

99 See European Commission, 'Managing the migration crisis: immediate operational, budgetary and legal measures under the European Agenda on Migration', COM(2015) 490 final/2. An comprehensive overview of these measures is offered by L. Den Hertog, 'EU Budgetary Responses to the 'Migration Crisis' – Reconfiguring the Funding Landscape', CEPS Papers in Liberty and Security in Europe No. 93, May 2016. The paper also makes some interesting remarks on the use of the financial leverage as an instrument of policy making.

100 *Supra* n. 45.

101 Council Decision 2015/1523 of 14 September 2015 establishing provisional measures in the area of international protection for the benefit of Italy and of Greece; Council Decision 2015/1601, *supra* n. 16. For a comment, see S. Carrera and E. Guild, 'Can the New Refugee Relocation System Work? Perils in the Dublin Logic and Flawed Reception Conditions in the EU', CEPS Policy Brief No. 332, October 2015.

The 2015 decisions, departing from an approach based on pure financial assistance, marked the first step towards a rebalancing of responsibilities for the reception of refugees and protection seekers.[102] Less affected Member States are requested to contribute not merely by providing financial resources but by undertaking to accept a share of refugees. The effectiveness of the scheme, however, has been undermined by its limited scope and by lack of implementation.[103] Additionally, Slovakia and Hungary, two of the Member States most strongly opposed to the adoption of corrective mechanisms and to the review of criteria for the allocation of asylum seekers, challenged the legality of the measures before the Court of Justice of the EU. Although the action was ultimately unsuccessful,[104] the fact that one of the applicants openly challenged the primacy of EU law is an almost unprecedented step that raises serious concern.[105]

In the effort to devise structural solutions to the design flaws of the Dublin Regulation, in April 2016 the Commission outlined possible options for its reform, identifying two alternative approaches.[106] The first would essentially retain the present system, but add a 'corrective fairness mechanism' in order to redress its unbalance. The corrective mechanism would draw from the experience of the 2015 relocation scheme and would be intended as an exceptional, emergency-related tool. Alternatively, the Commission envisaged a comprehensive overhaul of the Regulation and the establishment of a new system for allocating asylum application, whereby the criterion of first application or irregular entry would be replaced by allocation on the basis of a distribution key reflecting the relative size, wealth and absorption capacity of the Member States.

When it tabled its proposal for the recast of the Dublin III Regulation in May 2016,[107] the Commission chose a conservative approach. The proposal

102 B. Nascimbene, 'Refugees, the European Union and the 'Dublin System'. The Reasons for a Crisis' (2016) 1 *European Papers* 101, 104.

103 See S.F. Nicolosi, 'Emerging Challenges of the Temporary Relocation Measures under EU Asylum Law', (2016) *ELR* 338–61; B. Nascimbene, *ibid.*, 106–09. In its 'Fifteenth report on relocation and resettlement', the Commission indicated that 27,382 people had been relocated as of 4 September 2017, noting 'a continuous positive upward trend' but also reporting that Hungary and Poland had not relocated a single applicant (COM(2017) 465 final, 3). The Court of Justice of the EU also mentioned the lack of cooperation on the part of certain Member States as a factor that undermined the effectiveness of the relocation scheme (*Slovak Republic and Hungary v. Council, supra* n. 17, para. 223).

104 *Slovak Republic and Hungary v. Council, supra* n. 17.

105 Cf. B. Nascimbene, 'Il primato, l'Unione allargata e lo spazio di libertà, sicurezza e giustizia' (2016) *Rivista di diritto internazionale privato e processuale* 5, 19–20.

106 European Commission, 'Towards a Reform of the Common European Asylum System and Enhancing Legal Avenues to Europe', COM(2016) 197 final.

107 Proposal for a Regulation of the European Parliament and of the Council establishing the criteria and mechanisms for determining the Member State responsible for examining an application for international protection lodged in one of the Member States by a third-country national or a stateless person (recast), COM(2016) 270 final.

does not contain any major change regarding the allocation criteria nor their hierarchical sequence.[108] The only modification in this respect relates to the definition of 'family members', which would no longer require the existence of the family 'in the country of origin':[109] the deletion of the reference is meant to ensure the unity of families that have formed before entering the EU but after leaving the country of origin. Apart from this minor change, the proposal essentially replicates the criteria set out in Dublin III.[110]

Additionally, in order to increase the effectiveness of allocation criteria and discourage secondary movements, the Commission proposed to extend the responsibility of the Member State of irregular entry, suppressing the provisions that currently determine the cessation of responsibility under certain circumstances.[111] This means that the Member State identified according to the criteria laid down in the Regulation would be indefinitely responsible for examining the applications of third-country nationals who have long left its territory. Ironically, the concern for preventing secondary movements would result in the strengthening of purely national responsibility for asylum seekers.[112]

Such effect would be further exacerbated by the envisaged curtailment of the discretionary mechanisms existing under the Dublin III Regulation: the 'sovereignty clause' enabling a Member State to voluntarily undertake responsibility for an asylum application notwithstanding the criteria laid down in the Regulation, and the 'humanitarian clause' enabling a Member State to request another Member State to take charge of the applicant based on humanitarian grounds. If it were adopted as such, the proposal would drastically reduce the scope of both provisions, which could be applied only to achieve family reunification.[113]

In order to mitigate the consequences of this approach, the Commission proposal includes a corrective allocation mechanism, aimed at redistributing the applicants among the Member States according to objective criteria (Articles 34–43 of the proposal). Yet, Article 34(1) of the proposal makes clear that this mechanism would only operate under exceptional circumstances. In addition, the Member States would even be allowed, under certain conditions, to be excluded from participation in the corrective allocation mechanism in exchange for a financial contribution.[114] This possibility, along with the

108 See Articles 9–17 of the proposal.

109 Article 2(g) of the proposal.

110 Article 15 reiterates the criterion whereby the Member States of first irregular entry shall be responsible for examining the application.

111 See Articles 13 and 19 of Regulation 604/2013, *supra* n. 85.

112 A.J. Menéndez, *supra* n. 86, 405.

113 Article 19(1) and (2) of the proposal, respectively. For an overview and a critical appraisal of proposed modifications concerning the discretionary clauses see ECRE, 'Comments on the Commission Proposal for a Dublin IV Regulation COM(2016) 270', October 2016, p. 17.

114 See Article 37 of the proposal.

experience of the 2015 relocation decisions, suggests that the effectiveness of such a mechanism in achieving a more balanced allocation of responsibilities would likely be fairly limited.[115] In conclusion, in light of the features briefly outlined above, it appears that the proposal would not only fail to redress the shortcomings of the Dublin Regulation in terms of solidarity, but to a certain extent would even exacerbate their consequences by removing some elements of flexibility currently in place.

Compared to the Commission's approach, the European Parliament, which will have to decide on the reform together with the Council under the ordinary legislative procedure, has taken a more courageous stance, advocating a major departure from the Dublin III Regulation. On 19 October 2017, the LIBE Committee adopted a report on the recast proposal, suggesting numerous amendments to the Commission proposal. On 6 November 2017, the Parliament confirmed a mandate for interinstitutional negotiations based on the Committee's report.[116] Crucially, the Parliament suggested the replacement of the criterion of first country of entry with a permanent and automatic relocation mechanism, which would operate at all times – not only in times of crisis – and with no thresholds.

At the time of writing, however, it appears unlikely that the Council, which has thus far been unable to reach a common position, will agree with the suggested amendments. In a non-paper prepared following bilateral discussions with Member State delegations and presented on 27 November 2017, the Estonian Presidency of the Council proposed a solution far more in keeping with the Commission proposal, whereby the current responsibility criteria would remain applicable under 'normal circumstances'.[117] In turn, the Parliament's rapporteur described the Presidency's attempt to overcome the deadlock as 'very far from what could be an acceptable solution for the European Parliament'.[118]

---

115 D. Vitiello, 'Du vin vieux dans de nouvelles outres? Réflexions sur la proposition de Règlement "Dublin IV"' (2016) 1 *European Papers* 1235, 1248; S. Carrera et al., 'The European Border and Coast Guard. Addressing Migration and Asylum Challenges in the Mediterranean?', CEPS Task Force Report, 2017, p. 5.

116 European Parliament, Report of 6 November 2017 on the proposal for a regulation of the European Parliament and of the Council establishing the criteria and mechanisms for determining the Member State responsible for examining an application for international protection lodged in one of the Member States by a third-country national or a stateless person (recast).

117 See 'CEAS reform: state of play of negotiations on the Dublin IV Regulation', <http://www.asylumineurope.org/news/30-11-2017/ceas-reform-state-play-negotiations-dublin-iv-regulation> accessed 15.12.2017.

118 See European Parliament, 'Council plans on new Dublin rules far from acceptable', press release, 30 November 2017, <http://www.europarl.europa.eu/news/en/press-room/20171130IPR89211/council-plans-on-new-dublin-rules-far-from-acceptable> accessed 15.12.2017.

7. CONCLUSION: IS AN ALTERNATIVE APPROACH POSSIBLE?

Were the eventual compromise on the recast close to the European Parliament's position, it would do much to remove the above mentioned imbalances within the Dublin system. In the long run, however, an even more radical departure from the current approach might be preferable. A shift in responsibility from the national to the EU level has been advocated by some authors[119] and identified by the Commission as a possible outcome of the reform process in the long term.[120] According to the Commission, this could be done by increasing the competences and powers of the European Asylum Support Office (EASO), an agency established by Regulation 439/2010 in order to facilitate and coordinate practical cooperation among Member States in the field of asylum. In addition to such tasks, EASO could be given the power to process all asylum claims in the Union in accordance to a unified procedure: national branches of the agencies in each Member State would decide on the recognition of asylum or subsidiary protection status, subject to appeal to a central structure. After recognition, the refugees would be allocated among the Member States according to a distribution key.

More than the mere replacement of criteria for the allocation of responsibility, the creation of a fully-fledged EU mechanism for the processing of asylum application would likely contribute to redressing some of the current shortcomings of the CEAS. In particular, it would eliminate the current high divergence in recognition rates between different Member States, thereby removing a strong incentive for secondary movements. Other incentives would, of course, remain in place, since Member States also have different reception capacities and do not offer equal chances of integration to refugees, but their impact could be reduced either by then allocating the beneficiaries of protection according to objective criteria or by taking into account the applicants' preferences.

Such radical change in approach would also greatly reduce incentives for Member States not to apply the Dublin Regulation and other EU measures properly, since it is the inextricable link between entry and the allocation of responsibility that has provided a temptation for Member States at the external border of the Union to disregard their obligations.

Entrusting the examination of asylum application to an EU agency seems therefore the best way both to ensure compliance of the CEAS with the principle of solidarity and to improve its effectiveness. This option, however, may

---

[119] See E. Guild et al., *supra* n. 83, p. 58; H. Dörig and C. Langenfeld, 'Vollharmonisierung des Flüchtlingsrechts in Europa – Massenzustrom von Flüchtlingen erfordert EU-Zuständigkeit für Asylverfahren' (2016) *NJW* 1.

[120] European Commission, *supra* n. 106.

encounter some serious obstacles. Whereas legal objections can ultimately be overcome, political concerns are likely to prove more formidable hurdles.

From a legal perspective, the compatibility with primary law of a centralised procedure for the examination of asylum claims has been contested. While Article 78(2) TFEU grants the EU competence to lay down 'common rules' on asylum procedures, it is debated whether it permits a complete replacement of national asylum systems with a single EU mechanism. Some commentators have excluded this possibility by pointing to the wording of the provision, since the harmonisation of procedures seems to presuppose the continuing existence of national asylum systems.[121] Accordingly, a full unification of asylum procedures and the setting up of a federal agency competent for their management would require Treaty amendment.

This view, however, does not appear convincing. First, a contextual and teleological interpretation of Article 78(2) TFEU points towards a less strict conclusion. Harmonisation of asylum law is instrumental in the creation of a *common* asylum *system* (Article 67(2) TFEU): both the wording and the purpose of this provision, together with the absence of any express limitation as to the material scope of Article 78(2), suggest that full unification of asylum procedures and their management fall within EU competence.[122] Second, a broad understanding of the competence is also supported by the case law of the Court of Justice of the EU relating to harmonisation in the context of the internal market. The Court has consistently adopted a broad reading of the notion of 'measures of approximation' under Article 114(1) TFEU, holding that the adoption of common legal provisions is not the sole means to reach approximation[123] and that, in particular, an act based upon Article 114(1) TFEU can legitimately pursue harmonisation through delegation of certain powers to an agency.[124]

Of course, for such a measure to comply with primary law it would have to respect the principles of subsidiarity and proportionality. While the proportionality of the measure would depend on its actual content, exhaustive harmonisation in this field does not appear to pose problems with respect to the principle of subsidiarity, since it would remedy the fragmentation currently impairing the effective functioning of the CEAS.

---

121 K. Hailbronner and D. Thym, 'Legal Framework for EU Asylum Policy' in K. Hailbronner and D. Thym (eds.), *EU Immigration and Asylum Law. Commentary*, 2nd ed., C.H. Beck-Hart-Nomos, 2016, p. 1037.

122 See S. Peers, *EU Justice and Home Affairs Law*, 3rd ed., Oxford University Press, Oxford 2011, p. 308.

123 ECJ, Case C-359/92, *Germany v. Council*, ECLI:EU:C:1994:306, para. 37; ECJ, Case C-217/04, *United Kingdom v. Parliament and Council*, ECLI:EU:C:2006:279, paras. 43–44; ECJ, Case C-270/12, *United Kingdom v. Parliament and Council*, ECLI:EU:C:2014:18, paras. 102–05.

124 Case C-270/12, *United Kingdom v. Parliament and Council, supra* n. 123, paras. 78–80.

More importantly, the delegation to an EU agency of tasks related to processing asylum applications would require careful design in order to ensure that the conditions laid down in the *Meroni* doctrine are respected, namely that the delegation is limited to 'clearly defined executive powers' the exercise of which can be subject to strict review in the light of objective criteria determined by the delegating authority.[125] While it is true that additional difficulties could arise from the direct impact that its decisions would have on the fundamental rights and the personal freedom of applicants,[126] in the light of the rather flexible interpretation of the *Meroni* criteria that the Court gave in a recent case concerning the powers of the European Securities and Markets Authorities (ESMA)[127] the establishment of an EU agency responsible for processing asylum applications does not seem precluded.

Nevertheless, even if legally admissible, the proposal does not appear practicable in the short term merely for political reasons. In the current political climate, where the prospect of a further shift of power to the supranational level is highly unpopular in a large number of Member States, it is clear that calls for bold reforms are destined to remain unheard.

The consequence of sticking to a short-term logic, however, is that the failure to effectively address the challenge of solidarity is likely to further undermine the legitimacy of supranational law-making in the long run.

Writing on the tasks of the Convention called upon to draft a Constitutional Treaty for the EU, Joseph Weiler predicted that translating the rhetoric of solidarity into an effective constitutional principle would prove a hard choice.[128] We may no longer live in times of constitutional fervour, but the diagnosis is equally accurate *in dürftiger Zeit*.

---

125 ECJ, Case 9/56, *Meroni v. High Authority of the European Coal and Steel Community*, ECLI:EU:C:1958:7, 152.

126 M. den Heijer, J. Rijpma and T. Spijkerboer, *supra* n. 92, 639–40.

127 ECJ, Case C-270/12, *United Kingdom v. Parliament and Council*, *supra* n. 123, paras. 41–54.

128 J.H.H. Weiler, 'A Constitution for Europe? Some Hard Choices' (2002) 40 *JCMS* 563, 569–70.

3. EU FOREIGN POLICY AND OTHER EU EXTERNAL RELATIONS IN TIMES OF CRISIS: FORCING THE LAW TO OVERLAP?

Graham BUTLER*

1. INTRODUCTION

The European Union (EU) imposes on itself its own constraints in which it performs as an external actor, and yet, there is little acknowledgment of this imposed constraint. It is the migration crisis, an unexpected occurrence, which happens to have brought the fields of EU external relation law and migration law together. The EU's external border, on both land and sea, has brought vivid images of tightened borders through legal acts of non-traditional nature, namely, the resort to securitisation and militarisation. Challenges, such as mass irregular migration,[1] require more than just the individual responses of a few selected Member States that are directly affected by the issue. With thousands of persons attempting to reach the shores of EU Member States, and the perils such persons face on their journey, which has seen mass drownings in the Mediterranean Sea,[2] the EU and its Member States have not stood idly by. Instead, decisive action on a number of fronts has been imperative.

These responses to the migration crisis have been caught up in a multileveled legal architecture that, whilst complementary, can also compete with other interested stakeholders. Local responses, coupled with national efforts at Member State level and supranational coordination determination, make for a paradigm that is difficult to disentangle. The level of human smuggling and wider

* Aarhus University, Denmark. E-mail: gb@law.au.dk.

1 Throughout this chapter, the term 'migrant' or 'migrants' is used to define persons who have yet to fulfil the legal categorisation as either an asylum seeker or a refugee, and does not wish to cast distinctions as to whether persons are the aforementioned two categories, or so-called economic migrants. Similarly, 'traffickers' and 'smugglers' will be used as terms with a presumption of innocence.

2 'Migrants in the Mediterranean: The Numbers Nightmare', *The Economist*, 18.04.2015.

trafficking activity in the more troubled regions of the European neighbourhood pose new challenges that defy traditional convention. The profiteering from such unscrupulous activity poses a significant threat to the rule of law in the EU, and EU Member States more generally. Certain Member States, such as Greece and Italy, have been faced with a two-fold setback with the financial crisis along with being subjected to migration flows into the EU which, being on the EU's geographic periphery, have been unprecedented. Accordingly, the likelihood is that the EU would do everything it possibly can to stem the flow of irregular migration from third states, to alleviate such problems.

1.1. PROBLEMATISING LAW AND MIGRATION

Within the EU framework, there are legal complexities that need to be established when actionable responses are being considered. For example, at its broadest level, the external actions of the EU can be conducted from either one of two general categories of legal bases; that of the Common Foreign and Security Policy (CFSP) (including the Common Security and Defence Policy (CSDP)), or *non*-CFSP, the other areas of EU external relations. In simple form, CFSP can be said to be akin to an intergovernmental method of 'foreign policy' through the Council of the European Union, and the European Council. Contrastingly, *non*-CFSP external action is the supranational method, encompassing the regular array of institutions within the Union's actionable framework. Landmark judgments from the Court of Justice of the European Union in external relations cases centring on CFSP, such as in the *ECOWAS* (also known as '*Small Arms and Light Weapons*' or '*Legal Basis for Restrictive Measures*'),[3] *Mauritius*,[4] *Tanzania*,[5] *H v. Council*,[6] and *Rosneft*,[7] have all progressively framed the legal dimension of the EU's foreign, security, and defence policy actions in recent years in response to multifaceted challenges, particularly with regard to the nature and scope of international agreements that the EU enters into with third states.

In response to the migration crisis, a number of measures have been deployed under the foreign, security, and defence banner (CFSP) by the EU, in close

---

3 Case C-91/05, *Commission v. Council*, ECLI:EU:C:2008:288 ('*ECOWAS*').

4 Case C-658/11, *Parliament v. Council*, ECLI:EU:C:2014:2025 ('*Mauritius*'). See G. Butler, 'Pinpointing the Appropriate Legal Basis for External Action' (2015) 6 *European Journal of Risk Regulation* 323.

5 Case C-263/14, *Parliament v. Council*, ECLI:EU:C:2016:435 ('*Tanzania*').

6 Case C-455/14 P, *H v. Council*, ECLI:EU:C:2016:569.

7 Case C-72/15, *PJSC Rosneft Oil Company v. Her Majesty's Treasury and Others*, ECLI:EU:C:2017:236. See G. Butler, 'A Question of Jurisdiction: Art. 267 TFEU Preliminary References of a CFSP Nature' (2017) 2 *European Papers* 201. Furthermore, see G. Butler, 'The Coming of Age of the Court's Jurisdiction in the Common Foreign and Security Policy' (2017) 13 *European Constitutional Law Review* 673.

coordination and with the approval of its Member States. One of which has been *Operation Sophia*,[8] and its subsequent deployment. Similarly, there have also been *non*-CFSP measures utilised to stem the flow of migrants, and bring about lasting stability measures in the wider European neighbourhood. With these actions, a number of particular developments have been seen on the EU stage. First, learning fast on its feet, the EU's soft approach to coordinating Member State activities through bodies like Frontex has led to increased prominence and positioning of state actors in tackling the migration crisis. Secondly, on the other hand, the hard face of the EU military response reflects a different approach, demonstrating the potential inability of the EU in challenging scenarios to respond to immediate and present encounters in a timely and adequate manner. For the migration crisis, the need to combine foreign, security, and defence policies through CFSP; as well as migration matters through the Area of Freedom, Security, and Justice (AFSJ), through *non*-CFSP, are central to the discussion on the full approach of the EU to the migration crisis.

1.2. ISSUES AT STAKE

The internal and external dimension of the EU's responses through both the foreign, security, and defence policy sphere (CFSP), versus that of through the migration policies (*non*-CFSP), and the overlap between the two, potentially brings forth a conundrum on the overlapping nature of legal bases. This nexus of policy fields stemming from different legal bases, as well as stretching the premise upon which the EU's Treaties are crafted, makes new activity permissible, albeit on questionable legal grounds. This chapter brings together various conundrums that the EU and its Member States are facing from a number of different legal and policy angles. Section 2 explores the responses have been made in regard to the migration crisis, and section 3 examines the cooperative measures that have been taken in the context of existing legal bases. Section 4 looks at the Union's coordinated approaches, whilst section 5 determines the future legal issues associated with EU foreign policy law and EU external relations law responses to migration issues.

By examining the EU's response to the migration crisis through this framework, legitimate questions can thus be raised about the appropriateness of particular legal instruments for achieving certain public policy goals. As demonstrated, when foreign, security, and defence policy matters (CFSP) are

[8] Council Decision (CFSP) 2015/778 of 18 May 2015 on a European Union Military Operation in the Southern Central Mediterranean (EUNAVFOR Med) [2015] OJ L122/31; Council Decision (CFSP) 2015/972 of 22 June 2015 Launching the European Union Military Operation in the Southern Central Mediterranean (EUNAVFOR Med) [2015] OJ L157/51.

brought together into a coherent framework, it can be established how effective tools at each actors disposal can ensure that democracy, rule of law, and basic fundamental rights can be maintained, and even strengthened, in times of crisis.

2. RESPONSES TO THE MIGRATION CRISIS IN CONTEXT

The pretext for any discussion of the legal responses to the migration crisis, and particularly the EU foreign, security and defence policy responses, is to understand the wide variety of views held by both national governments within the Council, and between the citizens of respective Member States. Such conflicting responses to large migration flows from outside the EU have the capacity to cause large-scale inaction on a pan-European level. The paradoxical nature of how Europe ended up in a situation with hundreds of thousands of people running and swimming to its borders and shores is in contrast to the situation seen in the previous century. Over the duration of a 40-year period in the early twentieth century, Europe saw its own continent engage in not just one, but two world wars that tore the sole and essence of Europeanism apart. It was only external assistance both during and after the wars that helped European nations get back on their feet, coupled with entering into international dialogue in the form of the predecessor of the EU, in order to move onto a path of economic interdependency between Member States.

2.1. THE CHANGING TIMES

Coupling this twentieth century mischievousness of war, with emigration from the continent to the new world in the previous century, it can be construed that Europe was a place in which people left for new lives elsewhere. Now compare this to the twenty-first century. Europe is now facing the opposite situation, where it has become a destination for migrants coming from elsewhere. With the Convention Relating to the Status of Refugees 1951, Member States of the EU, like all other signatories, are in a position to allow persons on their territory to apply to the state in which they arrive for international protection. And yet, the Convention does not contain the mandate or obligation upon states to take measures to assist or make it easier for persons to apply for international protection in the first place. In fact, there is nothing in principle to prevent states (or international organisations) taking proactive measures to ensure the path to reaching their territory is made any easier.

The ongoing responses to the migration crisis are having profound implications for the EU and its Member States as a whole. Within the EU legal order however, the intersection of legal and policy fields are coming to the fore, and deserve closer examination in light of such contemporary events. The migration crisis has bonded together many fronts of the EU: the diplomatic element; the civilian response; and the military arsenal, in order to stem, and further prevent, the flows of migrants. The EU's progress has to be looked at in the context of whether the adopted approaches are seeking to produce short or long-term effects. Whereas short-term solutions are more politically interesting; it is only longer-term solutions which will prevent similar crises such as large-scale migration into Europe from occurring. The external dimension of the EU, and how it applies its laws beyond itself is an intriguing course of study, and one that has serious implications for how external crises come about, how responses are initiated, and ultimately executed.

With the emergence of an external dimension to European integration comes both expected and unexpected quagmires of law and policy that are constantly evolving in a polity that is consistently chartering a new course, despite criticism being levelled that it is bringing forward the criminal law aspects of irregular migration.[9] The EU, for better or worse, has become a true global player, and is reaching new heights for the external relations of an international organisation. Recalling that the EU is not a state,[10] this alone places a handicap on it which takes a toll in multilateral negotiations. However, the search by the EU for an increased global role has had the effect of the EU pushing migration and foreign policy closer together.[11] Thus, the EU is always in a stronger position when it is engaging with third states on a bilateral basis, and thus, has had to develop competence for its external policies. Accordingly, whilst migration has gradually fitted into this framework of external action, and has been situated in the primary field of Justice and Home Affairs, it has nonetheless become an important subject in EU foreign policy.

The migration crisis is multifaceted, touching upon the capabilities of the EU and its Member States in controlling its external borders, its internal borders, and its mechanisms for coping with unexpected events. The paradox of the present migration crisis is that the migration of persons between *internal* EU borders is not problematic *per se*, but rather, an activity that has been encouraged for EU citizens. However, very little has been done to broach the issue with regard to persons coming from outside the Union, *externally*, to inside the Union. This was in part due to the fact that migration of non-EU persons was not within the scope of EU law in its formative decades. The external effect of Europe's actions

9 T. Spijkerboer, 'Minimalist Reflections on Europe, Refugees and Law' (2016) 1 *European Papers* 533, p. 538.

10 Confirmed in Opinion of Court, Opinion 2/13, *Accession of the European Union to the European Convention on Human Rights*, ECLI:EU:C:2014:2454, para. 49.

11 P.J. Cardwell, *EU External Relations and Systems of Governance: The CFSP, Euro-Mediterranean Partnership and Migration*, Routledge, Abingdon 2009, p. 140.

are deserving of a critique, and of course have set precedent for emulating similar actions elsewhere. As the EU attempts to become a global leader on multiple fronts, the employment of its foreign, security, and defence policies in times of crisis is worthy of reflection.

The chain of events leading up to the migration crisis were also interlinked. Migration movements across the Mediterranean to Europe have been recognised long before the recent migration crisis.[12] Even before the certainty that the Treaty of Lisbon was going to be fully ratified as a ghostly legacy of the Constitutional Treaty, there were instances of migrants crossing the Mediterranean Sea, with the unnecessary loss of life through drowning being a real factor, even in 2009.[13] However, the numbers were comparatively low in contrast to the numbers seen from 2014 onwards. Accordingly, individual Member States were in a position to cope with this small-scale maritime migration, and unilaterally dealt with such issues by providing individual support to third states on a bilateral basis.

2.2. PRIMARY EU LAW

Migration as a term within EU law should be recognised as one referring to third-country nationals from non-EU Member States, and thus, is not be confused with EU citizens availing of their free movement and citizenship rights as enshrined within EU primary law. The legal backdrop of EU action is also bolstered by a number of reflective policy documents to guide the relevant actors in dealing with migration from the perspective of foreign policy. June 2016 saw the publication of the Union's Global Strategy by the European External Action Service (EEAS),[14] which has acknowledged the need to join up internal and external policies in order to be in a position to manage the phenomena of migration from outside the EU,[15] gravitating towards being inside the EU. Migration, despite having legal bases within the internal sphere of EU law that is not based on foreign policy provisions of the Treaties, is a policy area that is not

---

12 'European Security Strategy: A Secure Europe in a Better World (2003)', European Council, Brussels 2003.

13 See the examples pointed to in, V. Moreno-Lax, 'Seeking Asylum in the Mediterranean: Against a Fragmentary Reading of EU Member States' Obligations Accruing at Sea' (2011) 23 *International Journal of Refugee Law* 174; T. Spijkeboer, 'Stretching the Limits. European Maritime Border Control Policies and International Law' in M. Maes, M.C. Foblets and P. De Bruycker (eds.), *External Dimensions of European Migration and Asylum Law and Policy / Dimensions Externes du Droit et de la Politque d'Immigration et d'Asile de l'UE*, Bruylant, Brussels 2011.

14 'Shared Vision, Common Action: A Stronger Europe. A Global Strategy for the European Union's Foreign and Security Policy', European External Action Service, Brussels 2016.

15 *Ibid.*, p. 50.

strictly internal. Rather, it is externally focused.[16] Notwithstanding the attempts within EU primary law to lay the basis for common policies to exist across the EU, this is by no means a reality.

Migration is no simple area of law from an EU perspective. Migration and other migratory measures began to feature within the sphere of primary law in 1999 with the promulgation of the Treaty of Amsterdam. Prior to this, Member States chose freely, subject to their complete discretion, as to how their asylum procedures should work. Its initial flirtation was with the Treaty of Maastricht, when it was placed within the then third pillar. In external relations by contrast, the Treaty of Maastricht proposed splitting the external affairs of the Union and Communities across the newly formed pillars. Bringing together polices across pillars then was a challenge,[17] and had many legal constraints. Today, the image of the EU Treaties is slightly different. The field is to be found within the AFSJ provisions of the Treaties. For the United Kingdom, Ireland, and Denmark, each retain varying degrees of 'opt-outs', which came about in the Treaty of Maastricht-era, and retained in subsequent Treaties.[18] The last substantial amendment to EU law regulating migration was in the Treaty of Lisbon, which came into effect in 2009,[19] and which sets out the competences held by the EU either exclusively or on a shared basis between the EU and its Member States, and identifies where the EU plays a supporting role.

Prior to the Treaty of Lisbon, and for some time previously, the issue of migration of non-Union citizens to EU Member States had been cast under a spotlight as an area where intergovernmental coordination had taken hold. Yet even major reforms with the Treaty of Lisbon could not fully dismantle the effects of the pillars. CFSP issues, such as tactful political affairs, high politics, and wider issues of defence, were still sheltered from the normal external relations competences, such as trade and development. Foreign affairs, as a policy field, can be linked with different policies, but the legal structuring of the EU is designed in such a way that they are not meant to be crossed, or specifically intersected.[20] Saying that, however, the Treaties do not absolutely

---

16 P.J. Cardwell, 'Rethinking the Law and New Governance in the European Union: The Case of Migration Management' (2016) 41 *European Law Review* 362, 368.

17 S. Stetter, *EU Foreign and Interior Policies: Cross-Pillar Politics and the Social Constructions of Sovereignty*, Routledge, Abingdon 2007, p. 113.

18 See M. Hedemann-Robinson, 'The Area of Freedom, Security and Justice with Regard to the UK, Ireland and Denmark: The 'Opt-in Opt-Outs' under the Treaty of Amsterdam' in D. O'Keeffe and P.M. Twomey (eds.), *Legal Issues of the Amsterdam Treaty*, Hart Publishing, Oxford 1999.

19 Treaty of Lisbon: Amending the Treaty on European Union and the Treaty Establishing the European Community [2007] OJ C306/1.

20 Article 40 TEU: 'The implementation of the common foreign and security policy shall not affect the application of the procedures and the extent of the powers of the institutions laid down by the Treaties for the exercise of the Union competences referred to in Articles 3 to 6

delimit policy areas, nor impose a wall between policies or policy areas. This in turn entails the potential for the widening and broadening of different policies, depending on their deployment.

2.3. BASES OF LAW

Typically speaking, given the dynamic power structures that exist between both CFSP and *non*-CFSP, and the categories of competencies, in order to achieve agreement on any set of policies, compromises must be reached. The distribution of competencies between the EU and its Member States results in the juxtaposition of two versions of the EU: one that is able to tackle real issues, versus a helpless entity that is unable to provide solutions for modern and contemporary challenges. So much is new for the EU in terms of its external action in both CFSP and *non*-CFSP spheres in the post-Lisbon era with EU institutions, particularly the Parliament and the Council, having engaged themselves in disputes over the correct legal bases of international agreements.[21] In the *non*-CFSP sphere, it is the first time that the primary law of the EU through the Treaties has had an explicit legal basis for the external dimension of visa, asylum and immigration matters. For many years,[22] this had given rise to a theory that CFSP was undermining EU competences – that of *non*-CFSP external relations. As a result, overlap between these policy areas, perceived or actual, became a legal issue.

The crux of the migration crisis has been that the EU's external borders are controlled by the Member States, and not by the EU itself. It would be untrue to say that there is an 'EU border', given that the Schengen Area only covers 22 of the 28 Member States,[23] and therefore, there is no singular cohesive external

of the Treaty on the Functioning of the European Union. Similarly, the implementation of the policies listed in those Articles shall not affect the application of the procedures and the extent of the powers of the institutions laid down by the Treaties for the exercise of the Union competences under this Chapter.'

21 See S. Adam, 'The Legal Basis of International Agreements of the European Union in the Post-Lisbon Era' in I. Govaere and others (eds.), *The European Union in the World: Essays in Honour of Marc Maresceau*, Martinus Nijhoff Publishers, Leiden 2014; A. Ott, 'The Legal Bases for International Agreements Post-Lisbon: Of Pirates and the Philippines' (2014) 21 *Maastricht Journal of European and Comparative Law* 739; G. Butler, *supra* n. 4.

22 C. Timmermans, 'The Uneasy Relationship between the Communities and the Second Union Pillar: Back to the 'Plan Fouchet'?' (1996) 23 *Legal Issues of Economic Integration* 61; R. Baratta, 'Overlaps between European Community Competence and European Union Foreign Policy Activity' in E. Cannizzaro (ed.), *The European Union as an Actor in International Relations*, Kluwer Law International, The Hague 2002.

23 The United Kingdom and Ireland are not a party to Schengen, holding a formal treaty 'opt-out' for the existence of a Common Travel Area between themselves. See B. Ryan, 'The Common Travel Area between Britain and Ireland' (2001) 64 *Modern Law Review* 855.

border that separates EU from non-EU territory on its eastern and southern boundaries. Furthermore, the EU does not control the internal borders between Member States, as it is again left to the individual Member States to decide their political arrangement for borders within the context of the Schengen Border Code.[24] Notwithstanding the lack of formal direct control of the EU on Schengen borders, it does play a central role in shaping the regulation of these borders. For instance, the EU does have significant policy capabilities with regard to persons who are on the territory of an EU Member State, including legislating powers on settlement, residence, and returns. The sustainability of the Schengen Area, a system of policies aiming to achieve no physical border controls for ease of travel purposes in Europe, has consistently been questioned throughout the course of the migration crisis. The tight external land borders operated by the Schengen Area has resulted in migrants opting for risky and circumventive routes, very often assisted by smugglers. In response, the EU and Member States have refocused their attention. Rather than just looking at land borders, attention has also been paid to the Union's external borders on the high seas.[25]

3. COOPERATION AND LEGAL BASES

In order to bring about an effective response to the migration crisis, the EU has resorted to measures beyond those that find their legal basis in the migration articles of the Treaties. A noticeable method of indirectly influencing (and curbing) irregular migration from third states into the European neighbourhood has been external engagement primarily through direct engagement with third states on a bilateral basis, as opposed to the alternative, which would be in multilateral fora. With the EU having varied success as regarding its recognition in other international organisations,[26] the bilateral option has to date proven to be more effective. Many of the non-EU states also affected by the migration crisis have traditionally come within the remit of the European Neighbourhood Policy (ENP). The ENP was established in a time when there was relative harmony on

G. Butler, 'Not a "real" Common Travel Area' (2015) 54 *Irish Jurist* 155. The four other EU Member States that are not yet part of the Schengen Area, but may eventually be admitted, are Bulgaria, Croatia, Cyprus and Romania. The Schengen Area also includes four non-EU Member States, which are Iceland, Liechtenstein, Norway and Switzerland.

24 Regulation (EC) No 562/2006 of the European Parliament and of the Council of 15 March 2006 Establishing a Community Code on the Rules Governing the Movement of Persons across Borders (Schengen Borders Code) [2006] OJ L105/1.

25 T.E. Aalberts and T. Gammeltoft-Hansen, 'Sovereignty at Sea: The Law and Politics of Saving Lives in Mare Liberum' (2014) 17 *Journal of International Relations and Development* 439, p. 450.

26 See R.A. Wessel and J. Odermatt (eds.), *Research Handbook on the EU's Engagement with International Organisations*, Edward Elgar, Cheltenham 2018.

the EU's external borders. Since then, there have been a number of uprisings, which commenced in Tunisia,[27] reflecting a bubbling undercurrent that finally made its way into the mainstream of public dissatisfaction with the legal and political regime under which these neighbouring states were governed. As a result, these states experienced a variety of different outcomes: a maintenance of the existing *status quo*; transition phases; new settlements; and even, transitions to democracy.

The outcomes might not have been what the revolutionaries had hoped for, but the changes to governance demonstrate wider significance to keen observers of the region. Some of these North African states have borne the brunt of the migration flows from further afield and, since they are on the fringe of the EU's own territory, a mass number of migrants have accumulated on the continent's periphery. Thus, it is widely seen as a scenario requiring policy responses. Strengthening bilateral agreements with third states has been a key component in the EU's contribution to counteracting the migration crisis. The legal personality of the Union is now guaranteed through Article 47 of the Treaty on European Union (TEU), and its capacity to enter into international agreements is provided by Article 216(1) of the Treaty on the Functioning of the European Union (TFEU), closely governed by procedures laid down in Article 218 TFEU. Engaging with third states for the purposes of a migration partnership can cause a two-fold affect. First, the focus in the short-term may be on tackling the immediate measures to be taken, such as the prevention of drownings in the Mediterranean Sea. However, secondly, a deeper approach, such as eliminating root causes of migration can be focused on securing long-term collaboration that benefits both parties evenly. It appears that a long-term view only becomes clear when a crisis period arises.

3.1. THE NEIGHBOURHOOD

Egypt is just one of the states in question which has an Association Agreement with the EU.[28] As a framework agreement covering relations between the EU and Egypt, it allows for structured dialogue between the two partners.

---

27 See A. Abat i Ninet and M. Tushnet, *The Arab Spring: An Essay on Revolution and Constitutionalism*, Edward Elgar, Cheltenham 2015. J. Wouters and S. Duquet, 'The Arab Uprisings and the European Union: In Search of a Comprehensive Strategy' (2013) 32 *Yearbook of European Law* 320.

28 Council Decision of 21 April 2004 Concerning the Conclusion of a Euro-Mediterranean Agreement Establishing an Association between the European Communities and Their Member States, of the One Part, and the Arab Republic of Egypt, of the Other Part (2004/635/EC) [2004] OJ L304/38.

An area identified for closer cooperation has been migration data, in order to better determine the problem before correctly diagnosing the issues involved. The EEAS, a body primarily charged with structuring CFSP-related matters, has, in a '*non-paper*' suggested some *non*-CFSP proposals, such as highlighting the potential for closer contact between the European policy body, Europol, and Egyptian policing and border authorities.[29] The EU's legal responses of reaching 'agreements' with third states, from whom migrants are originating, are difficult to legally categorise, given they are not always international agreements or treaties in the traditional sense. Such agreements are not opened, negotiated or ultimately concluded according to the Article 218 TFEU procedure.

The EU is not just concluding bilateral agreements with North African states, as such action is also extended to regions further afield. For instance, in Mali, the EU has been adopting measures to combat irregular migration under the auspices of foreign affairs. In December 2016, the Dutch Foreign Minister concluded a '*joint communiqué*' on behalf of the EU with Mali,[30] flowing from the Dutch Presidency of the Council of the European Union in the first half of 2016. The Foreign Minister of the Netherlands was acting on behalf of the High Representative of the Union for Foreign Affairs and Security Policy. This '*joint communiqué*' was not a formal legal agreement, and thus no institutions of the EU were involved and, accordingly, their consent was not needed. As part of the '*joint communiqué*', EU Member States would be able to return Malians who have failed to demonstrate their asylum status within the EU back to Mali.

The conclusion of such an agreement, in the form of a '*joint communiqué*' with a third state, using a Member State as opposed to an EU institution as a negotiator, demonstrates two things: first, the unspecific delineation of what separates *foreign* policy and *migration* policy and, secondly, the lengths to which actors in Europe will go in order to combat the overall migration crisis. Third states such as Mali do not blindly sign up for receiving the return of their nationals without something in return. Instead, tangible returns are provided *quid-pro-quo*, as they engage in an 'arm-wrestling match' with the EU negotiators. Thus, in the present example, Mali would, in return, receive from the EU a general fall-back provision: capacity-building. The EU would be committed to improve and increase Mali's capabilities in relation to its security infrastructure, building upon the existing CSDP mission.[31]

It remains important to recall the distinction between a political agreement and an international agreement, with the former mandating no legal effects,

29 'Non-Paper: Options on Developing Cooperation with Egypt in Migration Matters', European External Action Service, Brussels 2016.

30 Government of the Netherlands, 'Koenders Concludes Migrant Return Agreement with Mali for EU' (11.12.2016).

31 Council Decision 2014/219/CFSP of 15 April 2014 on the European Union CSDP Mission in Mali (EUCAP Sahel Mali) [2014] OJ L113/21, as amended.

whilst the latter has a strong procedural aspect, with the firm intention of creating binding legal effects. A *joint communiqué* deliberately avoids the formal conclusion of an international agreement and instead is seen as a political agreement between one EU Member State and a third country. The legality of such an approach can certainly come into question when it is considered whether such deliberate shirking is in the spirit of European cooperation, and a Union which is based on the rule of law.[32] Problems with the *joint communiqué* with Mali are nonetheless beginning to emerge, whereby Mali, upon receipt of two individuals deported from France in December 2015, sent the two individuals back to France, owing to questions being raised over whether such persons were even Malian citizens at all.[33]

3.2. THE CFSP-MIGRATION LINK

CFSP in the Treaties is unspecific *per se*, and its scope has been delimited for its breadth by progressive judgments of the Court of Justice since its inception. This is notwithstanding the fact that the Treaties primarily envisage that it is to cover 'all areas of foreign policy'.[34] Given this lack of specificity for what CFSP actually entails, it could be seen as a flexible policy instrument,[35] and furthermore, there is no definitive time for when it is to be utilised as a legal basis for EU measures. Given this expansive interpretation afforded to it by the High Contracting Parties to the Treaties, can it be said that CFSP could be stretched as far as to include migration policies? Previously, CFSP possessed specific objectives,[36] but the Treaty of Lisbon merged both CFSP and *non*-CFSP objectives, thus presenting, in theory, a more uniform set of objectives to cover the breadth of EU external action, regardless of legal basis. This merger in and of itself can thus be said to have the potential to either widen or narrow CFSP, depending on the context to which an act capable of having legal effect was challenged. The present Article 21 TEU therefore encompasses all external objectives of the Union, cutting across both CFSP and *non*-CFSP.

Every individual action of the EU requires a legal basis in order to act. The underlying legal basis for action is furthermore predicated on the need for the

32 For a Union based on the 'rule of law' for its external policies, see G. Butler 'Implementing a complete system of legal remedies in EU foreign affairs law' (2018) 24 *Columbia Journal of European Law*.

33 'Mali Sends Back Migrants Deported by France', *BBC News* (London, 30.12.2016).

34 Article 24(1) TEU.

35 See S. Graf von Kielmansegg, 'The Common Foreign and Security Policy – A Pool of Flexibility Models' in T. Giegerich, D.C. Schmitt and S. Zeitzmann (eds.), *Flexibility in the EU and Beyond: How Much Differentiation Can European Integration Bear?*, Nomos and Hart Publishing, Oxford 2017.

36 Ex-Article 11 TEU.

action to be amenable to judicial review.[37] The linking of CFSP and the prevention of certain individuals from entering the EU has been done before. Whether this absolutely fits the legal category of 'migration' as per the Treaties is debatable, but through CFSP, the intergovernmental method has been used to introduce travel bans on persons of interest in the pursuance of EU foreign policy,[38] and has been done continuously following events in Ukraine in 2014,[39] and Libya in 2011.[40] These CFSP Decisions,[41] albeit within the ambit of EU foreign policy, set out in Articles 21–46 TEU, have distinct *non*-CFSP elements.

A prohibition on certain persons travelling to and from the EU entails everything from the prevention of entry, to the motion of transit of persons in the Union. It furthermore imposes an obligation, decided unanimously by the Member States through CFSP, for issuing visas and other forms of travel documents. Thus, a formal link between CFSP and migration policies is established, with recourse to a CFSP-only legal basis. It is not just CFSP and its 'specific rules and procedures' that have been entangled with migration.[42] Other elements of EU external relations stemming from the TFEU may too be caught up in migration-related matters. Such policies include development cooperation, and other associated EU's competences flowing from Articles 208–213 TFEU for relations with third countries. And yet the Union, going as far back as the Treaty of Rome included consideration for development with third countries, but this was not a policy in itself, *per se*.[43] Furthermore, whilst development cooperation still makes its way slowly towards better compatibility with other policies of the Union,[44] the coupling and complete linking of development cooperation and migration has not happened, despite both being areas that are *non*-CFSP.

For international agreements containing numerous actions, questions arise about the appropriate legal basis of such agreements. The preference for a CFSP

---

37 '*... must be based on objective factors which are amenable to judicial review*'. A phrase used by the Court of Justice time and again, but first seen in Case C-45/86, *Commission v. Council*, ECLI:EU:C:1987:163, para. 11. See A. Arnull, 'Legal Principles and Practical Politics' (1987) 12 *European Law Review* 448.

38 B. Martenczuk, 'Migration Policy and EU External Relations' in L. Azoulai and K. De Vries (eds.), *EU Migration Law: Legal Complexities and Political Rationales*, Oxford University Press, Oxford 2014, p. 100.

39 Council Decision 2014/145/CFSP of 17 March 2014 Concerning Restrictive Measures in Respect of Actions Undermining or Threatening the Territorial Integrity, Sovereignty and Independence of Ukraine [2014] OJ L78/16, as amended.

40 Council Decision 2011/137/CFSP of 28 February 2011 Concerning Restrictive Measures in View of the Situation in Libya [2011] OJ L58/33.

41 Prior to the Treaty of Lisbon, there were several types of legal acts adoptable under CFSP, such as Joint Actions and Common Positions, amongst others.

42 Article 24(1), second paragraph.

43 S. Peers, 'Case C-268/94, Portugal v. Council, (Development Policy), [1996] ECR 1-6177 (Full Court)' (1998) 35 *Common Market Law Review* 539, p. 539.

44 See M. Broberg and R. Holdgaard, 'EU Development Cooperation Post-Lisbon: Main Constitutional Challenges' (2015) 40 *European Law Review* 349.

legal basis, or a 'Community' legal basis pre-Lisbon, was desirable according to the *ECOWAS* judgment.[45] The Court of Justice said that building on the *acquis communautaire* was more suited by adopting a measure on an EC legal basis (now TFEU), rather than a TEU legal basis. The Treaty of Lisbon abolished the preference for a Community legal basis, thus, this point by the Court of Justice became moot after December 2009. Taking into account the *ECOWAS* judgment, could the same line of thinking by the Court of Justice be applied to a CSDP mission if the substance of *Operation Sophia* was challenged on appropriate legal basis grounds? Post-Lisbon, CFSP and *non*-CFSP legal bases cannot encroach upon one another according to Article 40 TEU,[46] and if pressed on clarifying this ability for mutual non-encroachment, it is a question that the Court of Justice would be reluctant to answer. The stuttering of handling dual legal bases,[47] and the uncertainty surrounding the possibility of using more than one legal basis for a certain action, given procedural incompatibility between CFSP and *non*-CFSP, is traceable to a principle feature of the legal structure of EU external relations, to the extent that both legal bases have never been specifically delimited.

3.3. OPERATION SOPHIA

Underlining the basis for the EU to act is the argument that combating and eliminating human trafficking and smuggling networks is a worthy endeavour. Thus, a combative role has been taken by the EU in the form of a military mission. *Operation Sophia* is a CSDP military mission established through a CFSP Decision of the Council.[48] This CSDP mission, through CFSP, was fully intended for cooperation, but not integration with *non*-CFSP aspects of EU policy. Saying that, CSDP has a multidisciplinary outlook.[49] According to Article 8(3) of

---

45 Case C-91/05, *Commission v. Council*, ECLI:EU:C:2008:288 ('*ECOWAS*').

46 Article 40 TEU: 'The implementation of the common foreign and security policy shall not affect the application of the procedures and the extent of the powers of the institutions laid down by the Treaties for the exercise of the Union competences referred to in Articles 3 to 6 of the Treaty on the Functioning of the European Union. Similarly, the implementation of the policies listed in those Articles shall not affect the application of the procedures and the extent of the powers of the institutions laid down by the Treaties for the exercise of the Union competences under this Chapter.'

47 See G. De Baere, 'From "Don't Mention the Titanium Dioxide Judgment" to "I Mentioned It Once, But I Think I Got Away with It All Right": Reflections on the Choice of Legal Basis in EU External Relations after the Legal Basis for Restrictive Measures Judgment' in C. Barnard et al (eds.), *Cambridge Yearbook of European Legal Studies 2012–2013: Volume 15*, Hart Publishing 2013.

48 Council Decision (CFSP) 2015/778 of 18 May 2015 on a European Union Military Operation in the Southern Central Mediterranean (EUNAVFOR Med) [2015] OJ L122/31.

49 For a recent study from an international relations perspective, see M.E. Smith, *Europe's Common Security and Defence Policy: Capacity-Building, Experiential Learning, and Institutional Change*, Cambridge University Press, Cambridge 2017.

the Decision, *Operation Sophia*, 'shall cooperate ... as appropriate, conclude arrangements with other Union agencies and bodies, in particular Frontex, Europol'. The very existence of *Operation Sophia* within the Mediterranean has a number of effects. It, first, increases the security presence of the EU in the region. Its mandate envisages three key phases of the military mission. For example, it is to 'support the detection and monitoring of migration networks through information gathering and patrolling on the high seas in accordance with international law'.[50] The subsequent second phase envisages a two-fold response, (i) to 'conduct boarding, search, seizure and diversion on the high seas of vessels suspected of being used for human smuggling or trafficking' in international waters,[51] but, also, (ii) under the premise of a UN Security Council Resolution or with the consent of a third state, to do the same in the territorial waters of a non-EU state. The third phase permits Union-mandated forces to, 'take all necessary measures against a vessel and related assets, including through disposing of them or rendering them inoperable, which are suspected of being used for human smuggling or trafficking, in the territory of that state, under the conditions set out in that Resolution or consent'.[52] The full breadth of the potential of *Operation Sophia* was thus clarified at an early stage, but how it would work in practice remained to be seen, given that the second and third phases required some level of third-party recognition for EU action, rather than the EU acting coherently with its own determined aims in mind. One of the underlying features of international law is the concept of jurisdiction. By operating an EU military mission in the Mediterranean Sea, the EU is indirectly ensuring that non-EU nationals never enter the jurisdiction of an EU Member State in the first place.

One of the common migration routes across the Mediterranean Sea has been the 'Central Mediterranean Route' (CMR), which is the maritime route between Libya to Italy. The popularity of this crossing point can be attributed to, amongst other things, networks of smuggling operatives in Libya.[53] *Operation Sophia* was not the first CSDP mission in the greater European area to attempt tackling the root underlying causes of migration. This follows the failure of the EU's Integrated Border Management Assistance Mission in Libya (EUBAM Libya), established in 2013,[54] to support Libyan authorities. Notwithstanding

---

50 Article 2(2)(a): Council Decision (CFSP) 2015/778 of 18 May 2015 on a European Union Military Operation in the Southern Central Mediterranean (EUNAVFOR Med) [2015] OJ L122/31.

51 Article 2(2)(b).

52 Article 2(2)(c).

53 Frontex, 'Central Mediterranean Route', 18.01.2017.

54 Council Decision 2013/233/CFSP of 22 May 2013 on the European Union Integrated Border Management Assistance Mission in Libya (EUBAM Libya) [2013] OJ L138/15.

the continued existence of the CSDP mission to date,[55] EUBAM Libya activities have largely stalled given *Operation Sophia*'s active presence. The Operation Commander of *Operation Sophia* stated in a report to the Political and Security Committee of the EU (PSC) and the EU Military Committee (EUMC) that the operation under his command has not contributed to additional migration in the Union via the CMR.[56] He went on to say that, of all the Search and Rescue (SAR) missions taking place in the region, his operation is responsible for a mere 13 per cent of all rescued migrants. The launching of a military operation by the EU, however, will not suffice. Coupled with the Union's CFSP response to the migration crisis has been the need for non-EU states to progressively undertake greater efforts to patrol their own maritime borders. As a result, the EU has assisted in upskilling local coastguard forces. For example, in Libya, *Operation Sophia* agreed with Libyan officials, two years into its mandate, to engage in the training of the local coast guard.[57] This engagement with the substantive migration aspects of EU policy are making the CFSP-migration link all the more apparent.

The EU's foreign, security, and defence responses to the migration crisis have unilaterally been to deter future flows of irregular migration coming to the shores of EU Member States. However, whilst appearing to be a deterrent, they are also potentially acting as an incentive for further incursions of irregular migrants. The growing together of the EU's foreign, security, and defence cooperation (CFSP) on a separate track compared to other policies (*non*-CFSP) have thus seen a legal phenomenon occur, in that the fields of policy that were intended to operate apart have in practice naturally come closer together. Taken collectively, this puts additional pressures on the rule of law in the EU that threatens the democratic institution should policies fail to meet the levels of effectiveness for which they were intended. Whereas scepticism has been expressed by one national parliament as to the possible success of the EU's *Operation Sophia*,[58] the foreign, security, and defence responses to the migration crisis to date have yet to see their full potential. The real challenge is now how future EU foreign, security,

[55] Last extended to August 2017 by Council Decision (CFSP) 2016/1339 of 4 August 2016 Amending and Extending Decision 2013/233/CFSP on the European Union Integrated Border Management Assistance Mission in Libya (EUBAM Libya) [2016] OJ L212/111.

[56] Council of the European Union, EUNAVFOR MED Op SOPHIA – Six Monthly Report, 1 January–31 October 2016 (14978/16) Brussels, 28 January 2016.

[57] See 'Operation Sophia: Signed the Agreement on Libyan Coast Guard and Navy Training', European External Action Service, Brussels, August 2016; 'Operation Sophia: Package 2 of the Libyan Navy Coast Guard and Libyan Navy Training Launched Today', European External Action Service, Brussels, January 2017.

[58] For the full report, see House of Lords European Union Committee, 'Operation Sophia, the EU's Naval Mission in the Mediterranean: An Impossible Challenge' (2016) 144, 14th Report of Session 2015–16.

and defence policies, and the array of legal instruments at the EU's disposal will be utilised to ensure migration flows are adequately controlled within the strict confines of both EU and international law. Once *Operation Sophia* was put into place in the Mediterranean, the principle of loyalty kicked in. The establishment of this undertaking by the EU, unanimously in the Council, ensured that under Article 4(3) TEU, that Member States are not in a position to undermine the EU's adopted position. Thus, individual actions by Member States outside the EU's established framework are prohibited, as they would undermine a determined aim of the EU derived from its primary and secondary law. It could thus be claimed that the non-appearance of CFSP-specific objectives makes CFSP a more difficult area to defend,[59] and conclusively determine. Article 22(1) TEU allows the European Council to adopt decisions relating to both CFSP and *non*-CFSP on 'strategic interests and objectives' of the Union, thereby reinforcing the future of external relations by bringing the fields of CFSP and *non*-CFSP closer together.

Just how forceful an effort has there been made to make a distinction between foreign, security, and defence measures (CFSP), versus that of migration measures (*non*-CFSP), from a legal perspective? To date, the Court of Justice has not had to make this distinction with regards to the migration crisis, and, generally, it has not been able to look into the substantive measures within a CFSP legal basis, given the curtailed jurisdiction in which it can do so. Furthermore, Article 43(1) TEU sets the guidance for what CSDP within the framework of CFSP is to be,[60] the scope of which may be wide. However, it does not appear to cover migratory matters. The EU has longed to be a prominent security actor. Notwithstanding its few competencies in the field given the prevalence of an explicit CSDP done under the ambit of the CFSP framework, it continues to strive for greater action in security when Member States agree to it. With an elaborate organisational subsystem homed within the Council, including the PSC,[61] the Union's CSDP missions of military and civilian nature are primarily

---

59 G. De Baere, 'The Basics of EU External Relations Law: An Overview of the Post-Lisbon Constitutional Framework for Developing the External Dimensions of EU Asylum and Migration Policy' in M. Maes, M.C. Foblets and P. de Bruyker (eds.), *supra* n. 13, p. 166.

60 Article 43 TEU: 'The tasks referred to in Article 42(1), in the course of which the Union may use civilian and military means, shall include joint disarmament operations, humanitarian and rescue tasks, military advice and assistance tasks, conflict prevention and peace-keeping tasks, tasks of combat forces in crisis management, including peace-making and post-conflict stabilisation. All these tasks may contribute to the fight against terrorism, including by supporting third countries in combating terrorism in their territories.'

61 For an overview of the work of the PSC, see D. Thym, 'The Intergovernmental Branch of the EU's Foreign Affairs Executive: Reflections on the Political and Security Committee' in H.J. Blanke and S. Mangiameli (eds.), *The European Union after Lisbon: Constitutional Basis, Economic Order and External Action*, Springer, Heidelberg 2012.

based in regions further afield than on the Union's immediate periphery.[62] In Delegations of the European Union,[63] the permanent diplomatic missions of the EU located in third countries, staffed by officials from the EEAS, are under the direction of the High Representative of the Union for Foreign Affairs and Security Policy ('High Representative'). Officials within these missions handle external issues that are of both a CFSP and *non*-CFSP nature. Accordingly, 2017 saw the deployment of two additional roles to relevant Delegations in relevant third states, with the addition of a European Migration Liaison Officer, and a European Border and Coast Guard Agency Liaison Officer.[64]

The overlapping nature of national competences, EU competences and competences shared between the two provide an ever-debatable discussion on the breadth of competencies, and the 'creep' of such competencies. To date, they have generally only been discussed in the context of competencies flowing away from Member States and to EU institutions. However, the Treaty of Lisbon imposed a new declaration annexed to the Treaties which allows for the repatriation of powers from the EU to Member States.[65] Whilst this Declaration has not yet been utilised to its full potential, there have been examples of intergovernmental instruments being used instead of competency repatriation. If an option is available that requires unanimous voting, and thus, a potential veto for each Member State, such as when launching a CSDP mission within the CFSP decision-making process, then this could be the preferred instrument. Ultimately, in light of the lack of migration measures in *non*-CFSP legal bases to effectively combat the migration crisis, it is foreign, security, and defence measures that are coming to the rescue of the EU as being a legal basis for response. CFSP is being conscripted to resolving matters of migration; a situation

---

62 See Chapter 5 (CSDP Military Missions) and Chapter 6 (CSDP Civilian Missions) in P. Koutrakos, *The EU Common Security and Defence Policy*, Oxford University Press, Oxford 2013.

63 G. Butler, 'The European Union and Diplomatic Law: An Emerging Actor in Twenty-First Century Diplomacy' in P. Behrens (ed.), *Diplomatic Law in a New Millennium*, Oxford University Press, Oxford 2017, p. 324.

64 European Commission, Annex to the Communication from the Commission to the European Parliament, the European Council and the Council: Second Progress Report: First Deliverables on the Partnership Framework with Third Countries under the European Agenda on Migration (COM(2016) 960 Final), Brussels 2016.

65 The key paragraph of Declaration 18 in relation to the delimitation of competences: '... When the Treaties confer on the Union a competence shared with the Member States in a specific area, the Member States shall exercise their competence to the extent that the Union has not exercised, or has decided to cease exercising, its competence. The latter situation arises when the relevant EU institutions decide to repeal a legislative act, in particular better to ensure constant respect for the principles of subsidiarity and proportionality. The Council may, at the initiative of one or several of its members (representatives of Member States) and in accordance with Article 241 of the Treaty on the Functioning of the European Union, request the Commission to submit proposals for repealing a legislative act. The Conference welcomes the Commission's declaration that it will devote particular attention to these requests.'

which is legally questionable and raises problems of adequate and appropriate legal bases. Furthermore, this, in turn, is bringing forward the unitary nature of EU law, where it is becoming increasingly difficult to mark different policies apart, making them increasingly indistinguishable.

4. A COORDINATED APPROACH?

In light of the migration crisis being fraught with indifference on what the EU response should be, the national responses have been stark. The underlying EU purpose, despite differences in internal opinions, has been to circle the square of different policies across the legal framework to deliver coherent policies.[66] Given that there is no legal basis in the Treaties for territorially defining the continent of Europe, delimiting the precise reach of what Europe is from a legal point of view is a moot point. Thus, the retreat from formal coordination responses through EU structures has been to return to national prerogatives to selectively derogate from the Schengen Border Code and patrol maritime boundaries. Thus, where coordination has occurred, it has been light. Frontex ('Frontières extérieures', the 'European Agency for the Management of Operational Cooperation at the External Borders') has been active during the migration crisis, with varying degrees of impact and effectiveness. Whilst it has made significant attempts towards establishing a common policy that secures a sustained external Schengen border with adequate controls,[67] the agency has been overwhelmed, understaffed and underfunded. Notwithstanding Frontex's legal mandate set down in EU Regulations,[68] the migration crisis alone led directly to the dissolution of this body. It was reincarnated as the new European Border and Coast Guard Agency as of mid-2016,[69] with a view to more effectively coordinating and managing a coherent EU response. This reawakening led to the continuation of all existing activities, but provided the Agency with an expanded mandate, including supporting national border forces of Member States when facing capacity challenges, and an increased ability to implement standards for the EU's external borders.

---

66 A. Łazowski and S. Blockmans, 'Constitutional Foundations and EU Institutional Framework: Seven Years of Working with Lisbon Reform' in A. Łazowski and S. Blockmans (eds.), *Research Handbook on EU Institutional Law*, Edward Elgar, Cheltenham 2016, p. 30.

67 For a thorough analysis, see R. Mungianu, 'Frontex: Towards a Common Policy on External Border Control' (2013) 15 *European Journal of Migration and Law* 359.

68 See B. Ryan, 'Council Regulation (EC) No 2007/2004 of 26 October 2004 Establishing a European Agency for the Management of Operational Cooperation at the External Borders of the Member States of the European Union' in K. Hailbronner and D. Thym (eds.), *EU Immigration and Asylum Law: A Commentary*, 2nd ed., C. H. Beck and Hart Publishing and Nomos, Oxford 2016.

69 Regulation (EU) 2016/1624 of the European Parliament and of the Council of 14 September 2016 on the European Border and Coast Guard [...] [2016] OJ L251/1.

4.1. MILITARY ACTION

In contrast to Frontex, at the coalface, the EU military operation was launched the previous year in 2015 to combat human smuggling and trafficking operations.[70] Its principal purpose, reflected in its mandate, is to identify, capture, and dispose of vessels used or suspected of being used by smugglers or traffickers of migrants. *Operation Sophia*, as previously indicated, saved over 16,000 lives in the initial months after being enacted.[71] Over a year later in July 2016 at the NATO Summit in Warsaw, the Summit's communiqué announced '*Operation Sea Guardian*' to complement the EU's *Operation Sophia*, and Frontex actions.[72] With the EU coordinating a response through naval missions long before other international partners, its previous naval mission in the Gulf of Aden in *Operation Atalanta*,[73] has proven that the EU has experience in conducting naval operations for alternative purposes, providing many lessons to be learnt.

Member States have a clear variety of different human rights norms.[74] The EU, however, must comply with the EU Charter of Fundamental Rights, in addition to the overall principles of international law. EU external relations law and EU law more generally complies with international law, although the legal orders and their respective compatibility have been under intense scrutiny.[75] This is particularly true after the *Kadi* saga that has been debated for over a decade.[76] Notwithstanding this overarching issue, the UN Security Council

70 Council Decision (CFSP) 2015/972 of 22 June 2015 Launching the European Union Military Operation in the Southern Central Mediterranean (EUNAVFOR Med) [2015] OJ L157/51.

71 For a full overview of the EU mission, its mandate and legal constraints, see G. Butler and M. Ratcovich, 'Operation Sophia in Uncharted Waters: European and International Law Challenges for the EU Naval Mission in the Mediterranean Sea' (2016) 85 *Nordic Journal of International Law* 235.

72 'Warsaw Summit Communiqué: Issued by the Heads of State and Government Participating in the Meeting of the North Atlantic Council in Warsaw, 8–9 July 2016', paras. 91–93.

73 See D. Thym, 'Transfer Agreements for Pirates Concluded by the EU – a Case Study on the Human Rights Accountability of the Common Security and Defence Policy' in P. Koutrakos and A. Skordas (eds.), *The Law and Practice of Piracy at Sea: European and International Perspectives*, Hart Publishing, Oxford 2014.

74 See N. Sölter, 'The Abyss of Complexity: Some Remarks on European and German Law in the Migration Crisis' (2017) 23 *European Public Law* 41, 45.

75 See R. Holdgaard, 'Principles of Reception of International Law in Community Law' (2006) 25 *Yearbook of European Law* 263. For the opposite way around, see R.A. Wessel, 'Flipping the Question: The Reception of EU Law in the International Legal Order' (2016) 35 *Yearbook of European Law* 533.

76 *Kadi I*, see Joined Cases C-402/05 P and C-415/05 P, *Kadi and Al Barakaat International Foundation v. Council and Commission*, ECLI:EU:C:2008:461. *Kadi II*, see Joined Cases C-584/10 P, C-593/10 P and C-595/10 P, *Commission and Others v. Kadi*, ECLI:EU:C:2013:518. See G. De Búrca, 'The European Court of Justice and the International Legal Order after Kadi' (2010) 51 *Harvard International Law Journal* 1.

('UNSC') Resolution 2240 (2015),[77] and Resolution 2292 (2016),[78] authorised the inspection and potential seizure of boats in international waters that are suspected of trafficking persons to European shores in haphazard unsuitable vessels. These tightly worded Resolutions have limited the scope of potential for EU action, given that the internal CFSP Decision envisaged a broader mandate, but the Resolutions to date have not authorised *Operation Sophia* to enter the waters of the Libyan State. All EU external action tackling the migration crisis is bound by the principles of *non-refoulement*.[79] This, of course, leads to debates surrounding the questionable activity regarding the EU's negotiating response with neighbouring states for effectively battling the migration crisis. Accountability and human rights compatibility are acknowledged issues in EU law,[80] so it is worth reiterating the Court of Justice's own words when it comes to respect for human rights. In *Kadi*, dealing with *inter alia*, restrictive measures ('sanctions') through both CFSP and *non*-CFSP systems, the Court of Justice said, citing earlier case law, that, 'respect for human rights is a condition of the lawfulness of Community acts … and that measures incompatible with respect for human rights are not acceptable in the Community'.[81]

4.2. THE LARGEST NEIGHBOUR

One of the responses to the migration crisis has been to engage with one of the Union's largest neighbours, Turkey, to take effective measures preventing third-country nationals from reaching the EU in the first place. The methods of how the EU and its Member States have engaged with Turkey was put under the spotlight in a recent case before the EU's General Court. It is notable that the EU–Turkey arrangements between 2015 and 2016 had been partly concluded outside EU structures, thereby ensuring executive leverage through the Council, and thus being kept away from the oversight and involvement of both the Parliament, and the Court of Justice. Or at least, that was what was attempted. The manner in which the EU–Turkey arrangements have been conducted has been a mix of both EU Member States acting at the European Council in its capacity as an EU institution and, separately, with Heads of State and Government meeting within the European Council.

---

77 Resolution 2240 (2015). Adopted by the Security Council at Its 7531st Meeting, on 9 October 2015. S/RES/2240 (2015).

78 Resolution 2292 (2016). Adopted by the Security Council at Its 7715th Meeting, on 14 June 2016. S/RES/2292 (2016).

79 For a discussion on this, see R. Mungianu, *Frontex and Non-Refoulement: The International Responsibility of the EU*, Cambridge University Press, Cambridge 2016.

80 See S.O. Johansen, 'Accountability Mechanisms for Human Rights Violations by CSDP Missions: Available and Sufficient?' (2017) 66 *International and Comparative Law Quarterly* 181.

81 *Kadi I*, *supra* n. 76.

The *NF and Others* case, filed at the General Court in 2016,[82] queried the legality of the 'EU–Turkey Statement' that had been agreed to by the 'European Council', and contested whether the statement in question was an international agreement. It was only with and since the Treaty of Lisbon that the European Council has been recognised as a standalone institution,[83] which, since *Pringle*, allows the Court of Justice to review its actions.[84] The European Council, defending itself for the first time as an institution in its own right before the EU judiciary, claimed that, notwithstanding the above, the Court of Justice did not have the necessary jurisdiction to hear the case, given its own Rules of Procedure.[85] Whilst Article 263 TFEU sets down that measures by Union actors in principle come within the scope of the Court of Justice's jurisdiction, it also must be in line with the intention to produce legal effects. Given the subject in *NF and Others* was a press release (the 'EU–Turkey Statement'), perhaps the initially broad thinking behind Article 263 TFEU has not been wide enough to capture all aspects of activity within the wider understandings of Union activity. With a press release on its own website,[86] the European Council as an institution claimed to not be the author of the statement, and on that basis, should not be considered a defendant.[87] The use of the European Council website to exert the positions of the Heads of State and Government meeting within the European Council certainly demonstrates the overlapping nature of what resulting documents and exertions belonged to whom. The argument of the European Council that it itself was not complicit is certainly not entirely convincing. Given the General Court was not entirely satisfied that the Member States were meeting their Turkish counterparts within the European Council, as standalone actors of international law, it is undoubtedly be a step backwards for the EU legal order, with Member States in a position to easily sidestep their obligations. Yet, the General Court did show some hesitation in reaching such a decision given the 'ambiguous wording' of the 'EU–Turkey Statement'.[88]

If the General Court's approach to the Rules of Procedure is similarly adopted by the Court of Justice on appeal, it would continue to chisel away on the maintenance of EU external action as a whole, including legal tools to support responses to the migration crisis. International agreements concerning migration matters are to be done through the Union's Ordinary Legislative

82 Joined Cases T-192/16, T-193/16 and T-257/16, *NF, NG and NM v. European Council*, ECLI:EU:T:2017:128, ECLI:EU:T:2017:129, ECLI:EU:T:2017:130.
83 Article 13(1) TEU and Article 15 TEU.
84 Case C-370/12, *Thomas Pringle v. Government of Ireland and Others*, ECLI:EU:C:2012:756, para. 31.
85 Rules of Procedure of the General Court [2015] OJ L105/1.
86 EU–Turkey Statement, 18 March 2016.
87 *Supra*, n. 82, para. 37.
88 *Ibid.*, para. 77.

Procedure. Whilst this 'EU–Turkey Statement' was not an international agreement,[89] it would have been *non*-CFSP in nature, as at no point was the Article 218 TFEU procedure on the opening, negotiating, and concluding of an international agreement attempted. Rather, the Member States were keen to avoid this at all costs. An appeal of the Order of the General Court to the Court of Justice deserves some merit, given that the 'EU–Turkey Statement' in question involved the inclusion of the Commission, which will ultimately monitor the implementation of the agreement. It could even be said that the chamber of the General Court had clearly not read the ERTA doctrine,[90] whereby the Council cannot merely act as a facilitator for Member States, but rather, as an institution in its own right. Given this development of a hands-off approach by the General Court on the 'agreement' itself, and the appeal that has been lodged,[91] the Court of Justice will play a pivotal role in the shaping of the EU's responses to tackling migration issues in the medium to long term, when looking at the implementation measures that will inevitably flow from the agreement. If the Court of Justice endorses the General Court's view, the detriment to the EU legal order would be that the EU Treaties and their effective means of democratic and judicial control would be undermined, and depend 'entirely on choices regarding the design instead of content made by Commission or Council'.[92]

4.3. VISAS AND RESIDENCE

Migratory measures within the scope of the EU Treaties are not included in primary law without stipulated reservations. Protocol No. 23 annexed to the Treaties,[93] specifies that persons entering Member States ... shall be 'without prejudice to the competence of Member States to negotiate or conclude agreements with third countries as long as they respect Union law and other relevant international agreements'. The exact scope of this Protocol is unclear in legal terms, but it nevertheless sends a clear signal by the Member States, in succinct terms, to the more supranationally-minded institutions, that progress

---

89 See G. Fernández Arribas, 'The EU–Turkey Agreement: A Controversial Attempt at Patching up a Major Problem' (2016) 1 *European Papers* 1097.

90 Case C-22/70, *Commission of the European Communities v. Council of the European Communities*, ECLI:EU:C:1971:32 (*European Agreement on Road Transport (ERTA)*). See C. Hillion, 'ERTA, ECHR and Open Skies: Laying the Grounds of the EU System of External Relations' in M. Poiares Maduro and L. Azoulai (eds.), *The Past and Future of EU Law: The Classics of EU Law Revisited on the 50th Anniversary of the Rome Treaty*, Hart Publishing, Oxford 2010.

91 Case C-208/17, *NF v. European Council*; Case C-209/17 P, *NG v. European Council*; Case C-210/17 P, *NM v. European Council*, pending (appeal lodged 21 April 2017).

92 T. Spijkerboer, *supra* n. 9, p. 552.

93 Protocol (No. 23) on external relations of the Member States with regard to the crossing of external borders.

in the field of external migration is a domain with reservation for Member States to continue exercising competence. Even so, the Treaties demonstrate, such as in Article 79(5) TFEU,[94] the intention to admit only third-country nationals who suit the economic conditions of Member States, by framing the wording of the Treaties around the employment market. Thus, it could be deduced that Union responses are not needed as such. This is further entrenched by Declaration 36 annexed to the Treaties, which affirmed the Member States intentions at the last Intergovernmental Conference (IGC) to preserve certain competences, continuing to allow Member States to 'negotiate and conclude agreements with third countries or international organisations in the areas covered by Chapters 3, 4 and 5 of Title V of Part Three in so far as such agreements comply with Union law'.[95]

Much recent discussion has focused on the migration crisis from a human rights perspective. That is, attention has been focused almost exclusively on the Dublin system, as well as the Common European Asylum System,[96] and the international system for alleviating the plight of migrants. The Dublin regime, which has seen incarnations of *Dublin I* and *Dublin II*, has failed. *Dublin III*,[97] has sought to allocate the responsibility of asylum seekers between Member States, based upon criteria set down, to the first Member State in which they entered the Union. During the migration crisis, it was clear that Member States were willing to let migrants pass through their territories with the intention of reaching other Member States; a policy decision that systematically undermined the *Dublin* regime altogether. For the Common European Asylum System,[98] the Ordinary Legislative Procedure is the method of decision-making in use. Similarly, a common immigration policy for the Union has the potential to be developed using the same decision-making process in a variety of scenarios envisaged by Article 79 TFEU, including establishing long-term visas and residence permits, inclusive of family reunification; defining the rights of non-Union citizens and their movement to and residence in other Member States; tackling illegal

---

94 Article 79(5) TFEU: 'This Article shall not affect the right of Member States to determine volumes of admission of third-country nationals coming from third countries to their territory in order to seek work, whether employed or self-employed.'

95 Declaration (36) on Article 218 of the Treaty on the Functioning of the European Union concerning the negotiation and conclusion of international agreements by Member States relating to the area of freedom, security and justice.

96 For example, see M. Wendel, 'The Refugee Crisis and the Executive: On the Limits of Administrative Discretion in the Common European Asylum System' (2016) 17 *German Law Journal* 1005.

97 Regulation (EU) No 603/2013 of the European Parliament and of the Council of 26 June 2013 Establishing the Criteria and Mechanisms for Determining the Member State Responsible for Examining an Application for International Protection Lodged in One of the Member States by a Third-Country National or a Stateless Person (Recast) [2013] OJ L180/31.

98 Article 78(2) TFEU and Article 78(2)(a)–(g) TFEU.

immigration and residence obtained unlawfully, including removal of such persons; and, finally, combating human trafficking.[99]

The Court of Justice is today in a position to be more responsive to the 'urgent' cases that appear on its docket than before. In 2008, a new accelerated procedure was made available through the Article 267 TFEU preliminary reference system, known as the *procédure préjudicielle d'urgence* (PPU).[100] In February 2017, Advocate General Mengozzi issued his Opinion in the *X and X* case,[101] a PPU case, where he believed the EU Visa Code adopted by the EU in 2009 was applicable,[102] and thus under certain conditions, that Member States in third countries should be obliged under the EU's Charter to issue visas to third country nationals on humanitarian grounds.[103] Whereas the Opinion of Advocate General Mengozzi can be said to have demonstrated considerable social conscience about how the EU should respond to certain issues, the Court of Justice found otherwise. In its judgment in March 2017,[104] the Court of Justice said that given that no measures have been adopted on long-term visas and residence permits based on Article 79(2)(a) TFEU,[105] it cannot be invoked in EU law for other purposes. Such measures continued to be within the scope of individual Member States national competence. The Court of Justice furthermore saw off a potential undermining of the entire EU asylum procedure,[106] thereby blocking a legal pathway for persons seeking access to the EU from a third state. The Court of Justice could be accused of adopting a sympathetic approach to the movement of EU citizens across EU borders, but that 'sympathy' does not extend to non-Union nationals moving across internal EU borders.[107] Therefore, if that judicial sympathy does not extend to persons already in the EU, then it certainly will not be extended to non-Union nationals who are outside the Union in the first place.

Expressing too much of a social conscience can result in the Court of Justice's loss of legitimacy to answer other legal questions. Whether the Court of Justice's judgment in *X and X* was reasonable or not is debatable, but the Member States'

---

99 Article 79(2)(a)–(d) TFEU.

100 See L. Clément-Wilz, 'La procédure préjudicielle d'urgence, nouveau théâtre du procès européen?' (2012) 48 *Cahiers de droit européen* 136.

101 Opinion of Advocate General Mengozzi in Case C-638/16 PPU, *X and X*, ECLI:EU:C:2017:93.

102 Regulation (EC) No 810/2009 of the European Parliament and of the Council of 13 July 2009 Establishing a Community Code on Visas (Visa Code) [2009] OJ L243/1.

103 Article 4 of the EU's Charter of Fundamental Rights ('Prohibition of torture and inhuman or degrading treatment or punishment'): 'No one shall be subjected to torture or to inhuman or degrading treatment or punishment'.

104 Case C-638/16 PPU, *X and X*, ECLI:EU:C:2017:173.

105 *Ibid.*, para. 44.

106 *Ibid.*, paras. 48–49.

107 P. van Nuffel, 'Having 'the Law' observed: The Role Played by the European Court of Justice in the Application of EU and International Law towards Third-Country Nationals' in M. Maes, M.C. Foblets and P. De Bruycker (eds.), *supra*, n. 13, p. 91.

rationale for backing the Belgian argument in the case was simple; the EU Visa Code was not intended for the purposes of mandating humanitarian visas to be issued by Member States through the EU. This has proven that, notwithstanding the efforts that have been made to provide for an explicit external competence in the field of migration through visa, asylum, and immigration policies in EU primary law; the these legal bases have not been availed of in full with EU secondary law.

5. THE PATH FORWARD

The newly created synergy of actors and policies in the migration crisis, working in tandem with one-another, leaves open the possibility for future cross-policy cooperation amongst different hierarchical actors to respond to pan-European crises. However, the political discourse on the migration crisis continues to be fraught. Matters of migration fall into a politically difficult area of public policy. EU migration policy remains a framework for sets of laws, which have yet to be fully completed. It is yet to be determined how far away the harmonisation of policies for catering for the entry into the Union of non-Union citizens may be, but it is looking increasingly less likely as the migration crisis rumbles on. Before the financial crisis, figures show that Europe was one of the most open regions in the world in terms of inward migration flows.[108] Stefan Zweig, in the midst of the Second World War spoke of the madness of borders in Europe, particularly given their 'artificial' nature, with how they were 'contrary to the spirit of our times that clearly wished for closer links and international fraternity'.[109] For the most part, they have been largely eliminated internally, but to the outside world, Zweig would likely be equally horrified to see how Europe is putting in place deterrents at its external European borders in order to protect the Schengen Area.

Interest in the topic of migration in Europe is increasing, and the research agenda is booming, with a range of publications reaching fruition, in response to the prolonged migration crisis. From whatever angle the field is approached, there is considerable discussion to be had regarding how migration is to be managed and enforced.[110] Europe has and will continue to be a territory with a

---

108 T. Piketty, 'Pour une Europe ouverte' [2015] *Libération*; T. Piketty, 'For an Open Europe' in T. Piketty (ed.), S. Ackerman (tr.), *Chronicles: On Our Troubled Times*, Penguin 2016.

109 S. Zweig, *The World of Yesterday: Memoirs of a European*, A. Bell (tr.), Pushkin Press 2011, p. 219. Originally published as S. Zweig, *Die Welt von Gestern: Erinnerungen eines Europäers*, Bermann-Fischer 1942.

110 For example, see T. Gammeltoft-Hansen and J. Vedsted-Hansen (eds.), *Human Rights and the Dark Side of Globalisation: Transnational Law Enforcement and Migration Control*, Routledge 2017.

'magnetic' effect, with people gravitating towards its borders and shores. Whilst lacking a comprehensive approach, with answers to the problems arising as a result of the migration crisis, there are faint signs of hope. In the same way that it can be argued that international law feeds off crisis,[111] the EU has arguably been on the opposite end of the spectrum. The EU's legal order has thrived in times of relative normality, and been stuck in a rut during times of crisis. Practice has shown that decision-making on the political level has been slow, and where decisions are made, this has been done on a compromised basis. This is unsurprising given the huge variation in national responses to the migration crisis, with Member States changing their position, such as Germany's 'open door' policy which was later closed and tighter restrictions in migration policy applied.

5.1. CHASING THE PRESENT

The reason why the CFSP and *non*-CFSP conundrum has only come to the fore recently is that migration measures now have an explicit basis within the Treaties. Yet, it is not a joined-up framework. The Treaties provide an incomplete set of tools, which hinders a coherent and effective holistic approach towards the migration crisis. Previous CFSP actions have imposed bans on particular individuals, thus excluding judicial review of the Court of Justice, which would have been one of the key motivators for CFSP in the first place, as opposed to the use of Article 352 TFEU.[112] Concern has previously been expressed on using CFSP for migration matters.[113] If the use of CFSP for migration is contrasted to other policies, some differences can be seen. For example, for restrictive measures, this is done through a two-fold system of, first, a CFSP Decision based on Article 29 TEU and, secondly, a *non*-CFSP Regulation, adopted on the basis of Article 215 TFEU.[114] For migration

---

111 See B. Authers and H. Charlesworth, 'The Crisis and the Quotidian in International Human Rights Law' in M.K. Bulterman and W.J.M. Van Genugten (eds.), *Netherlands Yearbook of International Law 2013: Crisis and International Law: Decoy or Catalyst?*, TMC Asser Press 2014. This builds on the previously published, H. Charlesworth, 'International Law: A Discipline of Crisis' (2002) 65 *Modern Law Review* 377.

112 Formerly Article 308 EC.

113 B. Martenczuk, 'Migration Policy and EU External Relations', *supra* n. 38, p. 100.

114 Article 215 TFEU: '1. Where a decision, adopted in accordance with Chapter 2 of Title V of the Treaty on European Union, provides for the interruption or reduction, in part or completely, of economic and financial relations with one or more third countries, the Council, acting by a qualified majority on a joint proposal from the High Representative of the Union for Foreign Affairs and Security Policy and the Commission, shall adopt the necessary measures. It shall inform the European Parliament thereof. 2. Where a decision adopted in accordance with Chapter 2 of Title V of the Treaty on European Union so provides, the Council may adopt

issues, such as the travel bans mentioned previously, no *non*-CFSP follow-up legal acts are necessary. How this is compatible with Article 40 TEU on the non-encroachment of CFSP and *non*-CFSP, post-Lisbon, remains to be seen.

The future potential of the EU as a problem-solving forum for the coordination of responses to unprecedented crises could be under threat. The established legal framework for EU external relations means reaction to external events will always be insufficient, which is undoubtedly a terrible prognosis. If there is no means to resolve issues, Member States will look elsewhere, albeit their options are inherently limited given some competencies are already shared with the Union. To prevent this legal fragmentation and disintegration from occurring, one solution could be greater linkage of CFSP and *non*-CFSP. As previously highlighted, if the European Border and Coast Guard Agency develops further, there will be a need for it to have interoperable solutions by linking it to other bodies of the Union,[115] such as the European Defence Agency (EDA). Consequently, a full interlinking of all the EU's actors at its disposal may be further warranted. Likewise, international agreements between the EU and third states to lock-in practices preventing irregular migration will be an eventuality. Article 220(1) TFEU states that the EU, 'shall establish all appropriate forms of cooperation', with UN bodies, the Council of Europe, the OSCE and the OECD, and 'shall also maintain such relations as are appropriate with other international organisations'. Accordingly, the EU may in future be edged into ensuring responses to crises are coordinated on a multilateral level in international fora.

Individually, Member States are competent to independently play a role in the migration crisis without resorting to collective measures, through CFSP or *non*-CFSP. But individual actions are unable to stop the root causes of irregular migration to Europe. Solution-based thinking has been and continues to be at the heart of what the EU is about. Yet, this goal has to be coupled with legal bases which are appropriate for achieving such ends. It is clear that foreign policy responses to the migration crisis through CFSP legal tools has been a short-term measure. The need for the EU to act, in whatever manner, is thus seen as the EU attempting to re-establish law and order on its external borders, whilst similarly, bringing stability, as far as possible, to the European neighbourhood. By invoking foreign policy measures, rather than merely relying migration measures under EU law, the aim is to prevent persons from migrating at all.

---

restrictive measures under the procedure referred to in paragraph 1 against natural or legal persons and groups or non-State entities. 3. The acts referred to in this Article shall include necessary provisions on legal safeguards.'

115 S. Blockmans, 'New Thrust for the CSDP from the Refugee and Migrant Crisis', CEPS paper No. 142, Brussels 2016, p. 14.

5.2. FORGING LEGAL CHANGE

As with every Treaty amendment that increases the potential scope of EU action, this widened vision for the EU is not always followed up with the requisite tools. Thus a vacuum is created. If the integrity of the EU's legal order is to be considered of primary importance, then the legal bases for the EU's action should be used appropriately. The coming together of CFSP and *non*-CFSP activity to achieve a comprehensive response should ideally be seen as an opportunity, rather than a legal hurdle that may cause unspeakable difficulties. Even more, the migration crisis has shown that *non*-CFSP tools have not been enough to provide a full EU response to a challenge, and in times of crisis, intergovernmental tools through CFSP have been resorted to. Foreign policy responses have been utilised as extended tools that encroach upon the more long-term intended uses of *non*-CFSP tools. For example, *Operation Atalanta* is fast approaching its 10-year anniversary as the first EU naval mission combating maritime piracy in the Indian Ocean. Whereas the EU's military mission, *Operation Sophia*, conducts its activities under the auspices of CFSP, the European Border and Coast Guard Agency (Frontex) has an equally difficult task on its hands on a *non*-CFSP basis. Much of its remit inevitably involves SAR, which itself poses questions about where to place migrants who have been rescued from unsuitable vessels for Mediterranean crossings.[116] The task of Frontex has been to compliment the AFSJ features of the Treaties. Yet, the Regulation giving legal effect and establishing the new European Border and Coast Guard Agency is conspicuous,[117] in that it is at pains to distance itself from any collaboration with military matters, notwithstanding that it has been called 'semi-military' in its new format.[118] Rather, the Regulation merely makes passing reference, by envisaging that the Agency will be able to, 'continue cooperation at an operational level with other Member States and/or third countries at the external borders, including military operations with a law enforcement purpose, to the extent that this cooperation is compatible with the actions of the Agency'.

Despite the disarray of refugee settlements systems that EU Member States have in place both before and in light of the migration crisis, looking elsewhere paints a much bleaker picture. The Convention Relating to the Status of Refugees of 1951 has been ratified by states neighbouring the EU, such as Egypt; however, in contrast with EU Member States, the full and follow-up implementation of these international principles through the national legislative framework have

---

116 See M. Ratcovich, 'The Concept of 'Place of Safety': Yet Another Self-Contained Maritime Rule or a Sustainable Solution to the Ever-Controversial Question of Where to Disembark Migrants Rescued at Sea?' (2016) 33 *Australian Year Book of International Law* 81.

117 Regulation (EU) 2016/1624, *supra*, n. 69.

118 S. Blockmans, *supra* n. 115, p. 2.

remained absent. In the Commission's 'Agenda on Migration', it accepted that to combat irregular migration to the EU, a multifaceted approach would have to be taken. Four policy areas were singled out: development cooperation, trade, employment, foreign and home affairs policies; which all come under different legal bases in EU law.[119] If anything, the overall response has been weak, and demonstrates the lack of overall coherence as regards the EU's ability to effectively combat challenges for which it is ill prepared. The political situation in Europe's wider neighbourhood continues to be perilous, which has knock-on effects in Europe; namely, that people will continue to avail of any means possible in order to make the trek to Europe.

Monitoring the passage of persons through both land and maritime means requires multifaceted responses, engaging a range of institutional actors and agencies and coordinating responses to fulfil desired EU objectives. Efforts must have sound legal bases in order to reach their maximum potential. Presently, the EU is not fulfilling this basic requirement. Rather than basing certain tasks exclusively on a CFSP legal basis, that is, more intergovernmentally than supranationally, the EU should invoke, as a matter of course, *non*-CFSP legal bases. This would ensure institutional plurality, giving greater legitimacy to its decision-making in tackling the migration crisis, by giving EU citizens through the Parliament a better say, whilst also ensuring proper judicial review of the legality of such policies by the Court of Justice. To date, there has been no attempt at a framework for achieving an agreement encompassing both CFSP and *non*-CFSP matters to respond to the migration crisis. One example of a specific international agreement stretching across the breadth of the Treaties encompassing multiple legal basis that have different procedural matters has been concluded,[120] although the legality of this has not yet been challenged.

5.3. BUILDING EUROPEAN LEGAL HERITAGE

The legacy of the Treaties in terms of migration is becoming clear. Apportioning responsibility to the EU, without the allocation of the necessary tools for acting, is by no means an efficient way to run the affairs of an enhanced international organisation of any description. This irony is seen not just in the context of the migration crisis, but also the financial crisis, where the lack of effective tools to

119 European Commission, *A European Agenda on Migration*, (COM(2015) 240 Final), Brussels 2016, p. 6.

120 See Council Decision (EU) 2016/123 of 26 October 2015 on the Signing, on Behalf of the European Union, and Provisional Application of the Enhanced Partnership and Cooperation Agreement between the European Union and Its Member States, of the One Part, and the Republic of Kazakhstan, of the Other Part [2015] OJ L29/1.

combat new challenges hampers the working nature of a *sui generis* international organisation. If anything, such lack of potential responses of the EU to crises points to the need for greater mechanisms for the EU to be entrusted with when difficulties arise. Coupled with this will be the need for Member States to free up their hold on competences where EU action is needed to solve the most pressing public policy issues of modern times. Some action is better than no action, even when there are overarching legal problems that are equally deserving of solutions. An existential challenge to the EU in the future, of similar magnitude to the migration crisis, is conceivably possible. Whilst the migration crisis was able to be brought within the bounds of EU foreign, security, and defence policy as a complimentary measure, in another crisis, the EU might not be so fortunate to have tools available to it.

4. THE MIGRATION CRISIS IN EUROPE: THE IMPLICATIONS FOR TRADE AND LABOUR IN A GLOBALISED CONTEXT

Maria CUDOWSKA*

The land flourished because it was fed from so many sources – because it was nourished by so many cultures and traditions and peoples.
Lyndon B. Johnson

1. INTRODUCTION

The interface between global policies in economic, social and migration related issues has become a focal point in today's discussion about the migration crisis and the path to a modern and synthetic integration. Hence, it may be appropriate to say that with the necessary governmental support, migration can have the power to drive economic growth and development in both home and host countries.[1] That being stated, international migration and international trade in goods and services both raise questions regarding the effect of trade liberalisation on incentives to migrate across countries, and the effects of international migration on the need for trade liberalisation.[2]

Throughout history there have been various instances of simultaneous trade and immigration liberalisation operations, as well as examples of a complete opposite nature, such as in the United States, wherein trade liberalisation has been coupled with immigration restrictions.[3] The current influx of migrants

* Faculty of Law, University of Białystok, Poland. E-mail: mcudowska@wp.pl.

1 International Migration Report, highlights 2015, p. 3, <http://www.un.org/en/development/desa/population/migration/publications/migrationreport/docs/MigrationReport2015_Highlights.pdf> accessed 18.07.2017.

2 J.S. BHANDARI, 'International Migration and Trade: A Multi-Disciplinary Synthesis' (2006) 6 *Rich. J. Global L. & Bus.* 113.

3 *Ibid.*

into the European Union (EU), followed by the so-called 'migration crisis', is not only a challenge for democracy, *per se*, but also a challenge for several EU institutions in terms of labour and economic policy. Also, as will be discussed in this chapter, the impact of migration on public finances cannot be overlooked in the long run, as this may jeopardise the financial stability of the entire European community.

What is important, however, is that the Organisation for Economic Cooperation and Development (OECD) countries have responded to emergency situations by scaling up public spending to process asylum applications and welcome refugees. In order to support countries of origin and transit, additional funding has also been made available at the EU and national levels alike.[4] Significantly, the labour markets in the EU, the European Economic Area (EEA) and Switzerland markets, will most likely (based on estimates) not suffer from the influx of refugees. To the contrary, the labour markets of the EU might take in as many as one million new workers by the end of 2016.[5]

According to the UN and its 2015 International Migration Report, the number of international migrants worldwide has continued to grow rapidly over the past 15 years, reaching 244 million in 2015, which is up from 222 million in 2010 and 173 million in 2000.[6] Bearing all of those facts and figures in mind, it is clear that the migration crisis is one of the main challenges that the European community will be forced to face in the near-to-immediate future. Immigration and labour policies, let alone economic and fiscal stability, are key to modern integration, and are currently Europe's greatest concern. While classical economists have long argued that trade and labour migration are functionally the same,[7] it is extremely difficult to separate the two for the purpose of this chapter since there is no comprehensive data. However, it is crucial to mention that among the many scholars who have explored and analysed this topic, the current debate on migration and economy is headed in three main directions:

1. In the short term, the need to provide food, shelter and first aid to refugees; costs will have to be shared between transit and destination countries alike (no benefits).
2. In the medium term, destination countries have to bear the costs of processing asylum applications, as well as other significant costs of social and economic integration (no benefits).

---

4 Migration Policy Debates, No. 8, 2015, <https://www.oecd.org/migration/How-will-the-refugee-surge-affect-the-European-economy.pdf> accessed 18.07.2017.

5 *Ibid.*

6 International Migration Report, *supra* n. 1.

7 J. Gordon, 'People Are Not Bananas: How Immigration Differs from Trade' (2011) 104 *Nw. U. L. Rev.* 1109.

3. In the long term, the refugee influx will address the pressing problem of the current European demographic trend of an aging population, and improve the ratio of active workers, contributing to innovation, entrepreneurship and GDP growth.[8]

Notwithstanding the fact that there may be other outcomes of the migration crisis in Europe, these arguments offer a simple, yet powerful, understanding of what may actually happen, regardless whether it will be in the long or short term.

This chapter is designed to map out and articulate many of the current problems that pertain to migration and trade, as well as analysing the issue of how migration effects labour markets across Europe. In order to fully understand, and appreciate the problem, several aspects of globalisation will be discussed in order to shed more light on, and to provide a better understanding of, the issues behind trade and migration. In doing so, this chapter attempts to demonstrate that migration has been a steady, yet unstoppable phenomenon for more than a decade, so much so that it has had a clear global effect on economies and trade policies across the globe. All in all, migration is an unrelenting part of today's global society; it drives social and economic change and, ultimately, it has the power to change our future at different levels and in different spheres of our lives.

2. TRADE AND MIGRATION: A HISTORICAL OVERVIEW

The examination of historical migration patterns goes far beyond the scope of this chapter; however, it should be highlighted that the history surrounding migration patterns is a critical aspect to understanding the various mechanisms that have developed over the years, which have an impact on various migration policies and labour markets in today's ever-globalised world. For the purpose of this chapter, the discussion will be guided by the more important historical events that have impacted migration patterns over the years and, ultimately, how this impact has affected states' various migration policies and labour markets.

First and foremost, the European migration after the Second World War, according to Zimmerman, should be differentiated between five phases:

1. The period of adjustment after the war (a period between 1945 and the early 1960s).
2. Decolonisation (a period between 1945 and the early 1960s).

---

8 European Parliament, 'Economic Challenges and Prospects of the Refugee Influx', Briefing Dec. 2015, <http://www.europarl.europa.eu/RegData/etudes/BRIE/2015/572809/EPRS_BRI(2015)572809_EN.pdf> accessed 18.07.2017.

3. Labour migration (from 1955 to 1973).
4. Restrained migration (from 1974 to 1988).
5. Dissolution of socialism and afterwards (since 1988).[9]

Significantly, the period of adjustment after the war, demographically speaking, brought about a new order as 20 million people became displaced and were forced to search for a new place to call home. For example, 12 million Germans were forced to leave Eastern Europe by 1950, with about 8 million migrating to West Germany.[10] Those previously unimaginable numbers perpetuated change both in the host nation and previously displaced persons' native homelands, and ultimately impacted the labour markets across Europe.

Following decolonisation, many Africans migrated to France, and with such movement, many transoceanic migrants ended up in Great Britain.[11] The reason behind this was the fact that many colonial powers, such as the UK, France, the Netherlands, Portugal and Belgium, lost their colonies in the years following the end of the Second World War:

- independence from Great Britain of India and Pakistan in 1947 and of Ghana in 1957;
- Congo's independence from Belgium in 1960;
- Algeria's independence from France in 1962.[12]

During these years, labour migration was driven by labour shortages which, importantly, induced openness and provided for an increase in labour migration. A famous example of this is Germany, which during this time was considered as a country that prided itself on taking in migrants from Turkey, Tunisia, Morocco, Portugal, etc. Also, net immigration to the North from the Mediterranean was estimated at about 5 million. Taking into account the historical migration waves, it is to be noted that current labour migration is more restricted than trade or foreign investment, and scholars have found difficulty in drawing a conclusion as to what the reasons for this phenomenon may be. With many international agreements governing trade and investment, the limited number of institutions governing and regulating the migration of workers across borders presents a stark contrast

9 K. Zimmermann, 'Tackling the European Migration Problem' (1995) 9(2) *J. Econ. Pers.* 46.
10 *Ibid.*
11 *Ibid.*
12 C. Dustmann and T. Frattini, *Immigration: The European Experience*, Norface Migration Discussion Paper No. 2012–01, p. 6, <http://www.norface-migration.org/publ_uploads/NDP_01_12.pdf> accessed 18.07.2017.

to the modern economic and labour trends.[13] Interestingly, the growth of BITs (bilateral investment treaties), especially in Europe, has contributed significantly to economic growth since the Second World War without any regulations whatsoever regarding labour migration. However, one may argue that without the labour force there would be no direct foreign investment, which would subsequently hinder economic growth and financial stability. In sum, labour migration, as defined and differentiated by Zimmermann, perhaps does not correspond to the modern concept of the occurrence, and calls for a redefinition.

In contrast to the third wave of migration just discussed, the period between 1974 and 1988 was characterised by a restrained approach to migration. It must be highlighted that during this time period, labour recruitment largely stopped, due to increased social tensions and the fear of economic recession after the first oil price shock.[14]

Zimmermann argues that the last period of mass migration following the dissolution of socialism was dominated by East–West migration, with a strong inflow of asylum seekers and refugees.[15] The fact that immigrants, refugees and asylum seekers most commonly seek refuge within the borders of the EU has to be treated very seriously, and consideration must be given to the various implications of this phenomenon, as will be elaborated on and discussed in greater detail throughout this chapter.

Social tensions and anxiety are inseparable elements of immigration, not only in the EU, but throughout the world as well. Interestingly, in eighteenth century America, Benjamin Franklin's 'Observations Concerning the Increase of Mankind',[16] may justify the inseparable link between migration and the social integrity of one's country. One could conceivably take Franklin's writing and studies of demography as racist, however, the core of his arguments lay somewhere between defending the social integrity of the United States and protecting the rights of the people who built the 'new' country of America. Franklin also expressed concerns that foreigners would take over America. Franklin believed that '[t]he number of purely white People in the World is proportionally very small' and, thus, the racial integrity of the continent might be compromised. In a way, it can be argued that Franklin's fears have shaped America's immigration history.[17] It is noteworthy that, based on the concept of the American exceptionalism, US enterprise has been shaped by cultural anxiety. This still remains an issue today, especially with the growing number

13 J. Gordon, *supra* n. 7, p. 6.

14 *Ibid.*

15 K. Zimmerman, *supra., n. 9.*

16 See B. Franklin, *America as a Land of Opportunity*, <http://www.digitalhistory.uh.edu/disp_textbook.cfm?smtID=3&psid=85> accessed 18.07.2017.

17 L. Orgad, 'Illiberal Liberalism Cultural Restrictions on Migration and Access to Citizenship in Europe' (2010) 58 *Am. J. Comp. L.* 53.

of Latino immigrants, and as evidenced by Donald Trump's presidency and attitude towards immigrants.[18]

Historically, the movement of people, and the social tensions that follow, are inherent to an ever changing and developing modern economic world. Today, labour markets operate in a different fashion as compared to the scheme implemented previously wherein labour workers from developing nations were relocating to developed nations in order to pursue business and employment opportunities. As a rule of thumb, this was the standard course of action taken by many labourers who resided in developing nations.[19]

It needs to be recalled that all kinds of migration, whether or not they relate to labour or any other basis for migration, are not regulated by comprehensive international mechanisms; rather, they are regulated by domestic procedures like visas and other migration-controlling policies. That stated, it is also necessary to consider how the international community decided to address some of the more pressing issues with respect to development and migration alike.

3. THE EFFECTS OF DEVELOPMENT ON MIGRATION

Migration and development is anything but a new topic.[20] It is also impossible to elaborate on migration without providing a substantial theoretical background; in discussing this, a better understanding of the interplay between migration and development will be gained. Throughout history, scholars and researchers have analysed this interplay, the oldest and most famous being Ravenstein, a nineteenth century geographer whose famous neo-classical equilibrium perspectives have been cited when discussing and dissecting migration and development. Ravenstein formulated the 'laws of migration', which seem relatively up to date with today's reality. According to the principles set forth by Ravenstein's 'laws of migration', migration is an inseparable part of development and one of the major causes for the migration is economics.[21] Neo-classical economics, at the macro-level, see the objectives behind migration being primarily geographical differences in the supply and demand for labour, whereas at the micro-level, the theory sees the migrant as an individual and a rational actor who decides to move on the basis of a cost-benefit calculation.

---

18 See 'To Detain More Immigrants, Trump Administration to Speed Border Hiring', *New York Times*, 12.04.2017, <https://www.nytimes.com/2017/04/12/us/trump-immigration-border-hiring.html> accessed 18.07.2017.

19 K.R. Zaidi, 'Harmonizing Trade Liberalization and Migration Policy through Shared Responsibility: A Comparison of the Impact of Bilateral Trade Agreements and the GATS in Germany and Canada' (2010) 37 *Syracuse J. Int'l. L. & Com.* 267.

20 H. de Hass, *Migration and Development: A Theoretical Perspective*, International Migration Institute, Working Paper No. 9, 2008, p. 5.

21 *Ibid.*

The so-called 'new economics of migration',[22] gives emphasis to the fact that migration of some family members may decrease dependence on the situation in a single labour market.[23] This may be important for developing countries and lesser developed countries alike, where the dependence on social security is very high and the where the social security systems are hardly operative.[24] Scholars have enumerated certain 'migration impeding factors', which generally block migration flows between First and Third World countries. Such factors include:

1. *Migration costs*. As there are a lot of costs connected to traveling in general, there are also a lot of costs connected to migration; such costs consist of not only direct expenditures and foregone earnings, but also psychological costs.
2. *Expected unemployment in the host country*. It is to be expected that migrants may or may not find employment in the host country, but it is also debatable whether their human capital is transferable.
3. *Uncertainty and the option value of waiting*. Vogler and Rotte[25] argue that an additional aspect is uncertainty, as economic and non-economic aspects can differ from expectations.
4. *Income valuation*. Moreover, it can only be determined in the future whether higher income drives migration, or whether short-term gains and the cost of migration make the wheel spin.
5. *Relative income situation*. In an environment where everyone has the same material status, the likelihood of migration is very low.[26]

The effects of development on migration are, therefore, specifically intertwined with trade and migration policy. To give an example, domestic economies rely on workers who could fill labour shortages in key industries; however, developed economies have a different understanding and viewpoint when it comes to labour and business investment. In short, they expect workers to remain in the host country while jobs are available and return home when those jobs are no longer available. In theory it is a win-win scenario for both the host country and the incoming migrants, as it provides the necessary workforce to fill labour shortages, while at the same time stimulating foreign investment and increasing domestic growth.[27]

---

22 O. Stark and D.E Bloom, 'The New Economics of Labor Migration' (1985) 75 *American Economic Review* 173.

23 M. Vogler and R. Rotte, 'The Effects of Development on Migration: Theoretical Issues and New Empirical Evidence' (2000) 13 *J. Popul. Econ.* 486.

24 *Ibid.*

25 *Ibid.*

26 These factors have been named and enumerated by M. Vogler and R. Rotte, *supra* n. 23, and are by no means exhaustive.

27 K.R. Zaidi, *supra* n. 19.

4. MIGRATION IN THE EU: FREEDOM OF MOVEMENT

The Treaty on European Union (TEU), and the Treaty on the Functioning of the European Union (TFEU) are the two main Treaties under which the European community currently functions. It has been critically important that, starting as a continent of wandering and displaced people, Europe should become a well-integrated economic market.[28] Therefore, as a consequence, the EU is said to be quite protectionist as it pertains to the free movement of persons. Such a contention is supported by the language contained in Art 45(2) TFEU, which states that:

> [F]reedom of movement shall entail the abolition of any discrimination based on nationality between the workers of the Member States as regards employment, remuneration and other conditions of work and employment.[29]

Additionally, the 'principles' of the EU Treaty include establishing a common market and an economic and monetary union, to promote throughout the Union a harmonious, balanced and sustainable development of economic activities, a high level of employment and social protection, a high degree of competitiveness and convergence of economic performance, and economic and social cohesion and solidarity among the Member States. The free movement of workers is key to achieving an economic union.

Therefore, if the EU has an overarching goal to protect the free movement of workers, stimulate trade, and encourage solidarity, what does that in turn mean for the migrants from third countries? Since the European Court of Justice has been sympathetically generous when interpreting and extending the free movement principles, and all of the benefits that arise thereof, to workers' spouses, former spouses and children, even after a worker has ceased to work, migrants not only have an incentive to work in the EU, but also to acquire EU citizenship.

5. MODERN TRENDS OF MIGRATION TO THE EU

Labour migration, along with family migration, family reunification and free-movement migration, is considered the bulk of overall migration flow in the EU.[30] Achieving stability and tackling the migration problem is a vital

---

28 F.J. Conte, 'Sink or Swim Together: Citizenship, Sovereignty, and Free Movement in the European Union and the United States' (2007) 61 *U. Miami L. Rev.* 331, p. 7.

29 Art 45(2) TFEU, formerly Art 39(2) of the EC Treaty.

30 International Labour Organisation, *The Contribution of Labour Mobility to Economic Growth*, Joint paper for G20 Labour and Employment Ministers' Meeting, Ankara, Turkey, 3–4 September 2015, p. 7, <http://www.ilo.org/wcmsp5/groups/public/---europe/---ro-geneva/---ilo-ankara/documents/legaldocument/wcms_398770.pdf > accessed 18.07.2017.

policy-related issue that needs to be addressed not only within the realm of the EU, but also worldwide. The EU has become extremely fragile when it comes to migration, as people often confuse labour migration with immigration or humanitarian migration.

With that in mind, the European Commission has announced the New Migration Partnership Framework, which is focused on reinforcing and continuing cooperation with third countries so as to allow for better management of future migration patterns countries in order to better manage migration. Saving lives at sea, increasing returns, enabling migrants and refugees to stay closer to their homes, and, in the long term, helping the development of third countries in an attempt to address the root causes of irregular migration, are key to the EU's current policies concerning and towards migrants.[31]

Notwithstanding the fact that in reality the number of migrants is more likely to increase rather than decrease in the near-to-immediate future, Vice-President Federica Mogherini highlights that saving lives and tackling some of the most crucial problems is '[a] responsibility Europe shares with the rest of the world',[32] meaning that only a united front is likely to be effective. Hence, a full and wide range of EU policy will be pursued in an effort to face the migration crisis. For instance, the EU will need to ensure that its focus and engagement is tailored to address the continuing problem of people dying in the Mediterranean Sea, and seeking to enable the refugees to stay close to home and avoid taking dangerous journeys. Next, the enhanced support strategy is designed to reinforce local capacity including border control, asylum procedures, counter-smuggling and reintegration efforts.

Given the fact that a major contributory factor in irregular migratory flows is irregular smuggling, praying on the desperate and vulnerable initiatives (including criminal measures) need to be undertaken to combat this problem. Certainly, the EU has contemplated and taken many steps to cooperate with different countries, yet substantial improvement of the situation is nowhere in sight. It needs to be highlighted that migration is a steady force, and the EU alone cannot, even through advanced policy making, combat all of the negative aspects of migration, whether legal or not. When analysing statistics regarding illegal border crossings into the EU in 2015, a picture of steady and major inflow of immigrants is revealed. For instance, 23,605 people crossed from Nigeria to the EU border irregularly during 2015.[33]

---

31 European Commission, 'Commission Announces New Migration Partnership Framework: Reinforced Cooperation with Third Countries to Better Manage Migration', Press Release, 07.06.2016, <http://europa.eu/rapid/press-release_IP-16-2072_en.htm> accessed 18.07.2017.

32 *Ibid.*

33 European Commission, Annex to the Communication From the Commission to the European Parliament, The European Council, The Council and the European Investment Bank on establishing a new Partnership Framework with third countries under the

Nevertheless, the data presented by the International Labour Organisation (ILO) shows that labour migration has declined continuously since the economic downturn, and fell by more than 10 per cent in 2012. It can be argued that this particular downturn of labour migration may be caused by some other external factors unrelated to wealth, such as decreasing birth rates worldwide. In countries such as Canada, Australia or New Zealand, which are considered traditional settlement countries, about 25 per cent of inflows of permanent migrants are primary applicants under the economic, skill or employment channels.[34] With that being said, the decline in labour migration is not a full reflection of migration, as substantial work-related migration occurs within the framework of free movement. Also, temporary labour migration, and its relation to free movement within the borders of the EU, can be an interesting example of incoherent data and statistics resulting from the number of seasonal workers who can move freely within the EU, and who simply disappear off the radar as the monitoring system simply does not register them at all.

What is more, the international trend of student mobility can also be a contributing factor to future employment rates, so much so that its effect can be as high as 20 to 30 per cent, depending on the host country. Interestingly, when analysing this phenomenon on a worldwide scale, the number of students enrolled in educational institutions outside their home country has doubled since 2000, to 4.5 million in 2012. It might have been expected that in the last five years these numbers would be even higher; however, this is not the case. Numbers have been steadily decreasing, especially in the OECD countries. Also, is noteworthy that more than half of all international students in the EU arrive from Asia.[35]

Therefore, it is crucial to answer the question: where are all of the migrants going? Estimates show that the United States still remains the most popular country for hosting immigrants, as it is housing close to 41 million foreign-born persons. As far as the EU is concerned, Germany, the United Kingdom and France follow with a combined total of 24 million migrants.[36]

Perhaps it is also vital to answer the question of what the migrants bring into the equation. For instance, the sharp difference between the developing countries and developed ones can be shown with a simple example – the population of the developing countries simply cannot afford not to work, as the availability of social protection is very limited.[37]

European Agenda on Migration, Brussels, 07.06.2016, <https://ec.europa.eu/home-affairs/sites/homeaffairs/files/what-we-do/policies/european-agenda-migration/proposal-implementation-package/docs/20160607/communication_external_aspects_eam_towards_new_migration_ompact_annex_1_en.pdf> accessed 18.07.2017.

34 *Ibid.*

35 *Ibid.*

36 *Ibid.*

37 International Labour Organisation, *World of Work Report 2014, Developing with Jobs*, Geneva 2014, p. 33, <http://www.ilo.org/wcmsp5/groups/public/---dgreports/---dcomm/documents/publication/wcms_243961.pdf> accessed 18.07.2017.

Statistics present an interesting relation between low incomes and high demographic growth – in the absence of significant social protection, low incomes and high demographic growth go together as it relates to the working age population in developing countries. Research also shows that the trend is more compulsive than in advanced economies.[38] Hence, people in the less developed nations tend to work longer and harder than the ones in the developed ones, and still they earn the bare minimum. Migrants provide for a better and stable economy, and ultimately they stimulate employment dynamics.

6. DIRECT AND INDIRECT EFFECTS OF IMMIGRATION ON ECONOMIC GROWTH

6.1. LABOUR MARKETS

Many argue that economic cooperation on an international level has been extremely hard to achieve. The so-called 'source countries' (emigration countries), and 'destination countries' (immigration countries), have different interests, to say the least, and most of these interests are either difficult or impossible to align.[39]

The rapidly increasing immigration flow that is reaching the shores, not only of the United States, but also the EU, has rekindled the debate over immigration policy on both continents alike. There have been major shifts in the national origins of the immigrant population, and a decline of skills in immigrant workers relative to the skills of native workers.[40] Although some may see this as a succession of unprecedented crises, immigration from lower income to higher income areas has actually been a steady force operating for over the last 50 years.[41] The impact that immigration has on labour markets, not only across the EU, but also globally, cannot be (and is not) undermined by the international community as it pertains to the liberalisation of the labour markets in general, as well as trade. Ever since the end of the Second World War, the wheels of social and economic change have been in motion. The General Agreement on Tariffs and Trade (GATT),[42] which was agreed upon in 1947, has contributed to a dramatic progress towards free trade in goods.[43]

Empirical data reveals, and a large quantity of the literature has investigated, the economic inequality between immigrant and native workers. Extremely

---

38 *Ibid.*, p. 34.

39 A. Bradford, 'Sharing the Risks and Rewards of Economic Migration, Symposium: Immigration Law and Institutional Design' (2013) 80 *U. Ch. L. Rev.* 29.

40 G.J. Borjas, 'The Economic Benefits from Immigration' (1995) 9(2) *J. Econ. Pers.* 3.

41 G. Peri, 'Immigrants, Productivity, and Labor Markets' (2016) 30(4) *J. Econ. Pers.* 3.

42 General Agreement on Tariffis and Trade, October 1947, hereinafter GATT.

43 H.F. Chang, 'Migration as International Trade: The Economic Gains from the Liberalized Movement of Labor' (1998) 3 *UCLA J. Int'l L. & Foreign Aff.* 371.

controversial studies from the early 1990s indicate that immigrants are generally in a disadvantaged position themselves, and the likelihood of them passing these disadvantages to their offspring are very high.[44] However, some evidence has been presented showing that immigrant competition has hurt the labour market opportunities of low-skilled nationals.[45] It is necessary to invoke the American example, although it has received substantial criticism, of estimating the impact of immigration by comparing labour market outcomes across cities. Card enlists three major problems connected to the cross-market approach:

1. An increase in the proportion of immigrants within a city does not necessarily raise the supply of low-skilled labour since nationals may move out in response to immigrant inflows.
2. Cross-sectional correlation between immigrant inflows and native wages may be upward-biased by local demand shocks that raise wages and attract in-migrants.
3. In the longer term, an immigration-induced increase in the supply of labour to a particular city can be diffused across the economy by intercity trade.[46]

6.2. ECONOMIC CONSEQUENCES

Researchers argue that the economic impact of migration is not uniform, especially with regard to economic growth, productivity and poverty alleviation alike. In order to understand why migration can have such a different impact in different areas, it must be understood that migration primarily has to do with the local context of migration, the nature of that migration and the intensity of the migration flows.[47] Yet, the short-term impact of migration is likely to be negative, as it may increase public sector spending.

For instance, reserves that were once intended to be used for the general community's health, education, housing and so on, may be spent differently, especially relating to the new influx of immigrants and their respective needs. Moreover, there has been speculation that a surge in the number of refugees may have an adverse effect on households. Specifically, this would relate to living standards, which may deteriorate, especially in semi- and unskilled labour sectors, due to depressed wages and higher prices. This is, of course, not considering the negative environmental impact on urban areas. Notwithstanding the negative impact on living conditions and such, the EU reports clearly

44 G.J. Borjas, *supra* n. 40.
45 D. Card, 'Immigrant Inflows, Native Outflows, and the Local Labor Market Impacts of Higher Immigration' (2001) 19(1) *J. Econ.* 22.
46 *Ibid.*
47 *Ibid.*

indicate that in the short run the focus has to remain on implementing effective management mechanisms. With such mechanisms in place, migrants can improve the flexibility and performance of the labour market as well as fiscal stability.[48] Regardless, a positive economic impact may be seen in the future, as economists argue that a large influx of refugees should not be perceived as an obligation or a threat – but rather as an opportunity.[49]

7. CONCLUSION

There is no question that immigration and migration in today's world has a vast impact on a host country's economic and labour markets, its society, its policies and any pre-existing migration issues the host country already faces. As this chapter has illustrated, migration has continued to steadily rise in the recent years and, because it has reached such a rapid pace, countries have been forced to adjust 'on the fly' as opposed to being able to gradually implement a system that will provide better results for the greater good.

Further, domestic labour markets will inevitably feel the effect of an influx of immigrants, as the markets will become overpopulated and the price of labour will be brought down. However, in the long term, immigrants may have a positive effect on a host country's GDP on the basis that, while immigrants may use many resources at the beginning, their 'demand' and dependency on the host country will likely decrease, thereby turning the immigrants into persons who contribute to the host country's GDP and ultimate growth. While there is, however, the potential for growth in the long term, large immigration numbers may prove to be costly on a host country in the short term, causing the country to suffer heavily due to depletion of the social security systems or causing chaos at the borders, thereby possibly decreasing seasonal income from tourism.

All in all, it is quite evident that the global rise in immigration numbers has affected many countries in various ways, whether it is through GDP alone, impact on the labour markets, or by affecting the previous policies that the nation had in place regarding immigration. It would be advantageous for host nations to develop new policies promptly in order to handle the rapid increase of immigrants adequately, as evidenced throughout history. Additionally, host countries must take into account how their policies going forward will affect the future growth and development of the nation as a whole, as well as how that nation's internal growth will affect today's globalised society.

---

48 An Economic Take on the Refugee Crisis – A Macroeconomic Assessment for the EU, p. 21, <https://ec.europa.eu/info/sites/info/files/file_import/ip033_en_2.pdf> accessed 31.01.2018.

49 J. Portes, 'Immigration Is Good for Economic Growth. If Europe Gets It Right, Refugees Can Be Too', <https://www.huffingtonpost.com/jonathan-portes/economic-europe-refugees_b_8128288.html> accessed 31.01.2018.

INVITED CONTRIBUTION

5. HAS THE MIGRATION CRISIS CHALLENGED THE CONCEPT OF THE PROTECTION OF THE HUMAN RIGHTS OF MIGRANTS? THE CASE OF *ILIAS AND AHMED V. HUNGARY*

Tímea DRINÓCZI* and Ágoston MOHAY**

1. INTRODUCTION

In this chapter, we try to – partly – answer the question that the editors have raised when laying down the concept of this volume, namely whether the increased presence of migrants and asylum seekers among the population of a country and the legal responses to this phenomenon has challenged the commonly accepted notions of democracy, the rule of law and fundamental rights in Europe. In recent years, across Europe and also in the Hungarian political sphere (which in turn strongly influences and determines the legislative activity of the Hungarian Parliament), migration is conceptualised as a threat to national security and public safety. This narrative has called for, and resulted in, the introduction of special measures, including the establishment of the 'crisis situation caused by mass-migration' and the modification of the laws on migration, the criminal procedure and the criminal codes, among other responses.

In this chapter we reflect on the question whether the migration crisis has challenged the human rights protection of migrants, with a particular focus on the Hungarian national context. We start with a hypothesis that the said crisis has caused a tendency to restrict the enjoyment of human rights in Hungary. The analysis of whether or not such a tendency exists requires examination of both national legislation and the jurisprudence of national and international courts. For the scope of this short chapter, we will restrict ourselves to a critical

* Faculty of Law, University of Pécs, Hungary. E-mail: drinoczi.timea@ajk.pte.hu.
** Faculty of Law, University of Pécs, Hungary. E-mail: mohay.agoston@ajk.pte.hu.

overview of the most relevant elements of the current Hungarian legislation on incoming migrants in light of a recent relevant judgment of the European Court of Human Rights (ECtHR), namely *Ilias and Ahmed v. Hungary* (2017),[1] in which the Court ruled against Hungary.

2. MIGRATION IN HUNGARY: THE *STATUS QUO*

2.1. RECENT DEVELOPMENTS IN THE HUNGARIAN REGULATION OF MIGRATION

Even before the *Ilias and Ahmed v. Hungary* judgment, there were several critical views expressed about the recent Hungarian rules intended to address the migration situation, culminating in the summer of 2015. These criticisms may be classified as follows. On the one hand, some of them challenged the constitutionality of the new 'crisis situation caused by mass-migration' (*tömeges bevándorlás okozta válsághelyzet* in Hungarian).[2] On the other hand, other commentators contested the existence (or, in any case, the unavailability) of data which allegedly justified the introduction of this crisis situation and, later on, its extension to the entire territory of Hungary.[3] Non-governmental organisations (NGOs) argued that some of the new rules are either unconstitutional or are in a clear breach of international obligations as they infringe human rights.[4] They further claimed that, from 2015, as a result of the new and modified legal acts, *inter alia*:[5]

- the institutional independence of the judiciary is questionable;
- property rights are affected and some environmental legal obligations do not need to be complied with;
- the law-making competences of the government have been extended;
- new related criminal offences have been created; and
- due process is not properly guaranteed and, in particular, the right to a legal remedy is no longer fully respected.

---

1 ECtHR, Case of *Ilias and Ahmed v. Hungary* (Application no. 47287/15), judgment, 14.03.2017.

2 T. Drinóczi, 'Special Legal Orders; Challenges and Solutions' (2016) 4 *Osteuropa Recht* 420. The first part of the description of the Hungarian laws in this chapter relies on this paper to a great extent.

3 Magyar Helsinki Bizottság, 'Tíz évre titkosították, miért is van most válsághelyzet' (05.04.2017). (The blog post of the Hungarian Helsinki Committee details the issue that the data underlying the introduction of the crisis situation has been declared classified for a period of 10 years.), <http://helsinkifigyelo.blog.hu/2016/04/05/tiz_evre_titkositottak_mitol_is_van_most_valsaghelyzet?utm_source=mandiner&utm_medium=link&utm_campaign=mandiner_migracio_201604> accessed 18.07.2017.

4 European Commission, 'Commission opens infringement procedure against Hungary concerning its asylum law' (Press release IP/15/6228), <http://europa.eu/rapid/press-release_IP-15-6228_en.htm> accessed 18.07.2017.

5 *Ibid.*

The last point raised requires a note of explanation. Applicants who are appealing against a decision rejecting an asylum or immigration application have been deprived of a right to refer to new facts and circumstances in the appeal proceedings and decisions are not automatically suspended in the case of appeals. The non-suspension of these proceedings means in practice that such applicants are effectively forced to leave the territory of Hungary before the time limit for lodging an appeal expires, or before an appeal has been heard. Moreover, in the judicial review of decisions rejecting an asylum application, a personal hearing of the applicants is optional. Finally, judicial decisions are taken by court secretaries/trainee judges (a sub-judicial level), which may raise the suspicion that institutional judicial independence is lacking.[6]

2.2. THE PUBLIC PERCEPTION OF MIGRANTS IN HUNGARY

Before embarking on our legal analysis, let us see first, what happened in early 2015 where Hungary faced an unprecedented influx of migrants entering its territory, legally or not. Table 1 presents a few statistics to illustrate this point.

Table 1. Irregular migration and requests for asylum in Hungary (2014–2015)

	July 2014	July 2015	January–July 2014	January–July 2015
Irregular border crossings	2,024	38,432	8,689	166,626
People smuggling	41	73	294	603
Applications for refugee status	1,258	19,480	5,382	72,200

Source: Hungarian Police.

Despite these data, no action was taken during the spring of 2015 in order to deal with the migration crisis through regulatory means. Instead, at the time, the Hungarian government started an internal, politically motivated and defensive anti-migration billboard campaign, and a so-called 'national consultation'.[7] It clearly neglected the fact that eventually people would reach the border and would enter the territory of Hungary in order to reach Western Europe. The billboard campaign and the 'national consultation' were successful political tools used to make the Hungarian population fearful of migration, or at least

6 The situation is complicated even further as the involvement of court secretaries/trainee judges in judicial decisions is permitted by the Fundamental Law itself. Due to the extra work-load of courts, newly appointed judges are allocated to this court.

7 See the Annex in this chapter, *National Consultation on Immigration and Terrorism*, published by the Prime Minister's Office (2015).

to develop increasingly negative attitudes thereto due to economic and security reasons. In particular, this latter consideration was stressed after the Cologne attack on New Year's Eve[8] and the subsequent terror attacks in Europe at the beginning of 2016.[9] The billboard campaign warned prospective migrants, at that time called 'economic migrants', in the Hungarian language, not to come to the country and not to take away the jobs of the Hungarians and, should they come, to observe Hungarian laws. In the public discourse, 'migrants' are constantly called 'illegal migrants', combining illegality and migration, and the term 'refugee' is seldom used – rather, it is avoided.

Against this background, the 'national consultation' questionnaire successfully combined the fear of losing employment and heightened security threats by implying their interconnectedness.[10] Those irregularly arriving in Hungary who committed crimes, such as thefts of food or otherwise damaging property, received huge media coverage.[11] Under these circumstances, it is not surprising that according to the Spring 2016 Global Attitudes Survey,[12] although many Europeans were concerned with security and economic repercussions of the refugee crisis, Hungarians made it to the top of the list, despite no terror attack having taken place in Hungary and Hungary being neither the destination country for migration nor a Mediterranean country. Hungarians scored highest in relation to the statements that 'refugees will increase the likelihood of

---

8 LiveLeak: 'Hungary's Orban Blasts "Dying" Europe for Migrant Crisis Self Denial' (31.01.2016), <http://www.liveleak.com/view?i=919_1454266501> accessed 18.07.2017.

9 The result was even a constitutional amendment on how to deal with a terror threat. See the Sixth Amendment to the Fundamental Law (14.06.2016), *Magyar Közlöny* [Official Journal] nr. 86 (2016).

10 See especially questions 3 and 6. As for public security reasons, beyond terror threats, there was no data supporting the assumption that public safety would be jeopardised by foreigners. According to the Prosecutor General's report from 2012, the figures were as follows: crimes committed: 472,236; crimes committed by foreign citizens: 4,756 (which is less than 1 per cent, although 60 per cent of this 1 per cent of perpetrators were citizens of neighbouring countries). It meant a total of 0.001 per cent of crimes, mostly burglary, were committed by foreigners. This is a figure which should have been the basis of any communication of public safety.

11 About the problem of the media freedom and neutrality see e.g. the Freedom House's country reports on Hungary. Freedom House, *Report (2015)*, <https://freedomhouse.org/report/freedom-press/2015/hungary> accessed 18.07.2017. Selection of key developments in 2016: 'In August, a leaked memo revealed that a public agency had instructed public television workers to avoid showing images of women and children in their coverage of the refugee crisis. In September, Hungarian police reportedly attacked at least seven international journalists covering the refugee crisis.' Freedom House, *Report (2016)*, <https://freedomhouse.org/report/freedom-press/2016/hungary> accessed 18.07.2017.

12 R. Wike, B. Stokes and K. Simmons, 'Europeans Fear Wave of Refugees Will Mean More Terrorism, Fewer Jobs. Sharp ideological divides across EU on views about minorities, diversity and national identity', p. 3, <http://www.pewglobal.org/files/2016/07/Pew-Research-Center-EU-Refugees-and-National-Identity-Report-FINAL-July-11-2016.pdf> accessed 18.07.2017.

terrorism in our country' (76 per cent), 'refugees are a burden on our country because they take our jobs and social benefits' (82 per cent) and 'refugees in our country are more to blame for crime than other groups' (43 per cent).[13]

It seems that it was not the Hungarian society that demanded stringent legislation towards migration in the first place but, rather, it was politically motivated. This motivation has subsequently been reflected in the public perception, and its formal engagement by political actors came after this. It is thus not surprising that there is not much public indignation regarding the treatment of migrants, save for NGOs and some private persons who have always been supportive towards the situation of migrants, especially in respect of their living conditions and the protection of their human rights.

2.3. HUNGARIAN LEGISLATION ON MIGRATION CLOSED THE STATE'S BORDERS *DE FACTO* AND *DE JURE*

The Hungarian government took formal regulatory action in late 2015 where proposals for legislative measures[14] were submitted to the Parliament in August, and adopted on 4 and 21 September 2015, respectively. These acts established both the *factual* and *legal* closure of Hungarian borders. By erecting the fence, the border was *de facto* closed, and – furthermore – by adopting modifications to, among others, procedural and criminal laws, borders were sealed *de jure*.

Pursuant to these laws, the so-called 'crisis situation caused by mass-migration' was introduced.[15] In concrete terms, a crisis situation is deemed to exist if the number of asylum seekers arriving in Hungary exceeds either an average of 500 per day over a month, an average of 750 per day over two consecutive weeks, or an average of 800 per day over a week. Additionally, a crisis situation may be declared if a situation related to migration emerges which poses a direct threat to public safety and the maintenance of law and order in a settlement, or poses a direct threat to public health.[16] The relevant governmental decree on this situation remains in force for a maximum period of six months, but its term may be extended if the circumstances that gave rise to it persist. Since the entry into force of the Act establishing the crisis situation caused by

13 Just to offer a comparative perspective, in those countries, which indeed have a high migrant population and have already suffered terror attacks, these figures are as follows: Germany: 61 per cent, 31 per cent, 35 per cent, France: 46 per cent, 53 per cent, 27 per cent.

14 Act CXL of 2015, *Magyar Közlöny* [Official Journal] nr. 124 (2015) and Act CXLIII of 2015, *Magyar Közlöny* [Official Journal] nr. 124 (2015).

15 For more specific rules, where the text of the translation of the rules introduced by Act CXL of 2015, see, <http://www.kormany.hu/en/prime-minister-s-office/news/government-declares-state-of-crisis-due-to-mass-migration-in-two-counties> accessed 18.07.2017.

16 This last provision will be applicable particularly if a disturbance or violence occurs at a reception centre or any other facility serving to shelter foreigners in a settlement or on its outskirts. As can be seen, it is quite a vague definition.

mass-migration, the crisis situation has not been cancelled but extended to the entire country, most recently until 7 March 2018, even though none of the conditions have been met.

The extension of the crisis situation raises doubts as to its legality. Therefore, when the crisis situation was extended for the first time in March 2016 to the entire country, the Helsinki Committee (Budapest) asked the Police and Immigration Office to make public the data and figures that were used to justify this extension. The Helsinki Committee based their request on available data, which showed that migration had in fact significantly slowed down and reduced in numbers. The Helsinki Committee justifiably took the position that the statutory preconditions for introducing the crisis situation had not been met. Such data and figures should be treated as public data pursuant to the Act on freedom of information,[17] yet the authorities categorised the data as classified. Therefore the Helsinki Committee was obliged to submit a petition to the National Data Protection and Freedom of Information Agency.[18] Finally, the issue of secrecy versus accessibility was essentially resolved by the Ministry of Justice one year later, in April 2017. The Ministry of Justice ordered the authorities to provide the data requested, as the interest of classification of the data was outweighed by the public interest of access to information. According to this document,[19] the number of irregular migrants (illegally entered into Hungary) between 15 September 2015 (entering into force of the law) and 4 March 2016 (last available data before the receipt of the request for information had arrived) was as shown in Table 2.

Table 2. Number of irregular migrants entering Hungary between 15 September 2015 and 4 March 2016

	In total	**Per day**
15 September–31 December 2015	189,720	1,762.2
1–31 January 2016	502	16.1
1–29 February 2016	2,290	78.9
1 January–4 March 2016	3,379	52.79

Source: Helsinki Committee, Response from Police and Immigration Office, <http://www.helsinki.hu/wp-content/uploads/valsag_anonim.pdf> accessed 03.08.2017.

It is interesting to note that the authorities did not take any proactive measures regarding the response to the right to information: they did not provide any additional data that was not included in the original request. Thus, we do not

17 Act CXII of 2011 on Informational Self-determination and Freedom of Information.
18 Magyar Helsinki Bizottság, *supra* n. 3.
19 Helsinki Committee, Response from Police and Immigration Office, <http://www.helsinki.hu/wp-content/uploads/valsag_anonim.pdf> accessed 03.08.2017.

have any further information about the legality of the extension of the crisis situation until September 2017, even though the right to access to this kind of data has already been acknowledged.

Furthermore, the Criminal Procedure Act (CPA) (1998)[20] was modified in the wake of legislative actions of 2015. As a result, it rendered the following provisions of the CPA inapplicable to migrants:

- translation of the indictment or its parts relating to the accused person into their mother tongue, national or regional language, which has to be submitted to the court along with the original indictment;
- translation of the court's ruling or decision or parts relating to the convicted person into that person's mother tongue, national or regional language, which also has to be delivered to the person concerned;
- rules regarding minors (in a regular procedure this would cover the following: taking the age of accused into consideration; involvement of a school teacher in the court proceedings as a lay member of the court; limited pre-trial detention; when deciding the execution of the sentence, judge decides on its place and method taking age into account; in correctional facilities, minors are separated from adults; and waiving of trial is not an option).

As it will be demonstrated by the judgment analysed below, some of these concerns raised by NGOs and the European Commission, and the questionable provisions of the CPA mentioned above were justified seeing that the ECtHR ruled against Hungary. The relevant national law applicable in the case of *Ilias and Ahmed* was the Asylum Act and the Immigration Act as modified by the CPA.[21] These statutes *inter alia* contain the principle of safe third country, rules on persons deserving special treatment and the principle of *non-refoulement*, the recognition of the Geneva Convention, the rights of the person seeking international protection, rules on asylum detention, admissibility and inadmissibility of the application for refugee status, and the role of the asylum authority. One of the decrees of the government[22] on the definition of safe countries of origin and safe third countries is also a crucially important source of law in the case at hand as it defines Serbia as a 'safe third country'[23] despite several reports and recommendations stating the opposite.[24]

20 Act XIX of 1998, CPA, *Magyar Közlöny* [Official Journal] nr. 23 (1998). See for an English translation, <https://ihl-databases.icrc.org/applic/ihl/ihl-nat.nsf/0/033d3f79294dc84ec1257163002cd383/$FILE/Act%20XIX%20of%201998.pdf> accessed 18.07.2017.

21 Act CXL of 2015, *supra* n. 14.

22 Government Decree 191/2015 (VII. 21), *Magyar Közlöny* [Official Journal] nr. 106 (2015).

23 Case of *Ilias and Ahmed v. Hungary*, paras. 31–33.

24 *Ibid.*, paras. 36–43. It may be noted that the European Commission recommended that Serbia be placed on a common EU-level list of safe countries of origin (cf. COM(2015) 452 final); however, the concepts of 'safe country of origin' and 'safe third country' are not the same in

3. THE *ILIAS AND AHMED* CASE

Mr Ilias and Mr Ahmed, two Bangladeshi nationals, arrived in Hungary on 15 September 2015 following transit through Pakistan, Iran and Turkey; they entered the territory of the European Union (EU) in Greece,[25] from where they travelled through Macedonia to Serbia. They finally arrived in the Röszke transit zone situated on the border between Hungary and Serbia.[26] According to the Hungarian regulations, they were required to stay inside the transit zone and were not allowed to leave travelling in the direction of Hungary. Their asylum applications (they first applied for asylum in Hungary) were rejected by the authorities as inadmissible on the grounds that Serbia was to be considered a 'safe third country' according to Government Decree No. 191/2015 (VII.21.). As a result the Hungarian asylum authority ordered the expulsion of the applicants from Hungary.[27] After unsuccessfully exhausting the internal legal remedy available, the applicants decided to take their case before the ECtHR in Strasbourg. The applicants essentially claimed that Hungary had violated their rights under Article 3 (prohibition of inhuman or degrading treatment – in relation to the reception conditions at the transit zone), Article 5 (right to liberty and security – in relation to the rules on leaving the transit zone), and Article 13 (right to an effective remedy) of the European Convention on Human Rights (ECHR).[28]

3.1. VIOLATION OF ARTICLE 3 ECHR

The ECtHR found that the reception conditions in the transit zone were not in contravention of Article 3 ECHR. The Court relied *inter alia* on a recent report by the European Committee for the Prevention of Torture and Inhuman or Degrading Treatment or Punishment (CPT), which had evaluated the conditions in the transit zone as acceptable; based on this assessment the Court considered that the living quarters and the sanitary and medical facilities were satisfactory.[29]

---

asylum law. See e.g. S. Peers, 'Safe Countries of Origin: Assessing the New Proposal', *EU Law Analysis*, 14 September 2015, <http://eulawanalysis.blogspot.hu/2015/09/safe-countries-of-origin-assessing-new.html> accessed 18.07.2017.

25 It seems from available data that the applicants did not ask for asylum in Greece, and have presumably not come into contact with Greek authorities. The Dublin transfer possibility was not raised in the legal dispute at all.

26 Case of *Ilias and Ahmed v. Hungary*, paras. 9–10.

27 *Ibid.*, para. 15.

28 The case has interesting connotations as to the relationship between EU law obligations and compliance with the ECHR as well, but this aspect will not be analysed in this chapter.

29 Case of *Ilias and Ahmed v. Hungary*, paras. 84–88. The ECtHR noted that there was, of course, 'an inevitable element of suffering and humiliation' involved in any custodial measure (see *Stanev v. Bulgaria*, Application no. 36760/06, para 204), but reminded that in itself, this will not automatically entail a violation of Art. 3.

The situation in the transit zone was thus neither inhuman nor degrading and did not amount to a violation of Article 3.

As regards Article 13, the applicants complained that there was no domestic remedy whatsoever at their disposal to complain about the standards of reception prevailing at the transit zone. The Court had to consider this claim regardless of whether the conditions were problematic or not, as this right is meant to guarantee an important procedural safeguard for individuals: the complaints raised by the applicants were not manifestly ill-founded and 'raised serious questions of fact and law' which required an examination as to the merits. The ECtHR found a violation of Article 13 (in conjunction with Article 3), as the Hungarian authorities had not indicated or made available any remedies by which the applicants could have submitted complaints as regards the conditions in the transit.

The Court did hold that there had been a violation of Article 3 with regard to the expulsion of the applicants to Serbia. The expulsion was based on the relevant Government Decree listing Serbia as a safe third country, establishing a presumption in this respect. The Court noted that Serbia had not automatically been considered as a safe third country by Hungary (in accordance with reports of various international institutions on Serbia) until 2015. The ECtHR also took into account the condemning evaluations of the asylum situation in Serbia by the United Nations High Commissioner for Refugees (UNHCR).[30] One of the main concerns with the expulsion to Serbia was, according to the Court, the risk of chain-*refoulement*.[31] Taking into account the practice of the relevant countries, it seemed very likely that the applicants would be expelled from Serbia to Macedonia, and finally to Greece, where they would face inhuman or degrading treatment due to the (still) quite serious shortcomings in the Greek asylum system (a possibility which the Hungarian authorities did not seek to rule out during the procedure).[32] Furthermore, the Court held that during the

30 Case of *Ilias and Ahmed v. Hungary*, para. 120. For the UNHCR report see: UN High Commissioner for Refugees, 'Hungary as a Country of Asylum. Observations on Restrictive Legal Measures and Subsequent Practice Implemented Between July 2015 and March 2016', <http://www.refworld.org/docid/57319d514.html> accessed 10.07.2017.

31 Chain-*refoulement* means subsequent *refoulement* of an asylum seeker by different states; i.e. a situation where even if *refoulement* of the asylum seeker is not a risk in the initial receiving state, but *refoulement* is likely to occur in a subsequent receiving state further along the 'chain' of expulsion. See N. Frenzen, 'Extraterritorial Refugee Protection' in A. Nollkaemper and I. Plakokefalos (eds.), *The Practice of Shared Responsibility in International Law*, Cambridge University Press, Cambridge 2017, p. 511. Regardless of certain criticisms in legal literature, chain-*refoulement* is a violation of international law in the same way that a (for lack of a better word) 'simple' *refoulement* is. See T. Molnár, 'The Principle of Non-Refoulement Under International Law: Its Inception and Evolution in a Nutshell' (2016) 1 *Corvinus Journal of International Affairs* 57.

32 Case of *Ilias and Ahmed v. Hungary*, paras. 121–23. The ECtHR noted that there seemed to be an 'improvement in the treatment of asylum-seekers in Greece conducive to the

asylum procedure, the applicants were provided with insufficient information.[33] Thus, due to inadequate procedural safeguards, the Court found a breach of Article 3, taking into account the real risk of the applicants being subjected to inhuman or degrading treatment.

3.2. VIOLATION OF ARTICLE 5 ECHR

The most thought-provoking part of the judgment is the interpretation of the situation in the transit zone in light of Article 5 ECHR. The applicants complained in this regard that their committal to the transit zone amounted to a deprivation of liberty devoid of any legal basis. The main argument of the Hungarian government was that since the applicants had been free to leave the territory of the transit zone in the direction of Serbia, they had not been deprived of their personal liberty at all; the government thus contested the admissibility of this claim.[34] The Court, after reiterating the objective and subjective factors for the assessment of restriction or deprivation of liberty from its case law, noted that the applicants were confined for over three weeks to the border zone in a guarded compound which could not be accessed from the outside, not even by their lawyer, and the applicants did not have the opportunity to enter Hungarian territory beyond the zone. The Court was of the view that – as applicants did not *choose* to stay in the transit zone – it could not be said that they had validly consented to being deprived of their liberty.[35] According to the jurisprudence of the ECtHR, the fact that it was possible for the applicants to leave voluntarily did not rule out an infringement of the right to liberty.[36]

---

gradual resumption of transfers to the country', yet this was not the case at the material time. Accordingly, the *ratio decidendi* of *M.S.S. v. Belgium and Greece*, Application no. 30696/09 still applies.

33 The applicants received a leaflet on the procedure but they were both illiterate. Furthermore, one of the applicants was, by mistake, interviewed in a language he did not understand. A translation of the decision in their case was produced (to their lawyer) only two months after the relevant decision had been taken, when the applicants were already outside Hungary: Case of *Ilias and Ahmed v. Hungary*, para. 124.

34 *Ibid.*, para. 49.

35 *Ibid.*, para. 54.

36 In *Amuur v. France*, Application no. 19776/92, the Court found that holding the applicants in the transit zone of Paris-Orly Airport was equivalent in practice, in view of the restrictions suffered, to a deprivation of liberty. The Court found that the mere fact that it is possible for asylum seekers voluntarily to leave the country where they wish to take refuge cannot exclude a restriction on liberty; furthermore, this possibility 'becomes theoretical if no other country offering protection comparable to the protection they expect to find in the country where they are seeking asylum is inclined or prepared to take them in' (para. 48). The same was held in the Case of *Riad and Idiab v. Belgium* (Applications nos. 29787/03 and 29810/03, para. 68). (Note that an earlier decision by the European Commission on Human Rights held in a similar situation that there was no deprivation of liberty as the applicants were entitled to

In accordance with Hungarian asylum law, if the applicants had left Hungarian territory, their applications for refugee status would have been terminated without an examination on the merits; and the applicants could not have left the transit zone in the direction of Serbia without the risk of refoulement. So accordingly, the confinement of the applicants to the transit zone amounted to a *de facto* deprivation of liberty, and the Court examined this claim on the merits as well.[37]

Article 5(1) ECHR requires that any detention be lawful and in accordance with a procedure prescribed by law; no detention shall be arbitrary. In the case at hand, the 23-day detention of Ilias and Ahmed was based, according to the Hungarian government, on sections 71/A(1)–(2) of the Asylum Act. These provisions refer back to section 5 of the Act, which states that asylum seekers have a right to stay in the territory of Hungary according to the conditions set out in the Act, and at a place of accommodation designated by the asylum authority. The Court ascertained that the national measure, under these circumstances, amounted to deprivation of liberty (irrespective of its classification in national law), yet found it 'quite difficult to identify in the provisions at hand any reference to the possibility of detention at the transit zone'.[38]

The applicants were deprived of their liberty without a formal decision, by virtue of an elastically interpreted general provision of the law; this practice did not comply with Article 5 ECHR and the relevant case law of the Court, and thus the ECtHR ascertained a violation of the right to liberty and security.[39]

4. EVALUATION OF THE IMPLICATIONS OF THE *ILIAS AND AHMED* CASE

The *Ilias and Ahmed* case demonstrates a clash between conflicting approaches to the migration and asylum crisis. On the one hand, the Hungarian approach to the situation, which notably manifests *inter alia* in a stringent border and asylum regime, places sovereignty and national security, as perceived by the government, at the forefront. This resulted, as we have seen, in insufficient procedural safeguards and, according to the ECtHR, a form of detention which is incompatible with

leave the state's territory at any time in the Case of *Saardi, Mourad and Semaan Mel-Tabah v. Austria* (Application no. 190066/91 [1992], not reported), analysed in P. Van Dijk and G.J.H. Hoof, *Theory and Practice of the European Convention on Human Rights*, 3rd ed., Kluwer Law International, The Hague 1998, p. 347. This Commission ruling had not been unanimously accepted and had already been criticised before the Court reconsidered this type of situation in *Amuur v. France*. (See C. Giakoumopoulos, 'Detention of Asylum Seekers in the light of Article 5 of the European Convention on Human Rights' in J. Hughes and F. Liebaut (eds.), *Detention of Asylum Seekers in Europe: Analysis and Perspectives*, Martinus Nijhoff Publishers, The Hague 1998, p. 169).

37 Case of *Ilias and Ahmed v. Hungary*, paras. 55–56.

38 *Ibid.*, paras. 65–66.

39 *Ibid.*, para. 68.

the Convention. It must be acknowledged of course that the Court cannot but approach the case at hand from the starting point of human rights.

The question can however be raised – as the editors of this volume have done – whether the intensity of the current situation has led, or will lead, to a more restrictive approach to human rights. After all, only four rights in the Convention are absolute (and thus cannot be restricted in a justifiable way);[40] also, the Court views the ECHR as a living instrument which must be interpreted in the light of contemporary circumstances[41] and the margin of appreciation doctrine provides some room for manoeuvre to national authorities.[42] The Court chose to uphold the level of protection of the rights at issue, obviously partly due to the absolute nature of the prohibition enshrined in Article 3.[43] In particular, the judgment is in line with the previous jurisprudence of the Court, reaffirming its earlier conclusions regarding 'international zones' as *quasi*-detention areas as well as the findings of the *M.S.S. v. Belgium and Greece* case,[44] and apart from condemning the Hungarian regulations, sent a rather clear message to Serbia as well.[45]

The *Ilias and Ahmed* judgment has been appealed by the Hungarian government.[46] It will be interesting to see how the Grand Chamber of the ECtHR interprets the case, although we find a reversal rather unlikely in light of the Court's consistent jurisprudence.

---

40 These are the right not to be tortured or to be inhumanly or degradingly treated or punished (Art. 3); the right not to be held in slavery or servitude (Art. 4(1)); the right not to be convicted for conduct which was not an offence at the time it occurred and the right not to have a heavier penalty imposed for an offence than the one applicable at the time the offence was committed (Art. 7(1)). See S. Greer, *The Margin of Appreciation: Interpretation and Discretion under the European Convention on Human Rights*, Council of Europe Publishing, Strasbourg 2000, p. 27.

41 A. Mowbray, *Cases, Materials, and Commentary on the European Convention on Human Right*, 3rd ed., Oxford University Press, Oxford 2012, p. 42.

42 Although the doctrine is mentioned neither in the ECHR nor its *travaux perparatoires*. See S. Greer, *supra* n. 40, p. 5.

43 The margin of appreciation has had a very limited role as regards Art. 5 as well. See J. Schokkenbroek, 'The Basis, Nature and Application of the Margin of Appreciation Doctrine in the Case-Law of the European Court of Human Rights' (1998) 19 *Human Rights Law Journal* 34.

44 As is known, in the *M.S.S.* case, the ECtHR found a violation of the Convention (Art. 3) by Greece and Belgium; the applicant in the case was transferred from Belgium to Greece as a result of the application of the 'Dublin II' Regulation of the EU. The *M.S.S.* case was later also referenced by the European Court of Justice, and may be considered as a catalyst for the reform of the Dublin Regulation. See P. Mallia, 'Case of M.S.S. v. Belgium and Greece: A Catalyst in the Re-thinking of the Dublin II Regulation' (2011) 30 *Refugee Survey Quarterly* 107.

45 P. Kilibarda, 'The ECtHR's Ilias and Ahmed v. Hungary and Why It Matters', *EJIL: Talk!* 20.03.2017, <https://www.ejiltalk.org/the-ecthrs-ilias-and-ahmed-v-hungary-and-why-it-matters/> accessed 18.07.2017.

46 Migrációkutató Intézet, 'Az Emberi Jogok Európai Bírósága Ilias és Ahmed kontra Magyarország ügyben hozott döntésének elemzése' [Analysis of the Ilias and Ahmed judgment by the think tank Migrációkutató Intézet], <https://www.migraciokutato.hu/hu/2017/03/27/az-emberi-jogok-europai-birosaga-ilias-es-ahmed-kontra-magyaroszag-ugyben-hozott-dontesenek-elemzese/> accessed 18.07.2017.

5. CONCLUDING REMARKS

Migration and asylum affairs have always had a security-related dimension (regarding the EU, one only needs to refer to the decades-long debate about the notion of 'Fortress Europe'),[47] and this dimension has come to the forefront due to the 'crisis-like' migration influx that peaked in 2015 but is still heavily on the European agenda, and it would not be too difficult to argue that the 2016 EU–Turkey migration deal is also centred around security instead of human rights;[48] the 'securitised' approach[49] further includes suggestions that asylum claims should be processed outside the territory of the EU.[50]

However, at the level of human rights institutions we have not seen a change in trend. States Parties to the ECHR are not realistically planning on leaving the Council of Europe and abandoning the common human rights heritage embodied in the ECHR. Compliance with Strasbourg judgments has also not changed in essence, regardless of the existence of ongoing delays or problems with implementation,[51] and certain (either politically motivated or technical) challenges to the authority of the Court's case law.[52] It is interesting to note that

---

47 The term 'Fortress Europe' is usually understood as meaning the legal measures aimed at preventing any irregular (economic) migration to Europe, while not providing sufficient accessible legal migratory avenues into the EU. (See e.g. Amnesty International, *The Human Cost of Fortress Europe: Human Rights Violations against Migrants and Refugees at Europe's Borders*, Amnesty International 2014, pp. 9–19.) Whether this notion is true, and whether it is a positive or a negative approach, has been debated in legal (and social sciences) literature for decades; for an early overview see A. Geddes, *Immigration and European Integration: Towards Fortress Europe?*, Manchester University Press, Manchester 2000.

48 For an analysis of the related risks see: J. Poon, 'EU–Turkey Deal: Violation of, or Consistency with, International Law?' (2016) 1(3) *European Papers* 1195, <http://www.europeanpapers.eu/en/system/files/pdf_version/EP_EF_2016_I_054_Jenny_Poon.pdf> accessed 18 July 2017.

49 For more on this issue in relation to Hungarian asylum policy in the context of EU law obligations see B. Nagy, 'Hungarian Asylum Law and Policy in 2015–2016: Securitization Instead of Loyal Cooperation' (2016) 17(6) *German Law Journal* 1033.

50 The possibility of processing asylum claims outside EU territory was potentially and indirectly alluded to even by the European Commission in the 2015 Migration Agenda (COM(2015) 240 final), though to be fair the final wording of the Agenda on this issue ended up much less concrete and much more cautious then a previously leaked version of the text; the UK has spoken in favour of such a solution, as have Hungary and most recently Austria. The UNHCR has also not excluded the possibility that multilateral cooperation in this regard could be possible. For analysis see A. Liguori, *The Extraterritorial Processing of Asylum Claims*, Jean Monnet Centre of Excellence on Migrants' Rights in the Mediterranean 2015, pp. 1–12, especially at pp. 2–5, <http://www.jmcemigrants.eu/jmce/wp-content/uploads/2015/07/The-Extraterritorial-Processing-of-Asylum-Claims-LIGUORI.pdf> accessed 18.07.2017.

51 See in this regard, Parliamentary Assembly of the Council of Europe, *Report on the Implementation of Judgments of the European Court of Human Rights* (09.09.2015), Doc. 13864.

52 Steering Committee for Human Rights (CDDH), *Report on the Longer-Term Future of the System of the European Convention on Human Rights*, 11.12.2015 (CDDH(2015)R84 Addendum I), pp. 31–59.

the 'infringement' mechanism of the Convention (cf. Article 46(3)–(5)) is still yet to be used by the Committee of Ministers; utilising it may assist in increasing the effectiveness of the implementation of the Court's judgments, and the provisions could potentially even be amended by the States Parties to introduce more effective sanctions.[53]

In *Ilias and Ahmed*, the ECtHR came to the conclusion that the detention of the applicants occurred *de facto*, as a matter of practical arrangement rather than based on a formal decision with reasoning; instead, the authorities deprived the applicants of their liberty 'by virtue of an elastically interpreted general provision of the law'.[54] Furthermore, due to the lack of any formal decision on their detention, the applicants were unable to challenge the lawfulness of the measure, and thus Article 5(4) ECHR was also infringed.

We find that even the most current challenges have not altered the approaches and attitudes towards human rights, and so the mainstream ethos has been and will be upheld: the existing rights and standards are, in principle, appropriate for the handling of current emergency or crisis situations, and no reinterpretation is necessary or warranted. Even though this latter statement was formulated by the Venice Commission in 2006,[55] and was not focused specifically on migration but on emergency situations, outside the scope of this chapter, we think that recalling this position is both worthwhile and legitimate. This is despite such reinterpretation being strongly demanded by some political actors.

---

53 *Report on the Implementation of Judgments of the European Court of Human Rights*, *supra* n. 51, p. 18.

54 Case of *Ilias and Ahmed v. Hungary*, para. 68.

55 Opinion No. 359/2005 of the Venice Commission on the Protection of Human Rights in Emergency Situations (Venice, 17–18.03.2006), p. 11.

ANNEX: THE NATIONAL CONSULTATION ON IMMIGRATION AND TERRORISM[56]

Published by the Prime Minister's Office

Please complete this questionnaire

1] We hear different views on increasing levels of terrorism. How relevant do you think the spread of terrorism (the bloodshed in France, the shocking acts of ISIS) is to your own life?

Very relevant   Relevant   Not relevant

2] Do you think that Hungary could be the target of an act of terror in the next few years?

There is a very real chance it could occur   Out of the question

3] There are some who think that mismanagement of the immigration question by Brussels may have something to do with increased terrorism. Do you agree with this view?

I fully agree   I tend to agree   I do not agree

4] Did you know that economic migrants cross the Hungarian border illegally, and that recently the number of immigrants in Hungary has increased twentyfold?

Yes   I have heard about it   I did not know

5] We hear different views on the issue of immigration. There are some who think that economic migrants jeopardise the jobs and livelihoods of Hungarians. Do you agree?

I fully agree   I tend to agree   I do not agree

6] There are some who believe that Brussels' policy on immigration and terrorism has failed, and that we therefore need a new approach to these questions. Do you agree?

I fully agree   I tend to agree   I do not agree

---

56 Source: <http://www.kormany.hu/download/9/a3/50000/Nemzetikonzultacio_mmkorrnel.docx> accessed 18.07.2017.

7] Would you support the Hungarian Government in the introduction of more stringent immigration regulations, in contrast to Brussels' lenient policy?

Yes, I would fully support the Government
I would partially support the Government
I would not support the Government

8] Would you support the Hungarian Government in the introduction of more stringent regulations, according to which migrants illegally crossing the Hungarian border could be taken into custody?

Yes, I would fully support the Government
I would partially support the Government
I would not support the Government

9] Do you agree with the view that migrants illegally crossing the Hungarian border should be returned to their own countries within the shortest possible time?

I fully agree I tend to agree I do not agree

10] Do you agree with the concept that economic migrants themselves should cover the costs associated with their time in Hungary?

I fully agree I tend to agree I do not agree

11] Do you agree that the best means of combating immigration is for Member States of the European Union to assist in the development of the countries from which migrants arrive?

I fully agree I tend to agree I do not agree

12] Do you agree with the Hungarian Government that support should be focused more on Hungarian families and the children they can have, rather than on immigration?

I fully agree I tend to agree I do not agree

INVITED CONTRIBUTION

6. EUROPEAN RESPONSES TO THE MEDITERRANEAN 'REFUGEE CRISIS' AND THE FEAR OF SAVING LIVES

Maria GABRIELSEN JUMBERT*

1. INTRODUCTION

Public and policy debates around how to respond to and tackle the so-called European 'refugee crisis' have been dense, and with seemingly few immediate solutions at hand. They have covered everything from how to receive migrants arriving on the shores of Europe, how to process asylum claims and how to integrate newly arrived migrants, to how to reinforce border controls, strengthen asylum processing capacities and improve or find mechanisms for returning migrants – whether still on their way to Europe or after their arrival. A key and recurrent issue within this debate, a sort of node between the administrative, security and humanitarian concerns, is the question of whether providing assistance and relief also creates a so-called 'pull-effect' by encouraging more migrants to make the perilous journey. The suggestion is seen as controversial and has been refuted in several studies, yet it appears to be particularly resistant, and remains an underlying assumption in many of the policies formulated by the European Union (EU) as well as national and local governments.

Indeed, much of the debate around how to respond to and tackle the refugees arriving in Europe is framed around the question: what assistance should be provided that does not send a signal that encourages more migrants to come? Most arguments in the debate can be organised along an axis between those who believe that rescue efforts do constitute a pull factor, and such rescue should thus be limited, and those who either claim they do not, or refute the question itself, emphasising that in any case providing such life-saving assistance is a fundamental moral and humanitarian duty. This chapter will look more closely

* Peace Research Institute Oslo (PRIO), Norway. E-mail: margab@prio.org.

at the nature of this debate, seeking to understand how the 'pull-effect' has become a key premise in the debate thereby influencing responses and stances taken by different stakeholders, at sea as well as on land. It takes part in a broader academic discussion, where the rising awareness over recent years of the human suffering entailed by the multiple attempts to defy European border control structures, and the following humanitarian forms of responses, have led to the conceptualisation of 'humanitarian borders'.[1] The concept of humanitarian borders designates the different forms of humanitarian government set up to respond to the suffering of migrants seeking to cross borders, notably to the so-called global North, who are prevented from doing so by different forms of border control. Attention has also been devoted in recent scholarship to how the security apparatus, with Frontex in the front seat, has sought to re-frame its border security interventions as tools to save human lives, in addition to being measures to control the borders.[2] In this discussion, we see that while the imperative to uphold basic obligations of search and rescue at sea is maintained, attention is increasingly devoted to showing the perils of proactive rescue operations. Essentially, this constitutes rescue operations as a security matter, and produces what could be called the 'fear of saving lives'.

2. FROM MARE NOSTRUM TO TRITON: THE EMERGENCE OF MARITIME RESCUE AS A 'PULL-FACTOR'

The debate about Mediterranean rescues as a pull-factor for migration kick-started when an increasing number of migrants and refugees arrived

---

1 P. Pallister-Wilkins, 'Interrogating the Mediterranean "Migration Crisis"' (2016) 21(2) *Mediterranean Politics*; P. Pallister-Wilkins, 'The Politics of Illegality in the Humanitarian Borderwork of Médecins Sans Frontières' (04.11.2015) *Border Criminologies*, <https://www.law.ox.ac.uk/research-subject-groups/centre-criminology/centreborder-criminologies/blog/2015/10/politics> accessed 25.08.2017; J. Jeandesboz and P. Pallister-Wilkins, 'Crisis, Routine, Consolidation: The Politics of the Mediterranean Migration Crisis' (2016) 21(2) *Mediterranean Politics*; W. Walters, 'Foucault and Frontiers: Notes on the Birth of the Humanitarian Border' in U. Bröckling, S. Krasmann and T. Lemke (eds.), *Governmentality: Current Issues and Future Challenges*, Routledge, New York 2011.

2 Border surveillance measures have often been framed as contributing to improved search and rescue operations, by Frontex and other agencies, in addition to their primary function of increasing overview and control over border areas. In addition, and as seen recently, border control at sea – and more specifically measures to prevent migrants from crossing the Mediterranean altogether – have been framed as 'humanitarian' as they aim to prevent people from embarking on the risky sea-route. See K.A. Franko and H. Gundhus, 'Policing Humanitarian Borderlands: Frontex, Human Rights and the Precariousness of Life' (2015) *British Journal of Criminology* 55; J. Rijpma and M. Vermeulen, 'Eurosur: Saving Lives or Building Borders?' (2015) 24(3) *European Security*; M.G. Jumbert, 'Control or Rescue at Sea? Aims and Limits of Border Surveillance Technologies in the Mediterranean' (forthcoming 2018) *Disasters*.

after Operation Mare Nostrum was set up. It was launched following the large shipwreck outside Lampedusa on 3 October 2013, where more than 360 migrants' lives were lost.[3] The disaster provoked a public outcry in Italy, with the Italian President Giorgio Napolitano referring to the sea drownings as a 'succession of true slaughters of innocents'.[4] Italy called for urgent international action, and the responses from the European level also expressed deep concern about the human tragedy unfolding. Jean-Claude Mignon, head of the Council of Europe's Parliamentary Assembly was quoted as saying: 'We must end this now. I hope that this will be the last time we see a tragedy of this kind, and I make a fervent appeal for specific, urgent action by member states to end this shame.'[5]

Operation Mare Nostrum was launched on 18 October 2013, coordinated by the Italian Ministry of Defence, which categorised it as a 'military humanitarian' operation.[6] It had a specific 'search and rescue' mandate and operated up to 400 nautical miles South of Lampedusa, and 150 nautical miles towards the East, thereby overlapping with both Maltese and Libyan search and rescue areas. It is estimated that the operation contributed to the rescue of approximately 140,000 people during its 12-month operational period.[7]

Italy continued to call for increased financial and material support for the operation from the other EU Member States during this year, as rescue needs continued to increase. Indeed, as stated by the International Organization for Migration (IOM), the number of migrants and asylum seekers arriving in Italy by sea quadrupled in 2014, from a recorded 42,925 arrivals in 2013 to 170,100 in 2014.[8] A connection was quickly made: the increase was thought to be due to the Italian rescue operation producing a pull-effect. The increase in the number of arrivals had, however, started before the launch of this search and rescue operation: an estimated 60,000 people crossed the Mediterranean sea, and 2,400 migrants lost their lives during the journey, in 2013,[9] rising from the

---

3 T. Brian and F. Laczko (eds.), 'Fatal Journeys: Tracking Lives Lost during Migration' (2014) *International Organization for Migration*, <https://publications.iom.int/system/files/pdf/fataljourneys_countingtheuncounted.pdf> accessed 25.08.2017.

4 L. Davies, 'Lampedusa Boat Tragedy is "Slaughter of Innocents" Says Italian President' (03.10.2013) *The Guardian*, <https://www.theguardian.com/world/2013/oct/03/lampedusa-boat-tragedy-italy-migrants> accessed 25.08.2017.

5 *Ibid.*

6 See the Italian Navy website, <http://www.marina.difesa.it/cosa-facciamo/operazioni-concluse/Pagine/mare-nostrum.aspx> accessed 25.08.2017.

7 ECRE (European Council on Refugees and Exiles), 'Mare Nostrum to end – New Frontex operation will not ensure rescue of migrants in international waters' (10.10.2014) News, <https://www.ecre.org/operation-mare-nostrum-to-end-frontex-triton-operation-will-not-ensure-rescue-at-sea-of-migrants-in-international-waters> accessed 24.08.2017.

8 IOM, 'Migrant Arrivals by Sea in Italy Top 170,000 in 2014' (16.01.2015) Press release, <https://www.iom.int/news/migrant-arrivals-sea-italy-top-170000-2014> accessed 29.08.2017.

9 T. Brian and F. Laczko, *supra* n. 3 and UNHCR (United Nations High Commissioner for Refugees), 'Mediterranean crossings more deadly a year after Lampedusa tragedy' (02.10.2014), <http://www.unhcr.org/news/latest/2014/10/542d12de9/mediterranean-crossings-deadly-year-lampedusa-tragedy.html> accessed 05.02.2018.

estimated total of 58,000 crossings and 1,500 deaths in 2011,[10] then considered a record high in the wake of the Arab spring (followed by a reduction in 2012). There was then a sharp increase between 2013 and 2014, with around 219,000 crossings and 3,283 deaths in the Mediterranean.[11] The numbers continued to increase after the termination of Operation Mare Nostrum and even increased further once the operation was replaced by more modest Frontex efforts.[12]

As Operation Mare Nostrum was being wrapped up, following repeated calls by Italy for increased assistance and European funds to continue to support the operation, to little avail, it was replaced by Operation Triton, under Frontex's leadership. Operation Triton did not have an explicit search and rescue mandate, and it was restricted to patrolling in a much smaller area than Operation Mare Nostrum. This was largely grounded in the need to limit the perceived 'pull effect' and to emphasise the border control function of such a patrol. As Frontex's Executive Director at the time, Gil Arias Fernandez, put it when the new operation was launched: 'I would like to underline that operation Triton focuses on border control and surveillance. Having said that, saving lives will remain an absolute priority for Frontex.'[13] The priorities were clear: the operation had a border control and surveillance mandate, but would respect its obligation to bring search and rescue – if a situation of distress occurred. Any vessel at sea however has an obligation to bring search and rescue to any other vessel in distress, under the United Nations Convention on the Law of the Sea (UNCLOS), so Frontex was merely stating that it would respect a basic legal obligation. However, in practical terms, the difference from its predecessor was crucial, as the restricted mandate also meant the Triton patrols were not properly equipped to conduct search and rescue operations and provide fundamentally life-saving support, nor did it patrol close to where most accidents occurred.[14] This can be read as a response to the supposed pull-effect of Operation Mare Nostrum.

The tone was different and sharper a few months later however, following two consecutive large-scale shipwrecks in April 2015. The new Frontex chief, Fabrice Leggeri, then stressed that Triton should not be used as a search and

---

10 UNHCR, 'Mediterranean Takes Record as Most Deadly Stretch of Water for Refugees and Migrants in 2011' (31.01.2017), <http://www.unhcr.org/news/briefing/2012/1/4f27e01f9/mediterranean-takes-record-deadly-stretch-water-refugees-migrants-2011.html> accessed 25.08.2017.

11 See IOM's Missing Migrant project, <https://missingmigrants.iom.int/mediterranean> accessed 25.08.2017.

12 E. Steinhilper and R. Gruijters, 'Border Deaths in the Mediterranean: What We Can Learn from the Latest Data' (08.03.2017), <https://www.law.ox.ac.uk/research-subject-groups/centre-criminology/centreborder-criminologies/blog/2017/03/border-deaths> accessed 29.08.2017.

13 Frontex, 'Frontex Launches Joint Operation Triton' (3.10.2014) *News*, <http://frontex.europa.eu/news/frontex-launches-joint-operation-triton-JSYpL7>.

14 M.G. Jumbert, *supra*, n. 2.

rescue operation, invoking the pull-factor. He is quoted as saying: 'We should not support and fuel the business of traffickers … What happened in the past was that if smugglers are sure that European boats are patrolling very close to the Libyan coast, then traffickers use this opportunity to advertise, and say to potential irregular migrants: "You will be sure to reach the European coast. It's very easy, European boats are patrolling not far from the Libyan coast, so let's jump into the sea and you'll see European boats very soon".'[15] After the argument was first used by Theresa May, then UK Home Secretary, to justify the UK staying out of Operation Triton, several other EU governments at that time also supported the same view – while organisations like the United Nations High Commissioner for Refugees (UNHCR), IOM as well as other NGOs were calling for increased search and rescue efforts.[16]

Shortly after the April 2015 shipwrecks however, Operation Triton II was launched, taking over from the first operation, with increased funding and an expanded range of activities, responding to the increased criticism regarding the lack of rescue capacities in the Mediterranean. A number of NGOs also began at that time to charter their own ships to conduct search and rescue operations at sea, and in June 2016 the rescue capacities were estimated to be at the same level as during Operation Mare Nostrum. In the second half of 2016, eight humanitarian NGOs were known to be operating in the Mediterranean, between Libya and Italy. They would not be held outside the old controversy for long: in early summer 2017, as the number of rescue operations and migrants arriving in Italy was again increasing, accusations against the humanitarian rescuers again began to flourish. In July 2017, Italy called for an emergency meeting with France and Germany, to assess how they could stem the 'pull factor' created by the mere presence of the humanitarian NGOs.[17] Later in July, Italy presented a Code of Conduct for the NGOs,[18] seeking to regulate the way they operated, notably banning rescue vessels from entering Libyan territorial waters, and calling on the NGOs to cooperate with the police to investigate human trafficking – for instance by accepting armed police on board their vessels. It also includes a requirement to disembark rescued survivors in a safe place, and not by transferring them onto other vessels – which in practice means

15 P. Kingsley and I. Traynor, 'EU borders chief says saving migrants' lives "shouldn't be priority" for patrols' (22.04.2015) *The Guardian*, <https://www.theguardian.com/world/2015/apr/22/eu-borders-chief-says-saving-migrants-lives-cannot-be-priority-for-patrols> accessed 25.08.2017.

16 *Ibid.*

17 P. Wintour, 'Italian plan to curb Mediterranean rescue boat charities "threatens lives"' (03.07.2017) *The Guardian*, <https://www.theguardian.com/world/2017/jul/03/anger-at-rules-plan-for-migrant-charities-in-mediterranean> accessed 25.08.2017.

18 'Code of conduct for NGOs involved in migrants' rescue operations at sea' (July 2017), Italy, <http://statewatch.org/news/2017/jul/italy-eu-sar-code-of-conduct.pdf> accessed 25.09.2017.

reduced capacity to conduct further rescues by several of the NGOs.[19] Three of the active NGOs accepted to sign the code, while the other five refused to,[20] notably invoking that such requirements would compromise their humanitarian neutrality, but also arguing that the new rules would lead to increased risk for migrants and increase the number of drownings, as Médecins Sans Frontières (MSF) underlined.[21]

3. EXAMINING THE DATA: MIGRANT ARRIVALS AND MORTALITY

The argument that rescue and life-saving activities leads to more people attempting the risky journey has been seen as controversial. On one hand, it is used to legitimate the non-rescue of persons in danger, yet at the same time, this argument is widely accepted and even taken for granted. The correlation has been examined closely in several recent studies.[22] One of the most central reports assessed the claims that Operation Mare Nostrum led to an increase in migrants crossing the sea, as well as the effects of the reduced search and rescue effort by the EU with Operation Triton. It concluded that the two large-scale shipwrecks outside Libya in April 2015, claiming well over one thousand lives, could be seen as a result of the EU's retreat from state-led search and rescue.[23] Another report examined the claim that the increasingly important role played by NGO rescue operations constitutes a pull-factor. It also concludes that there is no evidence of such a pull-factor, and that the argument ignores the broader picture, failing to take into account the types of political and economic crises that push people to flee – whether from their country of origin, or to flee further from transit countries such as Libya.

Another study conducted examines the data on migrant crossings across the different search and rescue (SAR) phases, dividing the period between 2014 and 2017 into three phases, of 'high SAR' activity during Mare Nostrum, 'low SAR' activity during the first phase of Triton, and 'high SAR' again during Triton II.[24] Disregarding other causes impacting on the number of migrants

---

19 E. Zalan, 'NGOs divided by Italy's new rescue code' (01.08.2017) *EU Observer*, <https://euobserver.com/migration/138656> accessed 25.08.2017.

20 Save the Children, the Malta-based Migrant Offshore Aid Station (MOAS) and the Spanish group Proactiva Open Arms signed the code. Médecins Sans Frontières, Germany's Sea-Watch, Sea-Eye and Jugend Rettet, and France's SOS Mediterranée abstained.

21 *Ibid.*

22 Among which, the two reports published by the Forensic Oceanography department at Goldsmiths, University of London: 'Death by Rescue' (2016) and 'Blaming the Rescuers' (2017) are based on the most extensive empirical data collection.

23 *Ibid*, 'Death by Rescue'.

24 E. Steinhilper and R. Gruijters, *supra* n. 12.

crossing the sea, it shows that arrivals did not decrease during the phase of reduced SAR; rather, this was the period with the highest number of arrivals – concluding that there was little or no impact on the number of attempts to cross. The mortality rates markedly increased during the low SAR phase, which they emphasise is largely due to the two large-scale shipwrecks in April 2015, and yet, as the above-mentioned report shows, this should not be seen as being unrelated.

4. A COMPLEX DEBATE REDUCED TO A DILEMMA REGARDING WHETHER OR NOT TO PROVIDE HUMANITARIAN AID

Placing the blame on the rescuers, or the services they provide, is neither a new nor a unique approach to the Mediterranean. Despite the connection being refuted, both in practice, with varying attempts in the last few years to reduce search and rescue capacities at sea, and in these different studies, it nevertheless continues to impact upon the way in which the 'dilemma' about how to receive refugees in Europe is viewed. It is seen not only at sea, but also on land in various European countries, with arrests or court cases brought against volunteers or citizens providing different forms of basic assistance to refugees, as seen in Norway, Italy, France, Hungary and Greece to name a few.[25] A telling example is a case where this 'dilemma' has become the nodal point of the controversy, in Calais, in Northern France. In October 2016, the French government dismantled the camp known as the 'Jungle', moving and resettling more than 8,000 migrants elsewhere in France. In the first months of 2017 local authorities struggled with how to respond to the slowly increasing number of migrant arrivals, again assembling close to the port connecting to the United Kingdom. For instance, an attempt to install showers for the migrants was prevented by the local authorities

[25] A few examples: In Italy, a British and two French volunteers were arrested in March 2017 while distributing food to migrants in the city of Ventimiglia close to the French border, see AFP/The Local, 'French and British volunteers arrested for giving food to migrants in Italy' (23.03.2017). In Norway, two volunteers were arrested when helping asylum seekers, scheduled to be returned to Russia, to leave a detention center and find shelter in a nearby church, see T. Nilsen, '"We had to help them"' (21.01.2016) *The Independent Barents Observer*. In Greece, five international volunteers were arrested in January 2016, charged with human trafficking by facilitating the illegal entry of migrants and refugees when seeking to rescue a boat in distress, see D. Leivada, 'Volunteers Helping Refugees in Greece Fear Government Clampdown' (04.02.2017) *Huffington Post*. In Hungary, activists were risking arrest by transporting asylum seekers, ruled illegal by laws passed in 2015, see L. Frayer, 'Risking Arrest, Thousands of Hungarians Offer Help to Refugees' (29.09.2015) *NPR*, <https://www.npr.org/sections/parallels/2015/09/29/444447532/risking-arrest-thousands-of-hungarians-offer-help-to-refugees> accessed 20.01.2018.

at first. The Mayor of Calais then attempted to introduce a ban on delivering food to the migrants, arguing that handing out meals constituted a security threat.[26] The proposal was subsequently overruled by a regional court, when 11 non-government organisations filed a complaint. The court ordered the local officials to establish 'several drinking fountains, toilets and showers' evoking the 'inhuman and degrading conditions' to which the migrants are exposed.[27] Yet, in the desperation to avoid the creation of a new 'Jungle' camp, the Mayor refused to abide by the court's decision.[28] The situation in Calais illustrates how the question of how to respond adequately to migrants and would-be asylum seekers is reduced to a dilemma whether or not to provide life-supporting aid.

5. THE 'PULL-EFFECT': EXPLAINING THE OTHERWISE INEXPLICABLE

A common element of the understanding of the 'pull-effect' in the two situations presented – search and rescue on the Mediterranean Sea and the Jungle camp in Calais – is the narrow focus on the situation, leaving out the broader picture. Were the situation seen to be a mathematical equation, it would be set up in such a way that the rescue operations and humanitarian assistance are seen as independent variables, and the number of migrants as a dependent variable, with a seemingly unlimited value. It is as if the broader picture, the different factors preventing, pushing, allowing or facilitating people to move, are too broad and complex, and cannot be changed in the immediate to short term by initiatives or measures from EU Member States. In this set-up, the activities of the NGOs become in and by themselves the explanatory factor and the cause of an otherwise incomprehensible situation: why so many people are risking their lives to reach Europe. The 'pull-factor' argument is used as the logical mechanism, explaining individual choices that are hard to fathom. This is even harder to fathom when the broader picture, the different factors driving (or preventing) people to move, is left out. Thus the 'pull-factor' supposedly created by NGOs providing rescue or basic assistance becomes both an explanation to the situation, and the part

26 A. Gentleman, 'Calais mayor bans distribution of food to migrants' (02.03.2017) *The Guardian*, <https://www.theguardian.com/world/2017/mar/02/calais-mayor-bans-distribution-of-food-to-migrants> accessed 25.08.2017.

27 France 24, 'French court orders Calais officials to provide migrants with water' (26.06.2017), <http://www.france24.com/en/20170626-france-calais-court-orders-officials-provide-migrants-aid-water-toilets> accessed 25.08.2017.

28 Liberation, 'La maire de Calais refuse d'appliquer les mesures d'aide aux migrants ordonnées par la justice' (27.06.2017), <http://www.liberation.fr/direct/element/la-maire-de-calais-refuse-dappliquer-les-mesures-daide-aux-migrants-ordonnees-par-la-justice_66669/> accessed 25.08.2017.

of the equation that needs to be addressed. In a situation framed as a crisis, this probably also appears as the part of the equation that it is easiest to address, rather than factors external to Europe.

Refusing to 'save lives', or at least reducing the capacity to do so, is not a straightforward endeavour, ethically, morally and independently from any political positioning. This may explain why those defending this approach also tend to base their argument on the claim that rescues, in and by themselves, produce greater risks for the migrants, stating that they encourage more people to embark on the perilous journey and because they supposedly allow the smugglers to push the migrants onto less seaworthy vessels, gambling on them being rescued at sea. A recent investigation by the UK House of Lords has shown that the EU's naval Operation Sophia is, instead, to be blamed for this, as its practice of destroying smugglers' boats has led them to use even less seaworthy vessels.[29] In addition to the argument of increased risks for the migrants themselves, the refusal to step up aid and rescue efforts is justified through narratives of the need to protect Europe: 'us', the local communities. This is facilitated through processes of 'othering' the migrants as not entitled to the same rights as European citizen, or even as potential threats, and through discourses where social goods are presented as zero-sum, in the sense that providing for the migrants will erode the social benefits for the rest of the host society.

6. CONCLUSION

Despite having been refuted in recent studies, the 'rescue as a pull-factor' argument remains powerful: it is widespread in both popular perception and policy debates on how to respond to the Mediterranean tragedy, and serves as a guiding principle in official responses to the crisis. The idea of the pull-effect created by search and rescue operations at sea emerged at a time where both rescue efforts had been stepped up, with the Mare Nostrum operation, and the arrivals of migrants continued to increase and entered the public European awareness.[30] This may also explain why the connection now remains so resistant in public and policy debates, even if the trends in the following periods have not confirmed this connection. The concept of 'rescue as a pull-effect' also allows a seemingly logical explanation to the otherwise inexplicable. By insisting on the

29 House of Lords, 'Operation Sophia, the EU's naval mission in the Mediterranean: an impossible challenge' (2016) 14th Report of Session 2015–16, HL Paper 144, <https://www.theguardian.com/world/2017/jul/11/eu-naval-tactics-operation-sophia-stop-people-smuggling-cause-more-deaths-report-says> accessed 25.09.2017.

30 M.G. Jumbert, *supra* n. 2.

risks posed to the migrants themselves, the argument becomes another form of moral compass, and a way to distance the argument from the complex situation at sea. In August 2017, the relatively sharp decrease in the number of migrants crossing the Mediterranean from Libya to Italy initially sparked optimism among Italian and EU policy makers and bureaucrats that what was seen was the success of different deterrent policies. The consequences of the EU's efforts to stem the flow of migrants across the Mediterranean, not only by regulating NGO rescue operations, but also through funding and training of Libyan coast guards, has however, since received increased attention. Some humanitarian NGOs, such as MSF, have drawn attention to the dire conditions in which would-be or returned migrants are detained. This could increasingly lead the 'broader picture', the multiple driving factors pushing or preventing people from fleeing, to be taken into account, rather than seeing migrants crossing the sea or arriving in Europe as isolated from this.

PART II

MIGRANTS, THEIR RIGHTS AND THE LIMITS THEREOF

7. ECONOMIC REFUGEES: AN ANALYSIS OF THE PHENOMENON IN THE CONTEXT OF THE EU MIGRATION CRISIS

Agnieszka PIEKUTOWSKA* and Elżbieta KUŻELEWSKA**

1. INTRODUCTION

The influx of migrants seeking protection in the European Union (EU), at levels unprecedented since the Second World War, has given rise to a question about the capability of EU Member States to host them. According to prevailing opinions, the majority of incoming migrants cannot be granted refugee status in the light of the Geneva Convention of 1951 because they are 'economic refugees', i.e. individuals who do not arrive in order to find shelter but, rather, to improve their economic situation.[1] The purpose of this chapter is to explain who economic refugees are and why they should not be identified with economic migrants. This is especially important as, in the view of the authors, the term 'economic refugee' has been wrongly and incorrectly applied both in the political discourse and media as a synonym of economic migration.

Although many scholars deal with the issue of economic migration,[2] relatively few works have been devoted to the phenomenon of economic refugees taking place in parallel to economic migrants. Economic migrants are persons who migrate in order to improve their economic status by finding employment in a host country. It should be emphasised that economic migrations are voluntary and unconstrained and such migrants are free to return to their country of origin. Economic migrants migrate not because they have a bad life but because

* Faculty of Economics and Management, University of Białystok, Poland. E-mail: piekutowska@uwb.edu.pl.

** Centre for Direct Democracy Studies, Faculty of Law, University of Białystok, Poland. E-mail: ekuzelewska@gmail.com.

1 Y. HAKIM, 'Migrant Crisis: "Hipster Right" Group Trying To Stop Rescue Ships', *BBC News*, <http://www.bbc.com/news/world-europe-40505337> accessed 07.12.2017.

2 Notably, W.R. Böhning, G.J. Borjas, Ç. Özden, T.J. Hatton and J.G. Williamson.

they want a better one.[3] On the other hand, an economic refugee is defined in the relevant literature as a person who treats migration as an escape from economic oppression. They are persons who escape from their country because the immense poverty they live in prevents them from satisfying their basic human needs. This situation concerns people who leave their countries due to threats that can be assimilated to those encountered by political refugees. The latter may flee due to terror, whereas economic refugees flee due to hunger. Toilsome conditions that frequently imply mental and physical suffering make economic refugees leave. However, the threat they experience is not individual in its nature, and that is why they cannot be granted political refugee status. The ensuing conclusion is that an economic refugee can be granted neither economic nor political refugee status within the meaning of the 1951 Convention on the Status of Refugees.

Hence the following questions arise: who are the migrants coming to the EU? Are they mostly economic refugees in the light of the present migration crisis in the EU? The main hypothesis assumes that migration of economic refugees is a self-restricting phenomenon that is not likely to increase.

Most definitions referring to economic refugees emphasise extreme poverty as the main reason for such a migration. Undoubtedly, a lack of income or low earnings preventing the satisfaction of basic human needs contribute to migration whose purpose is the improvement of living standards and financial situation. Continually increasing wage differences reinforce the migration pressure, particularly from poor to wealthy countries. Theoretically, people who do not have a chance to find employment in their country and provide their family with minimum existence may decide to emigrate.[4] Assuming such a thesis, we may draw a simple conclusion that citizens of the poorest regions of the world, such as Sub-Saharan Africa, will be characterised by the greatest mobility as they may benefit the most from migration. The statistical analysis carried out herein (a scale of migration from the poorest regions of the world, based on the World Bank data) will reveal that, in fact, this dependency does not occur.

The attempt to verify the above hypothesis requires the application of a statistical analysis based on Eurostat data of the structure of migrants seeking protection within the territory of the EU with regard to the criterion of citizenship. This method will facilitate the formulation of a conclusion according to which it will be shown that the migration of economic refugees is not increasing within the territory of the EU, despite the fact that approximately half of all applications for granting refugee status are rejected. The discussion in this

3 K. Kuciński, 'Migracje w teorii ekonomii' (2004) 15 *International Journal of Management and Economics* 10.

4 L.A. Sjaastad, 'The Costs and Returns of Human Migration' (1962) 70(5) *Journal of Political Economy* 80.

chapter is divided into five parts. Section 2 starts with the definition of economic refugees. Section 3 describes the relations between poverty and international migration and consequences for economic refugees. Economic refugees in the context of the EU migration crisis are discussed in section 4. Section 5 will draw some conclusions.

2. ECONOMIC REFUGEES: A DEFINITION

International migration is caused by several factors such as the situation regarding the job market, general economic situation, armed conflicts or cultural and religious circumstances. Although these causes often occur concurrently, individual incentives prompting a decision to leave may vary in intensity. A multifaceted nature of the migration phenomenon, including different reasons for international mobility, has brought the need to systematise it with the use of typology. And yet, typologies allow the systemisation of mobility only to a limited level.[5] The consequence thereof is a possibility of challenging the adopted divisions, for example into forced and voluntary migration. Richmond depicts the vague accuracy of this dichotomy, claiming that the absolute, simple and clear distinction into economic, social and political prerequisites of migration is wrong and unreasonable.[6]

For instance, a political conflict, which may result in flows of political refugees, will often cause deterioration of the economic situation and the native population may seek to improve their prospects by emigration.[7] On the other hand, in many countries political terror has its roots in economic collapse, and thus migrants from these regions may be both political and economic refugees.[8]

Assuming that the migration of refugees is shaped by both political and economic factors – because refugees also migrate to improve their living standards – according to Bodvarsson and Van der Berg, such migration may be analysed with regard to the economic model of migration, where flows are explained by wage level differences.[9] Other authors also straightforwardly

---

5 A. Górny and P. Kaczmarczyk, 'Uwarunkowania i mechanizmy migracji zarobkowych w świetle wybranych koncepcji teoretycznych' (2003) 49 *Prace Migracyjne* 10.

6 A.H. Richmond, 'Sociological Theories of International Migration: The Case of Refugees' (1988) 36 *Current Sociology* 8, 13–14; A.H. Richmond, 'Reactive Migration: Sociological Perspectives on Refugee Movements' (1993) 6(1) *Journal of Refugee Studies* 7.

7 P. Stalker, *Workers Without Frontiers: The Impact of Globalization on International Migration*, Lynne Rienner Publishers, Boulder, CO 2008, pp. 32, 97.

8 T. Simoes da Silva, 'Paper(less) Selves: The Refugee in Contemporary Textual Culture' (2008) 30(1) *Kunapipi – Journal of Postcolonial Writing and Culture* 68.

9 O.B. Bodvarsson and H. Van den Berg, *The Economics of Immigration. Theory and Policy*, Springer, New York 2013, p. 307.

indicate that refugees can be treated as economic migrants in the analysis because they are also committed to improving their financial situation.[10]

Since the reasons for migration overlap, it is not sufficient to distinguish only economic migrants on the one hand, and (political) refugees on the other hand, with regard to the complex issue of international mobility. As Lee indicates

> ... since we can never specify the exact set of factors which impels or prohibits migration for a given person, we can, in general, only set forth a few which seem of special importance and note the general or average reaction of a considerable group. Needless to say, the factors that hold and attract or repel people are precisely understood neither by the social scientist nor the persons directly affected.[11]

Complex and overlapping causes of international mobility not only in the European continent but also in other regions of the world[12] create difficulties in providing an explicit definition of the migration's character. It is worth adding that, depending on its nature, migration may provoke different attitudes within the communities of host countries. As Kukathas states, 'there are many refugees whose plight is more serious than that of most economic migrants; yet there are also many would-be economic migrants who face greater threats to their well-being than do some refugees. Not all economic migrants are in the same boat; nor are all refugees.'[13] Understanding the complex causes of international migrations have become a prerequisite for the distinction of new categories of migrants, an economic refugee (*réfugié économique*) being one of them. It is a term frequently used in connection with the migration crisis in the EU. Apparently, this term is not understood unambiguously. In the literature, an economic refugee is defined as a person who migrates to escape economic oppression.[14] An economic refugee is a person who leaves their country due to economic reasons, including extreme poverty preventing satisfaction of their basic human needs.[15]

---

10 G. Engbersen, 'Migration Transitions in an Era of Liquid Migration' in M. Okólski (ed.), *European Immigrations Trends, Structures and Policy Implications*, IMISCOE Research, Amsterdam University Press, Amsterdam 2012, p. 99.

11 E.S. Lee, 'A Theory of Migration' (1966) 3(1) *Demography* 50.

12 One of the main conclusions ensuing from the research on the phenomenon of migration in Africa entails that it is hard to determine a point where political migration finishes and economic migration starts, R. Mupedziswa, 'Africa's Refugee Crisis' in A. Rwomire (ed.), *Social Problems of Africa. New Visions*, Greenwood Publishing Group, Westport 2001, p. 194.

13 Ch. Kukathas, 'Are Refugees Special?' in S. Fine and L. Ypi (eds.), *Migration in Political Theory: The Ethics of Movement and Membership*, Oxford University Press, Oxford 2016, p. 258.

14 F. Gabor and J.B. Rosenquest, 'The Unsettled Status of Economic Refugees from the American and International Legal Perspectives – A Proposal for Recognition under Existing International Law' (2006) 41 *Texas International Law Journal* 277.

15 G. Lakoff and S. Ferguson, *The Framing of Immigration*, Rockridge Insitute, Berkeley 2006, p. 9.

Therefore they are also called '*réfugiés de la misère*'.[16] Furthermore, the above description embraces individuals who migrate due to threats similar to those faced by political refugees, that is, threats to life due to terror with regard to political refugees, and starvation in case of economic refugees. It is claimed that the conditions they encounter and stimulate them to leave are so extreme that they take a form of psychological and physical torture.[17] At the same time, the term 'economic refugee' seems to evoke associations which do not reflect the difficult situation of these people.[18] Moreover, the threat referring to economic refugees is devoid of individual character, and so these people cannot be recognised as political refugees.[19] Hence, an economic refugee may not be recognised either as an economic migrant or a refugee in the meaning of the 1951 Convention Relating to the Status of Refugees.

An economic migrant is defined as a person who migrates in order to improve their financial situation, taking a decision to migrate voluntarily whilst having the possibility to return to their country of origin.[20] Economic migrants migrate not because they have a bad life but because they want to improve it.[21] These migrants have a clearly defined purpose: to work and save their earnings, most often in order to return to their countries of origin: a significant, yet under-emphasised, part of international migration.[22]

What distinguishes an economic refugee from an economic migrant is the ability to depart voluntarily. An economic refugee takes a decision to emigrate due to necessity and sometimes oppression, whereas economic migrants take a decision to emigrate of their own free will. What connects economic refugees and economic migrants is a common objective (the economic incentive or prerequisite), which is a desire to improve their financial situation and the possibility to enhance the quality of their life.

What distinguishes an economic refugee from a political refugee in the meaning of the Geneva Convention are the reasons for leaving, which are economic in their nature rather than the consequence of persecution due to

---

16 P. Gonin and V. Lassailly-Jacob, 'Les réfugiés de l'environnement. Une nouvelle catégorie de migrants forcés?' (2002) 18(2) *Revue européenne des migrations internationals* 144.

17 G. Deschamps, 'Adaptation Économique des Réfugiés Indochinois de la Seconde Vague (1979–1980): l'Example du Québec' in K.B. Chan and L.-J. Dorais (ed.), *Adaptation linguistique et culturelle: L'expérience des réfugiés d'Asie du sud-est au Québec*, International Centre for Research on Bilingualism, Québec 1987, p. 61.

18 M. Islam, 'Natural Calamities and Environmental Refugees in Bangladesh' (1992) 12(1) *Refugee* 6–7.

19 E.K. Harris, 'Economic Refugees: Unprotected in the United States by Virtue of an Inaccurate Label' (1993) 9(1) *American University International Law Review* 269.

20 K.E. Cortes, 'Are Refugees Different from Economic Immigrants? Some Empirical Evidence on the Heterogeneity of Immigrant Groups in the United States' (2004) 86(2) *The Review of Economics and Statistics* 465.

21 K. Kuciński, *supra* n. 3, p. 10.

22 B. Nicholson, 'The Wrong End of the Telescope: Economic Migrants, Immigration Policy, and How it Looks from Albania' (2002) 73(4) *The Political Quarterly* 442.

religion or political opinions. Despite this, economic refugees and political refugees have forced departure in common, as a result of tense and unfavourable situation in the sending state that reinforces the decision to leave.

3. ECONOMIC REFUGEES: POVERTY AS A CAUSE AND BARRIER OF INTERNATIONAL MIGRATION

Definitions of an economic refugee underline that the cause of this type of migration is extreme poverty. Undoubtedly, a lack of income or low earnings preventing the satisfaction of basic human needs may be a strong stimulus to migrate in order to improve a financial situation.

Ravenstein's works on determinants of migrations from the end of the nineteenth century were a breakthrough and contributed to an increased number of studies on income as a cause of spatial mobility.[23] Ravenstein emphasised varied reasons for migration indicating, at the same time, that migration caused by, for example, political oppression or unfavourable climate cannot be compared in their range or scale to those which 'arise from the desire inherent in most men to "better" themselves in material respects'.[24]

The neo-classical theory of international flows of labour exerted a tremendous influence on the perception of migration and established grounds for the development of migration policy. In this sense, the main causative factor of migration are differences in wage,[25] an assumption which is based on the claim expressed by Hicks in 1932, according to which 'differences in net economic advantages, chiefly differences in wages, are the main causes of migration'.[26] In the light of this theory, poor, no income or low-income people may benefit the most from migration. Budnikowski emphasises that migration will occur provided its causes are considerably intense,[27] meaning that those persons who are absolutely unlikely to find employment in their country and provide their family with the minimum subsistence will be among the first to

---

23 M.C. Burda, W. Härdle, M. Müller and A. Werwatz, *Semiparametric Analysis of German East-West Migration Intentions: Facts and Theory*, Humboldt Universität zu Berlin, Berlin 1997, p. 2.

24 E.G. Ravenstein, 'The Laws of Migration' (1989) 52(2) *Journal of the Royal Statistical Society* 286.

25 D.S. Massey, J. Arango, G. Hugo, A. Kouaouci, A. Pellegrino and E. Taylor, 'Theories of International Migration: A Review and Appraisal' (1993) 19(3) *Population and Development Review* 433–44.

26 J. Hicks, *The Theory of Wages*, Macmillan, London 1932, p. 76 (quoted in Ö.B. Bodvarsson, N.B Simpson and Ch. Sparber, 'Migration Theory' in B.R. Chiswick and P.W. Miller (eds.), *Handbook of the Economics of International Migration*, Vol. 1A, North-Holland, Amsterdam 2015).

27 A. Budnikowski, *Międzynarodowe Stosunki Gospodarcze*, Polskie Wydawnictwo Ekonomiczne 2003, p. 157.

decide to migrate. Pritchett indicates that one of the five irresistible forces in the global economy creating growing emigration pressures, from poor to rich countries in particular, is increasing wage differentiation.[28]

The above may imply that citizens of the poorest regions of the world (Figure 1, left axis), such as Sub-Saharan Africa, will be characterised by the highest level of mobility because they may gain the most from migration. Yet empirical studies do not confirm such a relationship.[29] Poverty is an ambiguous factor explaining international migration because, on the one hand, a lack of income may stimulate migration whereas, on the other hand, it may block it.[30] As a result, poverty is, paradoxically, also one of the key barriers to migration, as it considerably limits its range. Whilst being strongly motivated to migrate, many potential migrants defined in the literature as '*would-be émigrés*'[31] nevertheless stay in their countries because they are 'too poor to migrate'.[32]

Figure 1. The issue of extreme poverty vs. migration scale in selected world regions

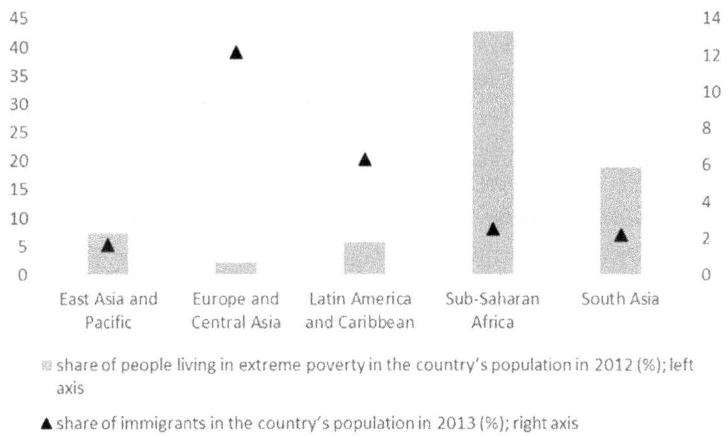

Source: Authors' own study based on: *Migration and Remittances Factbook 2016*, Global Knowledge Partnership on Migration and Development (KNOMAD), pp. 42–52; The World Bank, 2016, <http://data.worldbank.org> accessed 17.01.2017.

---

28 L. Pritchett, *Let Their People Come. Breaking the Gridlock on International Labor Mobility*, Center for Global Development, Washington 2006, pp. 5–6, 138.

29 Guriev and Vakulenko draw the same conclusion in their studies even though they focus on internal migrations in Russia. Studying interregional migrations in Russia, they proved that the poorest regions in this country are characterised by lower migration than richer regions, thus confirming that low or no income is a barrier to migration, S. Guriev and E. Vakulenko, 'Breaking Out of Poverty Traps: Internal Migration and Interregional Convergence in Russia' (2015) 43(3) *Journal of Comparative Economics* 640–42.

30 H.P. Van Dalen, G. Groenewold and J.J. Schoorl, 'Out of Africa: What Drives the Pressure to Emigrate?' (2005) 18(4) *Journal of Population Economics* 752.

31 T. Simoes da Silva, *supra* n. 8, p. 432.

32 T.J. Hatton and J.G. Williamson, 'Emigration in the Long Run: Evidence from Two Global Centuries' (2009) 23(2) *Asian Pacific Economic Literature* 22.

According to the data presented in Figure 1, regions seriously affected by poverty do not encounter a significant scale of migration (Figure 1, right axis).[33] The share of migrants in the population of Sub-Saharan Africa (at the level of 2.5 per cent) is significantly lower in comparison to migration from the countries located in the regions less affected by poverty. Among developing countries, the highest share of migrants is recorded in Europe and Central Asia (12.2 per cent in 2013), which also encounters the lowest poverty ratio.

This contradiction (i.e. low migration from the poorest countries) can be explained by migration costs. According to Hatton and Williamson,[34] despite the strong incentives to emigrate found in low-income countries, the majority of potential migrants do not leave because they cannot afford the cost involved in migration.

Nevertheless, opposite to the classical theory, increasing income in poor countries increases migration. The relation between wage levels and the scale of migration is not, in fact, linear, which contradicts the assumptions of the neo-classical theory.

Attempting to conceptualise the non-linear relation between development processes and the scale of migration from a given country, Martin and Taylor introduced the notion of the so-called 'migration hump'. It is a situation where growing economic development in a given country and decreased income differences entail a significant growth of migration in the first period thereof, whereas it is only in the later stages of economic growth that migration from this country decreases. The relation between increased salaries and the scale of migration in a given country is reflected by an inverted U-curve.[35]

It is worth indicating here that one of the causes of increased international mobility in the first phase of economic development are migration costs.[36] Shiff lists, among others, travelling costs or expenses connected with staying in the target country until finding employment. Having low income, migrants may not be able to pay these costs. If, however, wages grow thus enabling migrants to cover expenses connected with travel, the scale of migration will increase.

---

33 The conclusion of a low migration scale from the regions suffering strongly from poverty is confirmed by the analysis carried out at the level of the countries too (not just regions). There is a positive correlation between the income level and migration from 11 African countries that are most seriously affected by poverty, which means that migration scale is lower in lower income countries (opposite to the assumptions of the neoclassical theory of migration). A. Piekutowska, 'Migracje międzynarodowe a globalny problem ubóstwa' (2016) 13 *Zeszyty Naukowe Uniwersytetu Szczecińskiego* 27–37.

34 T.J. Hatton and J.G. Williamson, 'International Migration 1850–1939: An Economic Survey' in T.J. Hatton and J.G Williamson (eds.), *Migration and the International Labor Market 1850–1939*, Routledge, London–New York 1994, p. 9.

35 H. de Haas, 'Turning the Tide? Why "Development Instead of Migration" Policies Are Bound to Fail' (2006) 2 *International Migration Institute Working Papers* 26–27.

36 M. Schiff, 'How Trade, Aid and Remittances Affect International Migration' (1994) 1376 *The World Bank Policy Research Working Paper* 2–7.

The above entails an important conclusion, according to which the scale of migration of economic refugees is (self-)limited. Migration from poor countries may grow significantly in response to a considerable increase in their income[37] at the level sufficient to pay the costs of leaving. Yet, this situation does not reflect the present migration crisis in the EU. Such a conclusion may be confirmed, *inter alia*, by the analysis of the background of migrants (with regard to citizenship) wishing to enter the EU.

4. ECONOMIC REFUGEES IN THE CONTEXT OF THE EU MIGRATION CRISIS

A profound increase in the number of individuals applying for international protection in the EU (Figure 2) allows this phenomenon even to be called a migration crisis, undoubtedly one of the major challenges of European integration. Since 2010, the number of applicants has been constantly growing. In 2013, for the first time in 11 years, the number of applications for international protection exceeded 400,000. At the turn of 2014 and 2015, the number of applicants more than doubled: from nearly 627,000 to an unprecedented 1,323,000. It should be noticed that the dynamics of this phenomenon has varied amongst individual Member States. The greatest increase in the influx of people seeking protection in 2015 as compared to 2014 occurred in Finland and Hungary (an increase of 793.5 per cent and 314 per cent, respectively). At the same time, the

Figure 2. The number of applications for international protection in the EU in 1998–2015

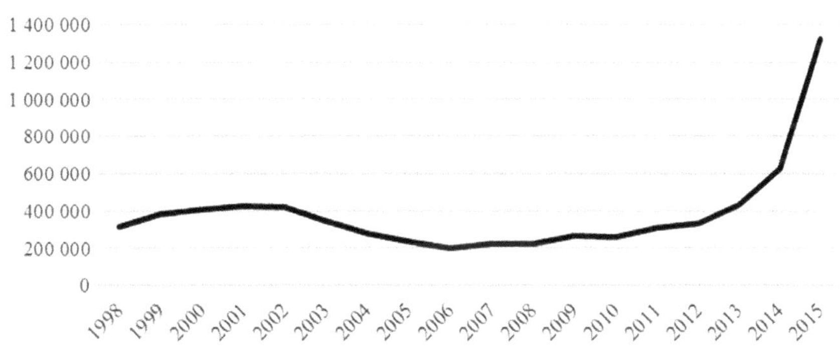

Source: Authors' own study based on: Eurostat, <http://ec.europa.eu/eurostat/data/database> accessed 15.01.2017.

[37] Assuming no change in other factors shaping migrations such as, e.g. migration policy. Migration policy and other legislative measures of host countries are a vital factor controlling international migrations. Despite strong incentives within sending states, migrations will not occur if potential host states do not decide to open their borders to foreign workers.

number of applications for protection decreased by more than half in Croatia (53.3 per cent) and by 28.6 per cent in Slovenia.[38]

Such an influx of migrants seeking protection within the EU territory, unprecedented since the Second World War, has evoked questions about the capability of the EU to host them. It has been claimed that most migrants cannot be granted refugee status because they arrive to improve their economic situation rather than to find shelter. Those taking part in political and social discussions even voice the opinion that the 'majority of migrants are economic refugees'.[39] Is it really true that the present migration crisis in the EU mostly embraces economic refugees, understood as people escaping from extreme poverty? Or perhaps they are economic migrants who migrate not because they have a bad life but because they want a better one? Attempting to answer this question requires more precise explanation of the background of migrants seeking protection within the EU with regard to the criterion of citizenship.

Out of 1,323,000 applications for international protection in the EU submitted in 2015, 82 per cent were filed by the nationals of 15 countries (Figure 3).

Figure 3. Main countries of origin of people seeking international protection in the EU in 2015 and the ratio of positive decisions granting international protection with regard to the applicant's citizenship

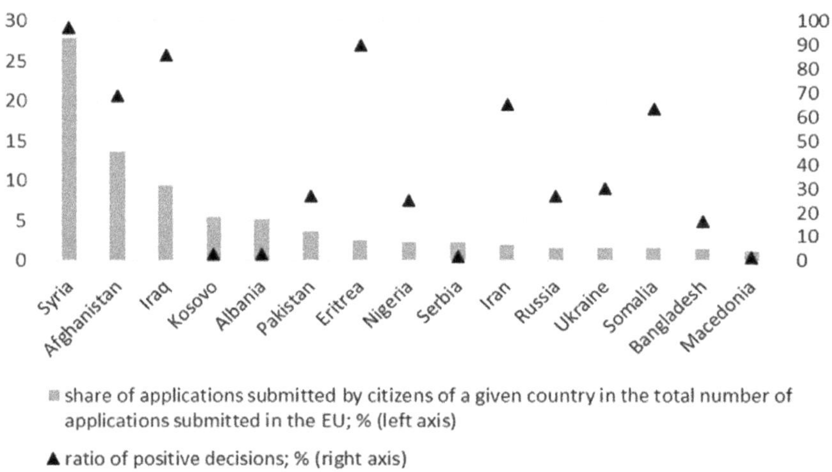

Source: Authors' own study based on: Eurostat, <http://ec.europa.eu/eurostat/data/database> accessed 15 January 2017.

---

38 Authors' own estimations based on, <http://ec.europa.eu/eurostat/data/database> [migr_asyappctza].

39 Y. Hakim, *supra* n. 1.

According to Figure 3 (left axis), the highest number applications in 2015 (similar to 2014 and 2013) were submitted by Syrians. They filed 27.83 per cent of all submitted applications. In second and third place, the highest number of submitted applications were made by Afghans and Iraqis. The group of 15 countries, whose nationals altogether submitted over 80 per cent of applications, also includes citizens of European countries (non-EU states) such as Albania, Kosovo, Serbia, Russia, Ukraine and Macedonia. In 2015, nationals of these countries submitted over 230,000 applications, i.e. 17.4 per cent of all filed applications.

Furthermore, it should be noted that there have been a significant number of rejected applications in the asylum procedure. Rejected asylum requests may indicate that seeking protection was not the purpose of all migrants arriving in the EU. Out of 597,680 decisions issued in 2015 in the first instance, as many as 48.11 per cent of applications were rejected.[40] At the same time we should notice that the ratio of positive decisions differs depending on the citizenship of individuals applying for protection (Figure 3, right axis). The highest ratio of positive decisions refers to applications submitted by the citizens of Syria (97.3 per cent), Eritrea (89.8 per cent), Iraq (85.9 per cent) and Afghanistan (69 per cent), i.e. countries where conflicts and/or persecution do occur. What is important, in four countries from the group of 15 sending states with regard to a number of submitted applications, the ratio of positive decisions does not exceed 3 per cent. These are applications submitted by the citizens of the countries located in Europe: Albania, Kosovo, Serbia and Macedonia. The ratio of positive decisions amounted to 2.62 per cent, 2.34 per cent, 1.6 per cent and 1.06 per cent, respectively. Such a low ratio of positive decisions just in this group of countries implies that most migrants from these states are not political refugees (according to the meaning of the Geneva Convention), nor are they economic refugees because they do not come from countries that are seriously affected by extreme poverty.[41] Therefore, they are most likely to be economic migrants who migrate to improve their financial situation. However, the analysis at the macro level provides only a general conclusion. Therefore, a small number of migrants from, for example, Kosovo might be economic refugees.

---

40 <http://ec.europa.eu/eurostat/data/database> [Eurostat, 2016].

41 Poverty level in these countries measured as the percentage of the population living on less than $1.90 a day, in the final year of the study amounted to the following levels: Albania – 1.1 per cent in 2012, Kosovo – 0.8 per cent in 2013, Serbia – 0.2 per cent in 2013, Macedonia – 1.3 per cent in 2008, The World Bank, *Poverty and Equity Database*, <http://databank.worldbank.org/data/reports.aspx?source=poverty-and-equity-database#> accessed 15.12.2016.

5. CONCLUSION

The EU faces a formidable challenge: creating a common supranational migration policy. Migration is not merely a geographical issue but rather a cultural and social problem. The influx of migrants and different approach to hosting refugees adopted by some EU Member States have undermined European solidarity whilst revealing increasing xenophobic attitudes and hostility to aliens (foreigners). Escalating migration embracing mainly economic migrants (not economic refugees) is resulting in stricter legal solutions regulating the Common European Asylum System.[42] The idea of solidarity was treated at the beginning of European integration as a manifestation of political will to enhance cooperation between European states. Its aim was to achieve two fundamental and very practical objectives: common economic benefits and closer political cooperation. The idea of solidarity intensified during the migration crisis in the EU. The migration crisis initially mainly involved refugees from the countries engulfed in war, that is, Syria, Iraq, Afghanistan and Eritrea. But as the war escalated, more and more people from other countries, or so-called stateless or displaced persons, the majority of whom sought better conditions to live and did not classify formally as refugees, started to arrive in Europe.

The economic analysis of international migration from the regions that are most severely affected by poverty leads to the conclusion that the migration of economic refugees is naturally limited. The regions suffering from extreme poverty do not experience a large scale of migration because potential migrants do not leave as they cannot afford the cost of migration.

What is more, the analysis of the background of individuals applying for protection within the EU territory has not confirmed the arrival of economic refugees in the EU despite the fact that nearly half of the applications for refugee status have been rejected. In the group of the main countries applying for protection within the territory of the EU, the highest ratio of rejected decisions regarded applications submitted by the citizens of countries not suffering from poverty. Migrants from these countries come voluntarily, not from regions affected by extreme, life-threatening poverty. Most migrants from these countries leave mainly to improve their financial situation and to enhance living standards. They do this of their free will. Since they do not come from the areas affected by extreme, life-threatening poverty, they are not economic refugees in the meaning of definitions provided by the literature. At the same time, due to restrictive and selective migration policies enforced by the EU and its Member States, applying for refugee status or irregular migration is, more often

---

42 European Parliament, *Enhancing the Common European Asylum System and Alternatives to Dublin*. Study for the LIBE Committee, Brussels 2015, p. 20.

than not, the only way for these people to access the European labour market.[43] Nevertheless, they should not be mistaken for economic refugees. The influx of different categories of migrants provokes various responses in the host countries' communities. The phenomenon occurring in the EU discussed here will be better understood if the relevant terminology is properly systematised and defined, which, in turn, will allow an assessment of the scale of this phenomenon.

43 It is worth emphasising that gradually increased restrictions imposed on entering a target country ensue an increasing number of illegal migrations, which entail negative phenomena of social exclusion and poverty encountered by both migrants and a host country. See further J. Harding, *The Uninvited: Refugees at the Rich Man's Gate*, Profile, London 2000.

8. DEFINING THE OFFENCE OF MIGRANT SMUGGLING: WHEN THE MIGRATION CRISIS REVIVES OLD DEBATES

Chloé BRIÈRE*

1. INTRODUCTION

In 2016, more than 300,000 migrants arrived in European countries through migration routes across the Mediterranean Sea, and more than 5,000 have been reported dead or missing. Although the numbers are slightly lower than in 2015,[1] the flows of migrants remain high, and there are uncertainties on whether the official statistics represent the whole picture. Behind these unprecedented, yet anonymous, numbers, it should not be forgotten that lives are at stake – people who are leaving their home countries in order to flee conflict and war, to escape serious human rights violations or poverty, or to seek better living conditions. These persons on the move may simultaneously fit into several categories, for example refugees, victims of human trafficking, smuggled migrants, asylum seekers and persons in need of international protection, economic migrants, etc. If they fall into one of these categories at the point they reach a border, they can, however, belong to another category when they reach their destination.[2] This change happens frequently as persons who start their journeys in a voluntary manner are also vulnerable to networks of labour or sexual exploitation.[3]

---

* Centre for European Law, Université Libre de Bruxelles, Belgium. E-mail: cbriere@ulb.ac.be.

1 According to the IOM, in 2015 it recorded 1,004,356 migrants arriving by sea, and 5,350 died, <https://www.iom.int/news/iom-counts-3771-migrant-fatalities-mediterranean-2015> accessed 08.04.2017. See also EUROPEAN COMMISSION, 'Report on the Follow-Up to the Leaders' Meeting on Refugee Flows Along the Western Balkans Route', COM (2015) 676 final: over 650,000 people crossing from Turkey to Greece in 2015, most travelling up through the Western Balkans to Central and Northern Europe.

2 M. MCADAM, 'Who's Who at the Border? A Rights-Based Approach to Identifying Human Trafficking at International Borders' (2013) 2 *Anti-Trafficking Review* 35.

3 EUROPEAN COMMISSION, 'EU Action Plan against Migrant Smuggling (2015–2020)', COM (2015) 285, p. 8.

When people take the decision to migrate towards Europe, this impacts the situation in their home countries, but also the situation in the countries through which they transit or those in which they finally settle. The unprecedented numbers of persons on the move have caused diverse reactions throughout the European states. Movements such as 'Refugees Welcome'[4] have led to demonstrations of solidarity and support for refugees. In contrast, extreme-right movements, such as Pegida in Germany, or the Front National in France, have criticised the massive influx of foreigners as a threat justifying closing down national borders. Beyond these strong positions, national public opinions and governments are still in the process of discussing and determining how best to answer to this situation, balancing the protection of fundamental rights and respect for laws concerning refugees, with the necessity to manage migration within the country, notably to ensure the smooth integration of the new arrivals into local society. Debates have also taken place at supranational level, as the institutions of the European Union (EU) have tried to ensure a certain degree of solidarity among Member States in welcoming and integrating these persons. These EU debates have addressed the possibility of designing and implementing a relocation system for asylum seekers,[5] the funding of programmes to integrate new residents, and the requirement of integration tests prior to obtaining a visa or a residence permit,[6] etc. Addressing all these issues at once will be impossible, and this chapter will focus on one particular debate: the definition of the offence of migrant smuggling.

This issue is linked to the importance of criminal networks in the current migration crisis. Indeed, the vast majority of the persons on the move who reach Europe have had recoursed to facilitation services, enabling them to enter irregularly in the territory of one EU Member State.[7] Criminal networks have

---

4 This slogan has turned into a website providing the possibility to offer housing to refugees in private accommodation, instead of camps. The website allows the registration of a flat share, support to find a new flatmate and ways to pay the rent. This initiative exists in Germany, Austria, Greece, Portugal, Spain, Sweden, the Netherlands, Poland, Italy, Canada, Czech Republic, Romania, Northern Ireland and Australia. Since the beginning of the project in November 2014, 930 refugees have found rooms in shared flats. See Refugees Welcome's website, <http://www.refugees-welcome.net/> accessed 08.04.2017.

5 Council Decision (EU) 2015/1601 establishing provisional measures in the area of international protection for the benefit of Italy and Greece [2015] OJ L248/80. The relocation system has been provisionally suspended for Sweden (Council Decision (EU) 2016/946 establishing provisional measures in the area of international protection for the benefit of Sweden [2016] OJ L157/23), and other EU Member States, such as Austria, have requested similar suspension (see for instance 'Austria to request exemption from EU migrant relocation system', *Euractiv*, 28.03.2017, <https://www.euractiv.com/section/justice-home-affairs/news/austria-to-request-exemption-from-eu-migrant-relocation-system/> accessed 08.04.2017).

6 See for instance ECJ, Case C-579/13, *P. and S.* ECLI:EU:C:2015:369, or ECJ, Case C-153/14, *K. and A.* ECLI:EU:C:2015:453.

7 Europol, 'Migrant Smuggling in the EU', February 2016, p. 2. See also Europol, 'Serious and Organised Crime Threat Assessment (SOCTA) 2017', pp. 49–51.

quickly adapted to this situation, and they have substantially increased their involvement in the smuggling of migrants. In practice, these criminal networks can provide a large variety of services, including the actual transportation or management of transportation of any person lacking a right to enter or transit a country of which that person is not a national; fabrication and/or provision of fake documents; the organisation of marriages of convenience; or other means to facilitate unauthorised entry, transit or residence.[8] These activities have emerged as a large, highly profitable and sophisticated criminal market, comparable to the European drug markets.[9] In 2015 alone, criminal networks involved in migrant smuggling are estimated to have had a turnover of between €4.7 and 5.7 billion.[10]

In order to reduce the attractiveness of this activity for criminals, and to limit the recourse to smuggling as a way to enter into Europe, criminal justice measures are essential, in so far as they participate in reducing the perception of low levels of risks for the perpetrators. Criminal law can indeed have a dissuasive effect, when its implementation ensures that smugglers are prosecuted and convicted for their involvement in this activity, and that the proceeds they earned are confiscated.

The efficiency of this criminal justice approach to the issue is unfortunately very much dependent on the shared willingness of all countries concerned by the phenomenon to combat it. States are called upon to play different roles. Given the cross-border nature of migrant smuggling, states need to cooperate with each other in order to dismantle the criminal networks and to trace the money. Such cooperation in criminal matters encompasses the collection of evidence within their territory for the purposes of criminal proceedings conducted in another state, or the identification, arrest and prosecution of smugglers operating in their territory. Notably, the EU Member States need to cooperate to dismantle the criminal networks enabling persons on the move to be smuggled from one Member State to another (secondary movements within the EU). Often these smuggling services are offered to move individuals from the Member State of entry, be it Italy, Greece or Spain, to the preferred country of destination, often the United Kingdom, Sweden or Germany.[11] Cooperation between EU Member States and third countries is also essential, especially for third countries crossed by the main migration routes, such as Turkey or Libya.

To combat criminal networks involved in migrant smuggling efficiently, a common definition of the offence of migrant smuggling constitutes an

---

8 European Commission, REFIT Evaluation of the EU legal framework against facilitation of unauthorised entry, transit and residence: the Facilitators Package (Directive 2002/90/EC and Framework Decision 2002/946/JHA), SWD (2017) 117 final, p. 4.

9 Europol, SOCTA, *supra* n. 7, p. 50.

10 *Ibid.*

11 Europol, 'Migrant Smuggling in the EU', *supra* n. 7, p. 6.

essential pre-requisite, especially in order to ensure that the requirement of dual criminality is met. This requirement implies that prior to the execution of extradition requests or mutual legal assistance requests, the requested state should verify that the crime charged in the requesting state is also found in its own national criminal law. This requirement applies to requests exchanged between non-EU states, but also to requests exchanged between EU Member States and third countries.[12] This principle does not apply to the execution of a European Arrest Warrant (EAW)[13] or a European Investigation Order (EIO)[14] exchanged between judicial authorities of EU Member States. Indeed, for these EU instruments implementing the principle of mutual recognition in criminal matters, the requirement of dual criminality has been waived for a list of 32 offences, which includes the facilitation of entry and residence.[15] Nevertheless, both instruments foresee that under certain conditions the executing authority can refuse to execute the EAW or the EIO if the conduct for which it has been issued does not constitute an offence under the law of the executing state.[16] Therefore, approximation of national definitions of the offence is crucial in order to ensure a common criminal justice answer to the phenomenon of migrant smuggling, and to foster cross-border cooperation in criminal matters. Similarly, efforts towards the approximation of the level of sanctions and of the investigative measures available are crucial in order to facilitate prosecution of the offence and cross-border cooperation to that end.

In this context, it is easy to envisage the willingness of states to adopt instruments aiming at approximating the definition of the offence, and other relevant elements. Efforts and initiatives pursuing these aims precede the current 'migration crisis', as some have been adopted in the late 1990s and early 2000s.[17]

---

12 See for instance Council of Europe, European Convention on Mutual Assistance in Criminal Matters, 20 April 1959, E.T.S. 30, Article 5(1)(a) 'that the offence motivating the letters rogatory is punishable under both the law of the requesting Party and the law of the requested Party'.

13 Framework Decision 2002/584/JHA on the European arrest warrant and surrender procedures (EAW FD) [2002] OJ L190/1.

14 Directive 2014/41/EU regarding the European Investigation Order in criminal matters (EIO Directive) [2014] OJ L130/1.

15 See EAW FD, Art. 2 and EIO Directive, *ibid*, Annex D. The dual criminality requirement may however apply to requests of mutual assistance made by Denmark and Ireland. These two States are not bound by the Directive on the EIO, and they can only rely on the 2000 EU Mutual Legal Assistance Convention (Council Act of 29 May 2000 establishing in accordance with Article 34 of the Treaty on European Union the Convention on Mutual Assistance in Criminal Matters between the Member States of the European Union [2000] OJ C197/1), which still requires dual criminality.

16 See EAW FD, Art. 4(1) and EIO Directive, Art. 10(g).

17 See in this regard the definition provided in Art. 27(1) of the Convention implementing the Schengen Agreement of 14 June 1985 between the Governments of the States of the Benelux Economic Union, the Federal Republic of Germany and the French Republic on the gradual

However, the adoption and implementation of these common definitions into national legal orders often faces obstacles linked to the sensitivity of the issue of migration and its close links with national policies on migration. This chapter will address the challenges faced in the elaboration of a common definition of the offence of migrant smuggling. The issue indeed raises conflicting arguments and positions, and the legislator, whether European or national, has to realise a delicate balance between them. The aim of this chapter will thus be to discuss how the legislators decide to define the offence of migrant smuggling, and how its decisions may encroach upon democratic principles. In doing so we will also attempt to determine whether the 'refugee crisis' has had any impact. First, we will analyse the choices made by the EU legislator (section 2), and we will then focus on the choices made by legislators of selected EU Member States (section 3).

2. DIFFICULTIES IN ELABORATING A COMMON DEFINITION OF THE OFFENCE OF MIGRANT SMUGGLING IN EU LAW

The origins of reflections on the importance of adopting a common definition of the offence of migrant smuggling date back to the late 1990s. At the European Council in Tampere, the Member States raised the 'need for a consistent control of external borders to stop illegal immigration and to combat those who organise it and commit related international crimes'.[18] The European Council indicated its determination to tackle illegal immigration, especially by targeting those who engage in trafficking in human beings and economic exploitation of migrants, and urged the adoption of legislation foreseeing severe sanctions against this serious crime.[19] In parallel, the European Community was participating in negotiations regarding the future United Nations' Convention against Transnational Organised Crime, and the future Protocol against the smuggling of migrants by land, air and sea.[20]

---

abolition of checks at their common borders [2000] OJ L239/19. See also the initiatives that preceded the negotiations of the United Nations' Convention against Transnational Organised Crime and its protocols, such as United Nations, Naples Political Declaration and Global Action Plan against Organized Transnational Crime (1994) A/49/748, para. 32; UN General Assembly, Resolution 52/85, Follow-up to the Naples Politcal Declaration and Gloabla Action Plan against Organized Transnational Crime (1997) A/RES/52/85, paras. 14–16; or UN General Assembly, Resolution 53/111, *Transnational Organised Crime* (1999) A/RES/53/111.

18 European Council, Tampere Conclusions, 15–16.10.1999, <http://www.europarl.europa.eu/summits/tam_en.htm> accessed on 08.04.2017, §2.

19 *Ibid.*, §23.

20 United Nations, Convention against Transnational Organised Crime, New York, 15.11.2000, 2225 UNTS 209, and Protocol against the Smuggling of Migrants by Land, Sea

As a preliminary remark, it should be noted that the instruments adopted within the United Nations and the EU do not use the same terminology: while the UN Protocol refer to smuggling of migrants, the EU instruments refer to the facilitation of irregular entry. These expressions cover similar factual situations, that is, when a person has recourse to the services of a criminal in order to enter, transit or reside irregularly on the territory of a state without having the authorisation to do so, and states are invited to criminalise similar behaviours. For the purpose of clarity, both expressions will be used in the discussion below, for the sole purpose of employing the expression corresponding to the instruments analysed.

2.1. COMPLEX NEGOTIATIONS

At the EU level, discussions on the definition of the offence started in June 2000, when the French Presidency published a proposal for a Framework Decision on strengthening the penal framework for preventing the facilitation of unauthorised entry and residence.[21] The text provided for a wide definition of the offence, as Member States were invited to criminalise 'the act of facilitating intentionally, by providing direct or indirect assistance, the unauthorised entry, movement or residence in its territory of an alien who is not a national of a Member State of the European Union'.[22] Criminalisation also concerned participation, instigation and attempt. The only exemptions from criminal liability proposed applied to persons with special links to the alien, either a relative in the ascending or descending line, brothers and sisters and their spouses; or the alien's spouse or the person who is known to cohabit with the alien.[23] The penalties foreseen included custodial sentences which might entail extradition for offences with aggravating circumstances, and other penalties such as the confiscation of the means of transport used to commit the offence, a prohibition on practising the activity in the exercise of which the offence was committed, and deportation if the convicted person was not a national of an EU Member State.[24]

---

and Air, Supplementing the United Nations Convention against Transnational Organized Crime, 15.11.2000, 2241 UNTS 507, Doc. A/55/383.

21 Council, Proposal from the government of the French Republic for the adoption by the Council of a framework Decision on strengthening the penal framework for preventing the facilitation of unauthorised entry and residence (2000) Council Doc. 9892/00, available on SEMDOC database.

22 *Ibid.*, Art. 1.

23 *Ibid.*, Art. 3.

24 *Ibid.*, Art. 4. The aggravating circumstances were the following: offence committed by a person belonging to a criminal organisation; purpose of the offence is trafficking in human beings or sexual exploitation of children, or is to allow the alien to work in contradiction with the rules applicable in the Member State in question.

This initial proposal raised several objections. Some were of a constitutional nature. The Council's legal service pointed out that by virtue of the rules concerning the allocation of Article 27 of the Schengen Convention between the first and third pillars, the proposal should be split into a Directive, under the first pillar, concerning the definition of facilitation of irregular entry, residence and movement, and a Framework Decision, under the third pillar, setting out the criminal penalties and rules on jurisdiction.[25] France thus proposed two new instruments known as the 'Facilitators' Package'. The proposal for a Council Directive was based on Articles 61(a) and 63(3) TEC (Treaty of Amsterdam version), and it contained a definition of the offence of facilitating unauthorised entry, movement or residence, and the exemptions, both of which remained unchanged.[26] The legal basis used belonged to the policy area of visa, asylum, immigration and other policies related to free movement of persons, and indicates, when read together with the first recital of the proposed Directive, that the goal of this package was to 'counter irregular immigration'.[27] The proposal for a Council Framework Decision was based on Articles 29, 31(e) and 34(2)(b) TEU (police and judicial cooperation in criminal matters) and, notably, it provided for penalties.[28]

Other objections were linked to the substance of the text and in particular to the constitutive elements of the offence and the exemptions envisaged. The French proposal did not follow the definition provided for in the Convention implementing the Schengen Agreement (CISA),[29] by virtue of which Contracting Parties undertook to 'impose appropriate penalties on any person who, for financial gain, assists or tries to assist an alien to enter or reside within the territory of one of the Contracting Parties in breach of that Contracting Party's laws on the entry and residence of aliens'.[30] The text further differed from the UN Protocol against Migrant Smuggling, which defined migrant smuggling as 'the procurement, in order to obtain, directly or indirectly, a financial or other material benefit, of the illegal entry of a person into a State Party of which the person is not a national or a permanent resident'.[31] Both the CISA and the

25 S. Peers and N. Rogers, *Immigration and Asylum Law: Text and Commentary*, Martinus Nijhoff Publishers, Leiden, Boston, 2006, p. 830.

26 Initiative of the French Republic with a view to the adoption of a Council Framework Decision on the strengthening of the penal framework to prevent the facilitation of authorised entry and residence [2000] OJ C253/6.

27 C. Ricci, 'Criminalising Solidarity? Smugglers, Migrants and Rescuers in the Reform of the 'Facilitators' Package', paper presented at the Migration and Law Network 2016 Conference 'Europe's Crisis: What Future for Immigration and Asylum Law and Policy?', 26–27.06.2016, p. 5.

28 Initiative of the French Republic with a view to the adoption of a Council Directive defining the facilitation of unauthorised entry, movement and residence [2000] OJ C253/1.

29 Convention implementing the Schengen Agreement, *supra* n. 17.

30 *Ibid.*, Art. 27(1).

31 UN Protocol Against the Smuggling of Migrants, *supra* n. 20, Art. 3(a).

UN Protocol insisted on the presence of a 'financial or other material benefit' in procuring the illegal entry of a person into a state. As indicated by the UN Office of Drugs and Crime (UNDOC), this element of 'financial gain' reflected the intention of the drafters that the criminal offences and sanctions established in accordance with the Protocol should apply to the smuggling of migrants by organised criminal groups, and not to mere migration or migrants, even in cases where it involved entry or residence that was illegal under the laws of the state concerned.[32]

Therefore, as the French proposal before the Council of the EU did not retain 'financial gain' as a constitutive element of the offence, and should the text remained unchanged, those who assisted asylum seekers and refugees out of humanitarian purposes, i.e. without the purpose of acquiring financial or material benefits, could be prosecuted for facilitation of entry, transit or residence. Strong concerns were expressed against the absence of reference to an element of 'financial gain'. For instance, the United Nations High Commissioner for Refugees (UNHCR) suggested that the definition of the offence should be narrowed to acts 'committed for the purpose of unlawfully acquiring financial or other material benefits'.[33] For the UN refugee agency, this element was 'essential to avoid that those assisting asylum-seekers and refugees purely out of humanitarian motives would risk criminal prosecution'. This was all the more crucial considering that asylum seekers 'generally rely on individuals and non-governmental organisations for information, advice and guidance as to the procedures to be followed in applying for asylum' (and they) 'are often dependent on the care and assistance of their own community or non-profit organisations during the initial period of their arrival in the asylum country'.[34]

The European Parliament also proposed several amendments to the French proposal, especially concerning the insertion of 'financial gain' into the definition of the offence of 'facilitation of unauthorised entry, movement and residence'. For the European Parliament, the general offence should be defined with an explicit reference to the commission of the offence *for purposes of direct or indirect gain*, which was justified for avoiding confusion between migrant smuggling and the humanitarian aid offered to enable people to flee

---

32 United Nations, Legislative Guides for the Implementation of the United Nations Convention against Transnational Organized Crime and the Protocols thereto, United Nations Publications, New York 2004, <http://www.unodc.org/unodc/fr/treaties/CTOC/legislative-guide.html> accessed 08.04.2017, p. 340, §28.

33 UNHCR, UNHCR comments on the French Presidency proposals for a Council Directive and Council Framework Decision on preventing the facilitation of unauthorised entry and residence, 22.09.2000, <http://www.unhcr.org/protection/operations/43662bd82/unhcr-comments-french-presidency-proposals-council-directive-council-framework.html?query=trafficking> accessed 09.04.2017, p. 3, point 8.

34 *Ibid.*

their country.[35] Along the same line of thought, the European Parliament proposed that exemption should be granted to associations, organisations and other legal persons acting for humanitarian reasons.[36] However, it is worth recalling that under the Treaty of Amsterdam, the Parliament had little influence over the content of these two proposals. The decision-making process for the adoption of a Framework Decision was in the hands of the Council of the EU, which would act unanimously, and was only bound to consult the European Parliament.[37] Directives in the field of migration, including the one in the Facilitators' Package, were negotiated during a transitional period of five years, and were adopted following the same procedure.[38] As a consequence, the discussions concerning the substance of the two proposals took place among the EU Member States.

The issue of inserting or omitting 'financial gain' as a constitutive element of the offence appeared very early at the core of the discussions within the Council. The argument in favour of omitting financial gain was linked to practical considerations, as requiring financial gain was considered too restrictive and raised a problem of proof.[39] Not requiring it was envisaged as a way to facilitate the investigation and prosecution of smugglers. Indeed, it might be difficult for the competent national authorities to rely on the assistance of the smuggled migrants, who might fear retaliation measures against themselves or their family if they cooperated with the authorities.

Yet, the positions of the Member States were diverse: some wanted to retain the requirement of financial gain (with possible exceptions), others not, while others felt that it should constitute an aggravating circumstance.[40] Some states also stressed that special treatment had also to be envisaged for humanitarian organisations, as well as for persons acting alone and not for financial gain.[41]

2.2. THE COMPROMISE FINALLY REACHED

As the two instruments were to be adopted unanimously, the negotiators were faced with the challenge of finding a definition of the offence, and exemptions, acceptable for all EU Member States. In order to accommodate the diverse

---

35 European Parliament, Report on the initiative of the French Republic with a view to the adoption of a Council Directive [... and] a Council Framework Decision ... (2000) procedure A5-0315/2000, doc. PE 294.244/rev, p. 8, amendment 8.

36 *Ibid.*, p. 10, amendment 11.

37 Articles 34 and 39 TEU (Treaty on European Union) [1997] OJ C340/145, pp. 164 and 167.

38 Article 67 TEC (Treaty establishing the European Community) [1997] OJ C340/173, p. 203.

39 Council, Draft Framework Decision on the strengthening of the penal framework to prevent the facilitation of unauthorised entry and residence (2000) Council Doc. 10859/00, p. 3.

40 *Ibid.*

41 *Ibid.*

positions expressed on the issue, the negotiations resulted in a complex compromise. The offences of facilitation of unauthorised entry, transit and residence are defined in Article 1 of the Directive,[42] and they can be summarised as follows:

- A person is criminally liable if he/she intentionally assists a third-country national to enter unauthorised, or transit across, the territory of a Member State (Article (1)(a)). His/her criminal liability can be engaged in the absence of a financial gain or any material benefit. However, the Framework Decision provides for the application of aggravating circumstances only when the offence was committed for financial gain.[43]
- A person is criminally liable if he/she intentionally assists, *for financial gain*, a third-country national to reside without authorisation within the territory of a Member State (Article 1(1)(b)).
- Member States have the possibility not to impose sanctions against persons, whether being individuals or organisations, assisting unauthorised entry and transit for humanitarian purposes (Article 1(2)). This clause is facultative and leaves a broad margin of discretion.

Regarding the penalties, the Framework Decision provided for 'effective, proportionate and dissuasive criminal penalties which may entail extradition' (Article 1(1)). Although this formulation is representative of second-generation instruments of EU criminal law, it remains weak and may fail to achieve the objective of approximation pursued. Penalties are provided for only when the offence of facilitation of unauthorised entry and transit is committed with aggravating circumstances. In this case, the penalty shall be a custodial sentence with a maximum sentence of not less than eight years (Article 1(3)). The text also includes a mandatory 'savings clause' for the Geneva Convention on refugees and other human rights rules related to refugee protection (Article 6),[44] but the provision is drafted in very general terms.

The compromise finally reached was heavily criticised. Some regretted the omission of 'financial gain' for the offences of unauthorised entry and transit, as it creates differences from the definition of the offence as provided in the UN Protocol, and it makes the scope of criminalisation at EU level very

---

42 Council Directive 2002/90/EC of 28 November 2002 defining the facilitation of unauthorised entry, transit and residence [2002] OJ L328/17.

43 Council Framework Decision of 28 November 2002 on the strengthening of the penal framework to prevent the facilitation of unauthorised entry, transit and residence [2002] OJ L328/1; Art. 1(3). The aggravating circumstances foreseen were offences committed as an activity of a criminal organisation and while endangering the lives of the persons receiving the assistance.

44 S. Peers and N. Rogers, *supra* n. 25, p. 831.

broad. Indeed, the offence as defined in the Directive can cover any form of assistance to enter or transit the territory of an EU Member State in breach of what is essentially administrative law (such as travel without appropriate documents).[45] The insertion of a facultative clause allowing Member States to provide for humanitarian exemption was not considered satisfactory. Because of its discretionary character, it undermines the objective of approximation of national criminal legislations and it results in institutionalising the existing divergences.[46] Furthermore, it does not redress the balance set out by the broad definition and criminalisation of migrant smuggling. Some authors considered that the EU measures 'essentially aim at deterring individuals and organisations from coming into contact and assisting any third-country national wishing to enter the territory of EU Member States'.[47]

Similar concerns are shared by the EU Agency for Fundamental Rights (FRA), which has conducted research looking at the use of criminal law measures to counteract irregular migration.[48] The Agency considers that the Facilitation Directive raises a number of fundamental rights challenges, as it 'fails to remind EU Member States of their obligation under international law to assist persons in distress at sea, regardless of their immigration status, nor that those who do so should not be punished under the directive'.[49] The criminalisation of the facilitation of stay done for profit also raises concerns, as 'it does not prevent Member States from also punishing acts not undertaken for profit, such as provision of humanitarian assistance to facilitate stay'.[50]

These illustrations of the sensitivity of the issue reveal the tension between the desire of Member States to provide strong criminal law measures, and the necessary respect for fundamental rights, and especially for international law on refugees. The existence of democratic checks and balances is necessary to ensure that all opinions are taken into consideration when elaborating EU measures against migrant smuggling. However, the legal framework applicable in 2002 fails to provide an adequate system of dialogues and counterweights, as the procedure remains in the hands of the most inter-governmental institution, the Council of the EU.

---

45 V. Mitsilegas, *The Criminalisation of Migration in Europe, Challenges for Human Rights and the Rule of Law*, Springer, Heidelberg 2015, p. 53.

46 A. Weyembergh, 'La lutte contre la traite et le trafic d'êtres humains' (2006) 1 *Revue internationale de droit pénal* 220.

47 V. Mitsilegas, *supra* n. 45, p. 53. See also E. Guild, *Criminalisation of Migration in Europe: Human Rights Implications*, Council of Europe, Commissioner for Human Rights, 39 (2009).

48 FRA, Paper 'Criminalisation of migrants in an irregular situation and of persons engaging with them' (2014), <http://fra.europa.eu/en/publication/2014/criminalisation-migrants-irregular-situation-and-persons-engaging-them> accessed 10.04.2017.

49 *Ibid.*, p. 15.

50 *Ibid.*, p. 16.

2.3. A NEED TO REVISE THE FACILITATORS' PACKAGE?

Since the adoption of the Facilitators' Package, that is, the Council Directive and Framework Decision discussed above, in 2002, the two instruments have not been revised. It could be argued that the entry into force of the Lisbon Treaty alone constitutes a reason justifying such revision, as the abolition of the pillar structure would enable the EU legislator to adopt the provisions defining the offence, the level of sanctions and other relevant elements in a single instrument. This would simplify the understanding of the EU measures against migrant smuggling. However, despite the abolition of pillars, the issue of legal basis would still arise. The text should be either based on a 'migration legal basis', such as Article 79(2)(d) TFEU,[51] or on a 'criminal law legal basis', such as Article 83 TFEU.[52] The choice would be crucial, especially considering that for EU criminal law directives, Member States benefit from a mechanism known as the 'emergency brake',[53] which does not exist in the field of migration. The issue is particularly sensitive, and may lead to annulment proceedings before the Court of Justice of the EU (CJEU).

Following a landmark judgment of the CJEU on the competence of the Community to provide for criminal law measures in Community instruments,[54] the European Commission has argued that the criminal law measures could have been introduced in the Directive defining the facilitation of unauthorised

---

51 The provision reads as follows: 'For the purposes of paragraph 1, the European Parliament and the Council, acting in accordance with the ordinary legislative procedure, shall adopt measures (in the area of) illegal immigration and unauthorised residence, including removal and repatriation of persons residing without authorisation.'

52 This provision, which constitutes the basis for the adoption of instruments approximating criminal laws, does not refer to smuggling as one of the euro-crimes for which the EU may adopt instruments. Nevertheless, it can be considered that an instrument could be adopted on the basis of Art. 83(2) TFEU, the so-called annex competence, as the adoption of criminal rules can be proved essential for the effective implementation of a Union policy. This provision reads as follows: 'If the approximation of criminal laws and regulations of the Member States proves essential to ensure the effective implementation of a Union policy in an area which has been subject to harmonisation measures, directives may establish minimum rules with regard to the definition of criminal offences and sanctions in the area concerned. Such directives shall be adopted by the same ordinary or special legislative procedure as was followed for the adoption of the harmonisation measures in question, without prejudice to Article 76.'

53 This mechanism is foreseen in Art. 83(3) TFEU, and it allows a Member States, which considers that a draft directive would affect fundamental aspects of its criminal justice system, to request that the draft directive be referred to the European Council. The legislative procedure is suspended, and the European Council has the possibility to discuss the text, and in case of consensus, can refer it back to the Council. In layman terms, this mechanism allows the suspension of qualified majority voting in EU criminal law, and enables a Member State to exercise a temporary veto.

54 ECJ, Case C-176/03, *European Commission v. Council of the EU (environmental crimes)* [2005] ECR I-07879.

entry, transit and residence.[55] As this judgment has been constitutionalised by the Treaty drafters, in Article 83(2) TFEU, the European Commission could eventually propose a new instrument based on a 'migration legal basis'. Furthermore, should the Council of the EU and the European Parliament agree on an alternative 'criminal law legal basis', the Commission could rely on its new competences to bring annulment proceedings before the CJEU. It has done this successfully in the field of transport policy, in which the Commission has sought the annulment of a Directive on the cross-border exchange of information on road safety related traffic offences, based on a 'criminal law legal basis', i.e. Article 87(2) TFEU on police cooperation.[56] The CJEU upheld its argument and annulled the text,[57] now replaced by a Directive adopted on the basis of the Union's competence to establish a common transport policy (Article 91(1)(c) TFEU).[58] The question of the adequate legal basis thus appears as a first challenge to be addressed when reflecting on the revision of the Facilitators' Package,[59] and this can possibly justify a certain restraint among the EU institutions and the Member States in proposing a new instrument.

Regardless of these legal considerations, the current migration crisis has placed the issue of migrant smuggling under scrutiny, and several have voiced their concerns about the relevance of the current EU legal framework. While some have expressed their desire to broaden its scope and/or increase the severity of the sanctions foreseen, others have advocated in favour of the consecration of the 'humanitarian exception' within EU instruments. More generally, the issue of migrant smuggling has become a topical one, and legislative reforms have been announced.

The European Commission for instance announced in its EU Action Plan against migrant smuggling,[60] that it 'will make, in 2016, proposals to improve the existing EU legal framework to tackle migrant smuggling, which defines the offence of facilitation of unauthorized entry and residence, and strengthen the penal framework'.[61] Such proposals 'will seek to ensure that

---

55 European Commission, 'Communication on the implications of the Court's judgment of 13 September 2005 (Case C-176/03 Commission v Council)', COM (2005) 583 final/2, p. 7.

56 Directive 2011/82/EU facilitating the cross-border exchange of information on road safety related traffic offences [2011] OJ L288/1.

57 ECJ, Case C-43/12, *European Commission v. European Parliament and Council of the EU* ECLI:EU:C:2014:298.

58 Directive (EU) 2015/413 facilitating the cross-border exchange of information on road-safety-related traffic offences [2015] OJ L68/9.

59 Complexity is further increased by the fact that, depending on the legal basis chosen, different Directorates General (DG) of the Commission might be responsible. Should a 'migration legal basis' be chosen, the DG Home would be responsible, whereas DG Justice would be competent if a 'criminal law legal basis' was selected.

60 European Commission, *supra* n. 3.

61 *Ibid.*, p. 3.

appropriate criminal sanctions are in place while avoiding risks of criminalisation of those who provide humanitarian assistance to migrants in distress'.[62] Similar announcement can be found in the EU Agenda on Migration.[63] The European Parliament acknowledged the intention of the Commission, and expressed the view that 'anyone who provides different forms of humanitarian assistance to those in need should not be criminalised and that Union law should reflect that principle'.[64] However, the publication of such a proposal is still awaited, and it seems to have been postponed to a distant future.

The Commission has, in the meantime, conducted an evaluation of the legal framework against facilitation of unauthorised entry, transit and residence, whose conclusions were published at the end of March 2017. The Commission acknowledged the challenges faced in evaluating the implementation of the instruments, partly due to the limited data available, but also due to the impact of the migratory and refugee crisis on the perception and responses to the phenomenon, which has added an extra layer of complexity.[65] On the insertion of the element of financial gain, the Commission pinpointed the arguments against its inclusion: the cash-intensive nature of the payment methods linked to smuggling makes it difficult to trace illicit financial flows and in turn to conduct investigations on the financial nature of the crime, and such difficulties would disproportionately hamper the investigation and prosecution of this crime, affecting states' legitimate interest to control borders and regulate migration flows.[66] The insertion of financial gain in the definition of the offences of irregular entry and transit was not discussed further, as the perceived risk of criminalisation and humanitarian assistance was considered as one of the main areas for improvement. Even though the Commission considers that 'limited evidence and information … do not allow to draw an accurate picture pointing to actual and repeated prosecution and conviction of individuals or organisations facilitating irregular border crossings or transit for reasons of humanitarian assistance', it recognises that fears about such perceived risk have been reported.[67] Nevertheless, given the context, marked notably by the adoption and implementation of the EU Action Plan against migrant smuggling, the Commission considers that 'at this point in time the Facilitators Package should be maintained in its present form [… and] the need for possible

---

62 *Ibid.*

63 European Commission, 'Communication "A European Agenda on Migration"', 13.05.2015, COM (2015) 240 final, 22 pages at p. 9.

64 European Parliament, Resolution of 12 April 2016 on the situation in the Mediterranean and the need for a holistic EU approach to migration, P8_TA (2016) 0102, para. 88.

65 European Commission, REFIT Evaluation, *supra* n. 8, p. 34.

66 *Ibid.*, p. 9.

67 *Ibid.*, p. 35.

legislative amendments to the Facilitators Package could be re-evaluated, once the implementation of the Action Plan has reached greater maturity'.[68]

Concerns have already been expressed concerning this latest position of the European Commission, especially concerning the remaining vagueness of EU law on those assisting migrants for humanitarian purposes. While awaiting a decision about the opportunity to revise the EU instruments, the Member States retain a wide margin of discretion and the possibility to criminalise humanitarian assistance. Some, such as Statewatch, a non-profit organisation monitoring the state, justice and home affairs (JHA), security and civil liberties in the EU, have considered this situation as problematic, since ensuring the effective implementation of the existing legal framework will do nothing to stop national authorities using the law against individuals and organisations engaging in humanitarian assistance to migrants.[69] From a democratic perspective, one can question whether the position expressed by the Commission answers the demands made by civil society. The public consultation organised by the Commission received an impressive number of replies (2,245 responses), and 92 per cent of the respondents considered that the EU should make it obligatory not to sanction facilitation of humanitarian reasons.[70] Yet the positions expressed at EU level remain as diverse as before. See, for instance, the debates within the European Parliament, considered to be the institution with a direct democratic legitimacy, at the occasion of the adoption of a resolution on the role of EU external action in addressing refugee and migrant movements.[71]

However, an initiative to propose a revision of the Facilitators' Package can only be made by the Commission, or at least eight Member States if they chose a 'criminal law legal basis'. In March 2016, the Council of the EU referred in its conclusions on migrant smuggling[72] to the respect of human rights and of those providing humanitarian assistance as essential parts of a comprehensive EU migration policy.[73] However, the text only invites Eurojust to identify and analyse the obstacles regarding prosecution and judicial cooperation, such as the differences between the Member States as regards the definition of

[68] *Ibid.*, p. 37.

[69] C. Jones, 'Hindering Humanitarianism: European Commission Will Not Ensure Protection for Those Aiding Migrants and Refugees' (2017) *Statewatch Viewpoint*, <http://www.statewatch.org/analyses/no-311-facilitation-directive.pdf> accessed 10.04.2017, p. 5.

[70] *Ibid.*, p. 4.

[71] European Parliament, Resolution of 5 April 2017 on addressing refugee and migrant movements: the role of EU External Action, P8_TA-PROV (2017)0124. See notably the references made to the issue of criminalisation of humanitarian assistance made by the MEPs M. Urban Crespo (GUE/NGL) and J. Lopez Aguilar (S&D). Transcription of the debates, <http://www.europarl.europa.eu/sides/getDoc.do?type=CRE&reference=20170404&secondRef=ITEM-014&language=EN&ring=A8-2017-0045> accessed 10.04.2017.

[72] Council, 'Conclusions on migrant smuggling', Council Doc. 6995/16.

[73] *Ibid.*, p. 2.

'illegal migrant smuggling' or the scope of the 'humanitarian exception'.[74] Given the silence of the Member States concerning the revision of the Facilitators' Package, it seems unlikely that they would exercise their right of initiative in this regard.

These decisions of the Commission and the Council will be difficult to remedy. The European Parliament has no right to initiative, and even though EU citizens can launch a European Citizens' Initiative,[75] or a petition,[76] their voices have little chance of changing the position of the EU institutions. In this context, in which neither the Commission, nor the Member States seem keen to open Pandora's box and to propose a revision of the current legal framework on facilitation of unauthorised entry, transit and residence, the discretion enjoyed by the national legislators is of crucial importance, and justifies an analysis of the national legislations on migrant smuggling, and more particularly of the potential influence of the migration crisis on the criminalisation of this behaviour.

3. IMPACT OF THE MIGRATION CRISIS ON THE NATIONAL DEFINITIONS OF THE OFFENCE OF MIGRANT SMUGGLING

In addition to their own national policies and legislations regarding migration, the EU Member States have since 2002 transposed and implemented into their national legal orders the definition of the offence as provided for in EU law. This has given an opportunity to realise a balance between their obligations under EU law, those under the UN Protocol against migrant smuggling, and those stemming from human rights instruments. The definitions provided for in national criminal codes constitute the results of the decision-making processes applicable at national level, as well as the channels available to their citizens to democratically express their views on the sensitive issue of migration. The scope of the offence demonstrates the approach taken on irregular migration, as well as on humanitarian assistance to migrants, and the position of a given state may change depending on a variety of factors, among which may figure the current refugee crisis.

74 *Ibid.*, p. 10.

75 A European Citizens' Initiative (ECI) 'Let'sfly2Europe: Enable safe and legal access to Europe for refugees!' was registered in September 2016, but it was withdrawn in December 2016. If it had received the backing of a million citizens from at least seven different Member States within one year of its registration, the issue would have to be put on the College agenda for discussion and action. For more information, see, <http://ec.europa.eu/citizens-initiative/public/initiatives/obsolete/details/2016/000001/en?lg=en> accessed 11.04.2017.

76 See in this regard an online petition calling for the EU to revise the Facilitation Directive to ensure that humanitarian actors are protected, which has been signed by 133,730 persons, <https://act.wemove.eu/campaigns/criminalising-humanity> accessed on 11.04.2017.

The following sections will be devoted to the sensitive issue of the definition of the offence of migrant smuggling in national criminal laws, and to the implementation of supranational/international definitions in national criminal justice systems. We will first analyse how the margin of discretion granted to national legislators has impacted the definition of the offence in national legal orders (section 3.1). Given the short time period between the peak of the crisis in summer 2015 and the time of writing of this contribution, we will attempt to assess whether the 'refugee crisis' has had an impact on the definition of the offence, that is, whether it has led to a deep reform of the national legislations and policies (section 3.2).

3.1. THE DIVERSITY OF NATIONAL LEGISLATION

All EU Member States have transposed in their national legal orders the offences of facilitation of unauthorised entry, transit and residence. Given the broad scope of this definition and the margin of discretion enjoyed by national legislators, most of the national definitions are considered to be in line with EU law.[77]

Concerning the offence itself, the Commission has indicated concerns linked to certain national provisions.[78] The Slovenian legislation is given as an example, as it provides that facilitation of entry or transit will be sanctioned only when it occurs in the form of repetitive acts. This additional requirement may undermine the investigation and prosecution of smuggling, as it imposes on national criminal justice authorities the necessity to demonstrate such repetitive character. In contrast, under the legislation applicable in Lithuania, the general offence of facilitation of unauthorised residence refers to third-country nationals who have crossed the border irregularly. This definition is narrower than the one provided for in the Directive, which refers to the assistance given to a person who is not a national of a Member State residing in that country in breach of the laws of the state concerned on the residence of aliens. The difference lies in the fact that the offence as defined in the Directive can cover the situation of persons who have entered the territory of that state legally, but who have extended their residence without possessing a valid permit. This refers, for instance, to persons who are assisted by smugglers abusing legal channels to facilitate entry or to legalise their residence, such as sham marriages, bogus paternity, false employment contracts, false medical visas, etc.[79]

Concerning the *modi operandi* followed by the smugglers, the definition contained in the Facilitators Package 'is broad and does not specify (those)

77 European Commission, REFIT Evaluation, *supra* n. 8, p. 14.
78 *Ibid.*
79 Europol, SOCTA 2017, *supra* n. 7, p. 50.

that can constitute the offence of migrant smuggling'.[80] This may reflect a decision of the EU legislator to preserve a certain flexibility, which is necessary to apprehend a criminal phenomenon like smuggling of migrants. Although some established smuggling *modi operandi* remain unchanged, such as the use of fraudulent documents, migrant smugglers have shown great versatility in the means of transport, concealment methods and technology they use.[81] Smugglers indeed seek to avoid detection and prosecution, and they thus adapt their techniques depending on the evolution of technologies, legislation and/or policy in a given country.[82] The use of fraudulent documents is referred to in the UN Protocol,[83] but not in the Facilitators' Package.[84] This silence of EU instruments does not prevent document fraud linked to irregular immigration from being widely sanctioned in national criminal laws. The Commission points out that in most of the Member States the provision or procurement of false documents is punishable in terms of facilitation of irregular immigration, either via general provisions (Belgium, Cyprus, France, Hungary, Lithuania, Poland, Sweden and the United Kingdom), or via specific provisions (Czech Republic, Greece, Spain, Finland, Croatia, Luxembourg and Slovakia). It also indicated that in two Member States, that is, Germany and Greece, the provision or procurement of false documents is considered a criminal offence in terms of facilitating third-country nationals' illegal residence in the country.[85] Concerning new *modi operandi*, such as sham marriages, several Member States reported that the current definition of facilitation of unauthorised entry, transit and residence is wide enough to allow sanctioning such type of conduct.[86]

---

80 European Commission, REFIT Evaluation, *supra* n. 8, p. 14.

81 Europol, SOCTA 2017, *supra* n. 7, p. 50.

82 *Ibid.*, *supra* n. 7, p. 50: 'Migrant smuggling networks heavily rely on social media to advertise smuggling services. Migrant smugglers make use of ride-sharing applications and P2P accommodation platforms to provide a cover for their smuggling activities. This leaves regular users at the risk of inadvertently becoming facilitators by unknowingly transporting or hosting irregular migrants.'

83 UN Protocol, *supra* n. 20, Arts. 3(c) and 4(b). The latter provision criminalises the production of a fraudulent travel or identity document, and the procurement, provision or possession of such document, when committed for the purpose of enabling the smuggling of migrants.

84 The Schengen Borders Code refers to the performance of checks on documents, but their issuance remains the competence of national authorities. To remedy the increased use of fraudulent documents, the Commission has recently published an Action Plan. See European Commission, *Action Plan to strengthen the European response to travel document fraud*, COM (2016) 790 final.

85 European Commission, REFIT Evaluation, *supra* n. 8, p. 14. For more details, including on the liability of the persons using false documents, see European Commission, Summary of EMN Ad-Hoc Query No. 2016.1036 – Existing legal framework on false documents (2016), <https://www.udi.no/globalassets/global/european-migration-network_i/ad-hoc-queries/com_ad-hoc_query_false_documents_final-summary.pdf> accessed 12.04.2017.

86 European Commission, REFIT Evaluation, *supra* n. 8, p. 14.

For sanctions, despite the vagueness of the provisions of the Framework Decision, the European Commission stresses that:

> all Member States impose criminal sanctions for facilitation of illegal entry and transit as a basic offence, while three of them provide for both criminal and administrative sanctions (Austria, Spain and Lithuania). Overall, the maximum limit of the custodial sentence can be of 14 years (United Kingdom), while the fine can go up to EUR 360 000. The administrative sanctions consist of fines of up to EUR 100 000 (Spain) and imprisonment of up to 60 days (Croatia). As regards facilitation of irregular residence, most Member States impose only criminal sanctions, whose maximums are similar to the ones applied to facilitation of unauthorised entry and transit. Only Spain and Lithuania provide for administrative sanctions, which consist of fines ranging from a minimum of EUR 72 (LT) to a maximum of EUR 100 000 (ES).[87]

The success of the approximation of the national criminal laws is understandable, as all Member States have supported the strengthening of the criminal framework against migrant smuggling. Many Member States are satisfied with the results achieved; with regard to the approximation of national laws, they considered that 'despite the existing differences, current national definitions are considered … to be sufficiently clear and broad enough to incorporate nearly all possible cases of smuggling of migrants'.[88]

The appreciation of the approximation of national legislations must be nuanced when examining the exemption from punishment for those assisting migrants for humanitarian purposes, and the requirement of financial gain for those assisting unauthorised residence. Concerning the facilitation of unauthorised residence, some Member States, such as Greece, France or the United Kingdom, go further than what is prescribed in the Directive and do not require any financial or material gain for the offence to be constituted. Others explicitly mention that the gain should be 'unfair' (e.g. Italy) or 'unlawful' (e.g. Czech Republic). On the other hand, several Member States provide diverse and scattered exemptions when the facilitation of irregular residence is carried out for humanitarian purposes (e.g. France), to a family member (e.g. Austria, France), or as a professional duty (e.g. Germany).[89] Turning to humanitarian assistance, it appears that only seven Member States (Belgium, Greece Spain, Finland, Italy, Malta and the United Kingdom) have included in their national laws an

---

87 *Ibid.*, p. 16.

88 ICF, *Evaluation and Impact Assessment Study on a proposal for a revision of the EU legal framework related to the facilitation of irregular migration (migrant smuggling)*, March 2016, p. 50.

89 S. Carrera et al., 'Fit for Purpose? the Facilitation Directive and the Criminalisation of Humanitarian Assistance to Irregular Migrants' (2015), study commissioned at the request of the LIBE Committee of the European Parliament, <http://www.europarl.europa.eu/RegData/etudes/STUD/2016/536490/IPOL_STU(2016)536490_EN.pdf> accessed 12.04.2017, pp. 30–31.

exemption from punishment for those assisting for humanitarian purposes the entry or transit of migrants.[90] According to the Commission, Belgium and Spain have adopted almost *verbatim* the language of the Directive on the inclusion of humanitarian assistance as a reason for non-incrimination, while other Member States have used different constructions.[91] In other states, such as Sweden or France, although a definition of humanitarian assistance is not provided by the law, national courts examine if any mitigating circumstances exist, or do not convict persons or associations providing such services.[92]

The results of these evaluations reflect the diversity of the positions taken by national legislators. It can be seen that the objective of approximation of national laws has not been achieved as successfully as hoped. Such discrepancies are regrettable, especially considering that they can incentivise smugglers to practice 'forum shopping'. The criminals involved in this activity may indeed be aware of these differences, and prefer to conduct their activities in countries with less severe laws, or with national authorities which give combating migrant smuggling a lower priority or which are less pro-active in this field. This is prejudicial to a common EU answer to, and fight against, migrant smuggling. Furthermore, coming back to the issue of financial gain, some EU Member States have adopted a definition of the offence conforming to the EU's definition, but not to the UN Protocol. Countries that have chosen not to integrate it in their national definitions can face obstacles when requesting cooperation from third countries, which may request the presence of a financial gain in order to qualify a behaviour as migrant smuggling. More generally, the diversity of the national transpositions illustrates how the issue of defining migrant smuggling remains highly sensitive and political.

---

90 European Commission, REFIT Evaluation, *supra* n. 8, p. 16.

91 *Ibid.*, fn 66: 'EL does not incriminate the assistance provided in view of rescuing a person at sea or of transporting a person under the need of international protection pursuant to the international law by captains and masters of ships and aircrafts as well as by drivers of any means of transport. IT adopted an explicit provision that recalls Art. 54 of the Penal Code, containing a general clause of non-criminalisation when the action is aimed at avoiding serious damage to the subject or the object of the action, as well as if conducted for the rescue and/or humanitarian help to foreigners, however present on the Italian territory. FI's relevant provision states that an act which, when taking into account in particular the humanitarian motives of the person committing it or his/her motives relating to close family relations, and the circumstances pertaining to the safety of the foreigner in his/her home country or country of permanent residence is to be deemed committed under vindicating circumstances and thus does not constitute arrangement of illegal immigration. MT provides the possibility not to institute proceedings on any person who aids or assists any other person in immediate situation of danger to land or attempt to land or transit through Malta, when such acts have been committed with a view to providing humanitarian assistance. UK's relevant provision provides for an exemption from punishment when the person is acting on behalf of an organisation which aims to assist asylum-seekers and does not charge for its services.'

92 ICF, *Evaluation and Impact Assessment Study*, *supra* n. 88, p. 29.

3.2. DOES THE REFUGEE CRISIS IMPACT ON THE DEFINITION OF THE OFFENCE AT NATIONAL LEVEL?

The positions expressed by the national legislators as described above are not cast into stone, and some states have changed their national legislation, notably to accommodate the lively discussions taking place at national level. A series of factors may have influenced the decision of national legislators to revise national definitions of migrant smuggling/facilitation of entry, transit or residence. Different elements can count among these factors, such as widely publicised criminal proceedings involving migrants, or persons assisting them generating strong reactions in the public opinion; and changes in the national political landscape (in particular general elections). The issue of migrant smuggling often turns into a dividing line between political positions, and the issue can sometimes appear in the political debate. However, despite the attention given to this issue, a certain consistency can often be witnessed in the position of a given state, and in this regard it might be difficult to conclude that the refugee crisis has had a determining influence on the way that the offence is defined in national criminal law.

Considering the sensitivity of the issue of migration, and especially of the provision of humanitarian assistance, some states have changed their national legislations, in circumstances independent from the so-called 'refugee crisis'. This is, for instance, the case in France.[93]

The criminalisation of assistance for unauthorised entry, transit or residence dates back to the 1930s, and despite successive reforms, the text has never referred to the element of the 'material gain', nor to a humanitarian exception.[94] When transposing the Facilitator's Package and the UN Protocol, the French government decided not to change the definition of the offence and the exemptions. The government considered that it was 'desirable that the principle of penalizing aid for illegal entry and residence should not be subject to any exception which might attenuate its scope or restrict its effectiveness'.[95] The text nevertheless introduces a new exemption, which can be viewed as a humanitarian exemption, yet only applicable to assistance to unauthorised residence.[96] In the meantime, organisations and individuals were conducting

---

93 For an overview, see J. Allsopp, 'Contesting *Fraternité*: Vulnerable Migrants and the Politics of Protection in Contemporary France' (2012) *Oxford Refugee Studies*, Research Paper n. 82, 3.

94 This is still the case today.

95 Assemblée Nationale, Rapport sur le projet de loi relatif à la maîtrise de l'immigration et au séjour des étrangers en France, rapport no 949 (2003) p. 37, <http://www.assemblee-nationale.fr/12/pdf/rapports/r0949.pdf> accessed 13.04.2017.

96 See Art. 21 III. 3. of the Ordonnance of 2 November 1945, which provided that assistance to unauthorised residence cannot give rise to criminal proceedings when it is given by any natural or legal person, where the act complained of was, in the face of a present or imminent danger, necessary to safeguard the life or physical integrity of the alien, unless there is a

activities, mainly at regional level, to support those accused/prosecuted for their actions supporting migrants. These persons were not necessarily directly accused of facilitation of unauthorised entry, transit or residence, but they were prosecuted for other offences.[97] Despite a lively debate in 2009, the creation of a consortium of NGOs and a draft bill put forward by the Socialist opposition, the text remained unchanged.[98] In 2011 it was amended,[99] but the amendment only concerned a change in the terms employed,[100] and the scope of the exemption remained interpreted restrictively by the national jurisdictions. Under this legal framework, persons and NGOs were subject to arrest, custody, indictment, prosecution or reminders of the law, which contributed to create a general climate of intimidation and pressure on all those who brought assistance. The offences for which they were prosecuted were labelled as '*délits de solidarité*' (solidarity offences), and the previously created NGOs-coalition lobbied again for a change in the law and/or the correct application of this humanitarian exemption.[101] The law was amended in 2012,[102] but although the insertion of a humanitarian clause was advocated for, the legislator decided to extend the scope of the exemption further. It now covers any natural or legal person who has assisted unauthorised entry, transit and residence of a third-country national, where the act complained of did not give rise to any direct or indirect compensation and consisted in providing legal advice or services of restoration, accommodation or medical care intended to ensure conditions decent living abroad, or any other assistance aimed at preserving the dignity or physical integrity of the person.[103] This change in the law does not necessarily satisfy advocates of organisations providing humanitarian assistance, as the current

---

disproportion between the means employed and the seriousness of the threat or whether it gave rise to a direct or indirect counterpart (translation by the author).

97 This was the case of E. Frammezelle, a former teacher belonging to an NGO providing assistance to migrants near Calais, charged for 'contempt of police' for protesting against police violence during round-ups of undocumented migrants, referred to in J. Allsopp, *supra* n. 93, p. 14.

98 J. Allsopp, *supra* n. 93, p. 15.

99 Loi no 2011-672 du 16 juin 2011 relative à l'immigration, à l'intégration et à la nationalité, JORF no 0139 du 17 juin 2011 page 10290, texte no 1.

100 The provision amended foresaw an exemption for persons assisting irregular residence. Whereas the previous version of the text referred to the assistance provided to protect the life or the physical integrity of a foreigner, the new text refers to the protection of the person of the foreigner.

101 See for instance Groupe d'Information et de Soutien des Immigré·e·s (GISTI), 'Si la solidarité devient un délit, nous demandons à être poursuivis pour ce délit!', press release, 23.03.2009, <http://www.gisti.org/spip.php?article1404> accessed 13.04.2017.

102 Loi no 2012-1560 du 31 décembre 2012 relative à la retenue pour vérification du droit au séjour et modifiant le délit d'aide au séjour irrégulier pour en exclure les actions humanitaires et désintéressées, JORF no 0001 du 1 janvier 2013, page 48, texte no 4.

103 See article L622-4 3, Code de l'entrée et du séjour des étrangers et du droit d'asile (Ceseda) [Code on the entry and stay of aliens and the right of asylum].

text of the law leaves a margin for interpretation to the judges, and persons continue to be prosecuted for having provided assistance to irregular migrants. This is for instance the case of individuals living the valley of the Roya, close to the Italian-French border, and who have since May 2016 offered assistance to migrants crossing the border by foot. Members of the association created by the inhabitants were tried in March 2017, including Mr Herrou, a farmer charged for having assisted unauthorised entry in the territory. The judges were relatively merciful, as, although the prosecutor asked for a suspended prison sentence of eight months,[104] they 'only' condemned him to a 3,000 euros' suspended fine, and no confiscation of his vehicle or limitation of his driving licence.[105] Mr Herrou was convicted for having facilitated the unauthorised entry of migrants to the French territory because he failed to establish the humanitarian character of his assistance for every migrant he assisted.

This French example illustrates how the issue of smuggling, and the non-prosecution of those providing assistance has been an ongoing debate for many years. The impact of the refugee crisis should not be underestimated, but it must be recognised to be only one of the factors influencing national debates and policies.

In contrast, other countries can be given as examples of countries where the national legislator has decided to amend the national criminal laws in reaction to the change in circumstances provoked by the refugee crisis. The reactions to the refugee crisis have been diverse, either in favour of the introduction of a humanitarian assistance, or in favour of more severe penalties.

On the one hand, Spain can be given as an example of a country introducing an exclusion of humanitarian assistance. The Western Mediterranean Route (from Morocco to Spain) has lost its importance compared to the Eastern Mediterranean route (from Egypt and Turkey to Italy and Greece) and the Central Mediterranean route (from Tunisia and Libya to Malta and Italy).[106] Nevertheless, Spain remains a country of destination for smuggling routes.[107] The country has also a certain sensitivity to the issue of migrant smuggling by

---

104 Libération, 'Cédric Herrou, le procès d'un geste d'humanité' (2017), <http://www.liberation.fr/france/2017/01/04/cedric-herrou-le-proces-d-un-geste-d-humanite_1539167> accessed 13.04.2017.

105 Le Figaro, 'Le tribunal de Nice clément avec Cédric Herrou, "passeur" humanitaire' (2017), <http://www.lefigaro.fr/actualite-france/2017/02/10/01016-20170210ARTFIG00085-le-tribunal-de-nice-clement-avec-cedric-herrou-passeur-humanitaire.php> accessed 13.04.2017.

106 N. Abdel Aziz, P. Monzini and F. Pastore, 'The Changing Dynamics of Cross-border Human Smuggling and Trafficking in the Mediterranean' (2015) *New-Med Research Network* 19.

107 See e.g. the case investigated by the Spanish and Polish authorities which revealed the existence of a migrant smuggling network exploiting irregular migrants from Pakistan in restaurants in Spain (see Europol, SOCTA, *supra* n. 7, p. 53).

sea, as for many years deaths at sea occurred regularly. The Spanish Criminal Code did not request financial gain to punish facilitation of entry, or the facilitation of stay,[108] but it was amended in 2015 to provide for an exclusion of humanitarian assistance of the scope of the offence of migrant smuggling (in force from 1 July 2015).[109] This amendment was not due to practical issues linked to the implementation of the Facilitators' Package, but it aimed to provide clarification of the legal framework in response to pressure from civil society.[110]

On the other hand, Hungary can be referred to as an example of a country that has changed its legislation towards more severe punishment. The situation of the country has been particularly affected due to its location: it is not only a country with external borders with the EU, but it is also a country located on the Western Balkans route. Migrants arriving in Greece travel towards their intended destination transiting through the Western Balkans, to re-enter the EU in Croatia or in Hungary. Budapest has become one of the main criminal hotspots for intra-EU movements,[111] especially for those willing to reach Germany. The response of the Hungarian government has been controversial, as it involved, notably, the construction of a fence at the border and changes to the criminal legislation. Before 2015 the Hungarian law was already strict: the Criminal Code provided for the criminalisation of illegal migrant smuggling[112] and the facilitation of unauthorised residence.[113] In 2015, the Hungarian Parliament adopted a law, which consisted of a range of amendments to the Criminal Code and Code of Criminal Procedure, with a view to rendering irregular entry through the Serbian border and the damaging of the newly built fence criminal offences, punishable by a term of imprisonment.[114] The new legislation also prohibits offering rides – even free of charge – to persons who have entered the country illegally and without the visa. The police and military have received extraordinary powers to search private homes if they suspect someone of

---

108 FRA, *Criminalisation of Migrants in an Irregular Situation and of Persons Engaging with Them* (2014), pp. 10 and 12, Figures 3 and 4. See Art. 318bis Criminal Code, <http://www.legislationline.org/documents/section/criminal-codes> accessed 19.04.2017.

109 Ley Orgánica No 1/2015 de 30 de Marzo de 2015 por la que se modifica la Ley Orgánica No 10/1995, de 23 de Noviembre de 1995, del Código Penal, BOE N°77, 2015, Sec. I, p. 27143, <http://www.wipo.int/edocs/lexdocs/laws/es/es/es179es.pdf> accessed 19.04.2017.

110 ICF, *Evaluation and Impact Assessment Study*, *supra* n. 88, p. 29.

111 Europol, 'Migrant smuggling in the EU', *supra* n. 7, p. 7.

112 Section 353(1) – any person who provides aid to another person for crossing state borders in violation of the relevant statutory provisions is guilty of a felony punishable by imprisonment not exceeding three years.

113 Section 354(1) – any person who provides aid for financial gain to a foreign national to reside unlawfully in the territory. Source: <http://www.legislationline.org/documents/section/criminal-codes> accessed 19.04.2017.

114 European Council on Refugees and Exiles (ECRE), *Asylum Information Database (AIDA), Crossing Boundaries, The new asylum procedure at the border and restrictions to accessing protection in Hungary*, September 2015, <http://www.asylumineurope.org/sites/default/files/resources/crossing_boundaries_october_2015.pdf> accessed 19.04.2017, p. 13 and pp. 21–24.

harbouring irregular migrants. The extent to which these laws will be enforced is difficult to assess. Some cases have attracted media attention, such as the case of a Hungarian man arrested – and finally acquitted – after using a local ride-share website, through which fuel costs are shared, to give lifts to refugees.[115]

The Spanish and Hungarian examples illustrate how the current refugee crisis has influenced the content of national legislations. Yet these two countries share a common characteristic. The crisis experienced in the last years has not fundamentally changed the content or the objectives of the national legislations and policies. It has, rather, served as a factor to justify amendments of the law, and very often these amendments have a strong symbolic value.

4. CONCLUSION

The definition of the offence of migrant smuggling is particularly representative of the consequences in European societies of the arrival of unprecedented numbers of migrants and refugees in recent years. Its representativeness can be attested through two elements.

First, the 'refugee crisis' has led to a certain legitimacy crisis of the EU. Whereas the scale of the migrant flows and the shared common interest in fighting irregular immigration called for a strong and united European answer, the main reaction of EU Member States has been the defence of national (or sub-regional) interests. The failure of the relocation scheme[116] is often quoted as an example, but the absence of a proposal aiming at revamping the Facilitators' Package can also be considered as negative. Notwithstanding the legal difficulties in the adoption of such an instrument, the EU institutions have not been able to convince Member States of the opportunity to revise these instruments, notably in order to introduce a humanitarian exception. This has led to a paradoxical situation, especially considering that an EU CFSP Mission (*Operation Sophia*) is active in the Mediterranean and is involved in search and rescue missions in high seas.[117] Although this mission's mandate is defined as contributing to the disruption of the business model of human smuggling and trafficking networks (Article 1(1)), the preamble of the text provides that the immediate priority is to prevent people from dying at sea. More critically, it preserves the margin of discretion of the Member States and the unequal treatment of those who assist migrants with a humanitarian purpose. Such situation is problematic

115 L. Frayer, 'Risking Arrest, Thousands of Hungarians Offer Help to Refugees' (2015), <http://www.npr.org/sections/parallels/2015/09/29/444447532/risking-arrest-thousands-of-hungarians-offer-help-to-refugees> accessed 14.04.2017.

116 On the Council Decision (EU) 2015/1601 and its difficult implementation, see *supra* n. 5.

117 Council Decision (CFSP) 2015/778 of 18 May 2015 on a European Union military operation in the Southern Central Mediterranean (EUNAVFOR MED) [2015] OJ L122/31.

when remembering that the 'crisis' was an opportunity for the EU to reaffirm the values on which it is based, especially the respect for fundamental rights. The sensitivity of the issue is so high that, in contrast, others are criticising the EU for not closing its borders and preventing the conduct of operations at sea. Its incapacity (or its shyness) to act is perceived as a paralysis, reproached both by those in favour of migration and those against it.

Secondly, moving to the national level, the refugee crisis is representative of the sensitivity of the issue, yet its impact must be nuanced by the observation that the issue of irregular immigration has been a topic for discussions for many years. The new context has not necessarily drastically changed the content of the national legislation, and the amendments that have occurred in the last two years are often marginal. Most importantly, the viewpoints of judges remain of crucial importance, as they are the ones able to interpret national legislations and, potentially, eventually acquit persons prosecuted for bringing humanitarian assistance to migrants. Yet relying on judicial interpretation may not be sufficient to ensure that those involved in assisting migrants do not fear prosecution. Civil society actors thus remain extremely involved in lobbying and campaigning for a change in the laws. Arguments linked to the principle of legal certainty have in this regard a certain weight. The efforts of the EU Member States thus seem to be oriented towards other objectives. The use of migration routes by terrorists in order to re-enter Europe has been a major source of concern, and the action plans developed at EU level have been much more ambitious in the field of counter-terrorism, including the creation of new forums for discussion, a revision of the EU legal framework, etc. Efforts have also been undertaken with regard to migration, but the focus remains still very much placed on the security dimension of the refugee crisis. This is regrettable, considering that the EU institutions and the Member States have been able in the past to adopt provisions foreseeing the non-prosecution of certain persons.[118] Should the political will be present, which is very unlikely, a similar provision could eventually be inserted in the future revised Facilitators' Package.

The sensitivity of the issue of migrant smuggling directly leads to a lack of consensus on how to approach it. Conflicting perceptions, arguments and positions can be found within each EU Member State, as well as within the EU as a whole. An important difficulty arises, linked to the realisation of a delicate balance between these divergent positions in the elaboration and implementation of the definition of migrant smuggling. Failing to realise such balance can become a challenge for democracy, especially if not all positions are taken into consideration by national and European policy-makers and legislators.

118 See for instance, the provision providing for the non-prosecution of victims of trafficking forced to commit criminal offences (Art. 8, Directive 2011/36/EU on preventing and combating trafficking in human beings and protecting its victims, and replacing Council Framework Decision 2002/629/JHA [2011] OJ L101/1).

9. THE COLLAPSE OF THE POLITICAL OFFENCE EXEMPTION IN EU EXTRADITION LAW: THE END OF POLITICAL ASYLUM?

Sibel Top*

1. INTRODUCTION

Extradition is a mechanism of international cooperation in criminal matters whereby a state (the requested state) surrenders a person to another state (the requesting state) that seeks the individual for trial or punishment for the perpetration of a crime. Extradition thus hampers alleged criminals from enjoying the impunity made possible by the crossing of a territorial border, where the jurisdiction of the requesting state does not apply.[1] Conversely, another mechanism that enables certain people to escape from the jurisdiction of a state exists, asylum. However, asylum is not a mechanism of international criminal law, as is extradition, and does not apply to alleged criminals. It concerns a particular group of people (asylum seekers) who have been subjected to persecution in their country and consequently moved across borders in search of protection in a safe haven.[2] Both mechanisms pertain to the relationship of an individual to a foreign territory, but they have evolved separately in two different fields of law. Nevertheless, developments in one field can affect the other. This chapter focuses on the changes in extradition law regarding the protection associated with political offences and their impact on the possibility of claiming political asylum.

---

* Fundamental Rights and Constitutionalism Research Group, Vrije Universiteit Brussel, Belgium. E-mail: sibel.top@vub.be. This chapter builds upon the author's master's thesis: S. Top, 'Réplique étatique à la sédition politique: de l'asile à l'extradition', Université Libre de Bruxelles, May 2014.

1 G. Gilbert, *Aspects of Extradition Law*, M. Nijhoff, Dordrecht 1991, p. 1.

2 UNESCO, 'Asylum seeker', <http://www.unesco.org/new/en/social-and-human-sciences/themes/international-migration/glossary/asylum-seeker/> accessed 27.07.2017.

For a long time, political offenders enjoyed a special status in extradition law: they were exempted from extradition. This meant that political offenders could benefit from an informal form of asylum, as they could stay in the country to which they had fled. Several reasons explain this political offence exception to extradition, not the least of which include the reluctance – for ideological reasons resulting from the French revolution – of states to surrender someone who would have risen up against despotism and tyranny, the need to avoid meddling in the internal affairs of their counterparts,[3] and the wish to avoid diplomatic tensions by extraditing the terrorist of today who – depending on the outcome of the struggle conducted – may well, tomorrow, become the leader with whom the state that granted the extradition will have to develop political relations.[4] As Honoré de Balzac phrases it, 'les conspirateurs vaincus seront des brigands; victorieux, ils seront des héros'.[5] In this regard, because of their particular nature, political crimes enjoy a special aura. They are not considered in the same way as ordinary crimes, which are associated with 'selfish' and 'vile' intentions. On the contrary, as Van Den Wijngaert describes them, such crimes are 'hyper-social' and 'altruistic', in the sense that their perpetrators are driven by a bigger purpose than their own personal interests; these acts are intended to serve the general well-being.[6]

However, over time, the protection associated with political crimes has not only weakened, but even disappeared from some institutional settings, such as the European Union (EU). In a context where the war on terror is at the top of the agenda, this development has significant adverse consequences on the asylum possibilities for political activists, as there are ever fewer offences that are considered to be 'political' and thus eligible for protection. This setback for potential political refugees takes place in a general context where, as will be outlined in this chapter, aliens are the primary target of the war on terror. Asylum seekers are thus not automatically perceived as vulnerable people in need of protection, but instead increasingly as potential terrorists.

This chapter will analyse the evolution of the protection associated with political crimes in extradition law by carefully scrutinising their development in connection with the context of their adoption, combining a legal approach

---

3 I.A. Shearer, *Extradition in International Law*, Manchester University Press, Manchester 1971, p. 166; B. Saul, 'Terrorism as a Transnational Crime' (2014) 14 *Legal Studies Research Paper* 1.

4 S.D. Bedi, Extradition in International Law and Practice, Bronder, Rotterdam 1966, p. 18. C. Van Den Wijngaert, *The Political Offence Exception to Extradition. The Delicate Problem of Balancing the Rights of the Individual and the International Public Order*, Kluwer, Deventer 1980, p. 3.

5 'The defeated conspirators become brigands; victorious, they become heroes' (translation of the author). H. De Balzac, *Une ténébreuse affaire: Scènes de la vie politique*, Éditions Furne, Paris 1846, p. 250.

6 C. Van Den Wijngaert, *supra* n. 4, p. 3.

with a historic political one. This will shed light on the purpose behind those changes, namely to fight terror, but also on their collateral victims. The choice has been made here to conduct this analysis first in the framework of the Council of Europe, and then in the EU. The reason for this relates to the fact that the political offence exception is a product of the European context and that the evolution of this kind of offence is best visible in its context of first appearance. Even though bilateral extradition agreements that EU Member States conclude with third countries do not go as far as the tools used *intra muros* concerning political crimes, they point in the same direction. The European example thus illustrates in a very clear way a tendency that is now widespread in democracies facing terrorism. The evolution of the legislation regarding political offenders in extradition law is a good indicator of how the need to combat terror impinges on the rights of potential asylum seekers. More generally, it shows how foreigners, including asylum seekers, are perceived today in Europe.

This chapter is divided into four parts. Section 2 gives a short timeline of the evolution of political crimes in extradition practices in the European arena, taking into account the context in which the most major changes took place. In section 3, the relationship of political offenders to terrorism is broached, with a view to broadening the debate to include other groups that are perceived as being connected to terrorism; namely foreigners. Finally, section 4 concludes by reflecting on the human rights as well as moral implications of such an approach to terrorism.

2. THE EVOLUTION OF THE PROTECTION ASSOCIATED WITH POLITICAL CRIMES IN EUROPEAN EXTRADITION LAW

2.1. COUNCIL OF EUROPE

The 1957 European Convention on Extradition, the first multilateral Convention on extradition adopted in the framework of the Council of Europe, was marked by a strong protection associated with political offences. Article 3 stipulates that '[e]xtradition shall not be granted if the offence in respect of which it is requested is regarded by the requested Party as a political offence or as an offence connected with a political offence'.[7] The only limitation to the political offence exception refers to the 'taking or attempted taking of the life of a Head of State or a member of his family',[8] a widespread Belgian legacy to extradition law ensuing from the assassination attempt in 1854 of Louis-Napoléon Bonaparte by

7 Article 3 of the European Convention on Extradition (ETS 24), 1957.
8 Article 3(3) of the European Convention on Extradition, *supra* n. 7.

two French nationals residing in Belgium.[9] The additional Protocol of 1975 to the Convention further specified the political offence by excluding war crimes and crimes against humanity from its scope.[10]

The guarantees associated with political offences thus remained largely intact until 1977, when the Convention on the Suppression of Terrorism marked an important turn in the definition of political offences. The reason for this shift cannot be understood in isolation from the political context surrounding the adoption of the Convention. Indeed, the late 1960s and 1970s saw the emergence and expansion of politically dissident movements following the 'years of lead' in Europe.[11] This political turmoil, later coupled with an ailing European economy, provided fertile ground for the apparition of independence movements in peripheral regions, such as Northern Ireland, the Basque country, Bretagne, Corsica, etc. In parallel to these separatist movements, political campaigners, sensitive to the Israel–Palestine conflict and inspired by the actions of the Black September Organisation,[12] started to develop and eventually turned into armed groups that advanced their political claims by using violence in European cities. The 1970s thus marked the birth of what is commonly called 'international terrorism'.[13] In this context, the drafters of the 1977 Convention wanted to equip judges with judicial tools that would enable them to tackle the problem of those armed groups that were considered as terrorist. To this end, the substance of the category of political crimes was considerably altered. The first article of the Convention provides a list of specific offences that no longer qualify as political and that are thus excluded from the protection associated with these kind of offences.[14] However, this change was not deemed to be enough and the legislators further added, in a subsequent article, that 'an act of violence, other

9 This clause is internationally known as the *attentat* clause. J.P. Grant and J.C. Barker, *Parry & Grant Encyclopaedic Dictionary of International Law*, Oxford University Press, Oxford 2009, p. 51.

10 Article 1 of the Additional Protocol to the European Convention on Extradition (ETS 86), 1975.

11 The 'years of lead' refer to a period of major political turmoil in Europe characterised by left and right-wing terror attacks across the continent. It started in Italy in the late 1960s, quickly spread to the rest of Western Europe and lasted until the early 1980s. P. Fabre and D. Fabre, *Histoire de l'Europe au XXème siècle (1945 à 1974) 2ème partie*, Complexe, Paris 1995, pp. 170–175.

12 Black September is a Palestinian terrorist organisation that was a special arm of the Fatah. It was named after the events of September 1970, where an armed conflict opposed the Palestinian Liberation Organisation to the Jordanian Armed Forces. It is known for its spectacular attacks, such as the assassination of the Jordanian Prime Minister, Wasfi al-Tall, in 1971 and the hostage-taking and subsequent assassination of 11 members of the Israeli team of the Olympic games in 1972. I. Fruchter-Ronen, 'Black September: The 1970–71 Events and their Impact on the Formation of Jordanian National Identity' (2008) 10 *Civil Wars* 255.

13 P. Fabre and D. Fabre, *supra* n. 11, pp. 167–222.

14 Article 1 of the European Convention on the Suppression of Terrorism (ETS 90), 1977.

than one covered by Article 1, against the life, physical integrity or liberty of a person' or 'a serious offence involving an act against property, other than one covered by Article 1, if the act created a collective danger for persons' may not be regarded as 'a political offence or as an offence connected with a political offence or as an offence inspired by political motives'.[15] As Weyembergh and Bribosia underline, the authors of the Convention used both the descriptive and enumerative methods, leaving very little room for an offence to qualify as political.[16] However, one safeguard – entirely left to the discretion of the states – introduced the possibility, at the time of the signature of the Convention, to reserve 'the right to refuse extradition in respect of any offence mentioned in Article 1 which it considers to be a political offence, an offence connected with a political offence or an offence inspired by political motives'.[17]

2.2. EUROPEAN UNION

A few years later, in 1985 the European Communities signed the Schengen Agreement aiming to abolish internal borders.[18] This came into force with the Convention implementing the Schengen Agreement, which was signed in 1990.[19] The removal of internal border control became possible thanks to the concomitant adoption of compensatory measures[20] that included, among others, mutual assistance in criminal matters.[21] The years ensuing the adoption of the Treaty of Maastricht, which integrated Justice and Home Affairs in the third pillar of the Treaty, saw the effective enhancement of mutual assistance in criminal matters, namely by the adoption of two conventions on extradition.

---

15 Articles 1 and 2 of the European Convention on the Suppression of Terrorism, *supra* n. 14.

16 E. Bribosia and A. Weyembergh, 'Asile et extradition: vers un espace judiciaire européen?' (1997) 1 *Revue Belge de Droit International* 79.

17 Article 13 of the European Convention on the Suppression of Terrorism, *supra* n. 14. In this regard, it is interesting to note that out of 46 states that ratified the Convention, 18 used the right granted by Article 13 to refuse extradition if the offence for which it is requested is a political one. Council of Europe, 'Reservations and Declarations for Treaty No.090 – European Convention on The Suppression of Terrorism', <https://www.coe.int/en/web/conventions/full-list/-/conventions/treaty/090/declarations?p_auth=joGjMypo> accessed 26.07.2017.

18 Agreement of 14 June 1985 between the Governments of the States of the Benelux Economic Union, the Federal Republic of Germany and the French Republic on the gradual abolition of checks at their common borders [2000] OJ L239/19.

19 Convention implementing the Schengen Agreement of 14 June 1985 between the Governments of the States of the Benelux Economic Union, the Federal Republic of Germany and the French Republic on the gradual abolition of checks at their common borders [2000] OJ L239/19.

20 W. Wagner, 'Building an Internal Security Community: The Democratic Peace and the Politics of Extradition in Western Europe' (2003) 40 *Journal of Peace Research* 704.

21 Chapter 2 of the Convention implementing the Schengen Agreement, *supra* n. 19.

If the first one, adopted in March 1995 and relating to the simplified extradition procedure between Member States, did not touch on political offences,[22] the second one, adopted in September 1996, changed the content of those offences in an extraordinary way. As for the 1977 Convention on the Suppression of Terrorism, the changes brought by the Convention of 1996 cannot be understood without considering the context of its adoption.

The wave of terrorist attacks shaking Europe which had begun in the 1970s continued until the 1990s. Euskadi Ta Askatasuna[23] (ETA), an armed Basque separatist organisation, participated to this flow of violent political activism in the attempt to achieve independence.[24] It is against this backdrop that the adoption of the Convention of 1996 relating to extradition between the Member States of the EU took place. Indeed, in 1993, Spain delivered an extradition warrant against two Basque activists, Moreno Ramajo and Garcia Arrantz, who had fled to Belgium. The non-binding opinion of the indictment division in Belgium was that the offences, for which their extradition was requested, were to be seen as political and did not qualify for the exceptions to the political offence exemption, outlined in the 1977 Convention. However, the Ministry of Justice took the opposite stance and ruled in favour of the extradition. In parallel to these proceedings, Garcia and Moreno lodged an asylum application in 1993 that was deemed admissible for further consideration. The Spanish authorities saw this acceptance for further examination of the asylum request as offensive, and regarded it as an 'unfriendly act'.[25] The asylum application was eventually rejected in 1994 on the grounds that the abuses committed by Spanish authorities against Basque militants were real, but constituted one-off events rather than a structural problem. The extradition request – which was put on hold until the decision on asylum was notified – was thus pursued, accepted and the consecutive appeal introduced by Garcia and Moreno was rejected. In order to counter the extradition, they thus lodged an application for suspension as a matter of extreme urgency before the Belgian Council of State. The Belgian Council of State ruled in favour of the couple, who ultimately, were not extradited to Spain.[26] The Spanish authorities viewed this decision as a suspicion raised by Belgian authorities about the democratic character of Spain. In this regard, Weyembergh and Bribosia argue that the decision of the

---

22 Council Act of 10 March 1995 drawing up the Convention on simplified extradition procedure between the Member States of the European Union [1995] OJ C78/1.

23 'Basque Fatherland and Liberty'. Council on Foreign Relations, 'Basque Fatherland and Liberty (ETA) (Spain, separatists, Euskadi ta Askatasuna)', <https://www.cfr.org/backgrounder/basque-fatherland-and-liberty-eta-spain-separatists-euskadi-ta-askatasuna> accessed 26.07.2017.

24 B. Galloux-Fournier, *Histoire de l'Europe au XXe siècle (de 1974 à nos jours)*, Complexe, Paris 1995, pp. 161–163.

25 E. Bribosia and A. Weyembergh, *supra* n. 16, p. 74.

26 *Ibid.*, pp. 75–76.

judge was based on the consideration that the offences for which the extradition was requested did not qualify as terrorist offences on the basis of the 1977 Convention; and therefore the ruling was not to be seen to be calling Spanish democracy into question.[27] Following these events, Spain actively worked both for the suppression of the political offence exemption in EU extradition procedures, and for the abolishment of the possibility of asylum in the EU for EU citizens.[28] The reason put forward for those changes related to the fact that they constituted an obstacle to mutual assistance in criminal matters as well as to the fight against terrorism.[29]

These events led to the adoption of the 1996 Convention, which generated the last and greatest shift concerning the political offence exemption in the EU. Indeed, not only did its Article 2 widen the grounds of extraditable offences; but its Article 5 abolished the political offence exemption among EU Member States for good by stating that 'no offence may be regarded by the requested Member State as a political offence, as an offence connected with a political offence or an offence inspired by political motives'.[30] The political offence exemption thus ceased to exist in the relations between EU Member States concerning extradition. As highlighted by Weyembergh and Bribosia, the relationship of this Convention to political crimes completely reversed the one of the 1957 Convention on Extradition.[31] This development was unprecedented and marked a new era in European extradition law.

This shift regarding political crimes in the EU was further maintained in the latest major tool adopted by the EU in terms of extradition: the European Arrest Warrant (EAW).[32] The Warrant, which had been the subject of negotiation

27 *Ibid.*, p. 76.

28 They eventually achieved the latter with the adoption of the Aznar Protocol, which was annexed to the Treaty of Amsterdam. Protocol (no 24) on Asylum for Nationals of Member States of the European Union, annexed to the Treaty of Amsterdam amending the Treaty on European Union, the Treaties establishing the European Communities and certain related acts [1997] OJ C340/305.

29 E. Bribosia and A. Weyembergh, *supra* n. 16, p. 76.

30 Article 5 of the Convention drawn up on the basis of Article K.3 of the Treaty on European Union, relating to Extradition between the Member States of the European Union [1996] OJ C313/12.

31 E. Bribosia and A. Weyembergh, *supra* n. 16, p. 78.

32 There is an extensive literature on the topic of the European Arrest Warrant. For further information, see L. Klimek, *The European Arrest Warrant*, Springer, Switzerland 2015; M. Platcha, 'European Arrest Warrant: Revolution in Extradition?' (2003) 11(2) *European Journal of Crime, Criminal Law and Criminal Justice* 178; S. Carrera, E. Guild and N. Hernanz, 'Europe's Most Wanted? Recalibrating Trust in the European Arrest Warrant System' (2013) 55 *CEPS paper in Liberty and Security in Europe* 1; S. Alegre and M. Leaf, 'Mutual Recognition in European Judicial Cooperation: A Step too Far too Soon? Case Study – The European Arrest Warrant' (2004) 10(2) *European Law Journal* 200; R. Blekxtoon and W. Van Ballegooij, *Handbook on the European Arrest Warrant*, T.M.C. Asser Press, The Hague 2005; E. Guild, *Constitutional Challenges to the European Arrest Warrant*, Wolf Legal Publishers, Nijmegen 2006.

for years before the 9/11 terrorist attacks in the United States, ended up being adopted in four months after the attacks.[33] The adoption of the European Arrest Warrant did not affect the definition of political offences, but it did significantly alter extradition between Member States, and turned it into a highly efficient fast-track procedure.[34]

The consequence of all the legal developments discussed above has been substantial for political offenders: in less than 50 years, their status went from strongly protected to almost automatically surrendered in the EU. The category of political offences in extradition law has thus undergone major changes in the last decades. The protection associated with these kinds of offences has diminished both in the framework of both the Council of Europe and of the EU.

3. THE AMBIGUOUS RELATIONSHIP BETWEEN POLITICAL CRIMES AND TERRORISM

As outlined in the previous section, the weakening of the protection associated with political crimes was achieved through the gradual 'depoliticisation' of offences, which, incidentally, happened in times where the need to fight terror appeared to be ever more pressing. Indeed, the major developments in extradition law concerning political crimes followed violent events, namely terror attacks. The war on terror thus seems to have also induced a war on the category of political crimes. This gives rise to one question: why has the war on terror affected the category of political crimes in extradition treaties?

3.1. THE DIFFICULTY IN DEFINING POLITICAL CRIMES

The difficulty in defining political crimes has been widely commented on in academic literature. None of the conventions on extradition studied in this chapter contains a definition of what is to be understood by 'political crime'. Conversely, the closest these conventions get to a definition of this type of offence resides in the enumeration of what is *not* included in the category of political crimes, thus providing a negative definition (i.e. the exclusion of elements from its scope) rather than a positive one (i.e. a description of its constitutive elements). Of course, there have been attempts to delimit the scope

33 S. Bot, *Le Mandat d'Arrêt Européen*, Larcier, Bruxelles 2009, p. 31.

34 Council Framework Decision of 13 June 2002 on the European Arrest Warrant and the Surrender Procedures between Member States – Statements made by certain Member States on the adoption of the Framework Decision [2002] OJ L190/1.

of such offences, namely through efforts to categorise the different crimes under different spectrums of 'political'. In this regard, many authors have embarked on the delicate task of providing lengthy descriptions of what constitutes, among others, a 'pure political offence', a '*délit complexe*', a '*délit connexe*', and of the different tests that exist to assess the political character of an offence.[35] Similarly, a distinction between 'objective' and 'subjective' theories has also been suggested in order to categorise those crimes. Supporters of the subjective theory consider that what matters in the definition of a crime as political is the intent of the alleged perpetrator (i.e. if the alleged offender had a political motive for the actions); whereas proponents of the objective theory support the idea that it is the nature of the entity that has been affected by the crime that determines if the offence is political or not (i.e. if the victim of the attack is a political entity).[36]

However, no substantial definition has been put forward so far because of the difficulty of such a task. Papadatos notes that the two essential characteristics attached to the notion of political crime is that they are 'relative' and 'indefinitely variable'.[37] Indeed, he attributes the 'relativity' of such crimes to their wide acceptance in our societies; acceptance that emanates from the perception of those crimes as 'hyper-social' and which is the result of the liberalism that reigned in Europe in the nineteenth century.[38] Furthermore, he describes the notion of 'political' as being utterly intangible. Papadatos rightly defines it as a prism through which everything can take political overtones rather than a substance that can be grasped.[39]

3.2. THE DIFFICULTY IN DISTINGUISHING POLITICAL CRIMES FROM TERRORISM

The problem raised by the lack of definition of political crimes becomes even more intriguing when one looks at the definition of terrorism. The EU adopted its own definition in 2002.[40] This means that at the time when all the instruments

35 See for instance C. Van Den Wijngaert, *supra* n. 4; Y. Chauvy, *L'Extradition*, Presses Universitaires de France, Paris 1981; G.S. Gilbert, 'Terrorism and the Political Offence Exemption Reappraised' (1985) 34 *International and Comparative Law Quarterly* 695; I.A. Shearer, *supra* n. 3; I. Stanbrook and C. Stanbrook, *Extradition: Law and Practice*, Oxford University Press, Oxford 2000; B. Galgani, 'Extradition, Political Offence and the Discrimination Clause' in S. Ruggeri (ed.), *Transnational Inquiries and the Protection of Fundamental Rights in Criminal Proceedings. A Study in Memory of Vittorio Grevi and Giovanni Tranchina*, Springer, Heidelberg 2012, pp. 167–191.

36 P. Papadatos, *Le délit politique: contribution à l'étude des crimes contre l'État*, Librairie E. Droz, Geneva 1955, p. 72.

37 *Ibid.*, p. 70.

38 *Ibid.*

39 *Ibid.*

40 It adopted a definition in its Council Framework Decision 2002/475/JHA of 13 June 2002 on combating terrorism that was amended by the Council Framework Decision 2008/919/JHA

presented above were adopted, no commonly agreed definition of terrorism existed. This is still the case at the global level, where there is still no common legal definition of terrorism.[41] The development of new legislation both on political crimes and on terrorism at a time when no definition was adopted for either of them could thus seem slightly – to say the least – problematic, especially when the states have preferred to 'depoliticise' 'political crimes' in conventions on extradition and on terrorism rather than give substantial definitions of political crimes and terrorism. This has been most clearly visible in the fact that the category of political offence exemptions has suffered the hardest hits in times of terrorist attacks. The comfortable use of two non-defined concepts is thus questionable, particularly in the field of law, where the terminology used is crucial in determining the rights to which individuals are entitled. The problem of denomination, and therefore, of delimitation between the two is thus of critical importance.

However, a delimitation would entail a clear difference. Are political crimes and acts of terrorism so different? Maybe not. As Van Den Wijngaert has highlighted, many among the crimes which are brought under international penal control (e.g. war crimes, genocide, hijacking, taking of hostages) are politically 'coloured', since they are often politically motivated and frequently situated within the frame of a political conflict situation. This problem is highlighted today as a consequence of the development of a transnational delinquency with political overtones: 'international terrorism'.[42] She further specifies that:

> from a broad, *sociological*, perspective, most of these acts of 'terrorism' can be considered as political offences because they are usually politically motivated and, in a majority of cases, ultimately directed against the state or a subdivision thereof. For this reason, they are political offences *lato sensu*; the inherent seriousness of most acts of 'terrorism' and the purpose pursued by the 'terrorists' do not affect this political character.[43]

The line between a political offence and a terrorist crime is thus somewhat blurred.

3.3. THE POLITICAL OPPORTUNITY

This blurriness between the two terms may seem at first sight as an impediment for lawmakers to legislate, but it was not. On the contrary, in the aftermath of

of 28 November 2008 amending Framework Decision 2002/475/JHA on combating terrorism [2008] OJ L330/21.

41 A.P. Schmid, 'The Revised Academic Consensus Definition of Terrorism' (2012) 6 *Perspectives on Terrorism* 158.

42 C. Van Den Wijngaert, *supra* n. 4, p. 21.

43 *Ibid.*, pp. 24–25.

the 9/11 attacks, the lack of a concrete definition and differentiation between the two terms cleared the lawmakers from the responsibility to engage in fastidious explanations on why the new measures to combat terrorism would affect, among other issues seemingly unrelated to it, political crimes. In the context of the sudden apparition of an urgent war on terror, the instruments adopted to tackle terrorism multiplied and strengthened.[44] The lack of distinction between the two seems to have been very convenient, since a clear definition of what is a 'political crime' would have constituted a shield against the repeated assaults on the protection associated with this category of crime.

In this context, potential political asylum seekers are the ones most affected by these developments in extradition law. As a matter of fact, the measures adopted in the EU in the aftermath of the 9/11 attacks primarily targeted foreigners. Indeed, besides the massive incorporation of anti-terrorism clauses in agreements with third countries at the time of the 9/11 attacks[45] as well as today,[46] many of the measures aimed at fighting terrorism actually intend(ed) to curb irregular immigration.[47] Berthelet goes even further by stating that EU Member States, in reaction to the attacks, had to tackle the issue of security and thus needed to identify what threatens security, to which they found an answer first in organised crime and, after 9/11, in terrorism, both embodied by the foreigner.[48] Identifying the foreigner as the danger to security enabled the authorities to concentrate their policies on individuals and not on a diffuse threat that would not be palpable, and therefore targetable. This projection of the cause of insecurity of EU citizens on the foreigner allowed the state to present this threat as coming from outside and endangering internal security. The inflow of migrants would thus coincide with the incursion of terrorism on the European territory. The minorities already on European soil would be the 'staging post' of newcomers, 'invading' Europe and 'spreading the word among their peers'.[49]

This discourse of asylum seekers coming to Europe and bringing (or being) terrorists is conveyed, among others, by the media. It is further relayed by politicians and high-ranking officials who sometimes 'just' hint it, but also, in

---

44 P. Berthelet, 'L'impact des événements du 11 septembre sur la création de l'espace de liberté, de sécurité, et de justice. Partie 2' (2002) 46 *Cultures & Conflits* 6.

45 *Ibid.*, p. 3.

46 In this regard, the very first sentence framed in the website of the EU fight against terrorism could not be more explicit on this issue. Indeed, it states that '[t]he security of the European Union is closely linked with the developments in other countries, particularly in the neighbouring states, and so the EU counter-terrorism strategy needs to be on a global scale'. European Union, 'EU Fight against Terrorism', <http://www.consilium.europa.eu/en/policies/fight-against-terrorism/> accessed 20.06.2017.

47 P. Berthelet, *supra* n. 44, p. 8.

48 *Ibid.*, pp. 6–7.

49 *Ibid.*, p. 7.

the worst case, say it out loud.[50] Even in the first case, they know what they imply, and they also know that their audience knows what they imply, and that the listeners will go halfway to meet them in the demagogical haven of their understatements. This behaviour is electorally very profitable and helps to disseminate fear among citizens of this 'diffuse' and 'omnipresent' threat, be it real or imagined. This, in turn, not only makes the ones in power seem indispensable in order to fight this, but also helps them legitimise more repressive policies, namely against immigrants.[51] As a consequence, and as pointed out by Soledad Saux, this can result in a policy that limits the immigrants' liberty without necessarily making the rest safer.[52] Even if terrorists use the migratory channels that the asylum seekers also use to access Europe, one should avoid conflating those two categories of people. As Bigo outlines, if politicians are unable to fulfil their role, they should not seek to re-legitimise their political power by creating an interior enemy.[53]

4. CONCLUSION

The continuous undermining of the protection associated with political crimes is a widespread phenomenon. The European example represents one of the most accomplished versions of this general tendency. In bilateral extradition agreements concluded with EU Member States, the political offence exception still exists, but states have sometimes used intricate tricks to circumvent it at their convenience in the past. They range from the use of 'alternative extradition procedures' such as abduction, kidnapping, disguised or informal extradition,[54] to the qualification of a political offence as '*complexe*' or '*connexe*' instead of 'pure', thus making extradition possible due to the generally non-binding character of this exemption in cases where the political offence is not a 'pure' one.[55]

As outlined in this chapter, the war on terror, with its self-explanatory power, has provided lawmakers and political authorities the opportunity to further fuel and accelerate this tendency without having to define the concepts

50 V. Bove and T. Böhmelt, 'Does Immigration Induce Terrorism?' (2016) 78 *The Journal of Politics* 573.

51 D. Bigo, 'Sécurité et immigration: Vers une gouvernementalité par l'inquiétude?' (1998) 31–32 *Cultures & Conflits* 1.

52 M. Soledad Saux, 'Immigration and Terrorism: A Constructed Connection. The Spanish Case' (2007) 13 *European Journal on Criminal Policy and Research* 57.

53 D. Bigo, *supra* n. 51, p. 11.

54 C. Van Den Wijngaert, *supra* n. 4, pp. 50–54.

55 M.D. Kielsgard, 'The Political Offence Exception: Punishing Whistleblowers Abroad', *EJIL: Talk!, Blog of the European Journal of Criminal Law*, <https://www.ejiltalk.org/the-political-offense-exception-punishing-whistleblowers-abroad/> accessed 22.06.2017.

of either political crime or terrorism, even though these are both widely used and intrinsically linked. The use of one term over the other largely depends on the context and purpose for which it is used. In order to combat terrorism, the latter has been preferred over the term 'political offence'. The impact of this shift on asylum seekers has been, as outlined in this chapter, substantial. As Berthelet underlines, after the 9/11 attacks, the general viewpoint, shared by several EU Member States, is that, in case of doubt, it is better to reject the asylum application of a person who has undergone real persecutions than to grant asylum to a potential terrorist.[56] Of course, EU Member States should not grant asylum to terrorists, and their desire to protect their citizens is more than legitimate, but even more than that, it is their *duty* to protect their citizens.[57] The difficulty in aligning measures protecting freedoms concomitantly with others that enhance security is not questioned, but the EU and its Member States should not 'throw the baby out with the bath water'. They should carefully evaluate the collateral damage of a policy before adopting it, and they need to take into account that the people whose lives might be part of this collateral damage are already vulnerable people whose vulnerability ensues from the very fact that they have already been part of the collateral damage elsewhere.

The general conflation of aliens, and *a fortiori* of asylum seekers, with terrorists is conveniently conveyed by high-ranking officials and politicians who build on the fears of their citizens in order to pass widely liberticidal measures. Incidentally, those repressive policies might affect not only EU residents, but also EU citizens. Indeed, this exclusion of 'aliens' is contagious to lawful residents who migrated to the EU, and to the following generations of 'immigrants' who – besides being 'second or third generation immigrants' – are also EU citizens who are experiencing – maybe not always actual, but surely symbolic – violence. This marginalisation of foreigners is a good indicator of the way in which aliens are currently perceived in the EU. This is detrimental not only to the EU's international reputation, but also to its legitimacy in representing values of 'respect for human dignity, freedom, ... equality, ... and respect for human rights, including the rights of persons belonging to minorities', which are values common to all EU Member States, societies where 'pluralism, non-discrimination, tolerance, justice, solidarity' should prevail.[58] Ironically, putting aside the moral issues at stake here, this abolition of the political offence exemption in order to protect European democracies from terrorism might directly backfire on some of the safeguards of democracies, such as whistleblowers.[59]

---

56 P. Berthelet, *supra* n. 44, p. 9.
57 Article 72 TFEU [2008] OJ C115/50.
58 Article 2 TFEU [2008] OJ C115/50.
59 M.D. Kielsgard, *supra* n. 55.

PART III

THE *STATUS QUO* OF MIGRATION IN EUROPE: SELECTED NATIONAL PERSPECTIVES

INVITED CONTRIBUTION

10. THE GOVERNANCE OF THE MIGRANT CRISIS IN ITALY

Lino Panzeri*

1. INTRODUCTION

The intensification of migrant flows from the Global South (from Africa and the Middle East in particular) in recent years has forced many European countries to realise that immigration is not a transitory condition, linked to single historical events such as the so-called Arab Spring, but a structural phenomenon to which Europe is called today to face up and to make long-term choices. In Italy, the relevance of this topic is further emphasised by its special geographic location, which makes the Peninsula the natural landfall for those who are escaping wars, famine, ethnic conflicts, religious persecution and other misery, looking for refuge and the hope of better living conditions. The aim of this chapter is to look into the legal impact of immigration from the Italian perspective. Section 2 will provide a historical overview of migration in Italy, both emigration and immigration. Taking into account recent experience, section 3 will outline the legislative developments that have occurred in the context of the ongoing migrant crisis with a view to making observations on issues that still need addressing in order to improve the reception and integration of migrants in Italy (section 4).

2. HISTORICAL PERSPECTIVES

Italy has been a land of emigration for decades. It has experienced three major waves. The first one, from the end of the nineteenth century to World War I, was brought about by the widespread poverty in the country (due to the demographic

* Department of Law, Economics and Cultures, University of Insubria, Como, Italy. E-mail: lino.panzeri@uninsubria.it.

growth and the agrarian crisis). Triggered by the same causes, there was a second wave, occurring between the two World Wars, which was partly contained by the limitations of the fascist Government. The third wave, between the 1940s and 1970s, was less intense, but nevertheless hundreds of thousands of Italians moved to other European and non-European countries during this time. It is estimated that more than 20 million people have emigrated from Italy over the course of a century.[1]

During the second half of the twentieth century, domestic economic growth has seen the drive for emigration fade away. Instead, since the 1990s, Italy has become a natural transitory or permanent destination for hundreds of thousands of migrants, seeking to either stay in the country or to reach – through Italy – other northern European countries.[2] The relatively new nature of the migration issue in Italy in comparison with other western European countries (such as France, where the first migration flows from Africa and the Middle East date back to at least the 1950s) has hindered its regulation, as the country's limited experience of immigration meant that very few legislative measures existed to regulate the status and social inclusion of immigrants.

The 1947 Italian Constitution provided for the right of asylum for political refugees only.[3] Moreover, the ordinary legislature refrained for decades from introducing a consistent set of rules on this subject. The legal status of foreigners continued to be regulated by the rather weak provisions of the Consolidated Public Security Laws (the so-called 'TULPS', dating back to 1931), which were consistent with fascist ideology and thus only aimed to protect public order and national security. However, even when the first legislation regulating migration and asylum came into force, it soon proved to be incomplete due to the lack of planning over the management of the phenomenon. Indeed, the first legislation on this subject, Law No. 943/1986 (the so-called 'Foschi' Law), only focused on the remedy of the condition of foreigners already residing in Italy, that is, of illegal migrants after they entered the country. The subsequent Law No. 39/1990 (the so-called 'Martelli' Law) introduced a new migration levels planning system designed to make sure the domestic labour supply can meet the demand for

1 Cf. P. Bevilacqua, A. De Clementi and E. Franzina (eds.), *Storia dell'Emigrazione italiana. Partenze*, Donzelli, Rome 2001.

2 On Italy's transition from a country of emigration to a country of immigration, cf. E. Rossi, 'Da cittadini vs. stranieri a regolari vs. irregolari. Considerazioni sull'evoluzione della disciplina giuridica dei non cittadini nell'ordinamento italiano' (2010) *Rivista di diritto costituzionale*, pp. 87 ff.

3 Section 10, para. 3: 'A foreigner who, in his home country, is denied the actual exercise of the democratic freedoms guaranteed by the Italian Constitution shall be entitled to the right of asylum under the conditions established by law.' On the constitutional debate regarding the legal status of foreigners, cf. G. Bascherini, *Immigrazione e diritti fondamentali. L'esperienza italiana tra storia costituzionale e prospettive europee*, Jovene, Naples 2007, pp. 105–08; on section 10, para. 3, cf. E. Cannizzaro and A. Caligiuri, 'Art. 10' in R. Bifulco, A. Celotto and M. Olivetti (eds.), *Commentario alla Costituzione*, III, Utet, Turin 2006, pp. 242 ff.

foreign workers, as well as some new types of residency permits. Nevertheless, it refrained from introducing any measures aimed at fostering the integration of foreigners, who were still regarded as temporary visitors.[4]

The entry into force of Law No. 40/1998 (the so-called 'Turco-Napolitano' Law, then merged into Legislative Decree No. 286/1998, 'Consolidated Immigration Laws') partially shifted the approach: in addition to some innovative measures (such as those on family reunion and on access of foreigners to healthcare), it introduced, for the first time, a system that set 'quotas' of immigrants to be periodically admitted in Italy (the so-called 'flow decree'). Moreover, in a bid to contain illegal immigration, it introduced the crime of 'facilitation and exploitation of illegal immigration' and 'administrative detention',[5] aimed at preventing migrants who were irregularly residing in Italy from escaping during the identification and forced repatriation activities.[6]

Only since the early 2000s has the presence of migrants been internalised as a long-lasting phenomenon. Most migrants are no longer looking for temporary employment opportunities before returning to their home countries. On the contrary, driven by the desire for better living conditions for themselves and their families, they intend to settle in Italy (or in other European countries).[7] This, however, requires a radical change and the adoption of multi-level social inclusion policies in areas such as education and training, healthcare, inter-linguistic and inter-cultural services, recognition and protection of cultural diversity, fight against exclusion and discrimination.

Italian society has often had a contradictory approach to expectations of new migrants. On the one hand, civil society has been increasingly engaged in hospitality activities (thanks also to a substantial network of voluntary associations). On the other hand, the resistance of Italian citizens to immigration has increased, fuelled by the uncontrolled growth in immigration and by the widespread perception that Italy is unable to effectively receive all the migrants

---

4 On the problems arising from the first legislation on the subject, cf. S. Castellazzi, 'Le implicazioni legislative del fenomeno sociale migratorio. L'evoluzione normativa in Italia' in V. Gasparini Casari (ed.), *Il diritto dell'immigrazione. Profili di Diritto italiano comunitario e internazionale*, I, Mucchi, Modena 2010, pp. 111–19.

5 The Law provided for the administrative detention to take place in specially designated 'Centres for Temporary Residence and Assistance' (CPTA), later renamed (2008) 'Identification and Expulsion Centres' (CIE). On 'administrative detention', its ineffective attempt to tackle illegal immigration and on the serious problems concerning constitutional legitimacy that it has posed, cf. D. Loprieno, 'La detenzione amministrativa dello straniero' in P. Fantozzi and D. Loprieno (eds.), *Profili multilivello di diritto dei migranti*, Rubbettino, Soveria Mannelli 2014, pp. 51 ff.

6 On the content of Decree No. 286/1998, cf. P. Bonetti, 'I profili generali della normativa italiana sugli stranieri dal 1998' in B. Nascimbene (ed.), *Diritto degli stranieri*, Cedam, Padova 2004, pp. 4 ff.

7 Information on the evolution of immigration in Italy can be found in the study conducted by C. Bonifazi, *L'immigrazione straniera in Italia*, Il Mulino, Bologna 2007.

who reach the country searching for better living conditions. This fear, often exploited by some political parties, has had an impact on a legislative level.

In this regard, Law No. 189/2002 (the so-called 'Bossi-Fini' Law) aims, on the one hand, to reduce the regular entry of foreigners in Italy by setting employment requirements, which would allow the migrants to provide for themselves and their families, and, on the other, to fight illegal immigration through the tightening of procedures for the expulsion of foreigners who illegally live in the country.

This restrictive approach towards foreigners has been further worsened by the 2008 economic crisis. The need to address growing unemployment and overall social insecurity, often put down to the presence of foreigners, led to the adoption of new measures inspired by the principle of 'zero tolerance'. Among them, Decree-law No. 92/2008, which was then turned into Law No. 125/2008, introduced the so-called crime of 'clandestinity' as an aggravating circumstance and is aimed at punishing foreigners solely on the grounds of their irregular presence. It is to be noted that the Constitutional Court subsequently ruled this norm to be unconstitutional (Judgment No. 249/2010), as the rigorous respect for fundamental rights implies the illegitimacy of more stringent criminal proceedings which are based on the personal qualities of the individual and derive from former conduct not related to the criminal offence; according to the Court, this would be an open breach of the principle of 'criminal offence'. In addition, Law No. 94/2009, containing the so-called 'Security Package', has further restricted the possibility to regularise the presence of foreigners, by providing for the granting of a residence permit to be subject to the foreigner's commitment to respect an 'Integration Agreement' (the so-called 'Permit with Penalty Points') and the granting of a long-term European Union (EU) residence permit subject to certain criteria, *inter alia*, language skills.[8]

Despite adopting such a restrictive approach, it has nevertheless proved to be insufficient in order to effectively address illegal immigration. Furthermore, it has only partially been compensated, over time, by the contribution from both regional and local authorities and the case law of the Constitutional Court. After the reform of Italian regionalism introduced by Constitutional Law No. 3/2001, regional and local authorities have an expanded mandate in this area, at least with regard to the domestic policies that directly impact on migrants, although

[8] On the 'Integration Agreement' in critical terms, cf. L. Pepino, 'Le migrazioni, il diritto, il nemico. Considerazione a margine della legge n. 94/2009' (2009) *Diritto, immigrazione e cittadinanza*, pp. 9 ff., and P. Morozzo Della Rocca, 'Entra in vigore l'accordo (stonato) di integrazione' in G. Caggiano (ed.), *I percorsi giuridici per l'integrazione. Migranti e titolari di protezione internazionale tra diritto dell'Unione europea e ordinamento italiano*, Giappichelli, Turin 2014, pp. 213 ff.

the 'immigration policy' continues to be an exclusive matter for the State.[9] They have taken compensatory measures in favour of immigrants on healthcare, social care and housing policies.[10] In a bid to guarantee the protection of migrants' rights, the Constitutional Court has maintained some regional laws recognising immigrants' rights and has prevented the introduction of discriminatory measures based on the legal status of the individual.[11]

3. THE EXPLOSION OF THE 2011 MIGRANT CRISIS

Within such an uncertain social and legal framework, political events in North Africa and Middle East, such as the conflict in Syria and the destabilising consequences of the Arab Spring, have exacerbated the current issue of immigration in Italy, both by changing its features and by creating situations of social tension.

First of all, both the number of foreigners who arrive in Italy and their condition has changed. In the past, most migrants were economic migrants who came to Europe to find better living conditions – and, as such, could be repatriated – whereas since 2011 many migrants are fleeing wars and persecution and are, therefore, entitled to international protection. This new direction of the immigration phenomenon requires the implementation of new intervention strategies. For instance, priority is no longer given to the adoption of social inclusion policies for long-term immigrants who are integrated due to the economic needs of the country; instead, more specific short to

9 'Immigration' (construed as the condition of the foreigner's presence in Italy) continues to be an exclusive matter for the State (section 117.2, Const.), but the competence of the Regions is now extended to many areas – health, education, social assistance – which also affect migrants who live in Italy. On the distribution of this subject-matter between the State and the Regions, cf. S. Castellazzi, 'La materia "immigrazione" e l'assetto delle competenze legislative tra Stato e Regioni' in V. Gasparini Casari (ed.), *supra* n. 4, pp. 173 ff., and F. Covino, 'Regioni e disciplina dell'immigrazione' in F. Angelini, M. Benvenuti and A. Schillaci (eds.), *Le nuove frontiere del diritto dell'immigrazione: integrazione, diritti e sicurezza*, Jovene, Naples 2011, pp. 389 ff.

10 See A. Gentilini, 'Tendenze della legislazione regionale, statutaria e ordinaria, in tema di migranti', in L. Ronchetti (ed.), *I diritti di cittadinanza dei migranti. Il ruolo delle Regioni*, Giuffrè, Milan 2012, pp. 55 ff.

11 See Judgment No. 432/2005, by which the Constitutional Court declared the unconstitutionality of a Lombard law that granted the right of free circulation on public transport for totally disabled people, but only for Italian citizens, thus violating the state rule that places Italian citizens on the same footing as legally residing foreigners in their 'enjoyment of social welfare benefits and services, including economic ones'. See also Judgment No. 133/2013, by which the Constitutional Court ruled illegal the regional Law of Trentino-Alto Adige/Südtirol No. 8/2011, as it set forth a family allowance to be granted only in favour of foreigners who had resided in the Region for at least five years.

medium-term needs are identified, such as (i) rescue operations for those migrants who are trying to reach the Italian coast; (ii) distinguishing those who can claim international protection as their lives are in danger from those who are economic migrants; (iii) offering hospitality to those who have arrived in Italy once their status has been acknowledged; (iv) introducing measures that are as inclusive as possible in order to avoid the rise of social tensions linked to the massive increase in the number of foreigners; and (v) relocating at least some of the refugees and expelling those who are not entitled to stay in Italy.

Secondly, the need for appropriate legal action to be taken in order to manage this epochal challenge also stems from growing hostility towards immigrants among the domestic population. For a long time, the ineffectiveness of measures aimed at expelling those who do not meet the requirements to remain in Italy (e.g. the lack of follow up to the decree of expulsion) has increased resistance to immigration within part of the Italian society. The participation of some irregular migrants in illegal activities has given rise to conflicts in some parts of the country and especially in big cities. More recently, in spite of the substantial involvement of civil society in the management of such situations, the pressure caused by the influx of hundreds of thousands of people reaching Italian ports aboard rescue ships (Brindisi, Pozzallo, Palermo, Salerno, Reggio Calabria) and by the long stay of many 'transiting migrants', who are attempting to reach other Northern European countries but have been prevented from crossing the border (Como, Ventimiglia), has further heightened social dissatisfaction – sometimes amplified by the media reporting of events involving irregular migrants – and an overall mistrust of the national and EU authorities and their ability to properly manage this complex situation.

In order to address this new crisis, which has been aggravated by the inadequacy of the current asylum system,[12] a new set of rules have been implemented under Legislative Decree No. 142/2015.[13] The Decree regulates the reception of asylum seeker applicants and introduces measures for the recognition of their status. It defines several levels of assistance: *rescue and first aid* (section 8) within 'hotspots', into which all incoming migrants are channelled and where, within a time limit of 48 hours (often exceeded), first aid and pre-identification activities will be performed;[14] *first reception* (section 9)

[12] On the problematic management of the crisis after 2011 due to current legislation, cf. F. Vassallo Paleologo, 'La fabbrica dell'emergenza immigrazione' in P. Fantozzi and D. Loprieno (ed.), *supra* n. 5, pp. 37 ff.; on the problems arising from the Italian reception system, cf. also P. Mori, 'Profili problematici dell'accoglienza dei richiedenti protezione internazionale' in G. Caggiano (ed.), *supra* n. 8, esp. pp. 429–30.

[13] Legislative Decree No. 142/2015 has implemented Directive No. 2013/33/EU, on standards for the reception of applicants for international protection, and Directive No. 2013/32/EU, on common procedures for granting and withdrawing international protection.

[14] Retention in 'hotspots' can limit the personal freedom and/or the freedom of movement. In this regard, the *Khlaifia* Judgment (European Court of Human Rights, Grand Chamber,

within First Reception Centres ('hubs'), where the necessary steps are taken to define the legal status of the applicant;[15] *second reception* (section 14) provided by the Protection System for Asylum Seekers and Refugees (SPRAR), which cooperates, on a voluntary basis, with local authorities.

In this way, the legislature has tried to implement a system that allows for both the satisfaction of the primary needs of migrants and for their integration across the national territory, in order to adopt effective inclusion policies once their refugee status has been established. However, the massive inflow of migrants has made this system so unsuitable that in order to satisfy the 'essential reception needs' the opening of temporary facilities has often become necessary, even through direct assignments without public invitation to tender (section 11). This measure has often been questioned due to the lack of transparency in the use of public money, as well as to the tensions it has caused between the Prefectures (in charge of providing housing for new migrants) and the local authorities, who are committed to reassuring citizens. In order to optimise the measures for the reception of international protection applicants and to highlight the contribution of the Regions and the local authorities, Legislative Decree No. 142 has introduced both a National Coordination Group (*Tavolo di coordinamento nazionale*) and Regional Coordination Groups (*Tavoli di coordinamento regionale*).

Despite the introduction of these legislative measures and the significant role played by local authorities in the management of the crisis, their effectiveness is still to be determined. The Legislative Decree failed in fact to contain the permanence of migrants in the reception facilities within reasonable time-limits. Moreover, the lack of available places in the SPRAR centres has required the opening of temporary facilities with a significant financial and, at times, social impact.[16] Above all, no system for social and labour integration of applicants who are granted international protection has been implemented, which could give rise to further social tensions.

The problematic management of the current migration situation has highlighted the need for a completely new approach that identifies complete and shared solutions to this phenomenon. Thus, the need for more thorough

Case 16483/2012, 15 December 2016) ruled that the detention of foreigners in closed centres (such as the 'Lampedusa First Care Centre'), or in case of immediate rescue or emergency activities due to the arrival of migrants, constitutes a detention without a legal basis and thus contradicts Article 5, para. 1, 2 and 4, of the European Convention on Human Rights.

15 Migrants should stay in these Centres for 'the time needed' to complete the set activities. However, in the situation where there are no places available in the Second Hospitality Centres, the length of time spent in the hubs may at times extend 'to a period of time that is strictly necessary for the transfer', without any time indication.

16 Cf. F. Biondi Dal Monte, 'La disciplina del diritto d'asilo tra accoglienza ed emergenza' in J. Woelk, F. Guella and G. Pelacani (eds.), *Modelli di disciplina dell'accoglienza nella' "emergenza migrazione"*, Editoriale scientifica, Naples 2016, pp. 92–95.

investigation into the causes of migration – to be identified with the unresolved disparities between the various regions of the world and the unfair distribution of resources – has long been recognised in the Italian scientific and political arena. This would imply strengthening of international cooperation, not only with transit countries (in particular, for coastguard services and fighting against trafficking in human beings, involving NGOs), but above all, supporting development cooperation by funding projects aiming to support the economies of the countries of emigration, which often have great potential. However, winning this challenge requires not only the transparent management of resources and measures, but also a medium to long-term perspective, as it may take a period of a few decades for the effects to be really felt. However, in the short term, it is necessary to adopt measures that can offer immediate responses.

At first, it was hoped that the crisis would be overcome by revising the procedures set forth in Legislative Decree No. 142/2015, with better resource management aimed at improving the management of flows and the speeding up of procedures for verifying refugee status. To this end, Decree-law No. 13/2017 (the so-called 'Minniti-Orlando' Decree), which has become Law No. 46/2017, has been brought into force in order to accelerate international protection procedures on the one hand and to strengthen the fight against illegal immigration on the other.

The text has reduced the time-limits for assessing international protection applications by simplifying the procedures that take place before the International Recognition Authority (the Territorial Commission). Furthermore, the Decree set forth that 26 Specialised Sections on Immigration (one for each Court of Appeal) will, among other activities, hear disputes concerning the measures of the Territorial Commissions. In this case, judicial protection is limited to a single merit degree, based entirely on papers and without the necessity for the individual to appear, giving rise to many issues concerning compliance with the Italian Constitution and the European Convention on Human Rights. This 2017 reform has also extended the network of detention centres for illegal immigrants (now 'Centres for Repatriation and Identification'), with measures that have been severely criticised by many NGOs, which have raised doubts about the constitutional legitimacy of these rules. Better results could be achieved by enhancing the 'multi-level governance' of immigration, that is, through the responsible involvement of the local authorities, which, despite the lack of available resources, have shown increasing concern about this issue, offering a contribution that compensates for state inactivity.[17]

---

17 Cf. F. Palermo, 'Dall'emergenza all'accoglienza attraverso l'integrazione della società. Primi spunti per un'indagine sul ruolo degli enti substatali' in J. Woelk, F. Guella and G. Pelacani (eds.), *supra* n. 16, pp. 11 ff., and L. Panzeri, 'Fenomeno migratorio e ruolo degli enti locali: prime note' (2018) *Osservatorio costituzionale*, pp. 1 ff.

4. OPEN ISSUES

Italy still needs to take some cultural measures in order to overcome the problems concerning the management of the migrant crisis that has developed over the last four to five years. It has become evident that the presence of migrants – even those who legally live in Italy – has not yet been fully accepted as an irreversible process. Regardless of the specific management of applicants for international protection – which, despite the emergency, is only a part of the migration phenomenon – the integration of more than 5 million foreigners in Italy requires measures encouraging social inclusion. These measures are inevitable, especially in favour of second generation immigrants, who will in future become an integral part of Italian society.

Amid the possible opportunities that development of measures aimed at social inclusion and integration would offer, there are still many obstacles, which are well demonstrated by the reform of the Law on citizenship. The current legislation on this subject, which dates back to 1992 and is still based on *jus sanguinis*, makes the process of granting Italian citizenship to children who have been born and raised in Italy very difficult. The adoption of new legislation based on *jus soli*, which has been under discussion for 13 years,[18] has recently given rise to strong political resistance, which is very likely to increase approaching the 2018 political elections.[19]

The achievement of this inclusive goal, which is considered to be inevitable in order to successfully deal with the irreversibility of immigration from the South of the world, requires two levels of intervention. First of all, internally, it calls for the overcoming of the current emergency approach in favour of a system that might stimulate the contribution of all government levels to the management of the immigration issue. Secondly, it implies the cooperation of all EU countries in addressing a crisis so far almost exclusively faced by the geographically most exposed countries, like Italy and Greece.[20]

To this end, the reform of the 'Dublin System' is crucial. As is well known, this system is based on the 'rule of first entry', which makes the country where international protection applicants first land (almost always Italy and Greece)

---

18 On the problems arising from the current legislation on citizenship for the integration of foreigners, cf., among others, L. Panella, 'Immigrazione e cittadinanza nazionale' in G. Caggiano (ed.), *supra* n. 8, esp. pp. 190–94.

19 The Gentiloni Government announced in July 2017 a new referral to the senatorial exam of the text due to the resistance of a Party of the majority (Alternativa popolare). However, as political elections are approaching (Spring 2018), it may be that most political parties will not be willing to support a project that could have a negative impact on the election.

20 See M. Savino, 'La gestione italiana della crisi migratoria: un primo bilancio' in F. Cortese and G. Pelacani (eds.), *Il diritto in migrazione. Studi sull'integrazione giuridica degli stranieri*, Editoriale scientifica, Naples 2017, pp. 41–43.

to be in charge of their acceptance. This system, conceived in a historically different time from the present,[21] prevents applicants from submitting their asylum application to another EU country (thus putting the entire weight of the crisis on two countries)[22] and this situation, from the Italian perspective, is no longer sustainable.

Measures shared so far, such as economic support for hotspots or coast-guarding, although important, are inadequate to manage the reception of hundreds of thousands of desperate people, whose integration calls for a fairer distribution throughout Europe. The involvement of the EU in managing the flows and, above all, in relocation (by overcoming the resistance of the Visegrad Group, including through the introduction of sanctioning systems) are goals pursued by the Italian Government with no positive outcome for the time being, but they can no longer be postponed.

This approach is necessary not only to improve the management of a phenomenon which, by its very nature, cannot be limited by boundaries (or, worse, by the construction of walls) but also because immigration is a challenge that Europe cannot ignore: the inadequate protection of migrants' rights undermines the foundation of the EU, that is the centrality of the protection of human rights. The resistance shown by some countries is contributing to widespread – sometimes amplified by the media – feelings of intolerance and xenophobia, which are difficult to eradicate and, above all, a growing anti-Europeanism which, in the absence of effective responses, could undermine the future of the European project, as demonstrated by the UK's decision to withdraw from the EU.

---

[21] On the evolution of the EU legislation on immigration and asylum, cf. M. Gestri, 'Immigrazione e asilo nel diritto dell'Unione europea' in V. Gasparini Casari (ed.), *supra* n. 4, pp. 45 ff.

[22] On the problems arising from the so-called 'Dublin System', see P. Bonetti, 'Accoglienza nell'emergenza: la recente evoluzione' in J. Woelk, F. Guella and G. Pelacani (eds.), *supra* n. 16, pp. 118 ff.

11. THE IMPACT OF THE MIGRATION CRISIS ON POLISH IMMIGRATION AND CRIMINAL LAW

Magdalena PERKOWSKA[*]

1. INTRODUCTION

The increased criminalisation of migration over the past decade leaves open the question of whether this is an appropriate policy response or whether the resulting policies can be described as over-criminalisation.[1] The immigration crisis in Europe, in addition to its social and humanitarian impact, has led to some legal consequences which are reflected in recent amendments to Polish immigration law. It must be noted that the example of Poland is not an exception when it comes to state responses to the perceived migration crisis. A very important regulation in question is the Act on Anti-terrorism, which was introduced in Poland on 10 June 2016, and gives the state licence to limit the rights of foreigners.

The main hypothesis presented in this chapter is that the amendments introduced into Polish law are disproportionate to the threat caused by immigration. The questions which will be discussed in this chapter are: (i) What is the scale of illegal migration to Poland? (ii) What is the scale of criminality attributable to foreigners in Poland? (iii) What are the latest amendments introduced into Polish immigration and criminal law to prevent the perceived threat? Drawing on the above, this chapter endeavours to answer whether the scale of illegal migration into Poland provides valid grounds for the introduction of the amendments to the law. Is it, for example, significant when compared with the situation in other European countries? What are the routes taken by immigrants to reach Europe and is Poland in fact 'on their roadmap'? This chapter looks at the question of whether or not the legal amendments to

* Chair of Criminal Law and Criminology, Faculty of Law, University of Białystok, Poland, E-mail: magdalena.perkowska@gmail.com.

1 J.M. CHACÓN, 'Overcriminalizing Migration' (2003) 102 *Journal of Criminal Law & Criminology* 616.

Polish law in the field of immigration and criminal law are necessary and if so, whether they are proportional to the perceived threat posed by migration and the criminality of foreigners.

2. ILLEGAL MIGRATION TO POLAND

In 2015, European Union (EU) Member States reported more than 1,820,000 detections of illegal crossings along the EU's external borders to Frontex. This number, the highest recorded, was more than six times the number of detections reported in 2014, which in itself was an unprecedented year. There are eight established routes of illegal migration leading to the EU.[2] Poland, as with every EU country that polices an external border, is also on the path of illegal migration. Poland's borders with the Russian Federation (Kaliningrad Oblast), Belarus and Ukraine, are part of the Eastern land border route that goes through Finland, Estonia, Latvia, Lithuania, Poland, Slovakia, Hungary and Romania. Poland does not have the longest section of the EU's external border compared to the other EU Member States. However, its unique position is that it borders three non-EU states. It is important to analyse whether in comparison to other routes, illegal migration places significant pressure on Poland's borders.

The annual Frontex analysis on migration at external EU borders, aside from cataloguing the number of people crossing and number of visas issued, provides data in respect of specific indicators (see Table 1). These encompass: (1) illegal border crossing between border check points; (2) clandestine entry at border check points; (3) persons using fraudulent documents; (4) decision on refusal of entry; (5) illegal stay; (6) return decisions issued; and (7) return decisions executed.[3]

Table 1. Illegal migration indicators in the EU

Indicator / Year	2011	2012	2013	2014	2015
Illegal border crossing between border check points	141,051	72,437	107,365	283,532	1,822,337
Clandestine entry at the border check points	282	591	599	3,052	3,642
Fraudulent document users	5,255	7,804	9,804	9,420	8,373

(continued)

2 These routes comprise: Central Mediterranean, Eastern Mediterranean, Western Balkan, Circular from Albania to Greece, Western Mediterranean, Eastern borders, Black Sea and Western African.

3 Frontex, *Annual Risk Analysis 2015*, Warsaw 2015, p. 12.

Table 1 *Continued*

Indicator / Year	2011	2012	2013	2014	2015
Refusal of entry	118,277	116,524	129,235	114,887	118,495
Illegal stay	350,948	344,928	345,098	441,780	701,625
Returns - decisions	231,385	269,949	224,305	252,003	286,725
Returns - executed	149,045	158,955	160,418	161,309	175,220

Source: FRONTEX, *Annual Risk Analysis 2015*, Warsaw 2015; FRONTEX, *Annual Risk Analysis 2016*, Warsaw 2016.

The year 2015 was marked by an unprecedented number of detections of illegal border crossings between border check points at the external borders, revealing a migration crisis in Europe of a scale that had not been seen since the Second World War. During 2015, three bottlenecks emerged: (i) the maritime border between Turkey and Greece; (ii) the Central Mediterranean border; and (iii) as a consequence of entry through Greece, the border with Western Balkan countries.[4]

Border crossing other than at border crossing points is only permitted at sections of the internal EU and Schengen area border by virtue of Article 22 of the Schengen Borders Code.[5] In 2015, the number of detected illegal border crossings between border check points even outweighed the number of detected illegal stays. Illegal stay is most frequently an outcome of illegal entry into EU territory but might also result from the extension of the stay when a visa or another residence permit expires. Clandestine entries (e.g. people hiding in vehicles to avoid border control) at border check points during border checks is an infrequent phenomenon in the European context. Likewise, the use of fraudulent documents by perpetrators at border check points is rare. Migrants who are identified by authorities as a result of illegal border crossing between border check points or illegal stay are issued return decisions, which can either take the form of voluntary or forced return.

Another indicator used in the Frontex statistics is refusal of entry into the EU issued by virtue of Article 14 of the Schengen Borders Code. This statistic shows the pressure of illegal migration at Europe's borders but not the status of illegal migration as such, as the refusal of entry prevents the illegal migration.

As Table 2 shows, Frontex identified eight routes used for illegal migration leading to Europe between 2011–2015. Most of them concern the Southern coasts of Europe. The year 2015 was marked by an unprecedented number of

4 FRONTEX, *Annual Risk Analysis 2016*, Warsaw 2016, p. 17.

5 Regulation (EU) 2016/399 of the European Parliament and of the Council of 9 March 2016 on a Union Code on the rules governing the movement of persons across borders (Schengen Borders Code) [2016] OJ L77/1.

foreigners who illegally crossed the external EU border between border check points on all of these routes.

Table 2. **Detections of illegal border crossing between border check points***

Routes / Year	2011	2012	2013	2014	2015
Eastern Mediterranean	57,025	37,224	24,799	50,834	885,386
Western Balkan	4,658	6,391	19,951	43,357	764,038
Central Mediterranean	64,261	15,151	45,298	170,664	153,946
Western Mediterranean	8,448	6,397	6,838	7,842	7,164
Circular from Albania to Greece	5,269	5,502	8,728	8,841	8,932
Eastern borders	1,049	1,597	1,316	1,275	1,920
Western African	340	174	283	276	874
Black Sea	0	1	148	433	68
Total	141,051	72,437	107,365	282,962	1,822,337

Source: Frontex, *Annual Risk Analysis 2016*, Warsaw 2016.

* Note: Data presented refer to the number of detections of illegal border crossing at the external borders of the EU. Illegal border crossings at the external borders may be attempted several times by the same person.

The Eastern Mediterranean route runs from Turkey to the EU by land and sea through Greece, Bulgaria and Cyprus. In 2015 a record number of illegal migrants (mainly from Syria, Afghanistan and Iraq) were detected, the majority of whom were detected at the maritime border.[6] In the years 2010–2011, this route was mainly used by nationals from Pakistan and Afghanistan but since 2012 Syrian nationals are the group most commonly detected.[7]

The Western Balkan route forms a transit route for migrants crossing the Greek–Turkish border, attempting to reach other EU Member States through Macedonia and Serbia. In the last two years most detections were reported at the Hungarian–Serbian border. In 2014, nationals from Kosovo, Afghanistan and Syria were the most prominent among those detected[8] but since 2015 most people detected are of unknown nationality or Syrian and Afghan nationals. The situation on that route has significantly changed year by year. The massive migration through the Hungarian border was only halted by erection of a fence at the Hungarian–Serbian border in October 2015. This forced the migrants to head for the Slovenian border and travel through Slovenia and Austria further to Western and Northern Europe.[9]

6 Frontex, *supra* n. 3, p. 18.
7 Frontex, *Annual Risk Analysis 2012*, Warsaw 2012, p. 14.
8 Frontex, *supra* n. 3, p. 22.
9 Frontex, *supra* n. 4, p. 19.

On the Central Mediterranean route, which runs from Tunisia and Libya through Italy and Malta, nationals from Eritrea, Nigeria, Somalia as well as a significant number of people of unknown nationality coming from sub-Saharan regions were detected. In the years 2012–2014 illegal migrants from Tunisia, Nigeria, Somalia, Eritrea, Syria and Central Africa were predominantly detected at this border section.[10] In 2015 the Eastern Mediterranean and Western Balkan routes became more popular due to the fact that Syrians prefer to choose the Balkan route.

The Western Mediterranean route runs from Eastern Africa to the EU via Spain (mainly through the Canary Islands). At present, nationals from Guinea, Algeria and Morocco are the largest group that attempt to reach Europe via this route.[11] Prior to 2012, nationals from Tunisia, Nigeria, Somalia and Eritrea prevailed.[12]

The circular route, running from Albania through Greece to the EU, was predominantly exploited mainly by Albanians and occasionally by nationals of other countries like Macedonia, Georgia and Kosovo. However, since 2010, illegal migration of nationals from Albania to the EU has been decreasing as the visa obligations that had previously been imposed were abolished by the EU.[13] The number of detected illegal crossings on the route remained stable in the years 2013–2015.[14]

Illegal migration on the Western African route, running from Senegal, Mauretania and Morocco to the EU through Spain (chiefly via the Canary Islands) concerns mainly migrants from Guinea, Côte d'Ivoire, Gambia and Morocco.[15] The Black Sea route, which runs to the EU from Turkey, Russia and Ukraine through Bulgaria and Romania, is mainly exploited by nationals from Afghanistan,[16] Syria, Iraq and Iran.[17]

The land route, which is described as the Eastern land or Eastern borders route, runs to the EU through Estonia, Finland, Latvia, Lithuania, Poland, Slovakia, Hungary and Romania; this route has recently been exploited by nationals from Afghanistan, Vietnam, Georgia and Syria.[18] In 2015 migrants started to use a new, so-called Arctic route, which runs from Russia to Norway and Finland.[19] Despite the total length of all the border sections (6,000 km),

---

10 Frontex, *supra* n. 3, pp. 18–19.
11 Frontex, *supra* n. 4, p. 21.
12 Frontex, *supra* n. 7, p. 14.
13 *Ibid.*, p. 19.
14 Frontex, *supra* n. 4, p. 17.
15 *Ibid.*, p. 21.
16 Frontex, *supra* n. 3, p. 19.
17 Frontex, *supra* n. 4, p. 17.
18 *Ibid.*
19 *Ibid.*, p. 21.

detections on this route tend to be lower than on other routes, possibly due to the long distances between major hubs and many countries of origin. Also, according to several reports published in 2014, visa fraud and counterfeit border crossing stamps tend to be a dominant *modus operandi* on this route, as opposed to detections of illegal border crossing. Detections of illegal border crossing remained stable, with 1,275 detections in 2014 (compared to 1,316 in 2013). Most detections were reported at the land border between Lithuania and Belarus. Most of these detections were of Vietnamese nationals arriving after transiting through Belarus. By contrast to other routes, large proportions of these detections were connected with the smuggling of goods rather than illegal migration. Regarding the border with Ukraine, Frontex monitors the situation, but in 2014 no important changes were noticed. Detections for illegal border crossing remain insignificant along all 'green border' sections with the Ukraine and the number of refusals of entry remained comparable to previous years.[20]

The statistical data presented above (Table 2) concerns the number of detections of illegal border crossings at the Eastern section of the EU land border (the Schengen area). Detailed analysis of the data referring to illegal migration onto the territory of Poland (including its borders) will be provided later in this chapter.

In accordance with the Polish law, illegal crossing of the Polish Republic's borders may constitute a petty offence or an offence in the form of a misdemeanour.[21]

By virtue of Article 49a of the Code of Petty Offences (1971)[22] illegal crossing of the border of the Republic of Poland constitutes a petty offence hence crossing the border of another country is not punishable. The principles of legal border crossing are prescribed by a number of legal acts such as the Act on Foreigners (2013)[23] and the Act on the Protection of the State Border (1990)

---

20 Frontex, *supra* n. 3, pp. 24–25. A similar analysis of the situation on routes of illegal migration leading to the EU was described in M. Perkowska, 'Nielegalna migracja w Europie – aspekty prawne i kryminologiczne' (2017) 12(3), *TEKA Komisji Politologii i Stosunków Międzynarodowych* pp. 59–75.

21 For more information on decriminalisation of illegal border crossings in the Republic of Poland, see M. Perkowska, 'Prawne i kryminologiczne aspekty dekryminalizacji przestępstwa nielegalnego przekroczenia granicy' in S. Pikulski, M. Romańczuk-Grącka (eds.), *Granice kryminalizacji i penalizacji*, Olsztyn 2013, pp. 505–15; A. Herzog, 'Zmiany w Kodeksie karnym w 2005 r.' (2006) 1 *Diariusz prawniczy* 54; R. Zawłocki, 'Kodeks karny śmietnikowy' in S. Pikulski, M. Romańczuk-Grącka and B. Orłowska-Zielińska (eds.), *Tożsamość polskiego prawa karnego*, Olsztyn 2011, pp. 78–79; A. Marek, *Kodeks karny*, Warsaw 2010, pp. 563–64.

22 Act of 20 May 1971, Code of Petty Offences, Journal of Laws 1971, No 12, item 114.

23 Act of 12 December 2013 on Foreigners, Journal of Laws 2013, item 1650.

(the Border Act).[24] Therein, mis-behaviour is liable to a fine of up to 5,000 PLN. However, if anyone who illegally crosses the border of the Republic of Poland with the use of violence, threats or deception, or in concert with others is liable to imprisonment for up to three years, according to Article 264 (2) of the Penal Code.[25]

The issue of illegal border crossing will be analysed further with regard to the Polish sections of both internal and external EU borders for a 10-year period from 2004–2014. The state border of the Republic of Poland is 3511.52 km long: 232.04 km of which is with the Russian Federation;[26] 104.28 km with the Republic of Lithuania; 418.24 km with the Republic of Belarus and 535.18 km with Ukraine; 541.06 km with the Slovak Republic; 796.04 km with the Czech Republic; and 489.37 km with the Federal Republic of Germany.[27] The sea border amounts to 439.74 km. The Polish section of the EU internal border is 1930.62 km, whereas the Polish section of the EU external border is 1580.77 km; thus the Polish section of the external EU border constitutes one quarter of the whole Eastern land route.

The data provided in Table 3 on the number of persons apprehended[28] after having crossed the border of the Republic of Poland illegally acts as an indicator of the so-called 'migration pressure'. In contrast to the Frontex data shown in Table 2, the data of the Border Guards concerning the persons apprehended encompass all cases of illegal border crossing, not just illegal border crossing between border check points. These data (apart from the data concerning, for example, the number of refusals on entry and the number of illegal stays) are, however, difficult to interpret, as they do not indicate the scale of illegal migration, but, rather, the efficiency of the actions taken by various services. Moreover, the number of foreigners who legalise their stay within the framework of abolition (for foreigners who had been staying in Poland illegally) or other mechanisms which allow them to regulate their legal status is a crucial indicator demonstrating the scale of illegal migration in Poland.[29]

---

24 Act of 12 October 1990, Borders Act, Journal of Laws 2015, item 930.

25 Art. 264(2), Act of 6 June 1997, Criminal Code, Journal of Laws 1997 No 88, item 553.

26 Covering the section which divides the territorial sea of the Republic of Poland and the Russian Federation – 22.21 km.

27 Covering the section which divides the territorial sea of the Republic of Poland and the Federal Republic of Germany – 22.22 km.

28 According to the definitions adopted by the Border Guard, apprehension may also mean detection, etc. It covers the cases of detection of a particular event and apprehension and detection of the person committing the act. It also encompasses the apprehension of people who have been accused of offences other than illegal crossing (e.g. forgery of documents). Komenda Główna Straży Granicznej, *Informacja o sytuacji na granicy państwowej, Działania Straży Granicznej w 2012 roku* (porównanie do 2011 roku), p. 2.

29 *Polityka Migracyjna Polski – stan obecny i postulowane działania*, Ministerstwo Spraw Wewnętrznych i Administracji Departament Polityki Migracyjnej, Warsaw 2011, p. 40.

Table 3. The number of people apprehended after having crossed the Polish sections of the external and internal EU borders illegally

Year	**External border**	**Internal border**
2004	1,085	4,592
2005	1,384	3,007
2006	1,464	2,393
2007	1,307	1,913
2008	3,452	2,096
2009	1,561	1,849
2010	1,361	988
2011	1,379	1,123
2012	1,657	1,591
2013	1,858	1,937
2014	2,124	2,787
2015	3,365	3,615

Source: The Border Guard Headquarters, <http://strazgraniczna.pl/pl/granica/statystyki-sg/2206,Statystyki-SG.html> accessed 20.02.2017.

Two milestones which determine the inflow of illegal migrants to Poland should be mentioned in the period analysed. These are 1 May 2004, when the Republic of Poland joined the EU, and 21 December 2007, when Poland fully implemented the Schengen *acquis*.[30] Another important factor, which affected the phenomenon of illegal border crossing, was the abolition for foreigners who had been staying in Poland illegally, which lasted from 1 January until 30 June 2012.[31]

It can be stated that illegal migration to and via Poland until 2007 mainly concerned the Polish section of the EU internal border, which confirms the statement that Poland is a transit territory for illegal migration in Europe.

The situation changed completely in 2008 when a considerable increase in the number of people apprehended at the EU external border was noted. This is of particular relevance when compared to the relatively constant number of people apprehended at the Polish section of the EU internal border. It should be highlighted, however, that until 2011, the number of people apprehended at the Polish internal section tended to decline, which was grounded in the fact that full implementation of the Schengen acquis started in 21 December 2007.

30 See A. Szachoń-Pszenny, *Acquis Schengen a granice wewnętrzne i zewnętrzne w Unii Europejskiej*, Poznań 2011, p. 270.

31 Abolition was introduced by Act of 28 July 2011 on the Legalisation of Stay of Some Foreigners in the Territory of the Republic of Poland and on amendments to the Act on Granting Protection to Foreigners in the Territory of the Republic of Poland and to the Act on Foreigners, Journal of Laws 2011, No 191, item 1133.

According to the data presented in Table 3 the highest number of people who crossed or attempted to cross the border of the Republic of Poland illegally was recorded in 2008.[32]

It was anticipated that the shift of the external border of the Schengen Area from the Polish Western border to its Eastern one, when Poland joined the Schengen Area, would result in an increased number of illegal migrants, which in fact was the case only in 2008, as the subsequent year saw a gradual drop in the number of foreigners apprehended for illegal border crossing. The significant growth which was recorded in 2008 might result from the fact that not all foreigners were aware of the legal requirements, such as the obligation to possess a visa to cross the border.[33]

Drawing on that, it might be argued that after joining the Schengen Area, Poland became attractive for third-country nationals and international criminal groups as a transit country to reach other EU Member States. Consequently, Poland strengthened its position as a kind of bridge between the East and the West.[34] Migrants wrongly presumed that crossing the Eastern border of the Republic of Poland would enable them to reach any EU Member States easily. Simultaneously, it is worth highlighting that Poland is increasingly perceived as the country of destination, which may lead to the conclusion that it is becoming more attractive in terms of labour market, remuneration or life and social conditions.[35]

In 2009, the Agreement on Local Border Traffic between Ukraine and Poland came into force,[36] which was supposed to facilitate border crossing for people living in the border area. However, it cannot unequivocally be stated that this agreement contributed to the drop in the number of persons detected while

---

32 M. Perkowska, 'Przekroczenie granicy państwa wbrew przepisom jako forma nielegalnej migracji' in W. Pływaczewski and M. Ilnicki (eds.), *Ochrona praw człowieka w polityce migracyjnej Polski i Unii Europejskiej*, Olsztyn 2016, p. 199.

33 M. Perkowska, *Przestępczość graniczna cudzoziemców*, Warsaw 2013, pp. 58–59.

34 See K. Laskowska, 'Przestępczość cudzoziemców w województwie podlaskim' (2003) 2 *Jurysta* 19; E.W. Pływaczewski, 'Problemy sprawców tzw. rosyjskojęzycznych na tle przestępczości cudzoziemców w Polsce' in O. Górniok (ed.), *U progu nowych kodyfikacji. Księga pamiątkowa ofiarowana profesorowi Leonowi Tyszkiewiczowi*, Katowice 1999, pp. 281–82. K. Laskowska, 'Przestępczość cudzoziemców w Polsce w latach 1989–2007 w świetle statystyk policyjnych – skala, dynamika, prognozy zagrożeń po wejściu do strefy Schengen' in M. Zdanowicz (ed.), *Polska w Schengen*, Białystok 2009, pp. 229–30.

35 Ministerstwo Spraw Wewnętrznych, *Raport o stanie bezpieczeństwa w Polsce 2012*, Warsaw 2013, s. 121. M. Perkowska, *supra* n. 32, p. 199.

36 Agreement of 28.03.2008 between the Government of the Repulic of Poland and the Cabinet of Ministers of Ukraine on the rules of Local Border Traffic, Journal of Laws 2008, No 103 item 858. See S. Dubaj, 'Uproszczenia w przekraczaniu granic – mały ruch graniczny' in A. Kuś and M. Kowerski (eds.), *Transgraniczny przepływ towarów i osób w Unii Europejskiej*, Lublin-Zamość 2011, p. 281 ff.

crossing the Poland–Ukraine border illegally in comparison to the preceding year (2008 saw the highest number of detected foreigners who illegally crossed the external border). The number of persons apprehended at the border section with Ukraine in 2009 and in the following years remained stable, at approximately 800 people detected.[37]

A slight increase was noted in 2012, particularly in the first six-month period when the abolition for people staying illegally in Poland entered into force. The increase was attributed to so-called 'abolition tourism', that is, an intensified illegal inflow of foreigners who were attracted by the possibility of legalising their stay in Poland but who did not, however, meet the conditions prescribed in the Abolition Act.[38]

Table 4. The number of people apprehended for crossing the border of the Republic of Poland illegally at the Polish section of the EU external border in the years 2004–2015

Nationality	Border section					
	Russia	Belarus	Ukraine	Sea border	Air border	Total
Afghanistan	0	64	73	2	27	166
Armenia	53	69	131	3	33	290
Belarus	5	1,375	24	13	38	1,455
China	1	60	153	0	43	257
Georgia	2	258	325	13	95	693
India	8	0	55	1	8	72
Moldova	18	34	863	3	62	980
Pakistan	1	21	115	1	19	157
Russia	587	612	340	50	56	1,550
Syria	3	3	35	1	183	224
Ukraine	32	54	10,481	71	954	11,592
Vietnam	0	78	516	3	32	629
Poland	296	270	606	681	325	2,178
Other EU states	56	70	87	80	33	326
Other third countries	86	243	399	42	606	1,428
Total	1,148	3,211	14,203	964	2,514	21,997

Source: The Border Guard Headquarters, <http://strazgraniczna.pl/pl/granica/statystyki-sg/2206, Statystyki-SG.html> accessed 20.02.2017.

---

37 At the border section with Ukraine, 881 people were detected in 2007, 2829 in 2008, 935 in 2009 and 965 in 2010. See M. Perkowska, 'Criminological Aspects of Local Border Traffic on the Polish Section of European Union's External Border' in M. Zdanowicz (ed.), *Local Border Traffic on the Polish Section of European Union's External Border*, Warsaw-Bialystok 2013, pp. 186–93.

38 M. Perkowska, 'Prawne i kryminologiczne aspekty abolicji dla cudzoziemców' (2015) 4 *Państwo i Prawo* 33.

At the Polish section of the EU external border, most people were apprehended at its longest section – at the border section with Ukraine; as a result, Ukrainian nationals constitute the largest number of people detected by the Border Guard for illegal crossing. The second largest section of the external border is the border section with Belarus, and Belarussians constitute the dominant group among those detected respectively; likewise Russians at the border section with Russia. It is an inevitable consequence of the fact that these border sections are mostly crossed by the citizens of Poland's neighbouring countries.[39]

However, it is worth stressing that a significant number of nationals of Moldova, Georgia and Vietnam were detected at the border as well. These people wish to join their communities who have been existing and functioning well in Poland for years, thus they use both regular and illegal migration channels to achieve this aim.[40]

It can be concluded from the data on the number of people apprehended for illegal border crossing at the Polish section of the EU external border that it is a marginal phenomenon when compared with the other sections of the EU external border, particularly the sea border sections. It is chiefly due to 'push' factors in the sending states (which recently have been Syria, Eritrea and Afghanistan), whose geographical routes run to Europe through its Southern borders. In addition, Frontex have reported some illegal border crossings between border check points by nationals of Vietnam, Afghanistan and Georgia at the Eastern land section of the EU external border, which reinforces the detections at the Polish section of the EU external border.

Table 5. The number of people apprehended for crossing the border of the Republic of Poland illegally at the Polish section of the EU internal border in the years 2004–2015

Nationality	Border section							
	Lithuania	Slovakia	Czech	Germany	Sea border	Air border	Total	State territory
Afghanistan	40	24	18	78	4	5	169	3
Armenia	50	0	11	122	5	1	189	38
Belarus	62	3	145	273	3	4	490	15
China	17	17	68	277	1	9	389	35
Georgia	147	23	56	470	35	9	740	9
India	17	26	28	142	3	27	243	12

(continued)

39 See M. Pogoda, 'Straż Graniczna w procesie dostosowania do wymogów Unii Europejskiej i strefy Schengen' in A. Kús and A. Szachń-Pszenny (eds.), *Wpływ acquis communautaire i acquis Schengen na prawo polskie – doświadczenia i perspektywy, Tom I- 10 lat Polski w Unii Europejskiej*, Lublin 2014, pp. 214–15.

40 M. Perkowska, *supra* n. 32, p. 201.

Table 5 *Continued*

Nationality	Border section							
	Lithuania	Slovakia	Czech	Germany	Sea border	Air border	Total	State territory
Moldova	19	64	127	555	0	0	765	14
Pakistan	15	30	22	174	5	105	351	32
Russia	140	283	478	2,744	26	1	3,672	61
Syria	8	36	16	198	14	23	295	1
Ukraine	50	215	3,093	6,016	154	45	9,573	206
Vietnam	389	54	274	309	2	2	1,030	189
Poland	70	448	1,385	1,353	12	11	3,279	23
Other EU states	379	557	1,432	864	36	0	3,268	55
Other third countries	222	117	378	2,649	141	143	3,650	222
Total	1,625	1,897	7,531	16,224	441	385	28,103	915

Source: The Border Guard Headquarters, <http://strazgraniczna.pl/pl/granica/statystyki-sg/2206,Statystyki-SG.html> accessed 20.02.2017.

Most people apprehended for illegal border crossing, in the discussed period (i.e. in the years 2004–2015), were recorded at the border with Germany – as many as 59 per cent of the total number of the people detected. Quite a significant number of people detected were noted at the border with the Czech Republic – 28 per cent of the total number of people apprehended at the internal border. The nationality of the perpetrators is comparable to that present at the Polish section of the EU external border. Ukrainians and Russians are the dominant group. The number of Ukrainians is similar to the number of people apprehended at the external border, whereas the number of Russians detected is almost three times as high as the number of people apprehended at the external section. Moreover, more citizens of China, Georgia, India, Pakistan and Vietnam were detected than at the external border (Table 5).[41]

An increase in illegal migration of Vietnamese nationals, who attempted to enter the territory of Poland at the border section with Lithuania as well as at the border sections with Ukraine and Belarus, was observed in the years 2014–2015. These attempts to cross the Polish and German border suggest transit migration.[42]

Illegal migration to Poland mainly occurs at overland sections of the external border (Tables 4 and 5). The apprehension of individuals at sea and

[41] *Ibid.*, p. 204.

[42] Ministerstwo Spraw Wewnętrznych, *Raport o stanie bezpieczeństwa w Polsce 2014*, Warsaw 2015, p. 103.

air border crossing points is rare. At sea border crossing points, migrants who wish to reach Sweden are detected.[43] The most popular air route has recently been via Istanbul to Warsaw, which was mainly used by nationals of Syria, Afghanistan and Iran travelling on fraudulent French, Austrian, Spanish and Greek documents. In addition, a new route (Cairo–Moscow–Cairo) has been recorded. This is used by Egyptian nationals who, on the return leg to Cairo, use the stop-over in Warsaw to apply for refugee status in the territory of Poland.[44]

The scale of illegal migration of Syrian nationals to Poland needs to be analysed in the present discussion on the perceived threat of illegal migration. The number of illegal migrants who are either nationals of Syria or stateless persons claiming Syrian nationality, has, in recent years, remained stable. Despite this, the perceived threat still exists. This is confirmed by, on the one hand, the high numbers of Syrians recorded in European statistics on the one hand and, on the other, no foreseeable prospects of their return to Syria due to the political instability there. Without doubt, Germany's asylum policy has played a pivotal role in shaping the illegal transit migration of Syrian nationals. Their main migration route runs from the Southern European countries through Austria and/or the Czech Republic/Slovakia to Germany and on to Scandinavian countries. Germany is both a destination and transit country for illegal migrants. It can be assumed that intensified activity on this route promoted the use of Poland as a transit country, which is confirmed by the increase in the number of Syrian citizens apprehended in 2015 (108 people were detected in 2014, rising to 175 in 2015). Also we cannot ignore the fact that criminal groups are now increasingly benefiting from illegal migration.[45]

Migration pressure revealed by the data provided by the Polish Border Guard concerning the refusal of entry into EU territory (Table 6) needs to be taken into consideration as well.[46] The refusal of entry can only be issued at the EU external border. The number of the refusals at the Eastern land border constitutes over 90 per cent (frequently almost 95–97 per cent) of all the cases at the Polish border (the remaining refusals are issued at air and sea border crossing points). The data included in Table 6 indicate that the number of refusals is significant. These refusals have mainly involved citizens of Ukraine, Russia, Belarus, Armenia and Georgia. In addition, nationals of remote countries such

43 Ministerstwo Spraw Wewnętrznych, *Raport o stanie bezpieczeństwa w Polsce 2013*, Warsaw 2014, p. 112.

44 *Ibid.* Perkowska, *supra* n. 32, p. 204.

45 Ministerstwo Spraw Wewnętrznych, *supra* n. 42, p. 103.

46 See Ministerstwo Spraw Wewnętrznych, *Polityka Migracyjna Polski – stan obecny i postulowane działania*, Warsaw 2011, p. 40. A. Szachoń-Pszenny, 'Uruchomienie Systemu Informacyjnego Schengen drugiej generacji w 2013 r. jako wzmocnienie bezpieczeństwa swobodnego przepływu osób i towarów' (2013) 5 *Monitor Prawa Celnego i Podatkowego*, pp. 191–99.

as Syria and Pakistan have also been reported to attempt crossing the border of Poland and the EU illegally.[47]

Table 6. Refusals of entry issued at the Polish section of the EU external border in the years 2009–2014*

Nationality	2009	2010	2011	2012	2013	2014*
Afghanistan	4	4	9	16	35	
Armenia	222	102	299	857	807	
Belarus	4,203	4,719	4,865	3,604	3,242	3,588
China	9	32	8	7	13	
Georgia	5,686	2,886	2,340	8,247	5,839	3,583
India	13	7	9	10	9	
Moldovia	125	87	129	110	101	
Pakistan	7	5	7	8	6	
Russia	3,348	3,530	2,679	3,589	10,056	5,133
Syria	2	2	15	95	76	
Ukraine	12,802	11,721	10,938	15,067	13,963	13,147
Vietnam	3	10	26	8	15	
EU Member States	1	0	1	7	0	
Other third countries	209	503	655	571	644	2,236
Total	26,634	23,608	21,980	32,196	34,806	27,687

Source: The Border Guard Headquarters. The data for 2015 were not available to the author while preparing the text.

* No detailed data on nationalities were obtained for 2014.

According to Frontex, in 2014, Ukrainians were the top ranking nationality for refusals of entry at the EU level. Among Member States, Poland reported the largest number of refusals of entry in absolute terms, mostly to nationals of Ukraine at the land borders. However, it is at the land border between Hungary and Serbia that the number of refusals of entry is the highest per passenger. This particular pressure is due to the higher passenger flow, following visa liberalisation in the Western Balkans, and the subsequent increased role of border control authorities in checking entry requirements, which was previously the responsibility of consular authorities.[48] Particular attention should be drawn to the fact that, for obvious reasons, illegal migrants who travel on sea routes cannot

47 M. Perkowska, 'Zagrożenie przestępczością na wschodniej granicy Polski – struktura i dynamika zjawiska' (2016) 41 *Politeja* 129.

48 Frontex, *supra* n. 4, p. 23.

be refused entry to the territory on which they land. Such migrants undertake travel at extreme risk, frequently on overcrowded and/or unseaworthy vessels, and sending them back would be inhumane as, in a worst-case scenario, it might well result in their death.[49] Refusal of entry is possible at overland borders, particularly along the Eastern section of the EU's external border, where refused entry may cause hardship, but does not directly place an individual's health or life at risk.

Illegal stay in the territory of Poland, under Article 495(1)(1) of the Act on Foreigners, constitutes an offence liable to a fine up to 5,000 PLN. The data shown in Table 7 indicate that the phenomenon was not significant; however, a rising trend can be observed as with other forms of illegal migration. Most people (approximately 60 per cent) who have been staying illegally in Poland are detected when they attempt to cross the external border to leave Poland for their country of origin. Most frequently, these are nationals of Ukraine and Belarus. On the other hand, one third of those staying illegally are detected inland, or at the sections of the internal border. These illegal stays mainly relate to the detected people's overstay in the territory of Poland.[50]

Table 7. Illegal stays in Poland in 2010–2014

Year	2010	2011	2012	2013	2014
Number of foreigners staying illegally	2,887	5,104	6,169	7,664	9,117

Source: The Border Guard Headquarters, <http://strazgraniczna.pl/pl/granica/statystyki-sg/2206, Statystyki-SG.html> accessed 20.02.2017.

If we compare the scale of illegal stays in Poland to the European context, it can be stated that this is a marginal phenomenon. The vast majority of illegal stayers in the EU were detected inland and so are presumed to be long-term overstayers as they were making no attempt to leave at the time of detection. The next most common location for detections of illegal stayers is at the air borders on exit, followed by the land borders where illegally staying migrants were leaving the EU or the Schengen area.[51]

49 For example, in 2015 118,495 people were refused entry to the territory of Poland at the EU external borders; 5,279 of these were at sea borders, which merely constitutes 4.5 per cent. Frontex, *supra* n. 4, p. 66.

50 Komenda Główna Straży Granicznej, *Informacja o sytuacji na granicy państwowej, Działania Straży Granicznej w 2014 roku* (porównanie do 2013 roku), p. 5; Komenda Główna Straży Granicznej, *Informacja o sytuacji na granicy państwowej* (Działania Straży Granicznej w 2010 roku), p. 5.

51 Frontex, *supra* n. 3, p. 30.

3. SCALE OF CRIMINALITY ATTRIBUTABLE TO FOREIGNERS IN POLAND

Three different data sources (i.e. the Police, the Border Guard and Customs) need to be analysed to discuss the criminality of foreigners to provide a realistic picture of the criminality attributable to foreigners in Poland.

The data presented in Table 8 indicate clearly that the criminality of foreigners detected in the territory of Poland is not significant. The detailed analysis carried out by Rzeplińska shows that foreigners most often commit the following offences: driving a motor vehicle while in a state of insobriety or under the influence of an intoxicant; forging and counterfeiting or altering a document with the intention of using it as authentic; labelling goods with fake trademarks; trading in goods bearing fake trademarks; trading in goods without Polish excise stripbands; unauthorised recording of works; and unauthorised dissemination of videograms. Foreigners are also involved in cases of corruption and theft; however, these offences are not very common.[52] The numbers show a declining trend in criminality of foreigners, except for 2013. The increase presented in 2013 results from the change in the system of data gathering rather than intensification of criminal activity of foreigners.[53]

Table 8. Suspects in Poland detected by the Police in the years 2010–2013

Year	Total	Suspected foreigners	Percentage of suspected foreigners in the total number of the suspects
2010	516,154	2,326	0.45%
2011	521,942	2,242	0.43%
2012	500,539	2,152	0.43%
2013	438,662	3,682	0.84%

Source: Police Headquarters. The data for 2014 and 2015 were not available to the author while preparing the text.

The data provided by the Border Guard and presented in Table 9 significantly changes the picture of criminality of foreigners as whole. The highest increase in number was noted in 2012 when the Agreement on Local Border Traffic with

52 I. Rzeplińska, 'Przestępczość migrantów w Polsce – historia i współczesność' in B. Namysłowska-Gabrysiak, K. Syroka-Marczewska and A. Walczak-Żochowska (eds.), *Prawo wobec problemów społecznych. Księga Jubileuszowa profesor Eleonory Zielińskiej*, Warsaw 2016, pp. 299–300.

53 M. Perkowska and E. Jurgielewicz-Delegacz, 'Zadania i funkcje kryminologii w systemie bezpieczeństwa', in R. Skarzyński, E. Kużelewska (eds.), *Bezpieczństwo. Dyscyplina nauki wobec funkcjonowania państwa*, Białystok 2018, p. 53.

Russia came into force.[54] It considerably affected the intensity of border traffic and consequently the number of people who attempted to cross the border illegally or smuggle goods increased.[55] The year 2012 was also marked by two crucial factors which determined the dynamics of the phenomenon. The first was the abolition for foreigners staying in Poland illegally, introduced in 2012. This led to so-called 'abolition tourism' manifested by illegal entries into the territory by nationals of non-EU states who wished to legalise their stay not only in Poland, but also in the EU.[56] Another factor related to the decreased efficiency of prosecuting illegal migration in Belarus in the respective year, which was a consequence of the fact that the Belarussian services concentrated on incoming, not outgoing visitors.[57]

Table 9. Suspects detected by the Border Guard in the years 2010–2013

Year	Total	Suspected foreigners	Percentage of suspected foreigners in the total number of the suspects
2010	5,693	3,536	62%
2011	4,962	3,070	62%
2012	6,062	4,162	69%
2013	5,029	3,256	65%

Source: The Border Guard Headquarters. The data for 2014 and 2015 were not available to the author while preparing the text.

In this context, offences committed by foreigners particularly include illegal border crossing and offences such as using counterfeited documents or documents belonging to another person, or obtaining a certification of a false entry in a document. Smuggling excise duty goods was less frequently detected by the Border Guard.

The number of suspected foreigners in the discussed period always outweighed the number of Polish suspects. The percentage of foreigners varied from 62 to 69 per cent of all suspects. Therefore, it can be concluded that border criminality in Poland is dominated by foreigners. Its dynamics depends on the dynamics of foreigners' behaviours. The activity of Polish citizens in that respect is insignificant, not exceeding the number of 2,000 suspects in the years 2012–2014.[58]

54 Agreement of 14.12.2011 between the Government of the Repulic of Poland and the Government of Russian Federation on the rules of Local Border Traffic, Journal of Laws 2012, item 814.

55 M. Perkowska, 'Dynamika i struktura przestępczości granicznej cudzoziemców w Polsce na podstawie danych statystycznych Komendy Głównej Straży Granicznej' in W. Klaus, K. Laskowska, and I Rzeplińska (eds.) *Przestępczość cudzoziemców. Aspekty prawne, kryminologiczne i praktyczne*, Warsaw 2017, p. 121.

56 See M. Perkowska, *supra* n. 38, pp. 33–49.

57 'Mniej szczelna granica polsko-białoruska' (2012) 26 *Biuletyn Migracyjny* 1.

58 M. Perkowska, *supra* n. 38.

As the data presented in Table 10 indicate, a rising trend was observed in the number of suspected foreigners until 2011, whereas the reverse trend has been noticed since 2012. In the period being discussed, most smugglers were detected at the Polish section of the EU external border. The ratio between the number of suspected foreigners at the sections of the external and internal EU borders varied from 3–4 per cent to 96–97 per cent.[59]

Table 10. Suspected foreigners detected by the Customs in the years 2010–2013

Year	Suspected foreigners				
	Total	at the internal border		at the external border	
		number	%	number	%
2010	63,353	1,813	2.86	61,540	97.14
2011	78,870	2,271	2.88	76,599	97.12
2012	65,987	2,082	3.16	63,905	96.84
2013	44,679	1,641	3.67	43,038	96.33

Source: Ministry of Finance. The author received data only for the period 2009–2013.

When analysing different forms of border criminality attributable to foreign nationals, it might be stated that it is not always marginal when compared to the criminality of Polish citizens. This is confirmed by the statistics provided by the Border Guard, which relate this criminality particularly to illegal border crossing or offences against the credibility of documents in connection with border crossing. On the other hand, the scale of illegal migration to or through Poland when compared to other migration routes running to and through Europe is insignificant.[60]

4. AMENDMENTS INTRODUCED INTO POLISH IMMIGRATION AND CRIMINAL LAW TO PREVENT THE THREAT

Immigration law today is clothed with so many attributes of criminal law that the line between them has grown indistinct. Scholars have labelled this the 'criminalisation of immigration law'. The merger of the two areas in both

59 M. Perkowska, 'Dynamika i struktura przestępczości granicznej cudzoziemców w Polsce na podstawie danych statystycznych Służby Celnej (Ministerstwa Finansów)' in W. Klaus, K. Laskowska and I. Rzeplińska (eds.), *Przestępczość cudzoziemców. Aspekty prawne, kryminologiczne i praktyczne*, Warsaw 2017, p. 169.

60 Frontex, *supra* n. 4, p. 21.

substance and procedure has created parallel systems in which immigration law and the criminal justice system are merely nominally separate. Criminal law seeks to prevent and address harm to individuals and society from violence or fraud, or evil motive. Immigration law determines who may cross the border and who may reside in the territory or must leave. Criminal law and immigration law primarily regulate the relationship between the state and the individual. Crimes committed by immigrants have influenced the direction of immigration law since its inception. Criminal and immigration law primarily serves to separate the individual from the rest of native society through physical exclusion and the creation of rules that establish lesser levels of citizenship. Moreover, the law often imposes both immigration and criminal sanctions for the same offence. Where a non-citizen violates immigration law that has been defined as criminal, or commits a crime that is a deportable offence, both incarceration and deportation may result.[61]

Accordingly, foreign nationals are punished for the offences created especially to control them i.e. the offences which in fact cannot be committed by the citizen of a particular country, which results in the significant overrepresentation of migrants in Western European prisons.[62]

The analysis of legal regulations and especially the amendments introduced into immigration and criminal law endeavours to answer the question of whether Polish regulations enter into the arena of 'crimmigration', a term created by Stumpf.[63] The 'crimmigration' merger has taken place on three fronts: (i) the substance of immigration law and criminal law increasingly overlaps; (ii) immigration enforcement has come to resemble criminal law enforcement; and (iii) the procedural aspects of prosecuting immigration violations have taken on many of the earmarks of criminal procedure.

Based on the analysis of this definition and the Polish system for the prevention of illegal migration, this chapter attempts to determine whether those legal provisions are necessary from a Polish perspective. Collectively, this embraces the detailed analysis of legal framework on foreigners, the Criminal Code and other acts.

The analysis of the amendments to the Polish criminal law in the context of 'crimmigration' should commence with decriminalisation of crossing the Republic of Poland's border in violation of law. Article 264(1) of the Criminal Code, stating 'Whoever crosses the border of the Republic of Poland in violation

---

[61] J. Stumpf, 'The Crimmigration Crisis: Immigrants, Crime, and Sovereign Power' (2006) 56(2) *American University Law Review* 376.

[62] W. Klaus, 'Cudzoziemcy niemile widziani. Detencja cudzoziemców jako przykład kryminalizacji migracji' in D. Pudzianowska (ed.), *Status cudzoziemca w Polsce wobec współczesnych wyzwań międzynarodowych*, LEXonline.

[63] J. Stumpf, *supra* n. 61, p. 381.

of the relevant regulations shall be subject to a fine, the penalty of restriction of liberty or the penalty of deprivation of liberty for up to 2 years', was repealed by the Act of 24 August 2005 amending the Act on Border Guards and some other acts.[64] However, simultaneously, Article 49a was introduced into the Code of Petty Offences stating: '§ 1.Whoever crosses the border of the Republic of Poland in violation of the relevant regulations shall be subject to a fine. § 2. Attempt and abetting are punishable'.[65]

The legislative, whilst providing reasons for these amendments in the criminal law, stated that in 2001 only 27 per cent out of some 4,000 instigated preliminary proceedings fell under Article 264(1) of the Criminal Code. The strictest form of punishment stipulated by Article 264(1), that is, deprivation of liberty (without suspending the sentence) was only imposed in 72 cases. The act specified by Article 264(1) of the Criminal Code, border crossing (i.e. entering and leaving the territory of the Republic of Poland illegally), is a typical violation of an administrative order. It is worth highlighting that the acts falling under Article 264(1) of the Criminal Code are considered petty offences according to the legislation of the Federal Republic of Germany, the Czech Republic and the Slovak Republic. In the context of Poland's accession to the EU, it appears appropriate to treat similar violations of law alike. The new regulation serves the purpose of rationalising prosecution and effective application of the principle that punishment is inevitable.

As Bojarski points out, border crossing nowadays is no longer of political character but usually relates to the desire of migrants from poorer countries to find better living conditions. Therefore, their acts cannot, in fact, be treated as serious offences, but rather as petty offences.[66] Moreover, as the national structure of Poland is of a homogenous nature with only a small proportion of foreigners present, immigration to Poland is minimal. Analysing the trends in migration of people applying for international protection, it can be definitely stated that only a few have decided to settle in Poland, with the vast majority treating the country as a transit point. This lack of interest results mainly from the relatively low standards of living in Poland when compared to the so-called 'old' EU Member States, but given that unemployment is falling and salaries are gradually rising, this situation may soon change.[67]

---

64 Act of 22 April 2005 on amendments of Act on Border Guards and other acts, Journal of Laws No 90, item 757.

65 Act of 20 May 1971, Code of Petty Offences, Journal of Laws No 12, item 114.

66 T. Bojarski, 'Kierunki zmian dokonanych w kodeksie karnym z 1997 roku. Charakterystyka ogólna' in T. Bojarski, K. Nazar, A. Nowosad and M. Szwarczyk (eds.), *Zmiany w polskim prawie karnym po wejściu w życie kodeksu karnego z 1997 roku*, Lublin 2006, pp. 30–31.

67 Ministerstwo Spraw Wewnętrznych, *Polityka migracyjna Polski – stan obecny i postulowane działania*, Warsaw 2011, p. 68. See M. Perkowska *supra* n. 21, p. 509.

This decriminalisation appears to be a positive change, as illegal border crossing shows a trend towards decline and is closely connected with the migration from the East to the West of Europe. Illegal border crossing does not pose any serious threat either to the Republic of Poland's public or legal order, provided it is not accompanied by other criminal behaviours such as using counterfeited documents, corruption or smuggling goods which is so common at the border.[68]

In addition, experience based on the practice of imposing punishments for illegal border crossing (as a basic offence) has shown that such decriminalisation is needed. The non-custodial punishments prevailed, that is, a fine, restriction of liberty or parole as a means of probation were applied.[69] Consequently, the fine stipulated under the present Code for illegal border crossing serves the purpose of the punishments which had been imposed under the earlier Criminal Code. The practice of imposing non-custodial punishments is particularly justified in the case of foreigners. It is worth underscoring that foreigners detected for illegal border crossing, or who have attempted to do, so constitute 95 per cent of the total number of people apprehended for these reasons since 2008. The fine is a penalty, which can be easily enforced, particularly as far as border criminality is concerned.[70]

Another step taken by the Polish legislature to prevent illegal migration was the implementation of Framework Decision of 28 November 2002 on strengthening the penal framework to prevent the facilitation of unauthorised entry, transit and residence[71] and Directive 2002/90/EC defining the facilitation of unauthorised entry, transit and residence.[72] Based on this, the law[73] penalised some actions undertaken for financial and personal benefits which include assisting illegal migration.[74] In addition, a stricter punishment was introduced for the offence stipulated by virtue of Article 264(3) of the Criminal Code (illegal border crossing arrangements) by determining its limits, that is, subject to deprivation of liberty for a term from six months up to eight years, according

68 M. Perkowska, *supra* n. 21, p. 514.
69 M. Perkowska, *supra* n. 33, p. 126.
70 M. Perkowska, *supra* n. 21, pp. 514–15.
71 Framework Decision of 28 November 2002, on strengthening the penal framework to prevent the facilitation of unauthorised entry, transit and residence (2002/946/JHA) [2002] OJ L328/1.
72 Council Directive 2002/90/EC of 28 November 2002 defining the facilitation of unauthorised entry, transit and residence [2002] OJ L328/17.
73 Explanatory memorandum to act changing Criminal Code and other acts, print No 2407, p. 14.
74 Art. 264a(1) of the Criminal Code: enabling and facilitating another person's stay in the Republic of Poland in violation of law.

to the requirements included in Article 1(3) of the Framework Decision.[75] According to Ćwiąkalski, Article 264a of the Criminal Code was a reaction to an increase in inflow and illegal stays of immigrants, which has resulted from Poland's increased attractiveness and would not be possible without other people's involvement in offering facilitation of illegal entry. Nevertheless, in exceptional cases the possibility of extraordinary mitigating or even waiving the punishment has been stipulated in that provision.[76]

According to the law, not every case of assisting in illegal migration requires imposition of the punishment stipulated under Article 264a(1) of the Criminal Code. In exceptional cases, where the perpetrator has not received any financial benefits, the court might, by virtue of Article 264a(2) of the Criminal Code, mitigate or even waive the punishment.[77]

Article 264(1) of the Criminal Code prescribes the basic offence, which somewhat specifies the provisions of Article 264(2) and (3) of the Criminal Code. Article 264 of the Criminal Code refers to the crossing of the Republic of Poland's borders illegally and assisting in such crossings, whereas Article 264a of the Criminal Code concerns the offence of illegal stays in the territory of the Republic of Poland. According to Pływaczewski, under Article 264a of the Criminal Code, it is the state border that receives direct protection against illegal crossing,[78] whereas the state security is protected indirectly.[79]

A person who intends to stay or stays in the territory of the Republic of Poland illegally (i.e. without legal entitlement) is criminalised under the aforementioned provisions, and only a foreigner, that is, anyone who does not possess Polish nationality,[80] fits into that category. Therefore, while Article 264a(1) of the Criminal Code does not expressly state that the provisions concern only foreigners, it can be concluded as such from the Act on Foreigners, which stipulates the rules and conditions attached to the stay of foreigners in the territory of the Republic of Poland.[81]

---

75 *Ibid.* W. Grzeszczyk, 'Zmiany w prawie karnym wprowadzone ustawą z dn. 16 kwietnia 2004 r.' (2004) 9 *Prokuratura i Prawo*, pp. 74–76, C. Nowak, *Wpływ procesów globalizacyjnych na polskie prawo karne*, Warsaw 2014, p. 335.

76 Z. Ćwiąkalski in A. Zoll (ed.), *Kodeks karny. Część szczególna, Tom II. Komentarz do art. 117–277 k.k.*, Warsaw 2013, p. 1454.

77 P. Gensikowski, *Odstąpienie od wymierzenia kary w polskim prawie karnym*, Warsaw 2011, pp. 182 ff.

78 E. Pływaczewski, in M. Filar (ed.), *Kodeks karny. Komentarz*, Warsaw 2012, p. 1197.

79 E. Pływaczewski and A. Sakowicz, in A. Wąsek and R. Zawłocki (eds.), *Kodeks karny, część szczególna. Tom II. Komentarz do artykułów 222–316*, Warsaw 2010, p. 534.

80 On the basis of Art. 2 of the Act on Foreigners.

81 R.A. Stafański, 'Przestępstwo umożliwienia lub ułatwienia nielegalnego pobytu (art. 264a k.k.)' (2005) 11 *Prokuratura i Prawo*, p. 8. M. Perkowska and E. Jurgielewicz, 'Zwalczanie nielegalnej migracji w polskim prawie karnym – wybrane aspekty implementacji prawa Unii Europejskiej' (2014) 15 *Białostockie Studia Prawnicze* 71.

Another step to implement EU law, namely Directive 2009/52/EC providing for minimum standards on sanctions and measures against employers of illegally staying third-country nationals,[82] in the scope of combating illegal migration is the Act of 15 June 2012 on Effects of Illegal Employment of Foreigners Illegally Staying on Polish Territory.[83]

Directive 2009/52/EC introduced a ban on the employment of third-country nationals who are illegally staying in the territory of the EU Member States. The term 'foreigner' was limited in the Act on Effects of Illegal Employment of Foreigners Illegally Staying on Polish Territory following Directive 2009/52/EC, if compared to the general term of 'foreigner' included in Article 2 of the Act on Foreigners. The Act on Foreigners and the Act on Employment Promotion and Labour Market Institutions, Article 2(1)(7), stipulate that a foreigner is every person who does not possess Polish citizenship.[84]

Moreover, the Act on Effects of Illegal Employment of Foreigners Illegally Staying on Polish Territory provides for penal and administrative sanctions imposed on employers who violate the ban, which include the liability of legal persons and, under certain circumstances, also financial liability of contractor if a subcontractor breaches the employer's obligations.

Statutory conditions for the legal employment of foreigners in Poland are prescribed in the Act on Effects of Illegal Employment of Foreigners Illegally Staying on Polish Territory and the Act of Employment Promotion and Labour Market Institutions.[85]

Under Polish law, the implementation of Directive 2009/52/EC resulted in increasing liability for illegal employment of foreigners. Article 2 of the Act of 15 June 2012 on Effects of Illegal Employment of Foreigners Illegally Staying on Polish Territory obliges the employer to demand from the foreigner before s/he starts working to produce a valid document, which authorises him/her to stay in the territory of Poland.[86]

The Act on Employment Promotion and Labour Market Institutions, by virtue of Article 120, penalises illegal employment of foreigners. It is a petty offence, which means employing a foreigner is in violation of law and is subject to a fine up to 3,000 PLN. In accordance with Article 2(2) of the Act on Employment

---

82 Directive 2009/52/EC of the European Parliament and of the Council of 18 June 2009 providing for minimum standards on sanctions and measures against employers of illegally staying third-country nationals [2009] OJ L168/24.

83 Act of 15 June 2012 on Effects of Illegal Employment of Foreigners Illegally Staying on Polish Territory, Journal of Laws 2012, item 769.

84 Art. 2(1)(7) of the Act on Foreigners, Journal of Laws 2011 No 191, item 1133.

85 Act of 20 April 2004 Act of Employment Promotion and Labour Market Institutions, Journal of Laws 2004, No 99, item 1001.

86 A. Drabek, *Nielegalne zatrudnienie w prawie polskim*, Warsaw 2012, p. 320.

Promotion and Labour Market Institutions, the foreigners who illegally perform the work are also liable, but the penalties are lower as they are subject to a fine up to 1,000 PLN. Thus, an increase in liability (for both migrants and employers) was reflected in the introduction of two new categories of offences and an aggravated type of petty offence.

Employing many foreigners who stay in the territory of the Republic of Poland without a valid residence permit or employing a minor foreign national staying in the territory of the Republic of Poland without a valid residence permit is subject to a fine or a restriction of liberty. A similar punishment is prescribed if a foreigner who stays in the territory of the Republic of Poland without a valid residence permit is persistently employed, provided that the offender's actions are closely connected with that person's economic activity.

Consequently, the liability for a petty offence under Article 120(1) of the Act on Employment Promotion and Labour Market Institutions has increased, as the legislator, in Article 9 of the Act of 15 June 2012 on Effects of Illegal Employment of Foreigners Illegally Staying on Polish Territory, criminalised the illegal employment of foreigners as misdemeanours. They appear to be 'split acts', but the subject matter is not identical. In the case of a petty offence the legislator used the term 'illegal performance of employment', whereas in the case of an offence, a causative act means 'employing many foreigners who stay in the territory of the Republic of Poland without a valid residence permit at the same time'. However, illegal performance of employment is a broader term as it encompasses both 'employment of many foreigners who stay in the territory of the Republic of Poland without a valid residence permit at the same time' and other cases such as legal stay but without a work permit.

The expression 'staying in the territory of the Republic of Poland without a valid residence permit' instead of 'illegal stay', which was initially proposed, is used in the contents of the Act, but is not employed in its title. It results from the necessity to indicate precisely the scope of liability of the entity who employs a foreigner and to exclude the liability of that entity when a foreigner fails to comply with conditions of stay or residence despite possessing a valid document, as the entity who employs a foreigner may not be aware of these circumstances, hence cannot be punished. In addition, Article 4(3) of Directive 2009/52/EC expressly states that an employer is not liable for employing a foreigner who illegally stays in the EU territory if the employer checks whether the foreigner possesses a valid document which authorises the foreigner to stay, keeps a copy of that document for at least the duration of the employment and notifies the competent authorities of the start of employment of the foreigner.[87]

---

87 Explanatory memorandum to the Act on Effects of Illegal Employment of Foreigners Illegally Staying on Polish Territory, p. 9.

Article 9 of the Act of 15 June 2012 on Effects of Illegal Employment of Foreigners Illegally Staying on Polish Territory includes a vague expression 'employment of a significant number of illegally staying third country nationals' and it might be problematic to assess how many foreigners are 'a significant number'. Some standpoints of the doctrine with reference to Article 140 of the Criminal Code and Article 164 of the Criminal Code may be used here to provide the interpretation in that respect.[88]

Another vague expression – 'under exploitative working conditions' – was used in Article 10 of the Act of 15 June 2012 on Effects of Illegal Employment of Foreigners Illegally Staying on Polish Territory, referring to employing a foreigner who stays in the territory of the Republic of Poland without a valid stay permit. This is considered as a misdemeanour punishable by up to three years in prison. However, the legislative further specifies what are understood to be exploitative working conditions.[89] These are conditions which demean human dignity and constitute a gross difference in treatment, particularly based on sex, from the working conditions provided to people working legally and which might affect the health and security of employees. The introduction of this Act is of key importance as illegally employed foreigners are not only exposed to violation of their basic employment rights, but also their fundamental human rights.[90]

Article 10 of the Act of 15 June 2012 on Effects of Illegal Employment of Foreigners Illegally Staying on Polish Territory also penalises employing a foreigner who has been subjected to the offence stipulated by Article 189a(1) of the Criminal Code.

Article 11 of the Act of 15 June 2012 on Effects of Illegal Employment of Foreigners Illegally Staying on Polish Territory prescribes an aggravated form of the petty offence stipulated by Article 120 of the Act on Employment Promotion and Labour Market Institutions, that is, persistent employment of a foreigner who stays in the territory of the Republic of Poland without a valid residence permit, but provided this work is not related to the employer's economic activity and which includes another ambiguous phrase: 'persistent'.[91]

The manifestation of increased criminal liability of employers who employ foreigners in violation of the law, introduced in Article 12 of the Act of

---

88 See Z. Ćwiąkalski, *supra* n. 76, p. 207. R.A. Stefański, *Przestępstwa przeciwko bezpieczeństwu powszechnemu i w komunikacji*, Komentarz, Warsaw 2000, p. 30. A, Marek, *Kodeks karny*. Komentarz, Warsaw 2010, p. 400. K. Buchała, in A. Zoll (ed.), *Kodeks karny. Część szczególna, Komentarz do art. 117–277 Kodeksu karnego*, Kraków 1999, p. 331.

89 Art. 10(3) of the Act of 15 June 2012 on Effects of Illegal Employment of Foreigners Illegally Staying on Polish Territory.

90 M. Duszczyk, 'Imigrant – pracownik. Przestrzeganie praw pracowniczych i potencjalne problemy na rynku pracy' in P. Dąbrowski and M. Duszczyk (eds.), *Przestrzeganie praw cudzoziemców w Polsce, Biuletyn Rzecznika Praw Obywatelskich w Polsce*, Warszawa 2012, p. 32.

91 M. Perkowska and E. Jurgielewicz, *supra* n. 81.

15 June 2012 on Effects of Illegal Employment of Foreigners Illegally Staying on Polish Territory, is the possibility of prohibition of accessing resources from European Structural Funds, the Cohesion Fund and the European Fund for Fisheries, as well as resources to implement Common Agricultural Policy and the obligation to reimburse any such resources obtained in the period of 12 months from delivery of the judgement for the perpetrators of acts falling into Article 9 and Article 10 of the Act of 15 June 2012 on Effects of Illegal Employment of Foreigners Illegally Staying on Polish Territory. These sanctions are similar to those which might be applied to a collective entity in accordance with Article 9 of the Act on Liabilities of Collective Entities.[92]

The newest amendment made in Polish criminal law is Article 259a of the Criminal Code, which introduces the new offence of illegal border crossing with the aim of committing an act of terrorism on the territory of another state.[93] This regulation is grounded in 10 June 2016 Anti-terrorism Act.

As pointed out in the explanatory memorandum to the draft Act (including very brief reference to criminal law), the said act, among other things, aims to introduce criminal law provisions following the Additional Protocol signed by the Republic of Poland with regard to the Council of Europe Convention on Prevention of Terrorism, concluded on 16 May 2005 in Warsaw.[94] Therefore, numerous amendments and new types of offences concerning the activities of the so-called foreign fighters were introduced. Article 4(2) of the Protocol states:

> Each Party shall adopt such measures as may be necessary to establish 'travelling abroad for the purpose of terrorism,' as defined in paragraph 1, from its territory or by its nationals, when committed unlawfully and intentionally, as a criminal offence under its domestic law. In doing so each Party may establish conditions required by and in line with its constitutional principles.[95]

---

92 Act of 28 October 2002 Act on Liabilities of Collective Entities, Journal of Laws 2002, No 197, item 1661.

93 Art. 259a of the Criminal Code states that whoever crosses the border of the Republic of Poland for the purpose of the commission of a terrorist offence in the territory of other state or the offence stipulated under Art. 255a or Art. 258(2) or (4) of the Criminal Code, i.e. distributing or publicly presenting content that could facilitate the commission of a terrorist offence or obtaining the access to the content with the intention that such an offence be committed, participation in a terrorist offence, receiving of training for terrorism, participation in an organised group or association whose purpose is to commit a terrorist offence, forming or leading an organised group or association whose purpose is to commit a terrorist offence is subject to the penalty of deprivation of liberty for the term from three months up to five years.

94 Council of Europe Convention on Prevention of Terrorism, concluded on 16 May 2005 in Warsaw, Journal of Laws 2008 No 161, item 998.

95 Travelling abroad for the purpose of terrorism means travelling to a state, which is not that of the traveller's nationality or residence, for the purpose of the commission of, contribution to or participation in a terrorist offence, or the providing or receiving of training for terrorism (Art. 1 para. 1 of the Protocol).

According to Article 259a of the Criminal Code, the offender who crosses the border has to manifest an intent to commit an offence in the territory of another state but, as Lach claims, this regulation is confusing. A doubt arises whether it refers either to entering or leaving the Republic of Poland. It may be assumed that both cases are criminalised. Any state, apart from the Republic of Poland, might be considered 'another state' according to these provisions. Therefore, both a person who leaves Poland to commit an offence in another state and a person who travels through Poland to reach another country to commit a terrorist attack are criminally liable. The Polish provisions are broader than the provisions of Article 4(1) of the Protocol which refer to leaving the country.[96] In order to be held criminally liable, it is irrelevant whether the border crossing was regular or illegal. In the latter case, Article 49a of the Code of Petty Offences is read in conjunction with Article 264(2) of the Criminal Code as they both relate to liability for crossing the Republic of Poland's border in violation of the law.

It may be argued that criminal prosecution solely based on expressions of motivation by an individual, and without more concrete manifestation of any intent to actually carry out a principal criminal act, would appear to criminalise expression and manifestations rather than objective criminal conduct. This risk is heightened where the conduct to be criminalised is an attempt to carry out the said prohibited conduct. The draft Protocol should have laid down a prerequisite of a sufficiently direct connection with a principal criminal conduct and stipulate that clear and unequivocal intent has to be established.[97] A similar approach was taken by the Ombudsman, who underscored that the provisions of Article 259a of the Criminal Code shift the liability significantly to the moment when the good has not yet been infringed, which raises serious doubts from the perspective of a democratic state based on the rule of law and the principle of proportionality. Moreover, the drafters did not provide persuasive arguments that prohibited acts shaped in this way are necessary, useful and proportional in the strict sense.[98]

The penalties introduced for the offence prescribed by virtue of Article 259a of the Criminal Code appear to be reasonable, bearing in mind the geographical location of Poland and transit routes running through Poland as well as illegal migration, smuggling of goods or movement of terrorists who wish to reach other European states. As indicated by the Border Guard, significant changes occurred in 2014 in the structure of illegal migration to Poland and new

---

96 A. Lach, 'Komentarz do art. 259a k.k.' in V. Konarska-Wrzosek (ed.), *Kodeks karny. Komentarz*, Warsaw 2016, LEXonline.

97 Amnesty International, Draft Additional Protocol to the Council of Europe Convention on the Prevention of Terrorism, 2015, IOR 60/1281/2015, p. 8.

98 Ombudsman, Opinia do projektu ustawy o działaniach antyterrorystycznych (print No 516), p. 19, <https://www.rpo.gov.pl/pl/content/projekt-ustawy-o-dzialaniach-antyterrorystycznych-opinia-rpo> accessed 16.01.2017.

priorities appeared in the mechanisms to combat this, grounded, among other things, in increasing activity by extremist groups of Islamic fundamentalists in Europe. Therefore, monitoring of traditional, refugee and economic migration from Asia and Africa and its prevention have acquired increased importance in the light of common security.[99]

Those who intend to reach other European countries in order to carry out a terrorist attack may exploit legal methods, which may encompass tourist trips or the possibility of requesting refugee status, as well as activities which seem on the surface to be legal, such as abuse of administrative procedures related to being granted a residence permit for a fixed period while legalising a stay in the territory of Poland, obtaining residence permits in connection with marriages of convenience, or fake enrolments at higher educational institutions as well as attempts to obtain permits to stay in Poland on the basis of incorrect information concerning their stay in other EU Member States (this is seen mainly in relation to the nationals of Asian countries).[100] These people use also illegal forms of documentation, which include using someone else's document ('look-alike' method) or travel documents obtained on the basis of counterfeited documents (obtaining the attestation of an untruth under false pretences).[101]

From the procedural point of view, it is crucial to prove the intent 'to commit a terrorist offence' provided for under Article259a of the Criminal Code. One question might be posed in this context. What elements of the perpetrator's behaviour or objects and documents possessed might prove those intentions? The fact that a foreigner produces counterfeited documents or uses someone else's documents or documents obtained under false pretences does not unequivocally mean that the individual plans to carry out a terrorist attack. As Amnesty International points out, defendants should not in any circumstances bear the burden of proof in establishing that their travel to or presence in a specific area would be for a legitimate purpose, in keeping with the principle of presumption of innocence. The burden of proof in criminal proceedings lies solely with the prosecution.[102]

The provisions of Article 10(1) of the Anti-terrorism Act need to be highlighted in the context of 'crimmigration' as they authorise the officers of the Internal Security Agency and the Border Guard to take fingerprints, record face image or non-invasively collect genetic materials to determine the foreigner's DNA profile. The officers may use this power when: (i) there are doubts regarding identity; (ii) there exists a justified suspicion of crossing Poland's border in violation of law or doubts regarding the declared objective of stay in the territory

99 Ministerstwo Spraw Wewnętrznych, *supra* n. 42, p. 102.
100 *Ibid.*, p. 104.
101 Ministerstwo Spraw Wewnętrznych, *supra* n. 43, p. 113.
102 Amnesty International, *supra*, n. 97, p. 8.

of Poland; (iii) there exists a justified suspicion that the person intends to stay in Poland illegally; and (iv) there exists a justified suspicion that the person was involved in a terrorist attack or participated in a terrorist training.

When discussing the said prerequisites, some important aspects need to be highlighted in the context of the threat of illegal migration and terrorism. The Act introduces the right to collect biometric data and DNA samples in the event of doubts regarding the identity of the individual or suspicion of illegal border crossing. It should be remembered that persons who cross the border in violation of the law frequently do not possess any documents that would confirm their identity (in the European context, this is usually seen when migrating on sea routes) and it is also closely connected with another negative phenomenon: 'bogus citizenship'. Bogus citizenship means that a foreigner who does not possess any identity documents declares citizenship of a country, which is, for example, at war or which has been affected by natural disaster, with the aim of increasing their chances of obtaining international protection such as refugee status. In this situation, the foreigner does not come from a region where he or she is at risk of suffering persecution or other events which would give grounds for such protection, except for economic migration. Therefore, collecting data or DNA samples is the only way to identify the person concerned or at least register this information (as frequently there is no data to compare). Such registration would then be used for future identification of the person in the territory of Poland, and in other EU states.[103]

Identification is of key importance in the context of refugee procedure, which is frequently abused in economic migration. Szulecka highlights that there are no measures which would facilitate monitoring the status of a foreigner who applied for international protection and whose proceedings were dismissed (dismissal would result from the fact that the applicant was neither interested in participating in the proceedings nor present in Poland). Although these dismissals are directly connected with the person's absence, it is not possible to tell whether foreigners have left Poland or stayed there illegally. The fact that there is no confirmed information as to what has happened to the people who were refused their applications in Poland or whose proceedings were dismissed makes the scale of any abuse difficult to determine. Nevertheless, the statistical data on refusals or dismissals serve as indicators confirming the abuse of procedures of international protection.[104]

---

[103] See W. Mądrzejowski and K. Wiak, 'Walka z przestępczością zorganizowaną na tle rozwiązań przyjętych w ustawie o działaniach antyterrorystycznych' in W. Zubrzycki, K. Jałoszyński and A. Babiński (eds.), *Polska ustawa antyterrorystyczna – odpowiedź na zagrożenia współczesnym terroryzmem*, Szczytno 2016, p. 410.

[104] M. Szulecka, 'Przejawy nielegalnej migracji w Polsce' (2016) 38 *Archiwum Kryminologii* 233.

Thus, the possibility of downloading the foreigner's data on the grounds of Article 10 of the Anti-terrorism Act will undoubtedly facilitate monitoring their stay in Poland or other EU states in the context of illegal migration and illegal stay, which was pointed out by the legislative in the explanatory memorandum attached to the Act. Furthermore, the adopted solutions aimed at data exchange with the third-country services seem justified in the context of the abolition of border controls based on the Schengen Agreement.[105]

The term 'suspicion of illegal stay or relation with a terrorist action' used in the said provision appears to be imprecise as the legislator did not even add an adjective 'justified' before the word 'suspicion', which could allow to refer to the doctrine and the judicial decisions while interpreting. For example, Article 17(1)(1) of the Code of Criminal Proceedings[106] could be quoted as it points to a substantive premise, which allows a criminal proceeding to be instigated. The phrase 'no data which would sufficiently justify the suspicion that prohibited act was committed' included in Article 17(1)(1) of the Code of Criminal Proceedings indicates the situation when insufficient evidence was gathered to prove the act was committed[107] or there are no sufficient data to claim that the act occurred.[108]

Some questions might be posed in this context. For instance, what behaviour demonstrates the intent of the perpetrator to stay in the territory of Poland illegally? Is it enough to cross the border in violation of the law, for example at a place which is not designated for that purpose, like the 'green line', or to use false or someone else's documents? To what extent is the suspicion sufficient when justified suspicion (i.e. supported by evidence) it is not required by the law?

In accordance with Article 10(1) of the Anti-terrorism Act, suspicion is a sufficient condition to collect biometric data and DNA samples but subsequent proceedings relating to illegal border crossing or terrorist offences as well as petty offences concerning illegal border crossing or illegal stay will require, under Article 17(1) of the Code of Criminal Proceedings and Article 5(1) of the Petty Offences Procedure Code, the production of evidence which justifies the suspicion of committing the offence. Hence, the decision to instigate a criminal proceeding will verify the legitimacy of this suspicion but will not cancel the data which have already been included in the relevant databases. In addition, a problem of consent or lack of consent for taking fingerprints or DNA samples arises. Neither the Anti-terrorism Act nor the Decree of the Prime Minister of

---

105 Explanatory memorandum to Anti-terrorism Act and other acts, Print No 516, p. 10.

106 Act of 6 June 1997 Code of Criminal Procedure, Journal of Laws 1997, No 89, item 555.

107 S. Steinborn in S. Steinborn (ed.), *Kodeks postępowania karnego. Komentarz do wybranych przepisów*, 2016 LEXonline.

108 T.H. Grzegorczyk, *Kodeks postępowania karnego. Tom I. Artykuły 1-467. Komentarz*, LEXonline.

25 July 2016 on collecting and transferring fingerprint images and genetic materials and recording the image of the face of a person who is not a national of the Republic of Poland[109] include any provisions thereon.

According to the provisions of the Code of Criminal Proceedings, only an accused person is obliged to undergo external examination, which includes photographing or collecting fingerprints or DNA samples.[110] However, by virtue of Article 192a(1) of the Code of Criminal Proceedings, it is possible to collect fingerprints, buccal mucosa swabs, hair, saliva, handwriting samples or take a photo of the person or record that person's voice in order to restrict the number of suspects or to assess the value of the disclosed evidence. Nevertheless, once the materials originally collected or recorded for a particular case are used, they have to be removed from the files and destroyed the moment they become unnecessary.

It is worth highlighting that the police, by virtue of Article 15(1)(3a) of the Police Act, may take fingerprints to identify persons of unestablished identity and to identify persons who wish to conceal their identity, if it has been impossible to establish identity by other means. Similar powers are conferred on the Border Guard under Article 10a(2) of the Act on Border Guard towards persons suspected to have committed offences prosecuted by public indictment as well as towards people of unestablished identity or those attempting to conceal their identity. On the basis of Article 13(10) and Article 13(24) of the Act on Foreigners, in the proceedings falling under the Act, like the proceeding on the obligation to return or while verifying the foreigner's legal stay (Article 295), the competent authorities may take fingerprints and record the foreigner's image.

The provisions of the Anti-terrorism Act go far beyond the provisions of the Code of Criminal Proceedings or of other acts, as collecting the data is not related to any procedure stipulated in the Act. In some illegal migration cases, the foreigner did not consent to have fingerprints taken. Could coercive measures be applied in this situation? It is not provided for in the current legislation but one should bear in mind that any limitation of human rights and freedoms may only be imposed by law.[111]

As the Ombudsman rightly points out, in the light of the provisions of the Act on the Protection of Personal Data,[112] personal data must be processed within the scope and subject to the procedure provided for by law; processing must be reliable

109 Decree of the Prime Minister of 25 July 2016 on collecting and transferring fingerprint images and genetic materials and recording face image of the person who is not a national of the Republic of Poland, Journal of Laws 2016, item 1102.

110 Art. 74 (2) of the Code of Criminal Proceedings.

111 Art. 31(1) of the Constitution of the Republic of Poland.

112 Act of 29 August 1997 on the Protection of Personal Data, Journal of Laws 2015, item 2135.

and transparent for the individual concerned and may serve exclusively specified purposes stipulated by law. It does not preclude any enforcement authorities from taking any preventive actions, conducting preliminary proceedings, detecting and prosecuting prohibited acts, or enforcing punishments if these actions are stipulated by law, are indispensable and proportional in the democratic society and take into consideration a particular individual's justified interest. The principle of reliable personal data processing laid down in the legal system of personal data protection means that individuals have to be informed on the risk, rules, securities and rights related to personal data processing and how they can execute their rights in that context. The purposes for personal data processing should be precise, justified and relevant at the moment of their collection. In addition, personal data should be adequate and appropriate in relation to the purpose for which they are processed. It should, in particular, be ensured that personal data gathered are not excessive and they are stored not longer than it is necessary to achieve the purpose of their processing. Personal data may only be processed if the purpose of the processing could not be achieved by other methods. To prevent the situation when the data are stored longer than needed, the administrator should fix the date when they are to be regularly reviewed or removed. In the Ombudsman's opinion, the Act does not explain if access to all the databases is really needed to accomplish its purposes, and does not confer any rights on the data subjects. In addition, it does not implement the principle of temporary restriction on the data storage, hence it breaches the fundamental principles of data protection.[113]

The Helsinki Foundation for Human Rights finds the provisions discussed above arbitrary towards foreigners as they exclude Polish citizens from the scope of Article 10 of the Anti-terrorism Act. If the Act aims to provide public security, a threat might be posed both by a foreigner and by a Polish citizen.[114]

A similar claim may be made with regard to Article 9 of the Anti-terrorism Act,[115] which authorises the head of the Internal Security Agency (ABW), in order to detect, prevent and combat terrorist offences, to take classified actions, for a period of up to three months, towards a person who is not a national of the Republic of Poland where there is a concern that this person might conduct terrorist activities. These actions encompass: (i) obtaining

---

113 Ombudsman, *supra* n. 98, p. 9.

114 Uwagi Helsińskiej Fundacji Praw Człowieka do projektu ustawy o działaniach antyterrorystycznych (Print No 516), p. 14, <http://www.hfhr.pl/ustawa-antyterrorystyczna/> accessed 18.01.2017.

115 Importantly, the head of the Internal Security Agency does not have to obtain any permission to take actions against foreigners. See J. Kurek, 'Ocena ustawy o działaniach antyterrorystycznych – wskazówki wynikające z orzeczenia BVERFG Z 20.04.2016 r. w sprawie 1 BRV 966/09 I 1 BVR 1140/09' in W. Zubrzycki, K. Jałoszyński and A. Babiński (eds.), *Polska ustawa antyterrorystyczna – odpowiedź na zagrożenia współczesnym terroryzmem*, Szczytno 2016, p. 435.

and recording the content of conversations and other information conveyed through telecommunications networks; (ii) obtaining and recording images and sounds of the people from the premises, the means of transport and from the places other than public spaces; (iii) obtaining and recording the content of correspondence, including the content of electronic correspondence; (iv) obtaining and recording data in digital data media, telecommunications terminal equipment and information and ICT systems; and (v) gaining access and control of the consignment composition. As it is rightly pointed out by Buczkowski, these provisions distinguish the legal status of people who are Polish citizens and enjoy the full protection of the law from the people who do not have this status and whose rights are restricted, which may infringe the principle of freedom and equality before the law based on Articles 31 and 32 of the Constitution of the Republic of Poland in conjunction with Article 37(1) and which ensures that people under the sovereignty of the Republic of Poland, hence foreigners, may enjoy freedoms and rights provided for in the Constitution. Moreover, the said provisions include imprecise, hence ambiguous, terms like 'concerns as to possibility of conducting terrorist activities'.[116]

Restricting foreigners' freedoms and rights is also included in the provisions of the Act on the Entry into, Residence in and Exit from the Territory of the Republic of Poland of Nationals of the European Union Member States and their Family Members (2006).[117] It relates to the decision on expulsion from the territory of the Republic of Poland when there is a concern that a person may conduct terrorist and espionage activities or is suspected of having committed these offences. The decision in question has immediate effect, which limits the right to appeal and the right to a fair trial.[118]

5. CONCLUSION

From the analysis of the migration situation in Poland conducted in the first part of this chapter, it may be concluded that illegal migration is an insignificant phenomenon. Taking into consideration its small scale, it can be stated that it does not pose a serious threat either to internal security or public order. Indeed, the number of people who cross Poland's borders in violation of the law, use counterfeit documents or stay illegally in the territory of the Republic

---

116 K. Buczkowski, 'Koncepcja kryminalizacji migracji a przepisy ustawy o działaniach antyterrorystycznych' (2016) 38 *Archiwum Kryminologii* 29. See P.K. Marszałek, 'Polskie ustawodawstwo antyterrorystyczne a prawa człowieka' (2016) XII *Studia Lubuskie*. 139.

117 Act of 14 July 2006 on the Entry into, Residence in and Exit from the Territory of the Republic of Poland of Nationals of the European Union Member States and their Family Members, Journal of Laws 2006, No 144, item 1043.

118 *Supra* n. 114, p. 22.

of Poland, constitutes merely a very small fraction of the percentage of the disclosed numbers in the EU, because Poland is still not a country of destination for migrants, particularly economic migrants. It also relates to the geographical location of Poland, which is not on one of the direct migration routes running from Syria, Afghanistan or any of the North African countries.

The low rate of criminality among foreigners in Poland results from the small number of foreign nationals who stay in the country, whether regularly or illegally. The offences committed relate mostly to border criminality, for example, the smuggling of excise duty goods, that is, acts against the interests of the State Treasury not against any particular personal rights protected by criminal law. Another type of criminal conduct encompasses crossing the border in violation of the law or offences against the credibility of documents related to border crossing but, as before, these are chiefly behaviours accompanying smuggling and not illegal migration.

With regard to the nationality of offenders, criminality in Poland has never been over-represented by foreigners. The number of foreigners suspected of taking part in criminal activity appears to be minimal even if we take into account the total data provided by the law enforcement authorities.

The following findings could be made to answer the question whether the amendments introduced into Polish law are disproportionate to the perceived threat posed by immigration.

Almost all of the discussed amendments introduced in the Polish legislation, which aim to prevent and combat illegal migration and terrorism, have stemmed from the implementation of international law, that is, the European Union and Council of Europe legislation, adopted by Poland. The only exception is the decriminalisation of illegal border crossing and thus the adopted legal solutions are a consequence of international agreements concluded by the Republic of Poland addressing regional and global policy in combating terrorism and illegal migration.

Penalising the arrangement and facilitation of illegal migration (including illegal stays) or the illegal employment of foreigners is justified and complies with the standards applied in other European countries.[119] The analysed provisions

[119] For example, it is worth highlighting that Art. L621-1 of the French Code of Entry and Residence of Foreigners and the Right of Asylum, which penalises illegal stay in France, was repealed as it mainly served the purpose of pre-trial detention of foreigners and was inconsistent with Art. 8(4) of Directive 2008/115/EC as it resulted in penalising for illegal stay instead of expelling foreigners hence put the accomplishment of the objectives set by the directive (i.e. effective policy on expulsion and repatriation of third-country nationals staying illegally) at risk. ECJ, Case C-61/11 PPU, – *El Dridi* [2011] ECR I-3015, paras. 59–60. See M. Perkowska, 'Francuski system zwalczania i przeciwdziałania przestępczości cudzoziemców' in W. Klaus, K. Laskowska and I. Rzeplińska (eds.), *Przestępczość cudzoziemców. Aspekty prawne, kryminologiczne i praktyczne*, Warsaw 2017, p. 498 ff.

penalise acts which in fact cannot be committed by nationals of a particular country. Therefore, those provisions cannot be considered too punitive or treated as control measures for foreigners.

The only exception in this context is penalising illegal border crossing with the aim of committing an act of terrorism on the territory of another state. Article 259a of the Criminal Code provides for punishment for having an intent to commit a prohibited act, regardless of whether or not steps have been taken to implement it.

However, the situation would be different with regard to the provisions of administrative law, particularly those of the Anti-terrorism Act. Several solutions were adopted which refer to foreigners even though a Polish citizen might pose a similar threat to security, i.e. the provisions of Article 9 and Article 10 of the Anti-terrorism Act. These provisions distinguish foreigners from Polish nationals, which directly contravenes the Constitution of the Republic of Poland.

Taking into consideration the threat to security and public order, an individual threat may be posed by either a regular migrant or an illegal migrant. Such a threat might also be posed by a Polish citizen, and therefore the introduction of a law which exclusively restricts foreigners' rights, which is not only contrary to the Constitution of the Republic of Poland, but also contrary to the European Convention on Human Rights, cannot be justified. Legal measures, which are used to prevent and combat criminality, must be targeted equally at both nationals of a particular country and foreigners who live there. The fact that a person does not possess Polish citizenship may not constitute grounds for undertaking procedural actions whose priority is crime prevention. Unfortunately, it can be seen that in this respect, Polish law is geared towards 'crimmigration'.

12. THE ROLE OF NGOs AS PARTNERS IN MIGRATION MANAGEMENT IN ESTONIA: A CASE STUDY

Lehte ROOTS*

1. INTRODUCTION

The past two decades have seen an increasing role for civil society and non-governmental organisations (NGOs) in all stages of public policy-making. With the shift from government to governance and the growing importance of concepts like 'trust', 'transparency' and 'openness',[1] governments have made efforts to improve the involvement of citizens and civil society organisations.[2] There is a wide consensus in the literature that, in addition to democratic values, public participation in policy-making also provides instrumental benefits like wider evidence base for policy decisions, reduced implementation costs, potential for innovation, increased competence and greater trust in government.[3] Since the end of the Second World War and especially in the post-Cold War era,

* Tallinn Law School, Tallinn University of Technology, Estonia. E-mail: Lehte.Roots@ttu.ee.

1 C. POLLITT and G. BOUCKAERT, *Public Management Reform: A Comparative Analysis – New Public Management, Governance, and the Neo-Weberian State*, 3rd ed., Oxford University Press, Oxford 2011.

2 Open Government Partnership Initiative, Communication from the Commission of 25 July 2001 'European Governance – A White Paper', COM (428), OJ 2001 C287/1.

3 S.R. FURLONG and C.M. KERWIN, 'Interest Group Participation in Rule Making: A Decade of Change' (2005) 15(3) *Journal of Public Administration Research and Theory* 353; K.E. HALVORSON, 'Assessing the Effects of Public Participation' (2003) 63(5) *Public Administration Review* 535; ORGANIZATION FOR ECONOMIC COOPERATION AND DEVELOPMENT (OECD), *Focus on Citizens. Public Engagement for Better Policy and Services*, Paris 2009; C. HARDY and N. PHILLIPS, 'Strategies of Engagement: Lessons from the Critical Examination of Collaboration and Conflict in an Interorganizational Domain' (1998) 9(2) *Organization Science* 217; G. JENEI and E. KUTI, 'The Third Sector and Civil Society' in S.P. OSBORNE (ed.), *The Third Sector in Europe. Prospects and Challenges*, Routledge, Abingdon 2008, pp. 9–25; H. WANG and M. WAN WART, 'When Public Participation in Administration Leads to Trust: An Empirical Assessment of Managers' Perception' (2007) 67(2) *Public Administration Review* 265.

NGOs have become key players in asylum policy by working closely with asylum seekers and refugees on the global and national level.[4]

An asylum seeker is a person who has fled his or her home and submitted a request to be recognised as a refugee, but has not yet been granted that status. Asylum policy in the context of this chapter refers to the framework of procedures related to the reception of asylum seekers and the processing of their applications. It forms only one part of the government's overall refugee policy.[5]

The right of asylum is a human right that is based on Article 14 of United Nations Declaration of Human Rights[6] and the United Nations (UN) Convention of 1951 of Refugees.[7] In many ways asylum seekers are one of the world's most vulnerable groups of people as they are 'between states' and 'the only tangible right they can assert … is the right to seek asylum'.[8] There have been claims that after the end of the Cold War, asylum policy in European countries has become pragmatic and state interests have become 'dominant in comparison with human right protection'.[9] In light of the current European migration crisis, this has become even more evident, as the influx of refugees has caused 'growing fragmentation of member States' national interests' and a decrease in solidarity which poses a threat to the underlying values of the European Union (EU) and, in the Baltic States, also to the security of Member States.[10]

These developments can also be seen in Estonia, where the high salience of the issue, minimal experience of processing asylum applications and the government's poor communication of decisions in this field has caused a decrease in the transparency, credibility and legitimacy of the government's actions.[11] Estonia has not had a lot of experience with asylum seekers, and consequently asylum policy related matters have not been a priority and policy-making in

---

4 E. Lester, 'A Place at the Table: The Role of NGOs in Refugee Protection: International Advocacy and Policy-Making' (2005) 24(2) *Refugee Survey Quarterly* 125.

5 J. Van Selm, 'European Refugee Policy: Is There Such a Thing?' (2005) *New Issues in Refugee Research, Working Paper* No. 115, UNHCR, pp. 1–23.

6 UN General Assembly, Universal Declaration of Human Rights, 10.12.1948, 217 A (III).

7 Convention relating to the Status of Refugees, Geneva, 28.07.1951, 189 UNTS 137.

8 J. Edwards, 'Asylum Seekers and Human Rights' (2001) 7 *Res Publica* 159, 160.

9 M. Kjaerum, 'Refugee Protection between State Interests and Human Rights: Where is Europe Heading?' (2002) 24(2) *Human Rights Quarterly* 513, 519; see also J. Doomernik and M. Bruquetas-Callejo, 'National Immigration and Integration Policies in Europe Since 1973' in B. Garces-Mascarenas and R. Penninx (eds.), *Integration Processes and Policies in Europe: Contexts, Levels and Actors*, Springer International, 2016; S. Heuser, 'Is There a Right to Have Rights? The Case of the Right of Asylum' (2008) 11(1) *Ethical Theory and Moral Practice* 3.

10 V. Veebel and R. Markus, 'Europe's Refugee Crisis in 2015 and Security Threats from the Baltic Perspective' (2015) 8(4) *Journal of Politics and Law* 254.

11 *Ibid.*

this field has been rather *ad hoc.*[12] However, statistics show that the number of asylum seekers entering Estonia is growing[13] and with the intensification of the European migration crisis, Estonia has also agreed to voluntarily accept refugees through resettlement and relocation programmes.[14]

The chapter aims to discuss the role of NGOs in the Estonian asylum policy development and implementation. In particular, the principal object of enquiry will be to analyse how NGOs were involved in the development phase of Proposal of the Law 81SE[15] amending the Act on Granting International Protection to Aliens and Associated Acts (AGIPA 81SE) that was adopted by the Parliament in March 2016. The Act on Granting International Protection to Aliens (AGIPA)[16] is the law regulating the Estonian asylum system. The role of NGOs in the two phases of the development and negotiations of the Proposal are discussed separately as there is evidence that there are differences in how Estonian government agencies and the Parliament committees have involved interest groups, including NGOs. The involvement of NGOs is analysed based on the following elements: the characteristics and function of NGOs; the perception of NGOs by the state; and the process for involving NGOs in law and policy development. The assumption is that the NGOs are mainly used as service providers and sources of information. However, can they be utilised better? Is the form of an NGO the correct way to outsource the responsibility of the state? What are the threats and strengths?

The chapter is structured in the following way: first, it will define the concept of NGOs by providing an overview of the different types of civil society organisations and their role in policy-making (section 2). Later it will look at how NGOs are involved in policy-making, what are the aspects of an in-depth involvement process, and in which cases the public involvement is reasonable (section 3). Criteria by which to analyse the public involvement process are also provided. The topic of NGO participation is then put into the context of asylum policy (section 4) before discussing the role of NGOs in influencing the asylum and migration policy in Estonia (section 5).

---

12 Riigikontroll, *Riigi ja kohalike omavalitsuste valmisolek võtta vastu rahvusvahelise kaitse taotlejaid ja saanuid* (2016), <http://www.riigikontroll.ee/Auditeeritavaile/Audititeplaan/L%C3%B5ppenudauditid/tabid/284/AuditId/336/language/et-EE/Default.aspx> accessed 29.05.2017.

13 Politsei- ja Piirivalveamet, *Rahvusvahelise kaitse statistika* (2016), <https://www.politsei.ee/dotAsset/218156.pdf> accessed 30.03.2017.

14 Siseministeerium, *Täpsustatud tegevuskava Euroopa Liidu ümberasustamise ja ümberpaigutamise tegevuste elluviimiseks*, 08.10.2015 (2015), <https://valitsus.ee/sites/default/files/content-editors/failid/vastuvotmise_tegevuskava_08102015.pdf> accessed 03.04.2017.

15 AGIPA 81SE was adopted by the Parliament on 16 March 2016.

16 Siseministeerium, *supra* n. 14.

2. DEFINING THE CHARACTERISTICS OF NGOs

In order to analyse the role of the NGOs, it is important to understand what NGOs are and how they can participate in the process of decision-making. As will be shown, the essence of NGOs identifies different capacities and limits in decision-making process.

Non-governmental organisations (NGOs) (also not-for-profit, third sector and voluntary organisations) are broadly defined as civil society organisations that are separate from the government and private sector.[17] This definition, however, does not explain the complexity of these organisations and the relationship between NGOs, the state and the market, which has led some authors to contend that the only thing the civil society organisations have in common is 'what they are not'.[18] Nevertheless, despite the 'fuzziness', 'changeability' and often the hybrid nature of civil society organisations,[19] there are still some mutual characteristics used to define them:[20]

1. *Autonomy.* Being apolitical and autonomous from the government (public sector) and the market (private sector), NGOs can be regarded as the essence of civil society organisations – 'their very raison d'être'[21] – since they are assumed to fill an area that the government is not covering and the market is not willing to cover.[22] Nevertheless, with the growing importance of privatisation and contracting-out resulting in NGOs becoming valuable service providers, the borders between the public, private and so-called 'third' sector are no longer clear.[23] Receiving public funding from the government has sometimes become inevitable for the survival of an NGO, although it can lead to a decrease in autonomy.[24]
2. *Serving the public good.* There is an unwritten agreement that NGOs are usually oriented towards voluntarily pursuing a mutually agreed collective

17 G. Jenei and E. Kuti, *supra* n. 3, pp. 9–25; J. Newman and J. Clarke, *Publics, Politics and Power. Remaking the Public in Public Services*, Sage Publications, London 2009.

18 T. Brandsen, W. van de Donk and K. Putters, 'Griffins or Chameleons? Hybridity as a Permanent and Inevitable Characteristic of the Third Sector' (2005) 28 *International Journal of Public Administration* 749, 750.

19 *Ibid.*

20 J. Casey, *Non-Governmental Organizations as Policy Actors: The Case of Immigration Policies in Spain*, Doctoral Thesis – Universitat Autonoma de Barcelona, Barcelona 1998.

21 L. Gordenker and T.G. Weiss, 'Devolving Responsibilities: A Framework for Analysing NGOs and Services' (1997) 18(3) *Third World Quarterly* 443, 444.

22 T. Brandsen, W. van de Donk and K. Putters, *supra* n. 18.

23 T. Brandsen and V. Pestoff, 'Co-production, the Third Sector and the Delivery of Public Services. An Introduction' in T. Brandsen and V. Pestoff (ed.), *Co-Production. The Third Sector and the Delivery of Public Services*, Routledge, Abingdon 2008, pp. 1–10.

24 E.A. Graddy and B. Chen, 'Influences on the Size and Scope of Networks for Social Service Delivery' (2006) 16(4) *Journal of Public Administration Research and Theory* 533.

purpose[25] which aims to produce or serve the public good and welfare of the people.

3. *Not profit seeking.* NGOs do not aim to seek profit, and even if they do make profit they obey the non-distribution constraint that allows re-investment but not distribution between members.[26]
4. *Strong reliance on volunteers.* The third sector is also called the voluntary sector; as the aim is to serve and care for others without making a profit, there must be a value-based incentive that motivates these people to participate. Nevertheless, NGOs can still have formal employees and often hire professionals to increase their capability to, for example, participate in policy-making.[27]

These characteristics give us an idea of the strengths and weaknesses of the NGOs that influence their participation in the political decision-making process. For example, the 'strong reliance on volunteers' is a negative aspect in respect of the engagement with political leaders, as volunteers are only temporarily attached to the NGO, and as a result may not be in a position to create long-term relationships, which require good communication and building of trust. NGOs as non-profit organisations can be seen as an asset, as the decision-making is not based on the financial aim or values of the organisation, though it is often intrinsically linked to the purpose of the NGO. So if the purpose of an NGO is to protect the rights of migrants they can be considered as watchdogs of those rights. For the sake of clarity, reference to NGOs in this chapter refers to all formally structured refugee and asylum seeker related non-profit organisations that are formed voluntarily and are not officially part of the government.

Nevertheless, Casey argues that all these characteristics should be looked at in a continuum and not in absolute terms.[28] There have been many attempts to systemise NGOs based on their field of activity, scale of operation, funding etc. One of the simplest classifications is by the World Bank,[29] which distinguishes between operational and advocacy organisations. Operational NGOs deliver services and carry out projects, while advocacy NGOs aim to defend a specific

---

25 I. Bode, 'Co-governance Within Networks and the Non-Profit – For-Profit Divide' in V. Pestoff and T. Brandsen (eds.) *Co-Production. The Third Sector and the Delivery of Public Services*, Routledge, Abingdon 2008, pp. 59–76.

26 G. Jenei and E. Kuti, *supra* n. 3, pp. 9–25.

27 L. Gordenker and T. G. Weiss, *supra* n. 21.

28 J. Casey, *supra* n. 20.

29 C. Malena, *A Practical Guide to Operational Collaboration between The World Bank and Non-governmental Organizations*, (1995) World Bank, Operations Policy Department, USA, <http://www-wds.worldbank.org/servlet/WDSContentServer/WDSP/IB/1995/03/01/000009265_3961219103437/Rendered/PDF/multi_page.pdf> accessed 12.03.2016.

cause by raising awareness, lobbying, monitoring and carrying out activist events.[30] Advocacy NGOs that have specific political interests and try to influence policy outcomes can also be defined as interest groups.[31]

In addition to simpler classifications, some authors have also constructed typologies of NGOs. Based on one of these typologies, four types of NGOs can be described: (i) self-benefiting; (ii) other-benefiting; (iii) advocacy; and (iv) service NGOs. In self-benefiting NGOs the members act to serve mainly the interests of themselves while, in contrast, other-benefiting NGOs serve a wider array of beneficiaries and often an altruistic purpose. Similar to the World Bank definition, advocacy NGOs either promote or defend individual or public interests and values. Service NGOs, on the other hand, aim to provide services that governments are either incapable or unwilling to provide.[32]

Although it is possible to distinguish NGOs based on certain characteristics, several authors agree that these organisations can also be a combination of different types and transform from one type to another. Nevertheless, distinguishing NGOs based on their characteristics and activities helps to draw conclusions about the dominating form of NGOs in a specific field of policy, which in turn can help better understand their role and relationship with the government. Estonian NGOs dealing with refugees seem to be more service delivery organisations, and sometimes also act in the field of awareness raising and lobbying.

3. THE PARTICIPATION OF NGOs IN POLICY-MAKING

3.1. THE ROLE OF NGOs IN POLICY-MAKING

Public participation in policy-making is an area of public administration which has been widely researched. It has been used in order to gain the perceived benefits of enhanced democracy, improved governance through producing better and more evidence-based decisions, increased legitimacy of government actions, active and better informed citizenry, and therefore increased trust in government.[33]

---

30 G. Jenei and E. Kuti, *supra* n. 3, pp. 9–25.

31 J. Beyers, R. Eising and W. Maloney, 'Researching Interest Group Politics in Europe and Elsewhere: Much We Study, Little We Know?' in J. Beyers, R. Eising and W. Maloney (eds.), *Interest Group Politics in Europe. Lesson from EU Studies and Comparative Politics* Routledge, Abingdon 2010, pp. 1–26.

32 M. Yaziji and J. Doh, *NGOs and Corporations. Conflict and Collaboration*, Cambridge University Press, Cambridge 2009.

33 M. Gramberger, 'Citizens as Partners', *OECD Handbook on Information, Consultation and Public Participation in Policy-Making*, Organisation for Economic Cooperation and Development, Paris 2001; H. Catt and M. Murphy, 'What Voice for the People?

Public participation can broadly be defined as any kind of interaction between citizens and the government. More narrowly it refers to 'the involvement of stakeholders in administrative functions and decision-making, which is achieved through the availability of participation modes, participation in functions, and participation in the decision-making process'.[34] Public participation in decision and rule-making is considered to show the authenticity of participation practices.[35]

NGOs usually participate in decision-making through either collaboration or confrontation, which represent the opposite ends of a scale.[36] Collaboration describes a relationship where NGOs and government actors genuinely cooperate in order to find a common solution. This can happen through regular meetings, formal consultations on planned legislation and also through delegating service provision to NGOs. The key aspect is that the government actually considers the opinion of the NGOs and sees their participation as beneficial.[37] Research has shown that this is more likely when policy-makers need information, expertise and support from NGOs.[38] According to Casey, collaboration is the preferred strategy for NGOs that do not seek to radically change the current policy and therefore want to 'maintain a proximity to decision-makers'.[39] NGOs that do not have the resources to oppose the state also seek cooperation. For NGOs that are dependent on state funding, cooperation with the government can also turn into compliance with the government. In the latter case, governments can use collaboration in order to control NGOs.[40]

The opposite of collaboration is confrontation, where NGOs oppose the current state of policy and try to influence it with demonstrations, negative media coverage, critical reports and in some countries even illegal actions like blackmail and terrorism.[41] A milder version of confrontation is contestation,[42]

Categorising Methods of Public Consultation' (2003) 38(3) *Australian Journal of Political Science* 407; R.A. Irvin, and J. Stansbury, 'Citizen Participation in Decision Making: Is It Worth the Effort?' (2004) 64(1) *Public Administration Review* 55; Involve, *The True Costs of Public Participation*, 2005, <http://www.involve.org.uk/wp-content/uploads/2011/03/True-Costs-Full-Report2.pdf> accessed 01.03.2016.

34 H. Wang and M. Wan Wart, *supra* n. 3, 271.

35 C.S. King, K.M. Feltey and B.O. Susel, 'The Question of Participation: Toward Authentic Public Participation in Public Administration' (1998) 58(4) *Public Administration Review* 317.

36 L. Gordenker and T.G. Weiss, *supra* n. 21; J. Casey, *supra* n. 20.

37 R. Lepa, E. Illing, A. Kasemets, Ü. Lepp and E. Kallaste, *Kaasamine otsuste tegemise protsessi*. Poliitikauuringute Keskus PRAXIS, Tallinn 2004, p. 120.

38 G. Abney and T.P. Lauth, 'Exchanges between Interest Groups and State Administrators' (1983) 15(4) *Polity* 593.

39 J. Casey, *supra* n. 20, p. 11.

40 C. Hardy and N. Phillips, *supra* n. 3.

41 J. Casey, *supra* n. 20, p. 61.

42 C. Hardy and N. Phillips, *supra* n. 3.

where NGOs are critical towards government actions even when they are partly dependent on government funding. The choice of these 'strategies of engagement'[43] depends on the political environment, the policy in question and the resources of the NGOs.[44] In spite of a certain level of hype around public participation and inclusive governance, increased participation and granting civil society organisations the right to influence decision-making may not always lead to the best results.[45] In some cases, simply informing or consulting with NGOs is more suitable due to the time constraints, limited amount of resources[46] and the possibility that too much power may be given to interest groups that are guided by their narrow interests.[47] In addition, the involvement of the public in decision-making also entails increased costs.[48] These costs may be monetary (increased expenditures relating to time, staff, administration, participant's expenses) but there may also be potential non-monetary costs (stress, uncertainty and conflict).[49]

When government officials consider that the participation process is too 'burdensome' or ineffective, for example when the issue is technical and there is no possibility of changing anything, they might involve NGOs only insomuch as is needed to seemingly comply with the regulation in force.[50] This, however, can create frustration among NGOs who realise that the decisions have already been made before they were involved.[51]

Therefore, it has been emphasised that it is important to inform those involved about the goal of the participation process, in order not to promise participation on issues that cannot actually be changed.[52] Nevertheless, even if issues are technical and NGO influence is minimal, it is still important that the process of involvement is fair, tries to find a compromise and does not harm the relationship between stakeholders. Involvement should not be a goal but a process.

---

43 *Ibid.*, p. 218.

44 J. Casey, *supra* n. 20.

45 A. Fung, 'Varieties of Participation in Complex Governance' (2006) 66 *Public Administration Review* 66.

46 A. Cornwall, 'Unpacking 'Participation': Models, Meanings and Practices' (2008) 43(3) *Community Development Journal* 269, 276.

47 R. Lepa, E. Illing, A. Kasemets, Ü. Lepp and E. Kallaste, *supra* n. 37, p. 25.

48 *Ibid.*, *supra* n. 37; p. 51; R.A. Irvin and J. Stansbury, *supra* n. 33.

49 Involve, *supra* n. 33.

50 R. Lepa, E. Illing, A. Kasemets, Ü. Lepp and E. Kallaste, *supra* n. 37, p. 32; More generally written in N.D. Woods, 'Promoting Participation? An Examination of Rulemaking Notification and Access Procedures' (2009) 69(3) *Public Administration Review* 518.

51 C.S. King, K.M. Feltey and B.O. Susel, *supra* n. 35.

52 OECD, *Focus on Citizens. Public Engagement for Better Policy and Services*, Paris 2009; A. Cornwall, *supra* n. 46.

3.2. ASSESSING THE EFFECTIVENESS OF THE INVOLVEMENT OF NGOs IN POLICY-MAKING

To assess the involvement of NGOs in decision-making, we can look at the involvement methods used, the process of involvement itself and the outcome of the decisions. Literature on public participation is rich with evaluations of different kinds of involvement methods.[53] The most common methods are: (i) provision of written comments on drafted laws; (ii) working groups; (iii) roundtables; (iv) public hearings; and (v) direct communication between stakeholders (officially or unofficially).[54] The selection of a specific involvement method is crucial to the effectiveness of the whole process, since different methods require certain sets of resources (such as time, and expertise) from those involved,[55] which should be taken into consideration.

The quality or 'depth' of participation has typically been measured using scales and typologies of participation. According to Arnstein, only partnership, delegated power and citizen control can be regarded as genuine participation, as only then is power distributed between stakeholders and citizens have an actual possibility to influence the decision. Similarly, White distinguishes between four types of participation – nominal, instrumental, representative and transformative – which differ, based on function and also on the interests of citizens and the government.[56] Nominal and instrumental participation are regarded by White as a display of participation where the main aim of the government is to legitimise its decisions (nominal) or use participation to increase efficiency (instrumental), while for the citizens it is mostly a cost. Representative and transformative participation move towards giving a voice to (representative) and empowering (transformative) citizens which, from the government's perspective, helps to create sustainable initiatives and empowered citizens, giving leverage to the citizens at the same time.[57] What Arnstein's and White's approaches have in common is that they are normative and suggest that the final aim should be full participation with citizens having power to influence decisions. As already mentioned, it is not always reasonable to give citizens full control over decisions. Among the more modern approaches that take this into consideration, continuums ranging from one-way information sharing to active participation are now widely used to measure the extent of involvement of NGOs.[58]

---

53 G. Rowe and L.J. Frewer, 'Public Participation Methods: A Framework for Evaluation' (2000) 25(1) *Science, Technology and Human Values* 3; J. Caddy, *Evaluating Public Participation in Policy Making*, OECD, Paris 2005.

54 S.R. Furlong and C.M. Kerwin, *supra* n. 3.

55 R. Lepa, E. Illing, A. Kasemets, Ü. Lepp and E. Kallaste, *supra* n. 37.

56 S.R. Arnstein, 'A Ladder of Citizen Participation' (1969) 35(4) *Journal of the American Institute of Planners* 216.

57 *Ibid.*

58 R. Lepa, E. Illing, A. Kasemets, Ü. Lepp and E. Kallaste, *supra* n. 37; A. Fung, *supra* n. 45.

For example, the International Association for Public Participation has developed a participation spectrum which shows what the goal of different levels of participation is and how the NGOs are engaged, in order to determine the role of NGOs in the decision-making process. They are categorised between five different levels – informing, consulting, involving, collaborating and empowering.[59] These levels refer to the extent to which NGOs can have a say in the decision-making process and how the government uses their suggestions. While informing is only one-way communication, consulting with the NGOs means that their opinions are requested and feedback is given on how their input was used. On this scale, the involvement of NGOs means that NGOs are constantly involved throughout the process and feedback is given on how public input influenced the decisions. Collaboration is described as continuous cooperation between government and NGOs in all phases of the decision-making process, with the incorporation of the NGOs' suggestions to the maximum extent possible.[60]

The actual depth and the method of involvement of NGOs is contingent upon various influence factors. The interaction between NGOs and governments is essentially a two-way process: the ability of NGOs to participate and the involvement of NGOs by the government. The applicability of these two approaches are affected by very similar factors. For instance, the extent to which NGOs may participate is mainly affected by their administrative capacity, access to decision-makers, affiliation to networks and perceived power. NGOs that lack in important resources like knowledge, experience and staff, are less likely to influence the final decision. In addition, it has been proven that formal and informal access to decision-makers is one of the key factors affecting the potential influence of NGOs.[61]

Consequently, if NGOs have well-developed social networks, they can mobilise similar views and be more efficient.[62] The perceived power of NGOs is also important, as research has shown that governments tend to offer participation opportunities to NGOs who are more significant than others.[63]

---

59 International Association for Public Participation (IAP2) *Spectrum of Participation*, 2014, <https://www.iap2.org.au/Tenant/C0000004/00000001/files/IAP2_Public_Participation_Spectrum.pdf> accessed 07.02.2018.

60 *Ibid.*

61 S. Nicholson-Crotty and J. Nicholson-Crotty, 'Interest Groups Influence on Managerial Priorities in Public Organizations' (2004) 14(4) *Journal of Public Administration Research and Theory* 571.

62 M.B. Platt, 'Participation for What? A Policy-motivated Approach to Political Activism' (2008) 30 *Political Behaviour* 391.

63 W.F. West, 'Formal Procedures, Informal Processes, Accountability, and Responsiveness in Bureaucratic Policy Making: An Institutional Policy Analysis' (2004) 64(1) *Public Administration Review* 66.

From the government's perspective, the involvement of NGOs depends also on the available resources, the procedural regulation in effect and the technicality and stability of the issue. When the issue in question is technical or highly stable and time is scarce, government officials will be less motivated or even unable to involve NGOs.[64] Also, if participation processes are not standardised in formal regulations and encouraged by politicians, this can cause political manoeuvring.[65]

Another set of evaluation criteria, which will be used in this chapter, has been developed by Rowe and Frewer,[66] who differentiate between acceptance criteria and process criteria. Accordingly, acceptance criteria are:

1. *Representativeness.* Public participants involved in the decision-making process should be representative of the target group that is affected by the decision.
2. *Independence.* The participation process should be unbiased and no-one should be under pressure.
3. *Early involvement.* Governments should involve the public as soon as practicably possible.
4. *Influence.* Those involved should have a genuine opportunity to influence the final decision. Public involvement should not be used to legitimise decisions that have already been made.
5. *Transparency.* The decision process should be traceable and essential information available.[67]

Criteria for an effective process of involvement are:

1. *Resource accessibility.* All participants should have relevant resources to take part in the involvement process. These include information, time and material resources.
2. *Task definition.* The involvement process should have a clear goal and all participants should be made aware of the reason for their involvement.
3. *Structured decision-making.* The decision-making process should follow necessary procedures and be understandable to all those involved.
4. *Cost-effectiveness.* The most suitable method for the specific policy question, participants and timeframe should be chosen.[68]

---

64 N.D. Woods, *supra* n. 50; A. Dür and D. Bievre, 'The Question of Interest Group Influence' (2007) 27(1) *Journal of Public Policy* 1.

65 H. Wang and M. Wan Wart, *supra* n. 3.

66 G. Rowe and L.J. Frewer, *supra* n. 53.

67 *Ibid.*, 11–15.

68 *Ibid.*, 15–17.

Although governments have increasingly established participation-related requirements that policy-makers are encouraged to follow, participation in decision-making still offers a lot of room for political manipulation.[69] Furthermore, whilst engaging NGOs and interest groups in policy-making has become a norm for most Western countries, practices differ substantially among governments and across policy fields.

4. THE ROLE OF NGOs IN ASYLUM POLICY-MAKING IN EUROPE

The international asylum system in operation today was set up shortly after the end of the Second World War, when the office of the United Nations High Commissioner for Refugees (UNHCR) was created, which is an intergovernmental organisation with a mandate to provide protection and assistance to all refugees worldwide.[70] Lavenex even claims that there has been an overall change in how asylum policy is framed. Instead of the human rights concerns that predominated the asylum system after the Second World War, the trans-governmental cooperation in asylum matters that emerged at the end of 1980s caused the securitisation of asylum which, according to Lavenex, 'was framed as a side issue of the single market project, with cooperation occurring only insofar as it was deemed necessary to safeguard internal security'.[71]

The European asylum system has gone through a lot of institutional changes since the Amsterdam Treaty, which tried to communitarise the area of Justice and Home Affairs. Qualified majority voting and, after the Lisbon Treaty, ordinary legislative procedure in decision-making have been introduced and the title has been changed to Area of Freedom, Security and Justice (AFSJ). This means that asylum policy has moved towards the supranational level, but nonetheless still remains a very sensitive issue for Member States, touching the very core of national sovereignty.[72]

Migration and asylum policy is directly related to the sovereignty of governments, when deciding who may enter its borders,[73] therefore, governments may be reluctant to 'entrust' civil society organisations with the power to decide

69 H. Wang and M. Wan Wart, *supra* n. 3, 271.

70 UNHCR, *Note on the Mandate of the High Commissioner for Refugees and his Office* (2013), <http://www.refworld.org/docid/5268c9474.html> accessed 13.03.2016.

71 S. Lavenex, 'The Europeanization of Refugee Policies: Normative Challenges and Institutional Legacies' (2001) 39(5) *Journal of Common Market Studies* 851, 860.

72 L. Roots, 'The Impact of the Lisbon Treaty on the Development of EU Immigration Legislation' (2009) *Croatian Yearbook of European Law and Policy* 261.

73 L. Roots, 'Irregular Migration in European Union after Lisbon' (2012) 6 *L'Europe unie/United Europe* 99.

on matters related to internal security. Internal security is traditionally a policy area that stays at arm's length in matters of public participation. This indicates that it can be difficult for NGOs to get involved in asylum policy-making. In addition, asylum policy-making is rather contradictory or even a constant tug-of-war between international norms and morality which tend to loosen asylum policy on the one hand and national interests tightening it on the other.[74] This can also be seen in practice: on the one hand, governments are motivated to offer protection to asylum seekers and EU standards in this respect are being improved,[75] but on the other hand, states are trying to minimise their burden by adopting legislation and implementation standards that would decrease their asylum recognition rate.[76]

In EU asylum policy negotiations, Zaun distinguishes between older and newer EU Member States, and correspondingly between states with a stronger or a weaker tradition of receiving refugees.[77] The difference lies between the strong regulators who negotiate anticipated domestic changes into the directives whilst weak regulators use EU level policy-making as a way to avert the political costs of doing so domestically and shift the blame onto the EU.[78] Either way, public debate on this matter is avoided, if possible, turning policy-making into a more closed process.[79]

Today asylum policy ranks high on the agenda in most of the European countries, as public opinion is influenced by the emergence of right wing populist movements across Europe,[80] therefore governments are under pressure to satisfy the public, making it hard for NGOs advocating refugee rights to participate in decision-making. The growth of refugee NGOs can partly be explained by the emergence of such restrictive asylum policies. As a result of the conflict between refugee policies and human rights laws,[81] there has been an incentive for the creation of a number of humanitarian and human rights organisations. The latter includes a significant number of refugee organisations

---

74 N. Steiner, *Arguing About Asylum. The Complexity of Refugee Debates in Europe*, St. Martin's Press, New York 2000.

75 UNHCR, *Moving Further Toward a Common European Asylum System. UNHCR's Statement on the EU Asylum Legislative Package*, June 2013, <http://www.unhcr.org/51b7348c9.html> accessed 15.03.2016; N. Zaun, 'Why EU Asylum Standards Exceed the Lowest Common Denominator: The Role of Regulatory Expertise in EU Decision-Making' (2015) 23(1) *Journal of European Public Policy* 136.

76 D.D. Toshkov, 'The Dynamic Relationship between Asylum Applications and Recognition Rates in Europe (1987–2010)' (2014) 15(2) *European Union Politics* 192.

77 N. Zaun, *supra* n. 75.

78 *Ibid.*

79 *Ibid.*

80 *Ibid.*; T.J. Hatton, 'European Asylum Policy' (2005) 194 *National Institute Economic Review* 106.

81 M. Kjaerum, *supra* n. 9.

and their activities.[82] NGOs working with refugees are most commonly other-benefiting service or advocacy organisations. It is important to understand how refugee NGOs participate in asylum policy and what their roles are. Based on the literature, it is possible to highlight the three most important roles taken by such NGOs.[83]

First, NGOs have become important service providers for asylum seekers both on the international and national level. Although it varies across countries, NGOs participate in arranging reception-related services such as support and mentoring services, help with cultural orientation, language courses, psychological support, provision of legal advice and other community-based services.[84] This is especially evident in countries that are engaged in the resettlement programme of the UNHCR. This is commonly described as being tripartite in nature – comprising the UNHCR, the destination state and NGOs.[85] If the state and NGOs work together to accept the asylum seekers or refugees, provide support services and later help integrate the newcomers into society, we can talk about co-producing or, more precisely, a model of co-producing and co-managing services for asylum seekers.[86] According to Brandsen and Pestoff, co-management differs from co-production insofar as the receivers of service (asylum seekers) do not participate in providing the service, though we see the collaboration between the state and the NGO.[87]

Casey and Winkler bring out four roles of NGOs[88] and the authors synthesised them into three main categories. When it comes to resettlement and reallocation, NGOs are producing and providing a service. Resettlement refers to the process where UNHCR acknowledged refugees are transferred from the host country to a third destination country, which agrees to accept them. In co-management, the NGOs and the government need to constantly exchange information and interact with each other in order to solve or forestall difficulties and adapt the service to fit the users.[89] When the NGOs are the main providers

---

82 E. Lester, *supra* n. 4.

83 E. Winkler, 'Voluntary Agencies and Government Policy' (1981) 15(1/2) *International Migration Review* 95.

84 International Catholic Migration Commission, *Welcome to Europe! A Comprehensive Guide to Resettlement*, 2013, <http://www.resettlement.eu/sites/icmc.tttp.eu/files/ICMC%20Europe-Welcome%20to%20Europe_0.pdf> accessed 14.05.2017.

85 A. Papadopoulout, B. Reviranus et al, *Comparative study on the best practices for the integration of resettled refugees in the EU Member States*. Directorate General for Internal Policies, Policy Department C., 2013, <http://www.resettlement.eu/resource/comparative-study-best-practices-integration-resettled-refugees-eu-member-states> accessed 13.03.2017.

86 T. Brandsen and V. Pestoff, *supra* n. 23, pp. 1–10.

87 *Ibid.*

88 J. Casey, *supra* n. 20; E. Winkler, *supra* n. 83.

89 T. Brandsen and E. Van Hout, 'Co-Management in Public Service Networks' in V. Pestoff and T. Brandsen (ed.), *Co-Production. The Third Sector and the Delivery of Public Services*, Routledge, Abingdon 2008, pp. 45–58.

of services for asylum seekers and interact with them on an everyday basis, we can presume that the government would be especially interested in collaborating with these NGOs. As third sector organisations are more flexible than the government,[90] it is also possible for them to produce innovative services and they are, therefore, also valuable partners for governments. Providing effective services and engaging asylum seekers in activities immediately after they have applied for protection is vital, since research has shown that staying in secluded accommodation for a long time severely hinders refugees' ability to regain the resources they need to integrate in the labour market once their asylum request has been granted'.[91] The danger of only focusing on providing services is that this can transform NGOs into quasi-market like organisations that do not deal with anything else.

Secondly, NGOs serve as maintainers of values and norms. Asylum policy and migration policy in general represents a policy area where decision-making is more dependent on the ideology and the prevailing values of the society than on scientific or technical considerations.[92] This watchdog role of the NGOs[93] is important as it controls government actions and uncovers wrongdoings; nevertheless on the other hand, it raises general awareness about refugee-related issues and human rights. The willingness of governments to improve the situation of asylum claimants also partly depends on the views of the people (not just the officials), NGOs have an important role in educating the public about asylum seekers and related issues to counteract the common negative media coverage of migrants.[94]

Thirdly, NGOs may also function as political actors. As discussed above, asylum seekers usually belong to the politically most marginal group of people, and therefore one of the main roles of NGOs is to serve as an intermediary between the asylum seekers and the state.[95]

Although asylum seekers and refugees can self-organise, this is limited to larger countries where there already is a community of refugees and enough social capital to organise. In countries that have a weak tradition in accepting

---

90 L. Gordenker and T.G. Weiss, *supra* n. 21.

91 L. Bakker, J. Dagevos and G. Engbersen, 'The Importance of Resources and Security in the Socio-Economic Integration of Refugees. A study on the Impact of Length of Stay in Asylum Accommodation and Residence Status on Socio Economic Integration for the Four Largest Refugee Groups in the Netherlands' (2013) 15 *International Migration & Integration* 431.

92 R. Hansen, 'Migration, Citizenship and Race in Europe: Between Incorporation and Exclusion' (1999) 35 *European Journal of Political Research* 415.

93 See more in C. Malena and V.F. Heinrich, 'Can We Measure Civil Society? A Proposed Methodology for International Comparative Research' (2007) 17(3) *Development in Practice* 338; T. Müller, 'Customary Transnational Law: Attacking the Last Resort of State Sovereignty' (2008) 14(1) *Indiana Journal of Global Legal Studies* 19.

94 T.J. Hatton, 'European Asylum Policy' (2005) 194 *National Institute Economic Review* 106.

95 E. Winkler, *supra* n. 83.

refugees and only a small number of asylum applicants, this is less likely, and Estonia is a clear example of such as country. Thus, advocating for asylum seekers rights in public debates and lobbying for comprehensive asylum policy in formal policy-making is needed from NGOs, in order to represent the perspective of asylum seekers in decision-making.

The role of the UNHCR as an important partner for NGOs dealing with advocacy is crucial; NGOs might be more effective at steering government actions in the desired direction at national level. In some ways, refugee NGOs have become 'extensions of the United Nations' on a national level.[96] In situations where governments might perceive the pressure of international human rights organisations as a threat to control policy-making,[97] national NGOs represent a legitimate instrument for influencing the government. In his extensive research on NGOs, Casey argues that although it is possible to distinguish between the different roles of NGOs, it is 'hard to separate the political role of NGOs from the other roles – or political NGOs from non-political – as almost all organizations take on some policy role'.[98] Even when an NGO is only focused on providing services, any attempt at trying to change the service can be considered to be an attempt to influence policy-making, even if indirectly.[99]

5. THE ROLE OF NGOs IN ASYLUM POLICY-MAKING IN ESTONIA

This section will describe the most prominent Estonian NGOs and identify the key characteristics of this corpus of NGOs, before looking at their participation in the development of asylum policy in Estonia. The analysis of the role of NGOs in asylum policy will discuss the involvement of NGOs in the drafting phase of AGIPA 81SE and the involvement of NGOs in the Parliamentary proceedings regarding AGIPA 81SE.

5.1. ASYLUM AND REFUGEE NGOS IN ESTONIA

Estonia's asylum legal framework is relatively new, as the first Refugee Law was only passed in 1997. As Estonia lacks in experience when receiving a significant quantity of asylum applications and there has only been a small number of applicants over the past 19 years, there are few NGOs active in the asylum

96 L. Gordenkert and G. Weiss, *supra* n. 21.
97 See more in K. Jacobsen, 'Factors Influencing the Policy Responses of Host Governments to Mass Refugee Influxes' (1996) 30(3) *The International Migration Review* 655.
98 J. Casey, *supra* n. 20, p. 52.
99 *Ibid.*, p. 59.

field in Estonia. Although there are some recently created NGOs that deal with refugee and asylum matters (MTÜ Pagula) and some NGOs who have a wider focus, but have also been involved in asylum-related projects (MTÜ Mondo, MTÜ Sõbralik Eesti), currently the most active NGOs are the Estonian Refugee Council (MTÜ Eesti Pagulasabi), the Estonian Human Rights Centre (Eesti Inimõiguste Keskus) and the Johannes Mihkelson Centre (Johannes Mihkelsoni Keskus). For this reason, the following analysis will only focus on these three organisations.

The oldest of the three organisations is the Johannes Mihkelson Centre (JMC), a non-profit organisation that was created in 1993. It has been dealing with asylum seekers and refugees for the past seven years. Currently the main function of the JMC in asylum policy is to provide a combined support service to people who have already received refugee status. A combined service means that, in addition to qualified support persons who help refugees with administrative issues and provide support in initial integration, the refugees can also turn to translators and psychologists. There are about 30 support persons who all receive compensation for their work. The service is provided on a project basis and is funded by the EU's Asylum, Migration and Integration Fund (AMIF) and the Ministry of the Interior. This means that JMC is in regular contact with the Ministry of the Interior through the project's steering committee meetings and by being obliged to present regular financial and activity reports to the Ministry. As the asylum seekers support service is, in essence, a social service, the JMC has a stronger cooperation with the Ministry of Social Affairs in this field. The asylum seekers support service is coordinated by a project manager and an assistant who are permanent employees of the JMC. The number of employees varies, and is subject to the management of different projects of the NGO. The JMC belongs to the SOLIDAR network and the Baltic Sea Network on Migration Issues.[100]

The Estonian Human Rights Centre (EHRC) is a foundation that was created in 2010 and from that same year it has been dealing with asylum seekers and refugees. The main aim of the EHRC is to stand for human rights and equal treatment in general.[101] The EHRC has been running a number of projects in relation to asylum seekers. During 2011–2015, the EHRC provided project-based legal aid to asylum seekers which was funded by the European Refugee Fund (ERF) and the Ministry of the Interior.[102] In 2012–2013, the EHCR conducted a public awareness raising campaign on asylum seekers and refugees during which on-line debates and university courses were organised. In addition to these activities, the EHRC, together with the Estonian Refugee Council, has made

100 <http://www.jmk.ee/> accessed 25.05.2017.

101 <https://humanrights.ee/> accessed 25.05.2017.

102 Eesti Inimõiguste Keskus, Pagulased. Lõppenud tegevused, 2016, <https://humanrights.ee/tegevused/pagulaste-oiguskliinik/> accessed 08.02.2018.

efforts to improve its advocacy skills and increase administrative competency to participate in asylum policy-making.[103]

The EHRC also publishes yearly reports on the human rights situation in Estonia, containing a separate section on the situation of asylum seekers and refugees in Estonia. The EHRC is monitoring the asylum application processing procedure and legal counselling of applicants in cooperation with the UNHCR.[104] The EHRC belongs to a number of networks. There are around 12 permanent employees working in the EHRC and also a network of volunteers.

The third organisation, the Estonian Refugee Council (ERC), is the only non-profit organisation in this field whose sole target group are asylum seekers and refugees. It was established in 2000 and has been the key organisation advocating on behalf of refugees and asylum seekers by reacting to the government's actions and decisions whilst at the same time proactively emphasising problems. The latter has been done by publishing reports and articles and presenting formal letters to the government. Since 2015, the ERC has published a yearbook on the Estonian asylum system in order to monitor the current situation.[105] In addition, the ERC also provides support service for refugees; however, in contrast to the EHRC, it is provided on a voluntary basis. Similarly to the EHRC, most of the ERC's activities are project-based. The activities conducted by the ERC have included projects for developing the capacity to offer humanitarian help, public awareness projects on refugees and racism, and preparing schools for supporting students who are refugees.[106] It has received some government funding through the National Foundation of Civil Society and from the Ministry of Foreign Affairs for humanitarian missions.[107] Currently the largest part of their activities is directed towards offering humanitarian help to refugees outside Estonia – in Ukraine, Lebanon and Turkey. However, in addition to project-based activities, the ERC also provides everyday support to asylum seekers and refugees, and organises events for both the target group and also for the wider public in order to raise awareness. The ERC has high network affiliation and is in regular contact with the UNHCR. There are about eight employees working in the ERC, of whom three are working outside of Estonia. All of the employees, except the chairman of the board, work part time.

Together, the three NGOs form the Roundtable of Refugee Organisations (RRO) that was jointly founded in 2013. The RRO is a cooperation network

---

103 *Ibid.*

104 Eesti Inimõiguste Keskus, *Varjupaigamenetluse monitoring*, 2016, <https://humanrights.ee/en/activities/varjupaigamenetluse-monitooring> accessed 12.04.2016.

105 Mtü Eesti Pagulasabi, *Varjupaiga aastaraamat 2014*, Tallinn 2015, <http://aastaraamat.pagulasabi.ee/> accessed 07.03.2017.

106 <https://humanrights.ee/materjalid/inimoigused-eestis-2014-2015/> accessed 29.05.2017.

107 Mtü Eesti Pagulasabi, *Majandusaasta aruanne 2014*, Tallinn 2015, <http://www.pagulasabi.ee/sites/default/files/public/2015_majandusaasta_aruanne.pdf> accessed 29.05.2017.

that aims to improve the Estonian asylum system through service development, promotion of integration, public awareness raising, advocacy for asylum seekers and participation in policy-making.[108] The JMC mostly considers itself to be a service provider for the government and therefore its role in the RRO is mainly to help amplify the voices of the ERC and the EHRC.

Although currently all three NGOs have a slightly different function, it is still possible to bring out some common characteristics.

First, all three NGOs are other-benefiting hybrid organisations that simultaneously provide services and advocate for refugees. Due to the small number of refugees in Estonia and their assumed lack of interest in government activities, none of the NGOs have asylum seekers or refugees as members and do not involve them when formulating formal positions.

Second, when looking at their size and administrative capacity, it could be said that compared to the average NGO in Estonia, all three NGOs are well-developed and professionalised, although smaller than the Estonian average.[109] The largest of the three is the EHRC which has the biggest budget[110] and which is also the only one with a written development strategy. The ERC is also gaining importance and in 2015 its budget increased multiple times.

Third, all three NGOs under analysis largely depend on project-based funding, which sets limits on how they can use their resources and hinders their ability to react to sudden changes.[111] None of the NGOs under analysis are involved with the government through strategic partnership and do not receive activity support.

Fourth, all the NGOs belong to the list of non-profit associations, foundations and religious associations benefiting from income tax incentives, which represent the organisations in Estonia that are considered to be serving the public good and therefore are not profit-seeking.[112]

Fifth, the sources of funding for the NGOs are mainly the Estonian government or EU funds. To a lesser extent, the ERC and the EHRC also receive funding from volunteers and other international organisations.

Another common characteristic for the JMC, the ERC and the EHRC is their high network affiliation on both the international and national level. All three NGOs belong to international networks that are useful for gaining information,

108 Pagulasorganisatsioonide Ümarlaud, *Eesti Pagulasorganisatsioonide Ümarlaua statuut*, Tallinn 2013.

109 E. Rikmann, L. Keedus et al, *Kodanikualgatuse institutsionaliseerumine Eestis 2014*, Tallinna Ülikooli Kodanikeühiskonna uurimis- ja arenduskeskus, Tallinn 2014.

110 Eesti Inimõiguste Keskus, *Majandusaasta aruanne 2014*, 2015, <https://humanrights.ee/app/uploads/2015/08/Aruanne-2014.pdf> accessed 14.04.2017.

111 M. Puurmann, 'Kodanikeühenduste rahastamine riigi poolt' (2004) 10 *Riigikogu Toimetised.*

112 E. Rikmann, M. Lagerspetz et al, *Kodanikualgatuse institutsionaliseerumine Eestis 2009/2010*, Uuringu raport. Tallinna Ülikooli Kodanikeühiskonna uurimis- ja arenduskeskus, Tallinn 2010.

guidelines and support in order to formulate positions, shed light on government malpractices, be more efficient in advocacy and to help develop services. In addition, the ERC and the EHRC are closely connected with the UNHCR. All three NGOs also have wide social networks on the national level. The RRO has regular quarterly meetings and the members are also constantly in touch with each other in their daily work. The NGOs all belong to the Estonian Roundtable for Development Cooperation and the EHRC also belongs to the Estonian Civil Society Organisations Union. From the government's side, the most important partners for the NGOs are the Ministry of the Interior and Ministry of Social Affairs. All the NGOs have personal contacts in the Ministry of the Interior, Ministry of Social Affairs and also in the Parliament. Communication with the ministries was frequent and both formal and informal. Other important partners for the NGOs, mainly in service provision are the Police and Border Guard Board, AS Hoolekandeteenused (welfare services) and local governments. As there is a small circle of organisations and people dealing with asylum matters in Estonia, people dealing with these issues are known to and communicate with each other. This means that the NGOs have good access to decision-making bodies.

5.2. THE PARTICIPATION OF NGOs IN ESTONIAN ASYLUM POLICY DEVELOPMENT

It is possible to distinguish between two periods of NGO participation in Estonian asylum policy: before and after the European migration crisis that started in 2015. The Estonian asylum policy before the crisis followed a conservative stance. The main participation methods used by the NGOs were formal letters, analytical reports and negative media coverage when necessary. In some ways, the participation strategy of the Johannes Mihkelson Centre has been an exception, since its strategy was always to seek participation through collaboration and, more narrowly, service provision. It is still possible to distinguish between the two periods. Before 2015, the development of support service was largely left in the hands of the JMC and almost no efforts were made to measure the actual effectiveness of the service and, therefore, NGOs lacked government input on what aspects should be improved. With the establishment of the resettlement and relocation programmes, this practice changed and the Ministry of Social Affairs became an important partner in co-designing the service.

The beginning of the European migration crisis and the adoption of the European Agenda on Migration in May 2015[113] also marked a clear shift in the Estonian government's political rhetoric on asylum policy. As a result,

113 European Commission, A European Agenda on Migration, Brussels, 13.05.2015, COM(2015) 240 final.

Estonia pledged to accept refugees through the quota system and make efforts to integrate them. In order to prepare the Estonian asylum system for resettled and relocated refugees, government ministries showed initiative by involving the NGOs in meetings, discussions and seminars. One of the biggest changes has been the initiation of monthly meetings for all social partners and government agencies involved in asylum policy, organised by the Ministry of the Interior since autumn 2015. These meetings include a very wide circle of organisations and although they are mainly for exchanging information, the meetings are perceived by the NGOs as being open and very constructive.

Taking into account the background of the development of Estonian asylum law and policy, the involvement of Estonian NGOs in asylum policy development will now be analysed with a particular focus on two areas that are indicative of a change in approach by the Estonian government and the subsequent response by NGOs: (i) the Drafting Phase of AGIPA 81SE and (ii) the Parliamentary Proceedings of AGIPA 81SE.

5.2.1. *The Involvement of NGOs in the Drafting Phase of AGIPA 81SE*

Notably, the elaboration of the Law Proposal 81SE amending the Act on Granting International Protection to Aliens and Associated Acts (AGIPA 81SE) began in 2013 when the recast asylum procedures and reception directives (2013/32/EU and 2013/33/EU, respectively) were announced in the Official Journal of the European Union. At this time, the main aim of the AGIPA 81SE was to harmonise Estonian legislation with EU law and it was meant to be a technical change with only a few places for discretion.[114]

The draft of AGIPA 81SE was developed in the Ministry of the Interior, although the Ministry of Social Affairs was responsible for harmonising clauses related to the Reception Directive. The NGOs were invited to make amendment proposals for the clean version of the law proposal when AGIPA 81SE was sent for the ministerial coordination round. The amendment proposals of all three NGOs were presented through the RRO and were mainly related to the processing of asylum applications. For example, the NGOs questioned the need for accelerated processing procedures and the way in which the concept of a safe third country was assessed during application proceedings. They also emphasised that the detention of asylum seekers should only happen when it is absolutely necessary and proposed setting up independent border monitoring of

114 Siseministeerium, *Seletuskiri välismaalasele rahvusvahelise kaitse andmise seaduse ja sellega seonduvalt teiste seaduste muutmise seaduse eelnõu juurde*, Tallinn 2015, <www.riigikogu.ee/download/9ef5069c-81c2-46ae-af74-f35e9f4bfd84> accessed 02.04.2017. There was a need to update the legislation in order to make it compatible with the EU directives, therefore it can be considered as a technical and not substantial change.

asylum procedures.[115] The nature of their suggestions was rather technical and the aim was not to completely alter AGIPA 81SE. The goal was to specify clauses so the regulation could not be interpreted to the detriment of the asylum seekers, ensuring that all applications would be processed fairly. Half of the proposals of the NGOs were partially accepted and other suggestions were rejected mainly for procedural reasons. At this stage, the NGOs received feedback on how their proposals were approved.

Although the coordination round of AGIPA 81SE was in spring 2015 and the deadline for adopting the directives into Estonian legislation was in July 2015, developments related to the migration crisis forced the Ministries of the Interior and Social Affairs to make last minute changes before AGIPA 81SE was sent to the Parliament. These changes related to the arrival of relocated refugees and included clauses that would give the government the right to decide on resettlement and relocation related matters and make Estonian language courses compulsory to all refugees.[116] Nevertheless, when AGIPA 81SE finally reached the Parliament, the Minister of the Interior stated that the amendment act was still '90% about harmonising European Union's directives'.[117]

5.2.2. The Involvement of NGOs in the Parliamentary Proceedings of AGIPA 81SE

After AGIPA 81SE reached the Parliament, the Constitutional Committee was made responsible for the passage of the law proposal. As the topic of refugees was extremely sensitive, the discussions in the Constitutional Committee's sessions lasted six months. During the first AGIPA 81SE meeting, the ministries introduced the law proposal and the Committee sent it to the plenary session for the first reading. After AGIPA 81SE passed the first reading, the RRO presented its proposals to the Committee. Although some of its comments concurred with the proposals presented to the Ministry of the Interior, there were also new suggestions related to the obligation of providing information and legal aid to asylum seekers on the border, and clarifications about how the accelerated process should be conducted. The RRO also proposed that in case the government wanted to make Estonian language courses obligatory, these should be free of charge.[118]

---

115 Pagulasorganisatsioonide Ümarlaud, *Kommentaarid ja ettepanekud seoses välismaalasele rahvusvahelise kaitse andmise seaduse muutmise seaduse eelnõuga*. January 2015, Tallinn, 2015.

116 Parliament recording 14.10.2015, at 14.00, <http://stenogrammid.riigikogu.ee/et/201510141400> accessed 10.04.2017.

117 *Ibid.*

118 Pagulasorganisatsioonide Ümarlaud, *Kommentaarid välismaalasele rahvusvahelise kaitse andmise seaduse ja sellega seonduvalt teiste seaduste muutmise seaduse eelnõule* (81SE). November 2015, Tallinn, 2015, <www.riigikogu.ee/download/b733cf58-2d92-4966-9604-710b40f4154e> accessed 24.04.2017.

Similarly to the ministerial level, the RRO's proposals were mainly technical and made suggestions on how to improve the wording of specific clauses so they could be clearly understood.[119] Based on their suggestions, it could be said that the main aim of the NGOs was to ensure that all asylum seekers had the right to fair processing of their application by competent officials who would base their decisions on individual claims. The representatives from the RRO and the UNHCR had the chance to represent their position in a separate Committee meeting. Shortly after meeting with the NGOs, the proceeding of AGIPA 81SE in the Committee was put on hold for the reasons of political differences that came to light when the Committee started to deliberate the amendment proposals of the Parliament parties. For three months, coalition parties met in working groups in order to find ideological compromises between themselves before continuing with the deliberations in the Committee. According to the Committee protocols, the main argument points were about where (in the host country or in Estonia) and how to process asylum applications received through relocation and resettlement schemes; how to stipulate the obligation to learn the Estonian language; and how much the social aid for refugees starting a new life in Estonia should be.[120] When the Committee met again in February 2016, the final decisions about all the proposals were made. Altogether, there were nearly 80 amendment proposals for AGIPA 81SE.[121] Compared to the first draft, AGIPA 81SE went through a lot of changes. It could be said that the underlying consideration of the Committee was to protect national interests and ensure that asylum seekers and refugees would be treated equally with Estonian citizens, without special treatment. The political deliberations were successful, as five out of the six Parliament parties eventually supported AGIPA 81SE.[122] The chairman of the Constitutional Committee stated that AGIPA 81SE was 'a good example of co-operation' and the Committee presenter added that the final version was 'in the best possible form we could achieve with our current knowledge'.[123] Not all stakeholders were that satisfied. According to the ERC and the EHRC, some of these changes were not in accordance with international laws, as they created possibilities for officials to reject applications without examining them in detail and made the right to receive international protection partly dependent on how well

---

119 *Ibid.*

120 Constitutional Committee, Protocols No. 27 and No. 29, 2016, <www.riigikogu.ee> accessed 24.04.2017.

121 Constitutional Committee, *Välismaalasele rahvusvahelise kaitse andmise seaduse ja sellega seonduvalt teiste seaduste muutmise seadus*, 81 SE II, 09.03.2016, <www.riigikogu.ee/download/0e6988a0-f6ab-464b-a55e-0ab7697f0ce5> accessed 01.05.2017.

122 Parliament recording 16.03.2016, at 14.00, <http://stenogrammid.riigikogu.ee/et/201510131000> accessed 10.04.2017.

123 Parliament recording 09.03.2016, at 14.00, <http://stenogrammid.riigikogu.ee/et/201603091400#PKP-18442> accessed 26.04.2017.

the refugee had integrated into society.[124] For example, according to Article 83 of the final version of AGIPA, the required level of language proficiency would be taken as a basis for deciding whether to extend the period of protection for refugees. The right to receive protection should only be decided on the bases of the actual need for protection. All these changes were included after the NGOs met with the Committee and they only received the final version of AGIPA 81SE two days before the second reading. After that, the NGOs turned to the media and criticised the Constitutional Committee for not involving them.[125] The EHRC claimed that the proceeding of AGIPA 81SE in the Committee was a case of 'bad legislative practice, as there was no involvement or public debate about the important changes made during the second reading in the Parliament'.[126] From the perspective of the Committee, this claim was an overstatement, as in reality the RRO had the chance to make its proposals and was involved. After the Act passed the third reading and was sent to the President for promulgation, the NGOs sent an appeal letter to the President as a last resort. They highlighted problems that in their opinion were against international norms and suggested that further discussions should be conducted.[127] The President did not accept their appeal and signed the Act.

Several conclusions about the role of NGOs in the Estonian asylum policy can be made when analysing the findings based on the definition of NGOs in Section 2.

First, when considering the main functions of the active NGOs in the Estonian asylum policy field, it can be said that there is an internal distribution of roles between the three NGOs and all three roles mentioned in the section 2 are represented. While the JMC is mostly a service-providing organisation, the EHRC currently acts as a 'watchdog' and the ERC could be regarded as the most political of the three, although advocacy is not its main activity. However, the function of the NGOs largely depends on the project they are currently conducting and as Casey highlighted, it is hard to separate their political role from their other activities.[128] All three NGOs advocate for the rights of asylum

---

124 Pagulasorganisatsioonide Ümarlaud, *Pöördumine seoses välismaalasele rahvusvahelise kaitse andmise seaduse ja sellega seonduvalt teiste seaduste muutmise seadusega* (81 SE), 21.03.2016.

125 Delfi, *Pagulasabi: pagulasseadus on rahvusvahelise õigusega vastuolus*' (2016), <http://www.delfi.ee/news/paevauudised/eesti/pagulasabi-pagulasseadus-on-rahvusvahelise-oigusega-vastuolus?id=73968449> accessed 14.04.2017.

126 Eesti Inimõiguste Keskus, *SA Eesti Inimõiguste Keskuse kommentaarid välismaalasele rahvusvahelise kaitse andmise seaduse ja sellega seonduvalt teiste seaduste muutmise seaduse-eelnõule* (81 SE II), 2016, <www.riigikogu.ee/download/aedd38a7-5648-4b9b-a578-c9a928e9a02e> accessed 24.04.2017.

127 Pagulasorganisatsioonide Ümarlaud, *Pöördumine seoses välismaalasele rahvusvahelise kaitse andmise seaduse ja sellega seonduvalt teiste seaduste muutmise seadusega* (81 SE). 21.03.2016.

128 J. Casey, *supra* n. 20, p. 59.

seekers and refugees voluntarily and try to stand for human rights and equality in general. This could also be seen, when analysing their participation in the proceedings of AGIPA 81SE. Most of the amendments made by the RRO were technical suggestions aimed to ensure the fair processing of asylum applications. Although there were some ideological differences between the NGOs and government actors on what could and should be considered as a legitimate reason for refusing to grant asylum, in reality the NGOs did not directly oppose the content of the directives or even the suggestions of the Parliament parties. They were, rather, challenging how the directives were incorporated into the Estonian legislation. During the proceedings of AGIPA, the RRO did propose shortening the time period before asylum seekers were allowed to enter the Estonian labour market,[129] which can be considered as an attempt to protect the specific interests of refugees; nevertheless in its last appeal letter to the President, it only pointed out problems related to the processing as important flaws according to its opinion.[130]

Therefore, we could say that from their own perspective, the role of the NGOs in the proceedings of AGIPA 81SE was to maintain values and norms, which coincides with the role of the UNHCR. Taking this finding and the tight communication between the ERC, the EHCR and the UNHCR into account, it could even be said that in the policy-making process, the NGOs, in some way, acted like an 'extension' of the UNHCR.

From the government's perspective, the role of the NGOs in asylum policy-making is somewhat different. As mentioned, there was a certain convergence of views between the NGOs and the Ministries of the Interior and Social Affairs after the migration crisis started and Estonia finally agreed to accept refugees through resettlement and relocation. In contrast, before the crisis, there was contestation and at times even conflict between the NGOs and the Ministry of the Interior, despite, at the time of the analysis, both sides describing their relationship as one of constructive collaboration. The reasons for this have been the change in the political rhetoric of the government and the realisation that in order to set up a viable reception system for resettled and relocated refugees, the Estonian government needs the help of the NGOs as service providers and sources of information.

Another important factor in improving the relationship between the NGOs and the ministries has been the initiation of monthly meetings for social partners

---

129 Pagulasorganisatsioonide Ümarlaud, *Kommentaarid välismaalasele rahvusvahelise kaitse andmise seaduse ja sellega seonduvalt teiste seaduste muutmise seaduse eelnõule* (81SE). November 2015, <www.riigikogu.ee/download/b733cf58-2d92-4966-9604-710b40f4154e> accessed 24.04.2017.

130 Pagulasorganisatsioonide Ümarlaud, *Pöördumine seoses välismaalasele rahvusvahelise kaitse andmise seaduse ja sellega seonduvalt teiste seaduste muutmise seadusega* (81 SE), 21.03.2016.

which have created a joint information space for all stakeholders and a platform for sharing problems. The involvement of the NGOs in the elaboration of AGIPA 81SE on the ministerial level confirms these tendencies. It could be said that, according to the International Association of Public Participation's analysis, the NGOs were involved as they had the opportunity to influence the outcome and received feedback on their inputs. The right to decide remained in the hands of the officials and the NGOs were not involved in all stages of the law proposal drafting (see, for example, the last minute changes discussed earlier).[131] Based on White's typology,[132] the involvement of the NGOs was therefore instrumental, since the expert knowledge and technical comments of the RRO were highly valued by the Ministry of the Interior and were incorporated as far as possible; nonetheless, for the NGOs the cost of the involvement process outweighed the benefits. At that time, AGIPA 81SE was still mainly about harmonising the recast EU directives with the Estonian legislation and therefore both parties considered the process to be suitable. As the content of AGIPA 81SE changed, the process of involving the NGOs also changed.

The intensification of the migration crisis during 2015 increased concerns among the public and turned the question of asylum seekers into a highly salient and political issue. This created a situation where AGIPA 81SE became an instrument to prepare Estonia for receiving refugees through resettlement and relocation. During the six months when AGIPA 81SE was discussed in the Constitutional Committee, it underwent several fundamental changes as a result of political compromises. It could be argued that the nature of these changes was to ensure the protection of national interests and internal security, and to discourage or even restrict (bogus) asylum claimants from entering the country. The fact that asylum-related matters are very political and even more so in a crisis situation, it was at times more important for the Constitutional Committee members to reach a political agreement and 'calm the society'[133] than focus on the interests of the target group or the suggestions made by the NGOs and the UNHCR. As the analytical findings indicated, the opaqueness of the process (caused by political deliberations outside the Committee meetings) and high salience made it harder for the NGOs to influence decision-making. The involvement of the NGOs on the Parliamentary level was only nominal and the NGOs did not have a genuine opportunity to influence the final decision. The Good Practice of Involvement of 2011[134] is used, when talking about the

---

131 International Association for Public Participation, *supra* n. 59.

132 S.C. White, 'Depoliticising Development: The Uses and Abuses of Participation' (1996) 6(1) *Development in Practice* 6.

133 A. Herkel, Parliament recording 09.03.2016, at 14.00, <http://stenogrammid.riigikogu.ee/et/201603091400#PKP-18442> accessed 26.04.2017.

134 Kaasamise hea tava, 2011, <http://www.epikoda.ee/wp-content/uploads/2012/03/Kaasamise-hea-tava.pdf> accessed 10.08.2017.

involvement process, which indicates that there is at least knowledge of its existence and the legal environment encourages involvement.

A problem that stood out throughout the process was that the Committee demonstrated poor communication with the NGOs by not explaining the goal of the involvement process, not providing information about the interim decisions, and not providing feedback. This seemed to create a misunderstanding about the concept of involvement which culminated with the NGOs turning to the media in frustration. The NGOs felt they should have had a bigger role in the decision-making process and were not sufficiently involved, since they were not involved throughout the political deliberations. At the same time, the Committee members stated that by providing the NGOs with an opportunity to present their views at the beginning of the process, the Committee had fulfilled its obligation and in the end it was the legitimate right of the elected officials to make the final decision. The reason behind this misunderstanding could be that the NGOs perceived themselves as maintainers of values or as 'watchdogs' in the policy-making process and therefore felt they had the right to be kept up to date during the whole process with an opportunity to make comments on the final decision. The politicians viewed them more as advocates for an interest group and did not perceive the usefulness of the NGOs' input as the ministries did. The voices of the NGOs in policy-making may be considered more important in the future as their experience, expertise and capacity grows, and the number of refugees in Estonia rises.

6. CONCLUSION

Public participation and the involvement of interest groups in policy-making have been high on the agenda for governments since the shift from government towards governance started in the late 1990s. As a result, NGOs have become important partners for government. This is especially the case in asylum policy, where NGOs have three main roles: service provision; monitoring of government practices; and advocating for the rights of refugees. As NGOs have close contact with refugees, they represent a viable source of information that could help governments make better decisions in the light of the growing migration crisis in Europe. The practice of involving NGOs differ substantially between governments and among policy fields. Asylum policy, in particular, is considered to affect the sovereignty of states and research has shown that asylum policy-making tends to be opaque and hard for the public to influence. In order to reach a well-considered decision, it is important to involve stakeholders and focus on making evidence-based decisions.

There has been a lot of research on public participation and the involvement of interest groups. Although it is not always practical to include the public in every minor technical decision, interest groups should have the right to be involved in decisions that directly affect them. The authenticity of participation ranges from one-way information sharing towards genuine participation which gives an opportunity for interest groups to have a dialogue with the government and a possibility to actually influence the final decision. An effective public involvement process should be transparent, allow equal access to stakeholders and make it possible for interest groups to explain their points of view.

The aim of this chapter was to analyse the role of the NGOs in asylum policy-making in Estonia by taking the adoption process of the AGIPA 81SE as an example. Using qualitative research methods, the analysis of the involvement of NGOs in the elaboration and Parliament proceeding phase was conducted. The findings show that the NGOs in the Estonian asylum policy are mainly small size other-benefiting hybrid organisations, characterised by dependence on project-based funding. At the same time, the organisations analysed in this chapter are highly networked and relatively professional compared to the average Estonian NGO. There are currently only three important NGOs in asylum policy field: Johannes Mihkelson Center, the Estonian Refugee Council, and the Estonian Human Rights Centre. Based on their current function, there is an internal distribution of roles between the three NGOs, although all of them are also active in advocacy.

The findings of the case study showed that there have been two significant periods of NGO participation in the Estonian asylum policy-making. Before the European migration crisis started, there was some conflict between the NGOs and the government's strict conservative asylum policy. Since Estonia agreed to participate in the resettlement and relocation scheme, the views of the NGOs and the Ministry of the Interior have somewhat converged. Nevertheless, from the government's perspective, the role of the NGOs has remained the same. The ministries perceive the NGOs as important service providers and a good source of information for decision-making. The usefulness of the NGOs input is not viewed in the same way at the Parliamentary level. Politicians do not perceive the NGOs as powerful actors in decision-making and see them more as advocates. As asylum policy related decisions are extremely political, reaching a political compromise was considered to be more important than the meaningful involvement of interest groups.

These tendencies have created an ambivalent relationship between the NGOs and the government. In setting up a reception system for resettled and relocated refugees, the NGOs are considered extremely important and the relationship between the NGOs and the ministries has become constructive. On the other hand, in decision-making, the role of the NGOs is more modest and their involvement is rather formal. As the NGOs themselves see their role in policy-making as protectors of equality and human rights, they are not satisfied with only nominal involvement and want a bigger role in policy-making. At a time when Estonia is faced with receiving more refugees than ever before, it is essential that misunderstandings between the stakeholders are avoided and all stakeholders cooperate towards a common goal. In order to prevent frustration among the NGOs, communication between decision-makers and the NGOs on the Parliamentary level should be improved. Parliamentarians should explain their motives and consult with NGOs during the preparation and decision making process.

The cooperation of NGOs in policy-making, legislation drafting and discussion is often related to the political will, which is sometimes lacking. In Estonia, NGOs have gained several competences via participation in everyday activities related to refugees and asylum seekers and the international cooperation and training provided by partners and UNHCR. This knowledge and increased competence of NGOs should be used by the ministries and Parliament in the policy-making process to come up with more efficient and effective solutions for immigration management. It can be also said, in conclusion, that NGOs have little political power to change the mainstream political decision which is to maintain a conservative asylum policy; however, they can point out the problems and support refugees in their struggles. The cooperation of NGOs and the government in dealing with the pressure of increased forced migration is essential in order to effectively tackle this situation.

13. LINGUISTIC INTEGRATION OF ADULT MIGRANTS IN THE ERA OF THE MIGRATION CRISIS

Halina SIEROCKA*

1. INTRODUCTION

According to the United Nations (UN) data, the number of international migrants reached 244 million in 2015 for the world as a whole, which represents a 41 per cent increase compared to 2000. Two thirds of all international migrants live in only 20 countries, starting with the USA, which hosts 19 per cent of all migrants, followed by Germany, the Russian Federation, Saudi Arabia, the United Kingdom and the United Arab Emirates.[1] With these new waves of migration and its diversity, the question may be asked whether there is a link between the migration crisis we are facing now and the level of migrants' integration (particularly linguistic integration) into host societies. Bearing in mind the fact that 'knowledge of the "host" language is seen as a barometer of migrants' integration in a particular society',[2] this chapter examines whether the language policies and requirements which have been introduced over recent years, and which are predominantly rooted in political responses to the migration crisis, affect the level of social cohesion and integration of immigrants into host societies. The chapter commences with discussion on the concept of linguistic integration in the context of migration in section 2. European policies for the linguistic integration of adult migrants are presented in section 3, followed by an outline of the language policies for migrants in European Union (EU) Member

* Białystok Legal English Centre, Faculty of Law, University of Białystok, Poland. E-mail: h.sierocka@uwb.edu.pl.

1 Trends in International Migrant Stock: The 2015 Revision. United Nations Department of Economic and Social Affairs, <http://www.un.org/en/development/desa/population/migration/data/estimates2/estimates15.shtml> accessed 24.03.2017.

2 C. ROS i SOLE, 'The Paradoxes of Language Learning and Integration in the European Context' in D. MALLOWS (ed.), *Language Issues in Migration and Integration: Perspectives from Teachers and Learners*, British Council, London 2014, p. 57.

States in section 4. The chapter concludes with an analysis of language learning, language requirements and adult migrant integration in Germany, France and the United Kingdom, which are the countries considered to be the top three destinations favoured by migrants.

2. THE CONCEPT OF LINGUISTIC INTEGRATION

The White Paper on Intercultural Dialogue[3] defines integration as 'a two-sided process and as the capacity of people to live together with full respect for the dignity of each individual, the common good, pluralism and diversity, non-violence and solidarity, as well as their ability to participate in social, cultural, economic and political life' and for a long time there existed a kind of European consensus regarding integration policy. Such consensus was reflected, for example, in respecting the language and cultures of origin of migrants; enabling migrants and their families to learn the language of the host country; or adjusting preliminary migrants' legal, social and economic conditions to the standards of the host country. Numerous scholars,[4] however, underscore the fact that, for various reasons, this consensus no longer exists. First, migration patterns have changed significantly since 1991 (after the collapse of the Berlin Wall) and have become more multifaceted. Secondly, new waves of migration and the social, economic and ethnic problems that arose as a consequence of this have resulted in hostile attitudes to foreigners, stirred on by extreme right-wing parties in particular countries and negative political discourse, which has led to the introduction of more restrictive requirements as far as immigration and access to citizenship is concerned. It appears, therefore, that integration nowadays is more and more often interpreted by public opinion in fact as assimilation.[5] Ros i Sole highlights[6] that many governments perceive migrants as an asset to society as long as they conform to the host community's language, culture

3 White Paper on Intercultural Dialogue – Living Together as Equals in Dignity, Council of Europe, 2008, p. 11, <http://www.coe.int/t/dg4/intercultural/source/white%20paper_final_revised_en.pdf>.

4 For example, C. Ros i Sole, *supra* n. 2, pp. 57–77; H.J. Krumm and V. Plutzar, *Tailoring Language Provision and Requirements to the Needs and Capacities of Adult Migrants*, Council of Europe, 2008, <https://rm.coe.int/CoERMPublicCommonSearchServices/DisplayDCTMContent?documentId=09000016802fc1c8>.

5 H.J. Krumm and V. Plutzar, *supra* n. 4, underscore that assimilation is complete adaptation to the language, behaviour and values of the host society with the consequential loss of the language(s) of origin, whereas in the process of integration both sides (migrants and the host country) are open to create foundation for living together respecting the diversity and the identity of the other.

6 C. Ros i Sole, *supra* n. 2, p. 60.

and way of life.[7] Consequently, the linguistic integration of adult migrants is frequently regarded as an obligation to learn the host society's language. Migrants are not only supposed to achieve the ability to communicate effectively in that language but are sometimes even expected to differ only minimally from fluent speakers of the majority language. This high level of proficiency in the official language proves the migrants' loyalty and allegiance to the host country and is equated with citizenship: 'someone who speaks French (well) is French'.[8] This approach is confirmed, for example, by an Ipsos MORI survey conducted in Great Britain in December 2013.[9] The respondents were asked what the most important factors are for migrants from other European countries to be accepted in British society: 69 per cent of the respondents felt that learning the English language was the most important thing to do, followed by getting a job and paying taxes (64 per cent) and not claiming benefits (48 per cent). In this vein, Beacco et al. comment, however, that real linguistic integration involves 'putting in place the conditions for a successful reconfiguration of the linguistic repertoires of adult migrants'[10] and can take different forms without causing alienation while, at the same time, preserving identity. Such linguistic integration might be passive (the adult migrants' linguistic competence in the majority language is inadequate to communicate effectively and they depend on other persons); functional (the adult migrants' linguistic repertoire is sufficient to allow them to manage relatively successfully in most of social, work-related and personal communication situations, but while retaining the prominent status of their language of origin); proactive (where adult migrants desire to improve their linguistic competences to better fit the host society); or it may *expand linguistic identity*[11] (i.e. the language of the host society starts to be part of the migrants' identity along with their language of origin, as adult migrants manage this repertoire with conscious effort). These forms of linguistic integration undertaken by adult migrants will relate directly to their life goals, educational and cultural background, and other factors. Such factors may well affect migrants' decisions whether nor not to alter their linguistic repertoire and, if so, to what extent.

---

7 A statement issued by Home Office in 'Knowledge of Language and Life in the UK for Settlement and Naturalisation', may serve as an example here: 'Effective integration of those who wish to adopt the UK as their home – including embracing a common language and an understanding of life in the UK – is important to continued good race relations and community cohesion and is a central part of the Government's managed migration policy, which benefits our society and economy'.

8 Council of Europe, *The Linguistic Integration of Adult Migrants: From One Country to Another, from One Language to Another*, Strasbourg 2014, p. 17.

9 Statista, The Statistics Portal, <https://www.statista.com/statistics/332551/european-migrants-accepted-into-british-society-survey/> accessed 24.03.2017.

10 By linguistic repertoire they mean a set of linguistic knowledge and skills (not only attributed to adult migrants) that we use in various areas of our life in different roles.

11 J.C. Beacco, D. Little and C. Hedges, *Linguistic Integration of Adult Migrants: Guide to Policy Development and Implementation*, Council of Europe, Strasbourg 2014, p. 15.

3. EUROPEAN POLICIES FOR THE LINGUISTIC INTEGRATION OF ADULT MIGRANTS

As previously mentioned, language is a crucial aspect of the many issues raised by migration, and particularly integration and maintenance of social cohesion. The Council of Europe has been a pioneer in addressing migration-related issues. Since the ratification of the European Cultural Convention in 1954, the Council of Europe has undertaken numerous activities to promote linguistic diversity and language learning in the field of education. These include elaborating standard-setting instruments and recommendations, which lay down the principles governing actions in the field of migration, together with language policy guidelines and reference tools developed to support their effective implementation. A great number of conventions, recommendations and resolutions have been adopted to facilitate the implementation of language policy, which cuts across various areas of integration like health, employment, education or participation in political life of the host countries. It is acknowledged that there are many more EU instruments adopted to promote integration, like the European Migration Forum, the European Integration Modules or the Asylum, Migration and Integration Fund, but they address the issue of linguistic integration only indirectly. Therefore, the discussion in this chapter will be limited to only the most important instruments.

The first resolution on this issue was adopted by the Committee of Ministers of the Council of Europe on 28 June 1968: Resolution (68) 18 on the teaching of languages to migrant workers. It stated that 'the home countries, immigration countries and public authorities and private bodies employing migrant workers should do their utmost to assist migrants wishing to learn the language of the reception country, and to facilitate the provision of the most effective types of language course'.[12] It was followed by the European Convention on the Legal Status of Migrant Workers (1977) which reads that 'migrant workers and members of their families … shall be entitled, on the same basis and under the same conditions as national workers, to general education and vocation training …' and that 'the receiving State shall facilitate the teaching of its language or, if there are several, one of its languages to migrant workers and members of their families'.[13] This aspect of integration was consequently included in the revised European Social Charter (1996): 'to promote and facilitate the teaching of the national language of the receiving state or, if there are several, one of these languages, to migrant workers and members of their families'.[14] The importance of education for migrants has been reasserted over time

12 Council of Europe Resolution (68) 18 on the teaching of languages to migrant workers.

13 Article 14(1) and (2) of the European Convention on the Legal Status of Migrant Workers. ETS 093.

14 European Social Charter (1996), ETS 163, Art. 19, para. 11.

in other soft-law instruments.[15] For instance, Recommendation No. R (82) 18 concerning Modern Languages states in its Appendix that Member States in the framework of their national policies and systems should promote the provisions of necessary resources for migrant workers and the members of their families 'to acquire sufficient knowledge of the language of the host community for them to play an active part in the working, political and social life of that community, and in particular to enable the children of migrants to acquire a proper education and to prepare them for the transition from full-time education to work'.[16]

In addition, considering that some knowledge of the language of the host country is indispensable for the migrants' adaptation to the host societies, the project Linguistic Integration of Adult Migrants (LIAM) was launched in 2012 by the Language Policy Unit of the Council of Europe to assist Member States in developing coherent and effective policies in keeping with shared Council of Europe values and principles and exchanging experiences, as well as to provide practical support for the effective implementation of policy and encouraging good practice and high standards in the provision of language courses. The LIAM website offers practical means of pooling and accessing useful resources which have been developed by a group of experts in various disciplines. The resources encompass official texts (e.g. Extracts from Conventions, Recommendations, Resolutions and Reports Related to Education and Integration of adult migrants adopted by Committee of Ministers; Parliamentary Assembly; Congress of Local and Regional Authorities),[17] guidelines (mainly on the linguistic integration of adult migrants)[18] and the main background papers and case studies describing specific approaches to courses, assessment, etc. In addition, some tools have been specifically developed within the framework of LIAM for learners and teachers (European Language Portfolio Model), language course providers (also addressing quality assurance), and those engaged in language learning for professional purposes.

Moreover, other valuable Council of Europe's initiatives concern organising intergovernmental conferences and conducting surveys. Three conferences

---

15 For example, Recommendation 786 (1976) on the education and cultural development of migrants; Recommendation No. R (82) 18 concerning Modern Languages; Recommendation CM/Rec (2008) 10 of the Committee of Ministers to member states on improving access of migrants and persons of immigrant background to employment.

16 Council of Europe, Committee of Ministers, Recommendation No. R (82) 18 concerning Modern Languages.

17 Committee of Ministers (CM), Parliamentary Assembly (PACE) and Congress of Local and Regional Authorities, *Adult Migrants: Integration and Education: Extracts from Conventions, Recommendations, Resolutions and Reports*, Revised 2017, <https://rm.coe.int/CoERMPublicCommonSearchServices/DisplayDCTMContent?documentId=0900001680306f0b> accessed 20.03.2018.

18 LIAM official texts and guidelines, <https://www.coe.int/en/web/lang-migrants/officials-texts-and-guidelines> accessed 24.03.2017.

(2008, 2010 and 2014)[19] have been held to date and they aim to offer the Council of Europe's Member States some insights into development of coherent and effective policies as well as practical support for their implementation. The surveys[20] carried out among its Member States on policy and practice focused on the linguistic integration of adult migrants, aimed to identify emerging policy trends in Member States and stimulate discussion on language requirements and language course provision in the light of shared principles.

The issue of linguistic integration of migrants is also addressed at the EU level. In 2004 the Common Basic Principles for Immigrant Integration Policy in the EU were adopted by the Justice and Home Affairs Council,[21] which were grounded in three handbooks on integration, jointly produced by representatives of the European Commission, Member States and civil society organisations. These principles provided the foundations for EU initiatives in the field of integration as the European Commission created a common framework for the integration of third-country nationals in 2005[22] and were reaffirmed by the European Council Conclusions of June 2014.[23] The principle that addresses the issue of linguistic integration of migrants directly is the fourth Common Basic Principle (CBP) stating that 'Basic knowledge of the host society's language, history, and institutions is indispensable to integration; enabling immigrants to acquire this basic knowledge is essential to successful integration'.[24] In addition, on 7 June 2016 the Action Plan was published, which provides Member States with a comprehensive framework to support their actions in developing and strengthening their integration policies and concrete measures which are to be implemented by the Commission in this respect. One of the actions included in the Plan,[25] which are considered crucial for integration, is 'education, including actions to promote language training, participation of migrant children to Early Childhood Education and Care, teacher training and civic education'.[26]

---

19 LIAM conferences, <https://www.coe.int/en/web/lang-migrants/conferences> accessed 24.03.2017.

20 LIAM surveys, <https://www.coe.int/en/web/lang-migrants/surveys> accessed 24.03.2017.

21 Common Basic Principles, <http://www.eesc.europa.eu/resources/docs/common-basic-principles_en.pdf> accessed 01.03.2017.

22 European Commission, *A Common Agenda for Integration Framework for the Integration of Third-Country Nationals in the European Union*, <https://ec.europa.eu/migrant-integration/main-menu/eus-work/actions> accessed 01.03.2017.

23 Council of the European Union, Conclusions of the Council and the Representatives of the Governments of the Member States on the Integration of Third-country Nationals Legally Residing in the EU.

24 Common Basic Principles, *supra*, n. 21.

25 Integration Action Plan, <https://ec.europa.eu/migrant-integration/main-menu/eus-work/actions> accessed 01.03.2017.

26 *Ibid.*

4. LANGUAGE POLICIES FOR MIGRANTS IN EU MEMBER STATES

Unquestionably, an ability to master the language of the host country contributes to successful integration and, as Extramiana and Van Avermaet highlight, language has become a key component of immigration and integration policies as a requirement for integration.[27] This is reflected in language policies towards migrants, which encompass three types of measures:

1. Specific requirements of second language (L2) competence (according to the Common European Framework of Reference) and Knowledge of Society (KoS) as prerequisites to acquire entry, residency and other rights in the host country.
2. Provision of official L2-KoS courses.
3. L2-KoS examinations.[28]

4.1. LANGUAGE REQUIREMENTS

The policies introduced were primarily aimed at facilitating the integration of migrants grounded in the fourth Common Basic Principle mentioned above and reflected a view of positive correlation between integration and mastery of the host country's language. However, a larger influx and presence of migrants over the recent years has resulted in introduction of stricter language requirements for them in numerous EU Member States, which is confirmed by the data collected in the third survey organised by the Language Policy Unit under the auspices of the Steering Committee for Educational Policy and Practice and conducted among 36 Council of Europe Member States.[29]

4.1.1. Admission to the Country

Nine out of the 36 countries participating in the survey (i.e. Austria, Albania, Germany, Finland (for Russian Ingrians), France, Liechtenstein, the Netherlands, Poland (only in the case of certain regulated professions) and the United

[27] C. Extramiana and P. van Avermaet, *Language Requirements for Adult Migrants in Council of Europe Member States: Report on a Survey*, Council of Europe, Strasbourg 2011, p. 8.

[28] S. Kluzer, A. Ferrari and C. Centeno, *Language Learning by Adult Migrants: Policy Challenges and ICT Responses; Policy Report*, JRC European Commission, 2011, p. 16.

[29] *Linguistic Integration of Adult Migrants: Policy and practice*, Final Report on the 3rd Council of Europe Survey presents key developments in language policy over the period of the three surveys undertaken between 2007 and 2013. <https://rm.coe.int/CoERMPublicCommonSearchServices/DisplayDCTMContent?documentId=09000016802fc1ce> accessed 03.03.2017.

Kingdom) impose pre-entry requirements with the aim of promoting the social and economic integration of new migrants by ensuring that they possess a basic level of proficiency in a/the language of the host country and have at least some knowledge of their new environment. Four of them provide (optional) language courses to intending migrants in their country of origin. These countries either require a language test to be passed or for the individual to attend an interview with a consular official when applying for a visa to demonstrate that the required level of proficiency has been achieved.

4.1.2. Language Requirements for Residence

According to the survey, in 22 out of the 36 states (i.e. 61 per cent) participating in the survey there is a legal obligation to demonstrate competence in a/the language of the host country in order to obtain a residence permit. Official language courses are provided in 14 of the 22 countries, but only in three of them is attendance obligatory. Interestingly enough, 11 of the 14 countries provide courses for migrants with special needs (those of basic literacy or with little formal education). As far as testing is concerned, migrants are obliged to take a language test in 12 of the 23 countries to be granted a residence permit. In three other states they can either take a language test or produce a certificate from the institution, which is authorised to issue the document confirming the required level of proficiency. The tests are linked to the Common European Framework of Reference for Languages (CEFR) scale and range from A1 to B1 levels. In four other countries migrants are required to demonstrate their linguistic competence during the interview with an immigration officer or to produce an appropriate certificate or diploma.

4.1.3. Language Requirements for Citizenship

Out of the 36 participating countries, 26 impose an obligation on migrants to demonstrate a particular level of competence in a/the language of the host country to obtain citizenship. Out of those 26 countries, 19 also attach language requirement to residence, whereas three countries introduce this language requirement to residence only and seven states attach a language requirement to citizenship only. Half of the 26 countries provide official language courses for migrants wishing to obtain citizenship but only in three countries is attendance compulsory. Migrants are obliged to take a language test in 13 out of the 26 states which have introduced a language requirement to obtain citizenship. In other countries they may take a test or provide a certificate from an accredited institution confirming that they have achieved the necessary level of proficiency. The required levels of proficiency range from A1/A2 to B1 of CEFR level.

Drawing on the key developments in language policy over the period of the three surveys undertaken between 2007 and 2013 and presented in the 2013 survey, it can be stated that stricter language policies and wider reliance of language tests have been introduced over the recent years, which somewhat reflects the negative reaction of public opinion and politicians to massive influx of migrants. As far as attaching a language requirement to residence and citizenship is concerned, there is an increase in the number of countries that impose this obligation if the 2007 and 2013 surveys are compared (respectively from 10 to 13 in case of residence permit and from 12 to 16 as regards citizenship). Interestingly enough, this increase is not reflected in the number of official language courses provided, as the number remained stable between 2007 and 2013.

4.2. DEVELOPING LANGUAGE TRAINING FOR ADULT MIGRANTS

Beacco states that:

> the diversity of migrants' languages is one aspect of the multilingual and multicultural nature of contemporary European societies. This diversity is reflected in the languages in their repertoires, the use of (one of) the language(s) of the host society (in the personal, social, working or other environments) and the use of the language(s) of origin or the languages in their repertoire[30]

and therefore the training provided must be diversified, related to the forms and stage of migration. In addition, Beacco highlights that special attention must be paid to quality and transparency in the development and organisation of language training for adult migrants as such training falls into responsibility of various stakeholders, who might not necessarily share the same approach to the issue in question and, additionally, due to the highly political dimension of migration issues.[31] Beacco outlines the standard general process for designing language courses and curricula for adult migrants, whose critical points are:

- identifying the language needs of new adult immigrants;
- recognising the educational cultures of new adult immigrants;
- limiting possible effects of institutional marginalisation arising out of training for new adult immigrants;
- organising course monitoring and quality control.[32]

---

30 J.-C. Beacco, *Adult Migrant Integration Policies: Principles and Implementation*, Council of Europe, 2008, p. 6.

31 J-C. Beacco, *The Role of Languages in Policies for the Integration of Adult Migrants*. Concept Paper prepared for the Seminar 'The Linguistic Integration of Adult Migrants', 2008.

32 *Ibid.*, pp. 20–21.

Nevertheless, as emphasised in the Council of Europe document, 'the linguistic integration of adult migrants: from one country to another, from one language to another', the practical implementation of the language policies that Member States adopt for adult migrants, among other things, depends on the particular Member State's general approach to developing language courses for migrants. The Member States first need to recognise their specific responsibilities in relation to the provision of language training for migrants,[33] which is not always the case.

Despite a number of efforts and actions taken while designing and implementing language programmes for adult migrants, there are a number of challenges and barriers that are to be faced in order to make these programmes work.[34] They concern:

- addressing migrants' needs in the context of their diverse educational and socio-cultural backgrounds;
- adapting content to migrants' skills;
- lack of positive incentives to encourage adult migrants to stay in a language course;
- increasing migrants' multi-literacy;
- supporting teacher training;
- lack of developed teacher training strategy;
- lack of good monitoring and evaluation policies;
- low host community involvement in the integration process to enhance migrants' L2 acquisition;
- overcoming migrants' language barriers after completing official courses;
- hostile attitudes toward diversity;
- the political, economic and financial contexts in the particular country.

These obstacles regarding the implementation and delivery of language courses prove that the process is challenging and might not always be successful in terms of achieving adequate linguistic competences by adult migrants, which might impede the process of migrants' integration into the host society.

4.3. LANGUAGE TESTING

The positive correlation between integration and mastery of the host country's language formed the foundation on which integration tests were introduced by

33 Council of Europe, *The Linguistic Integration of Adult Migrants: From One Country to Another, from One Language to Another*, 2014, p. 17.

34 C. Extramiana and P. van Avermaet, *supra* n. 27, pp. 22–26; S. Kluzer, A. Ferrari and C. Centeno, *supra* n. 28, pp. 25–30; E. Siarova and M.A. Essomba, *Language Support for Youth with a Migrant Background: Policies that Effectively Promote Inclusion*, Sirius Network Policy Brief Series, 2014, No. 4.

some of the Member States. The tests were initially introduced for citizenship purposes but, as the third survey data presented above indicate, over time they have become a common language policy measure adopted by a growing number of states and applied not only for citizenship, but also for residence or as a pre entry requirement. The use of these tests has provoked much discussion among academics,[35] politicians and officials of the Council of Europe institutions.[36] As pointed out in the Draft Resolution adopted unanimously by the Committee on Migration, Refugees and Displaced Persons on 4 June 2013, language testing might have two opposite effects. It may promote integration but it could also be 'a migration management mechanism to limit the number of migrants entering and/or remaining in the country concerned',[37] which is confirmed by 'a drop of at least 20% of people seeking family reunion in one member state and drop of 40% of those seeking or granted residence permits in another'.[38]

This correlation between integration and mastery of the host country's language is not always perceived as a positive one. An interesting discussion of the problem is provided by Shohamy.[39] The author claims that the use of language tests is grounded in false beliefs and assumptions, and frequently results in discrimination and violation of the rights of the immigrants at whom these policies are aimed. Shohamy highlights that language has become 'the major definer of national identity'; therefore, the knowledge and use of the language(s) of the state can be exploited legitimately as a criterion for classifying people. Thus those who do not or cannot master it are often perceived as 'outsiders to the national collective group and therefore cannot be considered equal members of the state'. Consequently, as she underscores, if immigrants do not acquire the host country's language, they are perceived as those are taking advantage of the economy of the country, and not willing to assimilate or having negative attitudes towards the state. However, as Shohamy highlights, it is not always the case as immigrants frequently lack both opportunities and access to instruction in the new language, and even if they are provided with suitable courses it may

---

35 For example, C. Ros i Sole, *supra* n. 2, pp. 57–77; E. Shohamy, 'Language Tests for Immigrants Why Language? Why Tests? Why Citizenship?' in G. Hogan-Brun, C. Mar-Molinero and P. Stevenson (eds.), *Discourses on Language and Integration: Critical Perspective on Language Testing Regimes in Europe*, John Benjamins, Amsterdam 2009, pp. 45–59 or H.J. Krumm and V. Plutzar, *supra* n. 4.

36 Resolution 1973 (2014) of the Parliamentary Assembly, Final version, *Integration Tests: Helping or Hindering Integration*? <http://www.assembly.coe.int/nw/xml/XRef/Xref-XML2HTML-en.asp?fileid=20481&lang=en> accessed 03.03.2017; Report of the Committee on Migration, Refugees and Displaced Persons (2013), *Integration Tests: Helping or Hindering Integration.*

37 Draft Resolution of the Committee on Migration, Refugees and Displaced Persons (2013), *Integration Tests: Helping or Hindering Integration.*

38 *Ibid.*

39 E. Shohamy, *supra* n. 35, pp. 45–59.

take them some time to acquire a new language, especially if they are adults and/or of basic literacy or with little formal education in their native language. In addition, there are many examples of immigrants who function well in the host community despite not knowing the language.

Testing has been implemented as a manifestation of standards, objectivity, productivity and motivational factor both for the learners and the teachers, and hence is widely used in different settings. Shohamy,[40] quoting Bourdieu,[41] claims that 'for bureaucrats, administrators and elite groups, tests symbolize social order; for parents, who often do not trust schools and teachers, tests provide an indication of control; and for various elite groups, tests provide a means for perpetuating dominance' and thus in the context of language policies towards migrants language, tests seem to provide legislatures with an easy and practical tool for carrying out such policies. Nevertheless, many scholars believe that language testing in the context of integration process might be counter-productive. As Krumm and Plutzar[42] state, 'passing a test indicates how well a person can manage the specific testing culture and demonstrate the specific linguistic skills tested – it says nothing about the person's integration process' and they provide further arguments which prove that language tests hinder rather than facilitate migrants' integration. First, tests focus on elements which are easy to test, hence intercultural elements of language learning and teaching are limited or ignored. Moreover, neither migrants' knowledge nor their plurilingualism can be appreciated in a test. Thirdly, they do not take into account the migrants' interests, background and contexts. Fourthly, the criticism has been made that the results of a single test will affect a high-stake decision. In addition, there has been too little research conducted to date to verify how effective and appropriate integration tests may be.[43] Here are some examples which, although not very representative, might be indicative.

The Centre on Migration, Policy and Society (COMPAS) at Oxford University conducted a study on Citizenship and Integration in the UK, which aimed at understanding the process of integration and acquisition of citizenship to improve policies and measures for the integration of migrants in the United Kingdom. The following conclusions were drawn:

1. Those applying for British citizenship were well-integrated in British society (being engaged in the labour market or civic life).

---

40 *Ibid.*, pp. 45–59.

41 P. Bourdieu, *Language and Symbolic Power*, Harvard University Press, Cambridge, MA 1991, p. 192.

42 See H.J. Krumm and V. Plutzar, *supra* n. 4, p. 8.

43 The Report of the Committee on Migration, Refugees and Displaced Person of 4 December 2013 (Doc. 13361).

2. Those who participated in the programme 'the path to citizenship' (which included language learning and citizenship ceremonies) liked the experience.
3. Integration into British society cannot be perceived as one-dimensional process but rather as multi-dimensional processes in various areas of life.[44]

On the other hand, the 2006 research commissioned by the Federal Ministry of Interior in Germany to check how integration courses might be improved indicated that despite 600 hours of tuition, approximately 40 per cent of all integration course participants were not able to acquire B1 level competence in German, and hence a more flexible system grounded in the assessed needs of learners was recommended.[45]

A comparative study of integration and naturalisation tests and their effects on integration in nine EU Member States[46] (INTEC Project) proved that successful integration depends on various other factors apart from knowledge of language and society. Interestingly enough, it was indicated that knowledge of the host country's language is not always indispensable in order to become integrated, particularly if the migrant lives in an environment where another language, for example English, is also used.

A Belgian (Flanders region) research showed that migrants who successfully completed an integration course could find work easier than those who did not. However, this evaluation proved that participation in the course did not significantly improve language skills or facilitate social contacts with Flemish-speaking Belgian citizens.[47]

The above concerns are also shared by the Parliamentary Assembly of the Council of Europe, who in their Resolution 1973 (2014) adopted on 29 January 2014,[48] states that

> rather than promoting testing, offering language courses and possibly obliging migrants to participate in these courses may offer greater advantages and develop their language skills without running the risk of excluding migrants. They may also promote integration as a two-way process, requiring an investment by both the host society and

---

44 The Centre on Migration, Policy and Society (COMPAS), <http://www.compas.ox.ac.uk/research/> accessed 03.03.2017.

45 See H.J. Krumm and V. Plutzar, *supra* n. 4, p. 9.

46 The Member States under study were: Austria, Belgium, Denmark, France, Hungary, Germany, Latvia, the Netherlands and the United Kingdom. T. Strik, A. Böcker, M. Luiten and R. van Oers, 'The Intec Project: Synthesis Report: Integration and Naturalisation Tests. The New Way to European Citizenship' in Y. Pascouau and T. Strik (eds.), *Which Integration Policies for Migrants?*, Wolf Legal Publishers, Nijmegen 2012, pp. 285–405.

47 See H.J. Krumm and V. Plutzar, *supra* n. 4, p. 10.

48 Resolution 1973 (2014) of the Parliamentary Assembly, Final version, *Integration Tests: Helping or Hindering Integration*? <http://www.assembly.coe.int/nw/xml/XRef/Xref-XML2HTML-en.asp?fileid=20481&lang=en> accessed 03.03.2017.

the migrants. Furthermore, testing of knowledge does not, as such, improve language skills and can only be effective if it is offered at the final stage of a language course provided by the host State.

The Council of Europe Member States are also invited to reconsider their approach to integration tests to make them a 'user-friendly integration tool'. For example, states are recommended to ensure that the language proficiency levels set in these tests are achievable (i.e. the language levels cannot be set too high and recognition of effort should be reflected over simply achievement) and the needs and abilities of those taking the tests are taken into consideration. Moreover, tests should not be the only method of assessment, and alternatives to tests should be searched for and monitored.[49] It was also pointed out in the Resolution that adequate financial support should be provided by the states for preparatory courses, wherever possible free of charge, as additional costs constitute a major barrier. In addition, particular attention should be drawn to pre-entry requirements and their impact on the right to family life thus 'failure could have the consequence of requiring further efforts but it should not lead to the denial of the right to family reunification'.

5. DISCUSSION OF LINGUISTIC INTEGRATION IN FRANCE, GERMANY AND THE UNITED KINGDOM

The experience of linguistic integration in the three different countries which are considered to be the top three destinations favoured by migrants (i.e. France, Germany and the UK),[50] might throw some light on the issue in question. All three countries participated in the 2007, 2009 and 2013 Council of Europe surveys and all of them, although to different extents,[51] conducted studies on the impact

---

49 In fact, some countries, according to the Report of the Committee on Migration, Refugees and Displaced Person of 4 December 2013, have adopted an alternative approach. For example, in Spain and Switzerland eligibility for citizenship is determined during the interview and the level of linguistic competence required is established on a case-by-case basis. On the other hand, in France failure to pass the test does not result in denial of admission but rather delays the admission, which decreases the negative impact on the family life of the person failing the test and their families.

50 Germany reported the largest total number of immigrants (884,900) in 2014, followed by the United Kingdom (632,000) and France (339,900). Moreover, the largest numbers of non-nationals living in the EU Member States on 1 January 2015 were found in Germany (7.5 million), the United Kingdom (5.4 million), Italy (5.0 million), Spain (4.5 million) and France (4.4 million). The statistics on migration and migrant population provided by Eurostat, <http://ec.europa.eu/eurostat/statistics-explained/index.php/Migration_and_migrant_population_statistics#Migrant_population> accessed 24.03.2017.

51 For further details: *Linguistic Integration of Adult Migrants: Policy and Practice: Final Report on the 3rd Council of Europe Survey* p. 41, <https://rm.coe.int/CoERMPublicCommonSearchServices/DisplayDCTMContent?documentId=09000016802fc1ce> accessed 24.03.2017.

of language policies on the social integration of adult migrants, which shows their considerable concern for the issue of migrants' integration and gives a solid background when analysing their language policies toward adult migrants during the migration crisis we are now facing. The analysis endeavours to answer whether (and to what extent) the language policies for adult migrants implemented in the examined states affect the level of their integration into the host society.

5.1. LANGUAGE POLICIES FOR ADULT MIGRANTS

According to the Final Report on the 3rd Council of Europe Survey,[52] all of the discussed countries introduced a language requirement for entry, residence and citizenship and all of them introduced adequate legislation in that respect.

5.1.1. Pre-entry Language Policies

As for pre-entry language requirements, all of the countries provide optional language courses. In Germany optional language courses (with A1 CEFR intended level) are offered, for example, by the Goethe Institute and private institutions in the country of origin both in the traditional form and as distance-learning and online courses. In France the CEFR level is not established and the optional language courses of 40 hours are held in the country of origin. However, no state courses are provided prior to entry in the UK. Courses partly financed from the European Integration Fund are available in some countries, including Pakistan and Bangladesh and in this case the cost to the beneficiary is reduced or they are free of charge.

As far as pre-entry testing is concerned, such a test is only required in the UK. The CEFR-level A1 test must be taken with an agency that has been accredited by the UK Home Office, but tests are available in most countries. There is no required language testing in either Germany or France. In Germany, migrants have to produce a certificate of language proficiency at A1 CEFR level, whereas in France, the level of language proficiency and the knowledge of the French society are evaluated, but the results of the evaluation are not taken into account for the delivery of a visa.

5.1.2. Language Policies for Obtaining a Residence Permit

Language courses for adult migrants seeking a residence permit are officially provided in Germany and France and they are mandatory. In France, they take

52 *Ibid.*

the form of A1 CEFR level courses which last 400 hours and are provided free of charge, whereas in Germany, courses are of 600 hours on average (between 400 hours for intensive courses and up to 900 hours for courses for special target groups) and no financial support is provided. Despite the language requirement imposed on migrants wishing to obtain a residence permit, no language courses are provided in the UK. No language test is required to obtain a residence permit in France, unlike in Germany and the UK. A B1 CEFR level test must be taken in Germany and an A1/B1 (reading, spoken interaction and production) test must be taken or a certificate obtained from attending a 'language with citizenship' course must be produced in the UK.

5.1.3. *Language Policies for Obtaining Citizenship*

All of the three countries provide the possibility of attending language courses; however, attendance of such a course (B1 CEFR level course, mainly listening and spoken interaction and production) is obligatory only in France. No specific information is available on language courses provided in the UK or Germany. Also, in all of the countries there is a requirement to take a language test at B1 CEFR level. In Germany, this might take a different form (language test as part of an integration course, B1 certificate or higher education and training course) and in the UK the alternative to a fee-based test might be a certificate obtained from attending a 'language with citizenship' course.

If we compare the data from 2007 and 2013, the following developments and tendencies can be observed:

- All of the countries retained a language requirement for entry, residence and citizenship.
- France introduced B1 CEFR level oral test for citizenship (the 2013 Council of Europe Survey) instead of an interview (the 2007 and 2009 Council of Europe Surveys).
- Germany laid down stricter requirements concerning the language tests for residence permits (from A1/B1 to B1), but at the same time provided different possibilities for demonstrating language proficiency in the case of citizenship.
- The UK slightly relaxed the language requirements concerning obtaining citizenship (in 2007 progress up to B1 was required, whereas in 2013 A1/B1 test was allowed and the possibility of presenting certificate obtained from attending a 'language with citizenship' course' was given as an alternative).

5.2. INTEGRATION POLICIES FOR ADULT MIGRANTS

Diverse tools may be exploited to assess the level of migrants' integration into host societies. One of these is the Migrant Integration Policy Index (MIPEX), which serves as a tool to measure policies to integrate migrants in all EU Member

States plus Australia, Canada, Iceland, Japan, South Korea, New Zealand, Norway, Switzerland, Turkey and the USA. It exploits 167 policy indicators, which are grouped in eight policy areas: labour market mobility, family reunion, education, health, political participation, permanent residence, access to nationality and anti-discrimination, which might help to evaluate what and how governments are doing to promote the integration of migrants. Countries are given scores (0–100) according to whether their policies are favourable or unfavourable to integration.[53]

According to the MIPEX data,[54] Germany appears to provide for the most favourable conditions for the integration of migrants if we take into account these eight policy areas. It scored 61 points, thus its policies might be described as slightly favourable (although being close to the 'halfway favourable' category). The integration policies of France and the United Kingdom were assessed as being halfway favourable, as each state scored 57 points. The discrepancy in the MIPEX overall score between the three countries is not huge (merely three points), therefore it seems that all of these countries provide comparable conditions for integration of adult migrants, although there are some areas in which they differ significantly.[55]

In this vein, the EUROSTAT statistics concerning the number of non-EU nationals being at risk of poverty and social exclusion might also be interesting to examine[56] as high numbers in that respect may reveal a low level of integration in the particular host society by migrants. The research on poverty and social inclusion in the EU was carried out within the Europe 2020 strategy, i.e. the EU agenda aiming for sustainable and inclusive growth to improve EU's economy and its competitiveness and productivity, with poverty reduction being a key policy component. The three sub-indicators, that is, monetary poverty,[57] severe material deprivation[58] and very low work intensity,[59] were exploited in the

53 Critically unfavourable – 0; unfavourable – 1–20; slightly unfavourable – 21–40; halfway favourable – 41–59; slightly favourable – 60–79; favourable – 80–100.

54 MIPEX 2015, Germany, <http://www.mipex.eu/germany> accessed 24.03.2017; MIPEX 2015, France, <http://www.mipex.eu/france> accessed 24.03.2017; MIPEX 2015, UK, <http://www.mipex.eu/united-kingdom> accessed 24.03.2017.

55 For example, in labour market mobility or permanent residence areas.

56 EUROSTAT, People at risk of poverty and social exclusion (population aged 18 and over), <http://ec.europa.eu/eurostat/data/database> accessed 05.02.2018.

57 People are considered at risk of monetary poverty when their equivalised disposable income (after social transfers) is below the at-risk-of-poverty threshold, which is set at 60 per cent of the national median equivalised disposable income after social transfers. This indicator does not measure wealth or poverty, but low income in comparison to other residents in that country.

58 The material deprivation rate is an indicator that shows the inability to afford some items considered by most people to be desirable or even necessary to lead an adequate life (rather than the choice not to do so).

59 The work intensity of a household is the ratio of the total number of months that all working-age household members have worked during the income reference year and the total number of months the same household members theoretically could have worked in the same period.

analysis of the headline indicator 'people at risk of poverty and social exclusion'. As Table 1 indicates, the highest number of non-EU nationals who are at risk of poverty and social exclusion in the years 2009–2015 is noted in France – an average of 53.95 per cent. The data appear to prove low levels of integration by migrants and although a 3 per cent decrease is observed in two consecutive years (i.e. in 2014 and 2015) we cannot draw the conclusion that this trend will continue in the subsequent years, particularly in the context of migration crisis we are now facing. The situation seems to be better in Germany (an average of 39.27 per cent of the migrants being at risk of poverty and social exclusion); however, a significant increase in the number (up 6.2 per cent) was noted in 2015, which may be expected to continue, taking into consideration the massive influx of migrants to Germany in recent years. The statistics show that the UK marks the lowest number of migrants who are at risk of poverty and social exclusion (an average of 34.32 per cent in this examined period); hence, we may assume that integration into the host society is most successful in the UK. In addition, it is not insignificant to note that the situation in the UK appears to be stable in the period under consideration.

Table 1. The percentage of non-EU nationals being at risk of poverty and social exclusion on the basis of the EUROSTAT statistics

Country	2009	2010	2011	2012	2013	2014	2015
France	55.5	56.1	57.7	54.3	56.1	50.5	47.5
Germany	38.4	41.8	42.4	32.5	40.4	36.6	42.8
UK	30.6	36.7	38.4	30.1	34.9	34.8	34.8

Source: Compiled by the author based on data from EUROSTAT, People at risk of poverty and social exclusion (population aged 18 and over), <http://appsso.eurostat.ec.europa.eu/nui/submitViewTableAction.do> accessed 28.03.2017.

Drawing on the above analysis of language and integration policies towards adult migrants in the countries examined, it cannot be clearly stated that the level of integration depends on the language policies implemented in the particular countries. Germany, whose integration policies have been assessed by MIPEX as the most favourable out of these countries, in 2013 introduced slightly stricter requirements concerning the language tests for a residence permit (from A1/B1 to B1 CEFR level), but this did not affect the number of migrants being at risk of poverty and social exclusion in the subsequent year (see Table 1). On the other hand, the language measures adopted in France are rather of moderate character and 'migrant-friendly' (e.g. no language test is required to obtain a residence permit or language courses are provided free of charge), but they do not seem to increase the level of integration, which is the lowest among all of the three countries. The UK appears to have most stable situation and the lowest rate of non-EU nationals being at risk of poverty and social exclusion, which might relate to (slightly) relaxed language requirements but, still, according to MIPEX data, UK is considered only 'halfway favourable' as far as integration of migrants is concerned.

6. CONCLUSION

Linguistic integration of migrants is a matter of serious concern for numerous stakeholders (academics, politicians or officials of various international organisations) who are aware that language plays a significant role in the process of individual and societal integration as it provides access to better job opportunities and eases social and political participation in the host communities. Despite the fact that various initiatives have been launched and instruments adopted to facilitate the process and that migrants acknowledge the vital importance of the acquisition of host society's language and attend tailored language programmes that are provided for them in the host countries, levels of linguistic integration of adult migrants remain low for large numbers of migrants. The analysed examples of language and integration policies in the top three destinations favoured by migrants (i.e. Germany, the UK and France), do not univocally indicate that the rate of integration depends on the language policies implemented in the particular country.

Undoubtedly, the problem of linguistic integration of adult migrants is worth further investigation, taking into consideration the scope and dynamics of the recent political changes. In the times of migration crisis and hostile political discourse towards migrants in many European countries, the word 'dialogue' takes on a new meaning and, as Beacco et al.[60] put it, 'the very word "dialogue" implies exchange, discussion, negotiation, even the resolution of potential conflict, and language is the necessary medium in which these different forms of dialogue are enacted' and this dialogue can positively affect the level of social cohesion and integration of immigrants into host societies.

---

60 J.C. Beacco, D. Little and C. Hedges, *supra* n. 11, p. 17.

www.ingramcontent.com/pod-product-compliance
Ingram Content Group UK Ltd.
Pitfield, Milton Keynes, MK11 3LW, UK
UKHW051920100926
8556IPUK00021B/1286

9 781780 686226